American Government and Politics

ENDORSEMENTS FOR *AMERICAN GOVERNMENT AND POLITICS*

Rob Singh has written a finely organized and informative textbook that combines to an unusually high degree analytical clarity, accessibility of style and form, and an enlightened scepticism about received wisdom. This is an admirable book.

Nigel Bowles, St. Anne's College, University of Oxford

Full of topical information and written with sparkling clarity, this book is a short-cut to excellence for the discriminating student.

Rhodri Jeffreys-Jones, Professor of American History, University of Edinburgh

In *American Government and Politics* Robert Singh provides an excellent introduction to the subject. His approach is wide ranging, his examples well selected and his style is accessible. It will make an ideal book for introductory and more advanced university courses on US government. I strongly recommend the book to teachers and students.

Desmond King, Mellon Professor of American Government, Nuffield College, University of Oxford

This is a well written and lively book that is an important addition to the ranks of textbooks on American politics. One of its many virtues is its recognition that the textbook today is useful to a student only if it links to the world of web-based resources. Highly recommended.

Alan Ware, Worcester College, University of Oxford

American Government and Politics

A Concise Introduction

Robert Singh

SAGE Publications
London ● Thousand Oaks ● New Delhi

For Exten, critic and friend

ISBN 0-7619-4093-6 (hbk)
ISBN 0-7619-4094-4 (pbk)
© Robert Singh 2003
First published 2003
Reprinted 2004 (twice), 2005

SAGE Publications Ltd
1 Oliver's Yard
55 City Road
London EC1Y 1SP

SAGE Publications Inc
2455 Teller Road
Thousand Oaks
California 91320

SAGE Publications India Pvt Ltd
B–42 Panchsheel Enclave
PO Box 4109
New Delhi 110 017

British Library Cataloguing in Publication data
A catalogue record for this book is available from the British Library

Library of Congress Control Number: 2002109397

Typeset by Photoprint Ltd., Torquay, Devon
Printed and bound in Great Britain by
Alden Press Limited, Osney Mead, Oxford

Contents

List of Exhibits and Tables

Preface

American politics provides a genuine challenge to study. On the one hand, the governmental and political system of the twenty-first century United States is especially complex and yet retains much of the original design penned by the 'Founding Fathers' in the eighteenth century. The distinctive belief systems of the American people, the pervasive influence of the US Constitution, the complex workings of federalism, the relative weakness of political parties, the pivotal relationship between White House and Capitol Hill, the powerful but limited role of the federal courts – all these make for a tremendously rich but especially complex body of information to master.

On the other hand, America's profound political, economic, military and cultural influence brings the nation 'closer' than most to those of us outside the United States. Students therefore typically enter the study of American politics with ideas, stereotypes and prejudices about both the nation and its people gleaned from films, music and books in ways unlike those of other nations. A mix of Madonna, *The Simpsons* and Hollywood treatments of subjects from JFK to Vietnam accord students an apparent familiarity with things American that brooks no comparison with other nations. Simultaneously, news coverage of the US invariably focuses on aspects that tend to personalize and sensationalize American public life: the president's particular intentions and indiscretions, seemingly routine outbreaks of gun violence, state executions, urban riots, political fanatics, and the cult of celebrity. It is hardly surprising, in the light of this, that many students enter US politics courses with a view that the president is the executive branch, the executive is the federal government, and the federal government is the government in America.

Beyond this, America is uniquely prone to academic criticism – even demonization – on the grounds of its singular military and economic position, self-conscious celebration of free market capitalism, and chequered record of respect for human rights and civil liberties. Within a discipline where leftist critiques are popular, if not predominant, the ease with which student prejudices can be confirmed makes America especially vulnerable to misleading, partial or biased characterizations. Among these are the notions that: Americans all own guns, hate communists, drive big cars, and don't vote; the president is in charge and can do what he likes, especially when it comes to war; Kennedy was a sleaze, Clinton was a sex-fiend, and Bush is a dunce; political parties don't exist in America, but the Democrats and Republicans are two right-wing parties with virtually no differences between them; elections are entirely based on personality, not issues; money rules; American cities are crime-ridden, drug-infested dens of iniquity; black Americans are all poverty-stricken and America is being taken over by Hispanics; most Americans are religious extremists and bigots; and Americans neither care nor know about the rest of the world and believe that the Middle East is Kansas.

Many facts therefore get lost before courses on US politics even commence: that most Americans do not own guns; that the supposedly free market is one of the most heavily regulated by government of all liberal democracies; that American political parties today are strongly partisan and differ at least as much as they agree on public policies; that the presidency is confronted by a myriad of competing and powerful political actors that impede his freedom of action; and that, long before September 11, 2001, the American public was more internationalist, pro-multilateral action, and willing to accept US military casualties than easy acceptance of the 'Vietnam syndrome' or the 'Body Bag effect' suggested.

The study of American politics should be dispassionate, balanced, and informed. But it should also be fun. The pages that follow hope to achieve both these ends and, thereby, to encourage further study of a unique national experiment in political, economic and social organization.

Acknowledgements

A large number of people participated in the development of this book, a few directly but most unwittingly. The first thanks that I should therefore offer is to the several hundred students whom I have been lucky enough to teach over the past 12 years at the universities of Oxford, Sussex, Dublin (Trinity College), Edinburgh, Glasgow and London. Lecturing and discussing American politics remains a genuine pleasure, all the more so for having enthusiastic, intelligent and critical students willing to engage in an open-minded fashion in the many issues that politics in the US raises.

The School of Politics and Sociology at Birkbeck College has offered a particularly welcoming and supportive home since my arrival there in 1999. I should thank in particular my colleague Bill Tompson, a Texan expert on all things Soviet and post-Soviet, whose many conversations have contributed enormously to my education about the States and much else besides. Birkbeck has a special mission and our students are overwhelmingly mature adults studying part-time. Each year has only added to my amazement at how impressive our students are, not simply in terms of their academic achievement but in managing to marry tough courses of study to coping with demanding jobs and personal responsibilities. Among the many who have helped to make teaching such a rewarding experience, I should especially thank Craig O'Callaghan, Andy Coath, Robert Dockerill, Paul Carabine, Tim Carlier, Gloria De Piero, Hazel Nyandoro, Lindsey-Jane Chiswick, Liz Rubenstein, Paula Clemett, and Martin Burke. I should also thank Kathryn Westmore, who offered extensive feedback on several chapters of this book and made several very helpful suggestions for revisions.

Another ex-Birkbeckian, Lucy Robinson, and the staff at Sage had sufficient confidence in the book and its companion volume, *Contemporary American Politics and Society: Issues and Controversies*, to take these twins on at a late stage of gestation and deliver them both – for which I'm enormously grateful.

1 Americanism

As we gather tonight, our nation is at war, our economy is in recession and the civilized world faces unprecedented dangers. Yet the state of our union has never been stronger.

President George W. Bush, State of the Union address, January 29, 2002

The society of happy, thoughtless philistines depicted by Huxley seems merely an exaggeration of today's America.

Judge Richard Posner on Aldous Huxley's novel, *Brave New World* (2001b: 260)

- **The Architecture of American Politics**
- **America's Social Base**
- **'Americanism' as an Ideology**
- **An Anti-Government Political Culture**
- **American Exceptionalism: how different?**
- **Conclusion**

Chapter Summary

The United States of America comprises a distinctive people and political system. Founded in a revolution against tyrannical government and unjust taxation, both American identity and the fabled 'American Dream' remain inextricably linked to the political values that originally informed the Declaration of Independence (1776) and the US Constitution (1787). These values – commonly referred to as the 'American Creed' – contribute to a political culture that is anti-authority and suspicious of government (the federal/national government in particular) and politicians generally. To be an American entails endorsing this Creed, and thereby acquiring an identity defined not by culture or language but political values associated with the classical liberalism of the eighteenth century: individual liberty, equality before the law, free markets, constitutionalism, democracy and a respect for the 'common man'. Partly as a result, America has known neither a pull between nationalism and ideology nor a genuinely influential socialist, fascist, communist, Tory, Christian Democratic or Social Democratic tradition. But profound conflict – regional, racial, ethnic, class-based and religious – has nevertheless existed through American history, deriving in large part from the conflicting values within the Creed. Americans often differ on how to apply those foundational values to day-to-day reality – so much so that since American citizenship is defined by values rather than blood, language or race, it is possible both to 'become' an American and act in 'un-American' ways. But in a complex society characterized by remarkable social diversity and heterogeneity in religion, region, race, ethnicity and incomes, the values articulated in the Declaration and the Constitution continue to provide a common focus for national unity and, ultimately, a powerful source of political stability. Despite attempts by some scholars to depict America as a loose collection of ethnic groups and hyphenated-Americans, the common values that unite the people of the United States mark the nation as enduringly different from those of other democracies. Moreover, as American responses to the terrorist attacks of September 11, 2001 demonstrated, what unites Americans not only remains far more profound and abiding than what divides them, but also sets them apart from the peoples of other nations.

The United States of America is one of the most studied but least understood nations in the contemporary world. Possessing the most extensive international influence of any nation and the most complex political system of any industrialized liberal democracy, it is perhaps not surprising that students of American politics often emerge from their studies with a view like the famous Dr Johnson's regarding the dog that walked on its hind legs: 'the remarkable thing is not that it walks badly, but that it walks at all'.

Similarly, after examining America's diverse social base and fragmented government, the remarkable pressures that exist on governing institutions and individual political actors, and the seemingly chaotic pattern of conflicts deliberately built into the heart of the system, the temptation is to wonder how and why the entire edifice does not collapse under the weight of the immense strains that it must absorb. In this respect, it remains a remarkable testament to the foresight of the Founding Fathers, and to subsequent generations of Americans, that the America of the twenty-first century stands in such remarkably robust political, economic, and social shape – the most politically, economically and

culturally influential, militarily dominant, materially prosperous and technologically advanced nation in the world.

At the same time, America continues to boast a history rich in contradictions and conflict. The Founding Fathers created a nation dedicated to liberty but resting substantially on human beings treated as property. The 'land of the free' sanctioned not only slavery but also, after its abolition, state-enforced racial segregation. The nation whose 'American Dream' of prosperity and freedom has been a beacon to millions of the persecuted and poor around the world exhibits extremes of wealth and poverty greater than any other industrialized country. America promised 'life, liberty and the pursuit of happiness' in its Declaration of Independence but implements capital punishment, imprisons more citizens than any other western nation (over two million), and sees a level of social dislocation that condemns millions to a life with neither adequate health care, education nor jobs. Though more Americans have died from gun violence since 1933 than were killed in all America's wars combined, by 2002 42 states had passed laws to allow the carrying of guns concealed on the person. A mass of pain as well as progress, Puritanism as well as prurience, America is simultaneously riveting and repellent to many outside its borders.

As these examples suggest, American politics is unlike that of any other nation – the product of a unique society, distinctive political system and particular people. America entered the twenty-first century with a Constitution written in and designed for the eighteenth. Despite the many changes that have occurred across its history, America possesses a system of constitutional government remarkably similar to that established in 1787 – simultaneously the object of envy and bafflement to outsiders and a source of immense pride and patriotism to Americans (in 1996, for example, *ABC News* asked a sample of Americans whether or not they agreed with the statement that 'Whatever its faults, the United States still has the best system of government in the world': 83 per cent agreed; 15 per cent disagreed).

But underneath that surface stability, American politics displays a complex and constantly changing character that defies easy categorization. This is not always apparent since, when many of us think about American politics, this often occurs in highly personalized ways: most obviously in terms of who happens to be president at the time. We are sometimes prone to thinking that American politics *is* the president, the president is the federal government, and the federal government is *the* government. This is understandable, especially in an era when television and the Internet provide us with intimate, personal and almost constant coverage of American political leaders that ranges from their favourite foods, pets and sporting activities to their preferred choice of underwear. In securing their independence from Britain, Americans decisively rejected a monarchical form of government, but as Head of State as well as Head of Government, the president symbolizes and personalizes America to those within and outside America. Leader of the most powerful nation on the planet and the only figure elected by a national constituency, the president possesses a unique political legitimacy to speak to and for the American nation.

As a result, we tend even to compartmentalize time according to presidents: 'the Kennedy era', 'the Reagan years', 'Bush's America'. Films and popular music regularly refer to presidents but rarely to members of Congress or Supreme Court justices: we watch *All the President's Men*, not *All the Members of the Senate Finance Committee*, *JFK* rather than *Earl Warren* (despite the fact that lawmakers and judges are frequently still serving long after the president has left the White House, and sometimes have at least as much political effect). But as the chapters that follow will emphasize, the president is only one player – albeit easily the most significant – in a supremely complex political system. Before assessing the government structures, politics and policy processes, we begin our analysis of America's divided democracy by examining the nation's distinctive 'social base'.

THE ARCHITECTURE OF AMERICAN POLITICS

One of the key features of American politics is the set of complex interconnections between its otherwise separate and distinct parts. It is impossible, for instance, to understand how American political parties work without knowing about the Constitution, how the president leads without knowing about Congress, or how interest groups lobby government without knowing about courts and bureaucracies. Equally, on specific issues and controversies, understanding why America has comparatively weak gun laws, lacks a national health insurance policy or executes large numbers of death row inmates can only proceed once the basics of the system of government and society are known. These connections are sometimes obvious, often subtle, but always important.

To make this task simpler, one way to 'conceptualize' American politics is presented in

Exhibit 1.1. This contains the 'architecture' of politics in the United States: the social base, governing institutions and intermediary organizations linking society and government together. The ongoing interaction of these three elements produces the politics and public policies (domestic and foreign) that directly and indirectly affect Americans' daily lives and those of millions outside America. By keeping in mind these three dimensions throughout the chapters that follow, the linkages between different aspects of American politics should become apparent. But in this chapter, we first concentrate on the social base, before moving on to the Constitution and institutions of government in Chapter 2.

AMERICA'S SOCIAL BASE

The 'social base' refers to the types of group that exist in society, including the key similarities and differences among them. The people of the United States share a common and distinctive identity as Americans, but they differ sharply according to distinct 'social facts': income, occupation (or class), religion, region, rural/urban/suburban location, race, ethnicity, gender and sexual orientation. Other significant divisions exist among Americans in terms of values, beliefs, and attitudes, not least regarding the appropriateness of government intervention to secure particular social, economic and political objectives (such as equality of opportunity). These dissimilarities receive expression not

Exhibit 1.1   A model of American politics

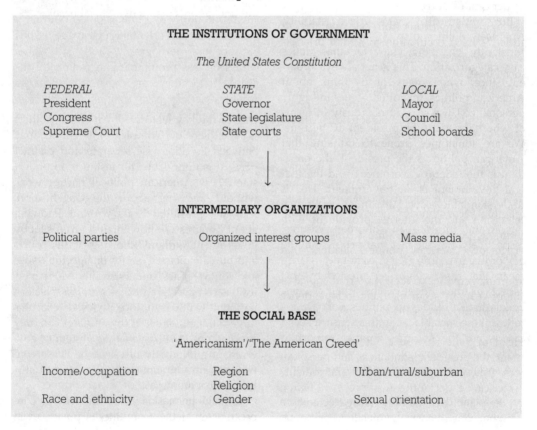

THE INSTITUTIONS OF GOVERNMENT

The United States Constitution

FEDERAL	*STATE*	*LOCAL*
President	Governor	Mayor
Congress	State legislature	Council
Supreme Court	State courts	School boards

INTERMEDIARY ORGANIZATIONS

Political parties   Organized interest groups   Mass media

THE SOCIAL BASE

'Americanism'/'The American Creed'

Income/occupation   Region   Urban/rural/suburban
                           Religion
Race and ethnicity   Gender   Sexual orientation

just in the marked differences between the individual 50 states but also within them.

Central to American society – and hence politics – is diversity. America's social base is especially rich and heterogeneous, at least as much as diverse nations like India and Brazil. Sometimes, though, the repetition of this observation can make us forget quite how unusual America has been, and remains. In terms of history and self-image, America is above all a self-consciously immigrant nation – not in the sense that most Americans today are new arrivals (though many are), but that the overwhelming majority trace their family histories to other parts of the world and an escape from political or religious persecution and economic disadvantage. Through successive generations, the mix of ethnicities and races that emigrated to America and then intermarried with Americans of still other backgrounds has produced an ever-richer diversity. When the other social factors that distinguish Americans from one another are added – from occupation to sexual orientation – America boasts an unusually varied social base.

America is so diverse that any American can display several social features at once. For example, despite their obvious differences, a heterosexual Baptist black woman company director living in a southern city centre displays the same social facts as a gay Catholic Hispanic male factory worker living in a Midwestern suburb: sexual orientation, religion, race/ethnicity, gender, occupation, region and rural/urban/suburban features, respectively. But the fact that people may be gay or live in a rural area does not necessarily mean that they will be so affected by this aspect of their identity that their values, beliefs and attitudes to politics will always reflect these social facts. In this sense, a social fact is not the same as another important term, a 'social cleavage'.

A social cleavage involves three conditions:

● A social division that separates people who can be distinguished from one another in terms of social facts like occupation or religion.
● Groups that are conscious of their collective identity and willing to act on this basis (as workers, African Americans or Catholics).
● The expression of these social facts or divisions in organizational terms (e.g. by a union, a civil rights group or a church).

Thinking about social cleavages explains much about the shape of American politics at a particular moment, and how and why politics changes. For example, without a religious cleavage, issues such as abortion or gay rights are less likely to be subjects of division. Why? Because millions who adhere to strong beliefs about the immorality of abortion and homosexuality would not mobilize politically, campaign or vote on the basis of this concern. (But, as Table 1.1 shows, Americans are a profoundly religious people.) Without a gender or sexual orientation cleavage, issues of abortion, pornography and gay rights would be less prominent and politically divisive than they are currently. Because America's social base is unusually diverse, more potential for such cultural as well as socio-economic conflict exists than in nations with fewer, less divisive, and less cross-cutting social cleavages.

America's being riven by more social differences in its base than almost any other modern industrialized liberal democracy does not necessitate that it is plagued by political divisions (though these have certainly been present and, at times, deeply divisive and violent, from the Civil War through industrialization era conflicts of the later eighteenth and early twentieth century to the civil rights struggles of the 1950s and 1960s). But, from a relatively homogeneous society in the eighteenth century, successive waves of immigration have left America as a kaleidoscopic mosaic of racial, ethnic, religious, regional and linguistic differences. The pressures that these have created have even caused some commentators to question the nation's prospects of survival and to argue that America is currently 'disuniting'.

Whether this break-up is so remains highly contentious. What is incontrovertibly the case, however, is that the citizen that we call an American today displays an impressive variety of accents, colours, creeds, religions and beliefs. Given this pronounced diversity, what force(s) can hold together such a seemingly discordant and fragmented society?

'AMERICANISM' AS AN IDEOLOGY

Since America's social base is so heterogeneous, the forces that bind the nation together and prevent its disintegration are sometimes obscure to outside observers. Yet these forces also exert a tenacious hold that has proven elusive to other nations containing a multitude of diverse social groups. Pressures of religious, racial and ethnic diversity brought about the collapse of states such

TABLE 1.1   Religion in American life

	Belongs to a church/ synagogue	Attended church/ synagogue in last seven days	Says religion is 'very important in their life'	Says religion can answer all/ most problems
All	69	42	58	62
Men	62	37	50	55
Women	74	46	65	68
Age				
<30	61	31	44	55
30–49	65	40	54	61
50–64	79	53	69	70
65>	75	50	72	63
East	68	39	55	56
Midwest	72	45	57	63
South	75	47	68	74
West	55	34	48	49
White	67	41	55	60
Black	82	50	82	86
College	70	44	53	58
No college	67	40	63	65
$50,000>	70	41	48	56
$30,000–$49,999	72	45	56	62
$20,000–$29,999	65	41	56	60
<$20,000	67	40	66	66
Protestant	72	45	65	71
Catholic	77	47	51	51

Source: Golay and Rollyson (1996: 190)

as Yugoslavia in the late twentieth century, threatened to cause the disintegration of India, Canada and Brazil, and pressured nations from Sri Lanka to South Africa. America, by contrast, has steadily absorbed, accommodated and transcended an impressive level of diverse influences from around the world. Far from precipitating its break-up, the capacity successfully to incorporate new immigrants into the American heartland has only reinforced the historic appeal of the fabled 'American Dream'.

The solution to this conundrum is conventionally located in the connection between the founding of the United States as a new republic in 1787 and the subsequent nature of American identity. America was born in a deliberate, self-conscious act of revolution, a revolution not simply against a nation – the British colonial power – but also against a form of oppressive government (the monarchy) and excessive taxation. The founding of the American state was therefore a deliberate attempt at establishing what the influential sociologist, Seymour Martin Lipset (1996), termed 'the first new nation'. The creation of national identity was linked to the formation of the state itself, and in particular

the values enshrined in the Declaration of Independence and the Constitution of the United States (see Exhibit 1.2). These values, crucially, were not so much ones of culture – language or religion – as ones concerning political ideas.

The essence of American identity was captured by the historian, Richard Hofstadter, when he argued that, 'It has been our fate as a nation not to have ideologies but to be one' (Lipset, 1990: 19). Whereas other nations have defined themselves in terms of certain organic notions like a common culture or language or blood ties (the German *Volk*, for example), Americans instead define themselves in terms of certain political ideas that they share. When new immigrants take the oath of allegiance, they profess agreement not with a certain type of blood, language or culture but with these shared political ideas. That represents their common 'heritage' as Americans. This means that adherence to certain normative values rather than the presence of existential or organic forces such as blood ties, language, skin colour or religion defines what it is to be an American and thereby eases the assimilation of otherwise

Exhibit 1.2   The Declaration of Independence (1776)

The Declaration of Independence is the best short introduction to American political thought. After years of colonial disputes, armed rebellions arose in several English colonies by July 1776. The Continental Congress that formed as a result formally accepted the Declaration on July 4 – subsequently celebrated as 'Independence Day' – by a 12 to zero vote, with New York abstaining (the state approved the measure five days later). The document was drafted mostly by Thomas Jefferson, who later claimed that he had been doing little more than expressing the 'common sense' of his age in affirming the existence of inalienable rights to life, liberty and the pursuit of happiness and the duty of the government to protect these rights:

> We hold these truths to be self-evident, that all men are created equal, that they are endowed by their Creator with certain unalienable Rights, that among these are Life, Liberty and the pursuit of Happiness. That to secure these rights, Governments are instituted among Men, deriving their just powers from the consent of the governed. That whenever any form of Government becomes destructive of these ends, it is the Right of the People to alter or abolish it, and to institute new Government, laying its foundation on such principles and organizing its powers in such form, as to them shall seem most likely to effect their Safety and Happiness.

disparate new immigrants as citizens of the United States.

In terms of political values, what makes American political thought distinctive is that it is wholly contained within the boundaries of one part of European thought: classical liberalism of the eighteenth century. Neither Tory conservatism (with its defence of aristocratic institutions and inherited privileges) nor Christian Democracy nor socialism, communism or fascism achieved a serious impact in America. With no feudal structure (hence no aristocracy or peasantry), Americans were 'born equal' before the law without having to undergo the types of democratic revolution commonplace in Europe. Instead, white adult males (but not blacks or women) possessed the suffrage from the outset, prior to America industrializing. Consequently, political conflict has occurred within the bounds of a 'liberal consensus' so pervasive as to make most Americans conceive of themselves as a non-ideological people: not as self-conscious exponents of classical liberalism but simply adherents to a given – 'Americanism'. This Americanism has been so dominant that any alternatives are at once undesirable, suspect and even 'un-American' in character (see Exhibit 1.3).

In comparative terms, the most distinctive aspect of the American Creed is its anti-government character. Whereas most ideologies legitimate established authority and existing government institutions, the Creed de-legitimizes hierarchical, authoritarian and coercive power structures, whether political or economic. Although writers such as Samuel Huntington (1981) argue that its values are too many and too often in conflict to constitute a coherent ideology like socialism or fascism, these inconsistencies – the fundamental clashes between freedom and equality, individualism and constitutionalism, majoritarian democracy and liberalism's respect for minority rights – have provided the flexibility by which Americans can simultaneously reaffirm their shared Creedal values and reject 'alien' ideologies as

inappropriate and unnecessary to resolving America's current problems.

No idea is more fundamental in this respect than freedom. The central term in American politics, 'freedom' is deeply embedded in the nation's history, pervades everyday language and is personified by cultural icons such as the cowboy. The Declaration of Independence lists liberty as one of the 'inalienable rights'; the Constitution announces its purpose as being 'to secure liberty's blessings'. America fought the Civil War, in part, to bring about a new freedom for slaves, the Second World War for the 'Four Freedoms', and the Cold War to defend 'the Free World' (those non-communist authoritarian states that were not renowned for individual freedom, such as Franco's Spain, Pinochet's Chile and apartheid South Africa, also counted as 'free' for America in the context of this struggle). The Bush administration's 'war on terrorism' was also framed not only as a fight to assure American national security, but also to preserve freedom after the terrorist attacks of September 11, 2001. Love of liberty has been represented by flags, caps, and statues, and acted out by burning draft cards and demonstrating for civil and political rights. If asked to explain or justify their actions, Americans frequently respond, 'It's a free country'.

That focus on individual freedom is nevertheless married to an abiding concern for the nature of American identity and real or imagined threats to it. Many official proclamations that represent America focus on the question of identity. The Constitution encourages the people to form a 'more perfect Union' and 'insure domestic Tranquillity.' The Pledge of Allegiance sees millions of schoolchildren daily declare: 'I pledge allegiance to the flag of the United States of America and to the republic for which it stands, one nation, under God, indivisible, with liberty and justice for all.' But, at the same time, other proclamations suggest difference. For example, the oath of allegiance – given to those being naturalized as citizens –

Exhibit 1.3   The American Creed

Freedom. The cornerstone of Americanism is a belief in individual liberty. This belief is a belief in 'negative liberty': freedom consists of being free from interference, not having the means to accomplish certain goals. As such, the priority is about unencumbered behaviour, whether in the economic or social sphere. In particular, a presumption exists against government interference with personal liberties, from the right to speak one's views (however offensive) to the right to own a firearm (however lethal).

Equality. Co-existing with a belief in freedom is the belief that every individual is born equal. This is not a matter of absolute equality in terms of wealth, condition or talent. Rather, it is a belief that no individual should be accorded special treatment simply by virtue of the family, class, religion or race he or she belongs to and that no one has the right to exercise such discriminatory power over another. However quaint many find it, Americans reject the idea of a British-style royal family. What this means – in theory, if less so in practice – is that all Americans are equal before the law, none is entitled to preferential treatment, and each is free to become unequal through his or her own efforts: a 'socialist conception of capitalism'.

Individualism. Each person has the right to act in accordance with his or her own conscience and to control his or her own destiny free from external restraint (except insofar as such restraint is necessary to ensure comparable rights to others). Rewards are seen as matching individual efforts. Failure to achieve economic or social progress is hence conventionally regarded as a matter of the individual's deficiencies, not the general social order or particular environmental conditions. The cultural dominance of Protestants for most of American history has powerfully reinforced an individualistic 'work ethic', embellished by folklore about how anyone – regardless of race, gender or religion – can become president.

Liberalism. Liberty takes precedence over power, such that individuals and minorities should be protected against, and free from, majority control. Certain rights guarantee particular areas of life that government cannot intrude on, and these – policed by the courts – ensure that government is 'limited' rather than majoritarian and, potentially, tyrannical or totalitarian.

Democracy. Americans reject arbitrary or monarchical government. Instead, government must be, as Abraham Lincoln put it, 'of the people, by the people and for the people'. Government ultimately rests on popular consent and the people have the right to withdraw that consent and hold those who govern to account through regular free and fair elections.

Property. A belief in property rights underpins a powerful commitment to free (but not unregulated) market capitalism. Without private property, appropriately safeguarded by the rule of law, there can be no individual freedom.

Constitutionalism. The power of government is to be limited through fundamental law, deriving ultimately from a divine authority and being 'higher' than any law passed by government, to which all citizens are subject equally. The US Constitution provides the cornerstone of democracy, constraints on government power, and the test by which its institutions, public officials and public policies are held to account.

declares the need to defend the Constitution and the nation's laws against 'all enemies, foreign and domestic'. As Exhibit 1.4 suggests, communists, psychopaths and sexual deviants need not apply for admission to the United States.

Exhibit 1.4 Becoming American

Anyone seeking to gain American citizenship must answer a series of questions. These give an indication of the kinds of individuals whom Americans – under the Immigration and Naturalization Service's guidance – seek to accept and refuse the privilege of citizenship:

- Are you or have you at any time been an anarchist, or a member of or affiliated with a Communist or other totalitarian party?
- Have you advocated or taught, by personal utterance, by written or printed matter, or through affiliation with an organization (a) opposition to organized government; (b) the overthrow of government by force; (c) the assaulting or killing of government officials because of their official character; (d) the unlawful destruction of property; (e) sabotage; (f) the doctrines of world communism, or the establishment of a totalitarian dictatorship in the United States?
- Have you engaged in or do you intend to engage in prejudicial activities or unlawful activities of a subversive nature?
- Are you afflicted with psychopathic personality, sexual deviation, mental defect, narcotic drug addiction, chronic alcoholism, or any dangerous contagious disease?
- Are you a pauper, professional beggar, or vagrant?
- Are you a polygamist or do you advocate polygamy?
- Have you committed or have you been convicted of a crime of moral turpitude?

The questions that are asked of prospective citizens give a good indication of these alien beliefs and degenerate practices. The cumulative result is that *being* American is not a given, a product of simply being born in a particular place or having a certain father or mother – being a citizen involves *becoming* an American. Certain values, beliefs and attitudes are intrinsic to American identity, while others are alien.

The corollary of becoming an American is that it is also possible to act in an 'un-American way'. (The US House of Representatives even had a permanent 'Committee on Un-American Activities' that lasted from 1938 to 1975.) But precisely because the American Creed is so diffuse, with different values competing against one another, Americans frequently disagree over what constitutes 'un-American' ideas or actions. Notoriously, during the later 1940s and early 1950s, McCarthyism identified and punished Americans who believed, or were suspected of believing, in communism – an ideology not only opposed to capitalism and democracy but also promoting 'Godless atheism'.

Since then, groups as diverse as anti-Vietnam protesters, black radicals, and even the federal government have been accused by some citizens of being 'un-American'. Few accusations could be more serious, damning and dangerous to careers, livelihoods and even lives.

One of the most important legacies of this aspect of Americanism is that admission to citizenship has frequently generated strong political conflicts. Americans have taken immense and justifiable pride in their nation being – with the notable exceptions of Native Americans and African Americans – a land of voluntary immigrants. But over American history, certain categories of immigrants have been decidedly unwelcome. Federal laws designed either to limit or to prohibit certain types of foreigner from becoming citizens have been as much a part of the nation's history as the admission of immigrants. In making and 're-making' Americans, illiberal practices have undermined the idealistic promise of liberal theories. Attempts to limit southern and eastern European immigration, combined with efforts to exclude non-white immigrants (such as the Chinese) and deny blacks basic citizenship rights, strongly reinforced the conception harboured by many Americans of their nation as a fundamentally white, Anglo-Saxon land from the 1920s to 1965. But this racialized conception of Americanism was and remains consistently secondary – in official accounts – to the universal Enlightenment values of reason, truth and law that inform the inclusive and democratic ideals of the American Creed.

That American ideals have been broached throughout the nation's history – that a theoretically colourblind Constitution has underpinned a practically colour-conscious polity – has not meant that they have been abandoned or even seriously eroded today. Quite the reverse: the idea of America has become the key battleground between traditionalists and progressives who wish to see their particular conception of Americanism realized in public policy. Traditionalists (epitomized by figures such as Ronald Reagan, John Wayne and Clint Eastwood) believe in America's uniqueness and its having set a shining example – a 'city upon a hill' – to the rest of the world; progressives tend instead to hold America's journey as only having begun and to advocate policies to make America 'live up to' its proclaimed ideals.

Perhaps the most striking example of the salience of the American Creed can be gleaned from the greatest blight on America's self-image: race. For even in the midst of the most brutal and barbaric conditions – slavery and state-enforced racial segregation in the South from the 1890s to 1965 – remarkably few black Americans turned to 'foreign' ideas like socialism or communism to challenge their brutal treatment. Instead, blacks before, during and after the civil rights movement of the 1950s and 1960s have appealed to the core values of the American Creed to try to convince their compatriots to make its idealistic promise of freedom, equality and justice a reality for all citizens.

Clearly, then, this notion of Americanism represents a vastly different set of ideas from those found elsewhere in the world. In France, for example, where the Tricolour flag is flown widely and where intense political divisions over the monarchy, class, region and religion have existed since 1789, political opponents rarely describe each other as 'un-French'. Even in the UK, it is possible to advocate the abolition of the monarchy without being called 'un-British' (unpatriotic, perhaps, but to be described as un-British strikes an odd tone). The reason is that the relationship between national identity and political values is far less intimate. It is close to impossible to imagine what an un-French activity (refusing to dress well or drink wine?) or un-British idea might be. By contrast, as President Woodrow Wilson remarked in September, 1919: 'America, my fellow citizens – I do not say it in disparagement of any other great people – America is the only idealistic nation in the world.'

One of the most important consequences of this Creedal passion is the intensity of American political conflicts. Many Europeans are baffled about why Americans disagree so heatedly when the differences between them appear comparatively minor. But it is partly because Americans adhere to notions of Americanism that anyone who departs from them is not simply a political opponent but is also compromising his or her national identity as a citizen. No conflicting pull exists between ideology (socialism, fascism, Christian Democracy), on the one hand, and nationalism (national identity), on the other. The two are instead synonymous – or, as President Clinton noted in his inaugural speech in 1993, 'There's nothing wrong with America that can't be cured by what's right with America.' What is right about America remains, however, something about which Americans themselves frequently disagree.

Americans, then, are among the most, not the least, ideological people in the world. They are not 'brain-washed' in the sense in which communist and theocratic regimes have attempted to indoctrinate their citizens in an ideology or religious faith, but through numerous mechanisms, Americans daily revel in a constant, quasi-religious celebration of their nation and its foundational values: the Declaration of Independence, the Constitution, the Founding Fathers, the four presidents immortalized on Mount Rushmore, the Bill of Rights, the Pledge of Allegiance, and the Stars and Stripes. Millions visit the capital, Washington DC, each year to admire the Dome on Capitol Hill, tour the White House, and visit the Lincoln and Jefferson Memorials and Washington Monument.

As Anthony King notes, 'No European country begins to accord either its governmental buildings or its defunct political leaders anything like such respect. Hardly anyone notices the statue of Winston Churchill in Parliament Square' (2000: 86). Where banknotes and coins in Europe depict abstract symbols or famous writers, painters, musicians or scientists, America's money is adorned with the Founding Fathers and government buildings. It is commonplace in suburban and rural towns to see the Stars and Stripes draped outside ordinary homes in a way that such patriotism is unthinkable in a Europe where nationalism cast a dismally dark history across the continent during the twentieth century. American politicians regularly invoke the names of Washington, Franklin, Jefferson, and Lincoln in ways unknown outside America to justify current policies (a British politician – of any party – invoking Hobbes, Locke or Burke to justify the National Health Service, railway reform or tax rises would be an oddity in every sense).

Despite their remarkable diversity, then, Americans remain bound to each other by this tenacious loyalty to a set of expressly political values derived from classical liberalism. Few other peoples exhibit such a self-conscious pride, confidence in the unique nature and the essential goodness of their national identity, and a marked orientation towards the future derived from a deep reverence for the past. The lure of the future, progress and the 'Promised Land' forms a constant theme in American history and language. Americans are demonstrably conservative in seeking the preservation of their existing political values and institutions. But the political ideas that they seek to preserve are liberal – even radical – in nature.

AN ANTI-GOVERNMENT POLITICAL CULTURE

As a result of this distinctive national identity, regardless of the particular historic reality (Depression in the 1930s, Vietnam in the 1960s and 1970s), the distinctive 'American Dream' has persisted. Many other nations have enjoyed periods of remarkable economic growth and offered their citizens startling levels of social mobility, yet we rarely talk of an 'Australian Dream' or 'Japanese Dream'. That we speak of an 'American Dream' suggests that there exists something special in the political arrangements of American democracy that allows for substantial freedom in the economic and social, as well as the political, realm. It is this common grounding in fundamental values that accounts for the shared outlooks and sometimes quizzical reception that Americans often encounter abroad – for whether white, black, Latino, or Asian, it is typically their shared Americanism that most immediately and forcefully strikes the foreign observer. Becoming American is a quasi-religious experience involving conversion and conviction. Americans believe themselves to be created equal and the most obvious manifestations of their values – shared convictions rooted in Americanism – suggests that in an important sense they remain correct.

In terms of practical politics, however, perhaps the most crucial aspect of this core identity is the extent to which hostility towards government in general, and the federal (national) government especially, has become pervasive. Owing largely to their revolutionary origins against the British colonies seeking to impose 'unjust' taxes on them and the fact that America was substantially populated by runaways from authority, Americans

Exhibit 1.5   Born in the USA: the political meaning(s) of Bruce Springsteen?

No American cultural icon personifies the powerful tensions inherent in Americanism more fully than Bruce Springsteen. In 1984, during a visit to New Jersey, President Reagan invoked Springsteen's name behind his strongly conservative brand of Republicanism:

> You are what America is all about. You didn't come here seeking streets paved with gold. You didn't come here asking for welfare or special treatment. America's future rests in a thousand dreams inside our hearts. It rests in the message of hope so many young people admire: New Jersey's own Bruce Springsteen. And helping you make those dreams come true is what this job of mine is all about.

The *Born in the USA* album had catapulted Springsteen into superstardom in 1984, the year of Reagan's landslide re-election. Its visual impact – a regular, jeans and white T-shirt-wearing blue-collar guy set against a backdrop of the Stars and Stripes – suggested the quintessential patriotic American. But the album's lyrics did not so much celebrate as censure America for its adventurism in Vietnam, mass unemployment, industrial decay, poverty and racism. That both left and right could celebrate Springsteen as an icon pointed to the gap between the enduring promise of American ideals contrasted with their partial or unrealized achievement in practice. As Jim Cullen noted, '. . . it is the job of the artist to remind us of who we are. When I listen to Bruce Springsteen I remember how to be an American' (1997: 202). It is difficult to imagine a comparable statement about remembering 'how to be British' or 'how to be Australian' through listening to popular music.

have never relinquished their suspicion of the dangers of excessive taxation and the coercive power of the state. Americans have been far more concerned about what government can do *to* them than what government can do *for* them (hence the popularity of firearms as preserving liberty as well as defending against criminals). Although this has been tempered at particular historical junctures, such as the Depression years following the 1929 Wall Street Crash, the basic antipathy has always been a potent force: 'The distinctive aspect of the American creed is its anti-government character. Opposition to power, and suspicion of government as the most dangerous embodiment of power, are the central themes of American political thought' (Huntington, 1981: 33).

Consequently, from the republic's founding to today, distrust of government has been a constant. Americans have been wary of government intervention, especially at the national level, even as the New Deal era

(1932–68) vastly increased the scope of that intervention in social and economic life. Physical distance from Washington reinforces the emotional and psychological distance that most feel towards the federal government (although even those in states neighbouring the capital – Virginia and Maryland – frequently feel distant from its actions). The federal government 'provides fewer services and benefits for its citizens than do the national governments of most other countries, with the result that Americans have a much smaller stake in their national government and its activities than do the citizens of most other countries in theirs' (A. King, 2000: 80). There exists no system of universal national health insurance, no national broadcasting service, little public housing, and low levels of income support for the poor (with a narrow range of eligible beneficiaries). America lacks a European-style 'welfare state' and what it possesses – principally, education – is organized and delivered at state and local levels with little federal involvement.

Americans therefore tend not to think of *the* government in the way that Britons think about the Thatcher or Blair governments. Instead, 'government' in general is seen as a tangible but distant entity and a force of at best limited worth. Table 1.2 notes four dimensions on which Americans typically express different attitudes towards government from the peoples of other nations. As the Republican Senator, Conrad Burns, noted, his constituents' attitudes towards the federal government were simple: 'Defend our shores. Deliver our mail. And we'll call you when we need you' (Esler, 1997: 287–8).

This does not mean that Americans do not accept government benefits. They do so in many forms, from taxpayer-funded public parks and monuments (such as the Statue of Liberty in New York City) through federal government regulation of airline safety and consumer products to subsidies for farmers and tax breaks for corporations. The federal government provides supremely efficient and powerful armed forces (the biggest single source of employment in America is the Department of Defense, or 'Pentagon'), a national postage service and old age pensions. Moreover, while America has known almost nothing comparable to the European experience of state ownership of industries such as steel, gas, electricity and water, as Table 1.3 notes, the extent to which government has become a strong regulatory force since Franklin D. Roosevelt's 'New Deal' is remarkable. The existence of thousands of regulations shaping where, how and what businesses can operate means that the term 'free market' is a misleading description of America's political economy.

Nor do Americans reject massive government expenditures or a strong government role across the board. For example, well before 9/11, the Department of Defense

---

TABLE 1.2   Public opinion on government in five democracies

Question	Percentage of those responding				
	USA	Canada	France	Germany	Japan
What about government's power?					
Too much	66	46	44	34	21
About right	30	44	41	41	13
Too little	4	6	16	11	47
Should government redistribute wealth?					
Yes	33	42	71	53	44
Mixed feelings	24	15	13	17	23
No	43	41	16	21	26
Should government provide jobs for all who need them?					
Yes	39	35	73	76	49
No	61	39	27	19	29
Should government provide a decent standard of living for the unemployed?					
Yes	48	65	82	78	58
No	52	31	18	14	22

Source: Gosling (2000: 141).

TABLE 1.3   The political economy of the New Deal

Programme category	Acronym	Origin
Traditional State		
Civil Works Administration	CWA	1933
Public Works Administration	PWA	1933
Civil Conservation Corps	CCC	1933
Works Progress Administration	WPA	1933
Tennessee Valley Authority	TVA	1933
Rural Electrification Administration	REA	1933
Soil Conservation Service	SCS	1935
Regulatory State		
Agricultural Adjustment Administration	AAA	1933
National Recovery Administration	NRA	1933
Securities and Exchange Commission	SEC	1933
Public Utility Holding Company		1935
National Labor Relations Act and Board	NLRB	1935
Fair Labor Standards Act	FLSA	1938
Civil Aeronautics Act and Board	CAB	1938
Redistributive State		
Federal Deposit Insurance Corporation	FDIC	1933
Bank holiday		1933
Home Owners' Loan Corporation	HOLC	1933
Devaluation		1934
Federal Housing Administration	FHA	1934
Federal Reserve reforms	FED	1935
Social Security Act	SSA	1935
Farm Security Administration	FSA	1935
Internal Revenue Service	IRS	1935
Organizational State		
Judiciary reform		1937
Executive Office of the President	EOP	1939
Budget Bureau	OMB	1939
White House staff		1930s
Administrative law		1930s
Federal Bureau of Investigation	FBI	1940s
Joint Chiefs of Staff	JCOS	1940s

Source: Lowi (1995: 37).

received in excess of $240 billion per annum during the 1990s – approximately 15 per cent of the total federal budget. Thirty-eight states and the federal government allow state executions (capital punishment), one of the most powerful endorsements of state action conceivable. Approximately two million Americans are incarcerated in prisons (though some of these are privately owned and run). Even when concern about inflation

TABLE 1.4 Selected federal laws of the 1970s

Year enacted	Statute
1969–70	Child Protection and Toy Safety Act
	Clean Air Amendments
	Economic Stabilization Act
	Egg Products Inspection Act
	Fair Credit Reporting Act
	Mine Safety and Health Act
	National Environmental Policy Act
	Occupational Safety and Health Act
	Poison Prevention Packaging Act
	Securities Investor Protection Act
1971	Economic Stabilization Act Amendments
	Federal Boat Safety Act
	Lead-based Paint Elimination Act
	Wholesome Fish and Fisheries Act
1972	Coastal Zone Management Act
	Consumer Product Safety Act
	Education Amendments Preventing Sex Discrimination
	Equal Employment Opportunity Act
	Federal Election Campaign Act
	Federal Environmental Pesticide Control Act
	Federal Insecticide, Fungicide, and Rodenticide Act
	Federal Water Pollution Control Act Amendments
	Marine Mammal Protection Act
	Marine Protection, Research, and Sanctuaries Act
	Motor Vehicle Information and Cost Savings Act
	Noise Control Act
	Ports and Waterways Safety Act
1973	Agriculture and Consumer Protection Act
	Economic Stabilization Act Amendments
	Emergency Petroleum Allocation Act
	Endangered Species Act
	Flood Disaster Protection Act
1974	Atomic Energy Act
	Commodity Futures Trading Commission Act
	Consumer Product Warranties Act

TABLE 1.4 *continued*

Year enacted	Statute
1974	Council on Wage and Price Stability Act
	Employee Retirement Income Security Act
	Federal Energy Administration Act
	Hazardous Materials Transportation Act
	Housing and Community Development Act
	Pension Reform Act
	Privacy Act
	Safe Drinking Water Act
1975	Age Discrimination Act
	Energy Policy and Conservation Act
	Equal Credit Opportunity Act
1976	Consumer Leasing Act
	Medical Device Safety Act
	Toxic Substances Control Act
1977	Clean Air Act
	Clean Water Act
	Federal Mine Safety and Health Act
	Safe Drinking Water Act
	Surface Mining Control and Reclamation Act

Source: Lowi (1995: 55–6)

and unemployment was especially widespread during the 1970s, federal regulation of the marketplace increased to encompass matters from toy safety to marine life (see Table 1.4). And when the federal government shuts down, as it did in November 1995 as a result of a stalemate between President Clinton and congressional Republicans, Americans were aghast. In preserving national security, imposing law and order, and regulating how businesses operate, government has achieved an extensive and highly influential role (albeit, in regard to business, one that strongly reinforces many Americans' basic antipathy to the state).

But while Americans clearly accept a role for government and have either supported or acquiesced in its expansion since 1933, this does not alter a political culture where government in general, and the federal government especially, are seen as necessary burdens to be tolerated and limited, not celebrated and expanded. Compared to Europe, where experience of tyrannical government encompassed mass exterminations in Nazi Germany and Soviet Russia, American attitudes towards the state are markedly more unfavourable. When Ronald Reagan quipped in 1980 that the most troubling words in the English language were, 'I'm from the government and I'm here to help', he found an instinctively positive response from millions of his compatriots.

One important result of this anti-governmental individualism is that, at its extreme, hostility towards the state can assume forms of suspicion, fear and hatred. Government is frequently seen as responsible for causing problems rather than solving them. Conspiracies and cover-ups – the real ones that have occurred such as Vietnam and Watergate fuelling the imagination of many others that have not – have therefore formed a marked presence in American politics.

When asked in 1994 to describe the biggest threat to the nation, two out of three Americans answered 'Big Government' (in 1954 only 16 per cent named government as a threat). Opinion polls in 2000 showed that three out of four voters did not trust government 'to do the right thing' when making decisions, and hostility to government survived even the response to September 11.

A second aspect of the anti-government sentiment, reinforcing suspicion of those occupying seats of power, is that politics and politicians do not rate highly among American affections. A succession of political scandals – from Watergate to the collapse of Enron in 2001 – confirmed Americans' suspicions about politics as a 'dirty business'. As Table 1.5 notes, politicians rank above only prostitutes in the public's view of their ethical standards. Mayor Quimby's ethically challenged character in *The Simpsons* epitomizes many Americans' conviction that politics is anything but a noble calling to public service. Ironically, the political values bequeathed Americans by the Declaration and Constitution make them simultaneously proud of their system of government but suspicious of

Exhibit 1.6   From Red Scare to Fed scare: American conspiracies

From 1947 to 1991, America was pre-occupied by the Cold War against international communism. One of the less positive consequences of its end was an outpouring of new targets for American fears, many to be found at home. In particular, the federal government has become the focus of conspiracy theories. Assassinations (JFK, Malcolm X, RFK, Martin Luther King), cover-ups (Vietnam, Watergate, Iran–Contra, Whitewater, Enron), and the FBI monitoring of public figures from presidents and civil rights activists to artists such as Frank Sinatra and John Lennon, suggested deliberate wrongdoing in the highest places. During her husband's evasions over Monicagate in 1998, Hillary Clinton attributed his political problems not to zipper trouble or perjury but to a 'vast right-wing conspiracy'. In popular culture, TV programmes such as *The X Files*, and films such as *Conspiracy Theory, Murder at 1600, Enemy of the State* and *Arlington Road* had plots featuring individuals and agencies within government as the authors of malign schemes against their own gullible and unwilling people. That the evidence for such sinister schemes is frequently flimsy does not matter much either to its purveyors or consumers since, as Richard Hofstadter once observed of 'the paranoid style' in American politics, the greatest evidence for the existence of a successful conspiracy is, paradoxically, the complete absence of any evidence.

TABLE 1.5 Respect in American life for a sample of occupations

Question: 'How would you rate the ethical standards of people in the following fields?'

Occupation	Very high/high (%)	Occupation	Very high/high (%)
Scientist	73	Journalist	28
Teacher	73	Federal worker	28
Clergy	72	Lawyer	24
Farmer	70	Stockbroker	24
Doctor	69	Union leader	24
Engineer	63	Professional athlete	22
Judge	63	Insurance executive	20
Military officer	59	Actor	17
Police officer	52	Politician	15
Banker	36	Prostitute	7

Source: *National Journal*, June 3, 2000, p. 1775.

those seeking, wielding and occupying positions of power within it.

Politics, then, is built into American identity in ways quite unlike those of most other peoples – even as many Americans themselves express neither interest in politics nor faith in politicians. No nation has succeeded so spectacularly – though many (not least Nazi Germany and communist states) have tried – in building political values into the hearts and minds of its people. Paradoxically, it is this Creed that simultaneously unites and divides them. For these values do not necessarily lead to similar views emerging on specific questions. For example, should freedom trump equality on affirmative action? Should respect for minority rights (liberalism) encourage judges to strike down laws passed by majorities of legislators in elected assemblies that infringe them (democracy)? The very consensus on fundamental values as a whole frequently leads to dissensus and division on specific issues where they are applied in practice.

This means that it is possible to identify distinct ideological tendencies in America but the differences between these occur within a basic range of consensus on fundamental values that is broad – such differences as exist are matters of degree rather than nature. Conventional approaches to the division in modern (post-1933) American politics distinguish between 'liberals' and 'conservatives' – now broadly to be found in the Democratic and Republican parties, respectively. But it is more accurate to identify four distinct tendencies in American politics: liberals, conservatives, libertarians and populists. In essence, the differences can be captured by thinking about whether it is desirable to have government 'on our backs', 'in our boardrooms' and 'in our bedrooms.' Exhibit 1.7 captures this in diagrammatic form on two axes: a vertical axis that pits the values of freedom and equality against each other along an economic dimension; and a horizontal axis pitting liberty against order along a social dimension.

Liberty and equality, then, provide the basic touchstones of American political

Exhibit 1.7   Ideology in America: backs, boardrooms and bedrooms

EQUALITY

Liberals	**Populists**
Pro: Government actions to promote equality, e.g. more spending on public housing and affirmative action programmes	*Pro*: Government actions to promote equality, e.g. minimum wage laws and health care programmes
Anti: Government actions that restrict individual liberties, e.g. baning flag-burning or sexually explicit movies	*Pro*: Government actions that impose social order, such as banning flag-burning or 'obscene' movies
On backs and in boardrooms, out of bedrooms (Al Gore)	On backs, in boardrooms and bedrooms (Perot; Pat Buchanan)

LIBERTY ———————————————————————— **ORDER**

Libertarians	**Conservatives**
Anti: Government actions that interfere with the market, e.g. affirmative action or 'socialized medicine'	*Anti*: Government actions that interfere with the market, e.g. affirmative action, health care, social programmes
Anti: Government actions that restrict individual liberties, such as censorship or anti-gay laws	*Pro*: Government actions that impose social order, e.g. bans on pornography, flag-burning, same-sex marriages
Off backs and boardrooms, out of bedrooms (Jack Kemp)	Off backs and boardrooms, and in bedrooms (George W. Bush)

FREEDOM

conflict. In terms of broad partisan identities and competing arguments on specific issues, political disagreement tends to revolve around these core values of the American Creed. Once these competing dimensions are taken into account, it becomes easier to understand how Americans with competing views co-exist in the two main parties, with conflicts within the parties traditionally as widespread and important in American politics as those between them (a theme we return to in detail in Chapter 3).

AMERICAN EXCEPTIONALISM: HOW DIFFERENT?

American exceptionalism – the notion that America is either different or unique, if not superior, to other nations – has an impressive historical record. The lack of a feudal tradition, absence of a serious socialist movement, dominance of classical liberal values, and resilience of the Creed together marked out America as distinctive. In its strongest sense, exceptionalism suggested a uniqueness that fitted well with prosperity, stability and (with the crucial exception of Vietnam) impressive military success. More modestly, America appeared at least different from elsewhere. But that difference has been double-edged: the aspirational values of Americanism can encourage lawlessness among many to achieve the ends of material success that appear to be denied them by legal means. Nevertheless, the centrality of America's founding values to social, political and economic life seemed clear.

This is less so today. During most of the twentieth century, the responsibilities and size of government agencies increased substantially in developed industrial nations. The history of the state in Europe, Australia and Asia over the last 100 years has been one of almost continual expansion into areas – social insurance, health care, economic management, education, environmental protection – where once its role was strictly limited. America is no exception. One can even argue that since its tradition of *laissez-faire* capitalism was so robust previously, the embrace of a government role in regulating the market has been that much more significant in America. Even prior to September 11, claims that, as Bill Clinton put it in 1996, 'the era of big government is now over' were not fully correct.

Similarly, the question that was for so long applied to America – 'why is there no socialism?' – can now be applied equally to most industrialized democracies. As Exhibit 1.8 shows, social scientists differ on the reasons why America has not seen a successful socialist party. Some focus on the nation's sociology or history; others on its political system. Either way:

> The absence of a European aristocratic or feudal past, a relatively egalitarian-status structure, an achievement-oriented value system, comparative affluence, and a history of political democracy prior to industrialization have all operated to produce a system which remains unreceptive to proposals for class-conscious leftism. (Lipset, 1996: 109)

But in Europe and Australasia, where influential political parties retain the labels 'socialist' or 'labour', the content of these parties' programmes no longer challenges market capitalism. In this sense, the left in general has been 'Americanized'. If there exists an anomaly among industrialized democracies, it is not the lack of a socialist party but more the absence of a significant Green party that is of consequence in America (no Greens, for example, sit in the US Congress).

One can therefore argue that, to the extent that some convergence has occurred between America and other western nations, the appropriate metaphor is that of a convoy:

> In a convoy, ships sail together, though often spread over a considerable area of ocean. Sometimes ships in the convoy move at slightly different speeds, and perhaps . . . in different directions. By and large, however, the ships move at much the same speed in the same direction. The relationship between the United States and other advanced industrialized countries has been similar. In terms of the development and contraction of government agencies, the United States is toward the rear of the convoy. Yet it is part of the convoy, and the direction in which the American state heads is in the direction of the convoy's other members. (Wilson, 1998: 131)

Whether knowingly or unknowingly reflecting such an approach, popular journalists regularly speak of 'Americanizing' trends at work in Europe. Some of these are political (the decline in the scope and intensity of ideological conflict between the main political parties, technological developments in campaigning – such as faxes, computers and the Internet – and governing, such as political advisors and focus groups). Others are cultural: the spread of American clothes, food, film, literature, art, music and even language. On this view, then, a convergence is occurring that makes Europeans and Americans increasingly similar. As the old phrase once had it: 'An Englishman is much like an American, with the volume turned down.'

Exhibit 1.8 Why no socialism?

SOCIETAL EXPLANATIONS

- The absence of feudalism minimized the existence of class consciousness around entrenched social divisions and reinforced the individualist ethos of American political culture.
- Americanism or the American Creed came to be 'surrogate socialism', in which the 'liberal tradition' was rapidly entrenched as the dominant public philosophy: promoting a 'socialist conception of capitalism' in which each American is free and equal to become unequal.
- A value system emphasizing individualism and revolutionary, anti-government values undermined popular belief in government or the state as a benevolent or effective agent for beneficial social change.
- A steady rise in living standards helped to reinforce the appeal of the 'American Dream' and the design of American political institutions. As Werner Sombart remarked in 1906, 'all Socialist utopias came to nothing on roast beef and apple pie'.
- The poorest fifth of Americans are concentrated among relatively marginalized groups with a low propensity to vote, thereby undermining the prospects of state-sponsored measures for equality of outcome receiving hearings in government.
- Productivity, increased access to education and increased opportunities for upward social mobility after the Second World War reinforced the sense of a uniquely blessed nation.
- Many Americans exhibit a propensity for geographic movement and migration within the United States, leading to a relative lack of the type of stable community roots in which class-conscious movements traditionally prospered.
- A multi-ethnic and multi-racial immigrant society ensured that:
  - (i) the upward mobility of native-born whites was helped by a racial and ethnic division of labor.
  - (ii) the working class was fragmented, with race and ethnicity becoming 'wedge' issues dividing peoples with otherwise similar economic interests.
  - (iii) a large Catholic working class (especially with Irish and Italian roots) developed that was strongly resistant to socialism.

POLITICAL EXPLANATIONS

- The early attainment of the suffrage by white propertied males, predating industrialization and the struggles for socialism that typically accompanied it in Europe, undermined the basis for a left-wing party or movement.
- The US Constitution and the plurality electoral system encouraged a presidential focus to national politics and institutionalized a bias against third parties or candidates (e.g. the New Deal, the racially and culturally conservative American Independence Party of 1968, and Ross Perot in 1992).
- The flexibility of the two-party system helped to co-opt or respond to discontent, with one or both main parties embracing any insurgent movements.
- Repression (Red Scares in 1919, McCarthyism in late 1940s/1950s) helped to punish 'subversives' and discourage others from joining their ranks.

Even if this is true, however, America remains tenaciously 'different': the expressly political values that make up American identity; the deeply unfavourable view of power,

Exhibit 1.9 Explaining American exceptionalism

Although this chapter has emphasized the importance of values to American political development, many academics disagree on their centrality. Social scientists have explained American 'difference' in competing approaches:

- *Sociological approaches.* Class – or the relative absence of class-consciousness – is often noted. America lacked a feudal structure that pitted aristocrats against peasants. The notion that all persons are created equal (even if they end up unequal) was more plausible than in Europe. Another related aspect is upward social mobility. Americans are used to enjoying greater affluence and better standards of living than their parents. Finally, the existence of pronounced economic inequality plays a key role: in no other nation do such extremes of wealth co-exist with such a pervasive conviction that this is a positive sign of a healthily functioning system (1 per cent of Americans own 39 per cent of national wealth compared to 25 per cent in the UK).
- *Institutional approaches.* The chief explanation of exceptionalism can be attributed to the design of America's political institutions. For example, federalism, the separation of powers, staggered elections and the plurality electoral system have produced a remarkably stable two-party system that has proven impenetrable by third-party challenges. Another example of institutional effects is that the responsibility for taxing and spending decisions in Congress lies with different committees. Lawmakers – and the public – are therefore not faced with the need to reconcile decisions on both as they are in the UK or France.
- *Multiple traditions.* Writers such as Rogers Smith, Gary Gerstle and Desmond King have argued that race and ethnicity have played a more central role in structuring American politics and preventing America's emergence as a genuine democracy until 1965 than is conventionally acknowledged. They stress that competing traditions to the official Creed (or civic nationalism) – especially ones based on racialized conceptions of American identity – require recognition to understand fully America's development.
- *Path dependency.* A final approach to American development emphasizes the extent to which nations become locked into particular 'paths' that are only broken by traumatic national or international crises. In this view, since the Civil War, America has faced many profound problems but none of a scale and nature that have achieved a radical shift in the basis of the American political, social or economic order.

authority, and their embodiment in government; and the profound religious commitments and activism that still strongly underpin most Americans' values and beliefs. Together, these features distinguish America strongly from its democratic peers. The movies, music and food consumed in Paris and Prague may be increasingly similar to those in Pittsburgh and El Paso but that cannot mask the substantial gulf in values, beliefs and attitudes that separates America from the rest of the world. Equally, while the communications revolution has brought Birmingham, England and Birmingham,

Alabama closer in some respects, they remain to all intents and purposes different worlds for their respective inhabitants.

CONCLUSION

Politics is a dynamic, not a static, process – especially in America. Too often, its dynamism can be neglected in focusing on the structural features of government that suggest an excessively formalistic, static and unchanging picture that stresses 'government' at the expense of 'politics'. We can isolate as separate categories the social base, governing institutions, and intermediary institutions for purposes of academic analysis. But the 'down and dirty' reality is that these three dimensions feed into each other continuously, producing a complex democratic system that, despite its apparent continuity in governing arrangements, is constantly facing challenge and undergoing change.

This chapter has emphasized the foundational values that Americans adhere to since these shape their attitudes, beliefs and behaviour in profound and complicated ways. In turn, the governing institutions that generate public policy do so through responding to each other and the mass public. The latter are conveyed to the corridors of government power – executive, legislature and judiciary – through political parties, interest groups, bureaucratic agencies and the mass media. How far the Framers of the Constitution and subsequent generations of Americans have succeeded in their original goals – not least in reconciling the need for effective government with respect for individual freedoms and rights – is a question to which the rest of this book offers some answers.

FURTHER READING

Seymour Martin Lipset, *American Exceptionalism: A Double-Edged Sword* (1996) is an excellent summary of the key ideas.

Graham Wilson, *Only in America? The Politics of the United States in Comparative Perspective* (1998) gives a useful summary of the theoretical and empirical work on exceptionalism.

Eric Foner, *The Story of American Freedom* (1998) is an elegant and readable history of the key American values from the republic's origins to today.

Michael Foley, *American Political Ideas* (1991) provides an elegant discussion of the several (conflicting) values that underpin Americanism.

Desmond King, *Making Americans: Immigration, Race, and the Origins of the Diverse Democracy* (2000) is a scholarly study that details the importance of race and ethnicity in defining who can be classified as American.

Anthony King, 'Distrust of Government: Explaining American Exceptionalism', chapter 4 in Susan J. Pharr and Robert D. Putnam (eds), *Disaffected Democracies: What's Troubling the Trilateral Countries?* (2000) is a lucid and elegant analysis of the sources of American suspicion of government.

QUESTIONS

- Can anyone become an American?

- To what extent and why is the notion that Americans dislike government a myth?

- 'It has been our fate as a nation not to have ideologies but to be one.' If so, how do we account for the pronounced political conflicts that have occurred in America?

- Are the forces that divide Americans more powerful than those that unite them?

- In what respects, if any, is America still 'exceptional'?

2 The US Constitution

We've got a fantastic Constitution.

> President George W. Bush, January 15, 2002

I do not believe that the meaning of the Constitution was forever 'fixed' at the Philadelphia Convention. Nor do I find the wisdom, foresight and sense of justice exhibited by the Framers particularly profound. To the contrary, the government they devised was defective from the start, requiring several amendments, a civil war and momentous social transformation to attain the system of constitutional government, and its respect for individual freedoms and human rights, we hold as fundamental today.

> Justice Thurgood Marshall, Bicentennial of the Constitution, 1987

- Origins: What did the Founding Fathers want to Achieve?
- Why has the Constitution endured so long and changed so little?
- Constitutional Amendment and Judicial Adaptation
- Interpreting the Constitution
- An Aid to Social Change or a Barrier?
- Conclusion

Chapter Summary

The Constitution of the United States is the single most important feature of American government and – with the Declaration of Independence – the foundation of national unity. The Constitution's significance to politics is immense. Its intimate connection with the republic's founding means that American identity is inherently tied to the original document establishing a new and distinctive political settlement. Partly as a result,

America's pronounced political stability owes its greatest debt to the Constitution. Founded on a pervasive fear of majority tyranny, the Constitution sought to achieve a representative and republican system of government and an effective national government. But simultaneously, it also divided, limited and checked the power of government generally and the three branches of the federal government in particular. Akin to an elaborate game of 'paper, rock, scissors', any one branch can hamper the actions of another. Although the document has only been formally amended 27 times since 1787 – despite over 10,000 bills having been introduced in Congress to do so – the Constitution's apparent changelessness masks its 'unofficial' adaptation by federal and state courts. Despite the many academic criticisms that have been made against it (not least its alleged inappropriateness for governing a twenty-first-century society), the Constitution remains revered by Americans. More than any other nation, political life is pervaded by the need for all branches of government, public officials and public policies to adhere to the federal Constitution's provisions as supreme – the key guarantor of the rule of law and the preservation of political freedom, democracy and limited government.

Despite near-universal American pride in their form of government, the term 'democracy' can be found in neither the Declaration of Independence nor the Constitution of the United States. More than any other constitutional democracy in the contemporary world, however, the Constitution is seen by most Americans as safeguarding a supremely democratic form of limited government in which the exercise of tyrannical power – whether by an individual, an elite or a mass of citizens – is prevented. American government and politics today, as much as in 1787, cannot be understood without first understanding the federal constitution (each of the 50 states also possesses its own state constitution).

As Michael Foley (1991) observes, if 'Americanism' is a secular religion, the Constitution provides its holy writ and the courts its high priests. So important is the document that it surfaces with a familiarity and frequency in everyday talk in ways that the French, German or British constitutions are seldom heard of in France, Germany or the UK. Revered by most Americans and reviled by few (if any), even those who criticize individual parts of the document invariably defend its overall design and marvel at its remarkable capacity for endurance. If acting in an 'un-American' fashion is a grave matter of political heresy, then violating the Constitution – the most elemental of 'un-American' acts – is tantamount to treason.

Exactly why such intense emotion and universal reverence should continue to be stirred among millions of citizens by a short piece of parchment composed over 200 years ago by an elite group of propertied white Anglo-Saxon men whose original conception of democracy explicitly included neither women nor blacks is sometimes perplexing for non-Americans. To explain this, the chapter examines the Constitution's origins, content and aims, and the methods by which its goals were addressed. Finally, we look at the arguments as to whether America has prospered because of, or despite, its Constitution, and assess the main criticisms of a document whose enormous influence contrasts so sharply with its short length.

ORIGINS: WHAT DID THE FOUNDING FATHERS WANT TO ACHIEVE?

A Brief History

The United States originally began as a settlement of 13 colonies on the northeastern seaboard of America, subject to the rule of the

British crown. Each colony had some amount of self-government and was mostly independent of the others. Until the late 1700s British political authority had relatively little effect on day-to-day life, but the passage of a series of acts to gain revenue for the British by taxing the colonists – to pay for war debts – prompted a popular American revolt under the banner of 'no taxation without representation'. (Antipathy to taxes remains powerful today.) By 1776, the Second Continental Congress asked Thomas Jefferson to write what became the second most famous and influential document in American history: the Declaration of Independence. The Declaration eloquently expressed the colonists' frustrations with seemingly arbitrary British rule and set out the Enlightenment ideals of the consent of the governed and natural rights (including life, liberty and 'the pursuit of happiness'). Thereby, the Declaration provided the catalyst and rationale for the revolutionary War of Independence against the British.

But it was another document, the Articles of Confederation, adopted in 1781, that established a new system of government for the 13 independent states under a confederal system. Similar to the structure of the United Nations today, the confederation allowed each individual state its own power and autonomy, with citizenship a state matter and the federal government possessing no real authority over either the states or individual citizens. The national government was hence too weak to function effectively, with no separate executive branch, no judicial branch and a unicameral Congress. The confederation's national government had no power either to impose taxes or regulate commerce between individual states. With no tax-raising power it could neither pay war debts nor provide an adequate national defence. Such major problems rapidly became apparent and prompted the establishment of the Constitutional Convention of 1787 to devise another set of arrangements by which the states could better be governed.

The Convention, held in Philadelphia, comprised 55 delegates from 12 of the 13 states (all but Rhode Island). Their deliberations encompassed many difficult political issues: whether political representation should be based on population or equality, whether slavery should be allowed, and how to account for slaves in determining population levels (notoriously, they compromised on slaves as 'three-fifths' of a person). Heated disputes occurred over the powers of the central authority, whether the main economic focus of America should be agricultural or mercantile (and the degree of protectionism desirable) and whether the foreign policy of the new nation should be internationalist or insular. Those delegates favouring strong central institutions – a virtual unitary state – shrewdly adopted the title of 'Federalists', while their opponents – who favoured a loose confederation of individual states – defined themselves (effectively by default) as 'Anti-Federalists'.

Neither side secured an unambiguous victory at Philadelphia. The majority of delegates produced a plan that dealt exclusively with the relative authority of the new central institutions and rejected the idea of formal guarantees of the rights of either the individual states or citizens. But the process of ratifying the new Constitution forced the Federalists to concede the main demand of the Anti-Federalists and establish a 'Bill of Rights' (the former's arguments are captured in *The Federalist Papers*, popular tracts of the time designed to secure support for the new document). The essence of this settlement was, then, a compromise based on the failure of the pure Federalist agenda. The Framers also considered the merits of a parliamentary system of government, proposed under the Virginia Plan, whereby the legislature would choose the executive (as in the UK), or the New Jersey plan, where an Electoral College would select the executive. In rejecting the Virginia Plan, the Framers embraced a distinctive form of democracy that set America apart from other nations.

But the Framers' greatest fear was that pure democracy would degenerate into a form of tyranny of the majority, or mob rule. Influenced by the ideas of the political philosophers Locke and Montesquieu, the solution they devised was to fashion a representative democracy that provided for individual liberty by limiting the power and authority of the majority. From Locke, the Framers took the notion of rights and the idea that government power should be limited, not untrammelled. From Montesquieu, they took the notion that the three powers of government – executive, legislative and judicial – should be separated among different branches of government. Rather than implement the type of clear and consistent separation favoured by Montesquieu, however, they devised a series of 'checks and balances' so that no one branch of government could possess a monopoly over its particular power. The result was a system that accords each branch of government the necessary power to prevent the other branches from absorbing more power, and that further checks the power of government as a whole.

Part of the explanation for why the Framers are frequently seen as political geniuses – even, or especially, today – is that the Constitution is the oldest codified constitution still in use, its intricate design and complex checks and balances representing a uniquely American contribution to the art of democratic governance. The Philadelphia compromise between Federalists and Anti-Federalists sought to establish an effective federal government (which was absent from 1781 to 1787) but also to divide, restrict, limit, check, and balance that national government's powers, based on five central and related principles:

- The Constitution subordinates the elected 'political' branches of government to

Exhibit 2.1   Key events in the evolution of American democracy

Philosophical influences on the Framers of the Constitution
Montesquieu and the doctrine of separation of powers
Locke and the principle of limited government

British laws and taxes that led to the Declaration of Independence

1764	Sugar Act (Repealed by Parliament in 1766)
1765	Stamp Act (revised by Parliament in 1766)
1767	Townshend Duties (taxes on a range of imported goods, including tea)
1776	Declaration of Independence
1776–81	War of Independence
1781–87	Articles of Confederation

The Constitutional Convention

1787 (May)	Representatives convene in Philadelphia
1787 (July)	Virginia Plan is presented and ultimately rejected
1789	Constitution voted on and ratified by the individual states
1791	Bill of Rights ratified by the individual states

The democratizing of American government

1865–70	13th, 14th and 15th Amendments to the Constitution grant citizenship to the former male slaves
1920	19th Amendment grants all women the right to vote
1964–65	Civil rights legislation helps African Americans overcome local restrictions on voting in the South
1971	26th Amendment grants 18-year-olds the right to vote

itself, as the fundamental law of the nation. Executive actions and laws must hence conform to the Constitution's provisions.

- The Constitution divides and balances powers among the legislative, executive and judicial branches: *legislative* power is assigned to Congress under Article I; *executive* power is delegated to the president under Article II; and *judicial* power, or the power to interpret laws, is entrusted to the Supreme Court under Article III. But each branch has only incomplete control of its particular governmental power, with the institution of 'checks and balances' (see below).
- The Constitution restricts the power, authority and activities of the national government in respect of individual citizens through the Bill of Rights (the first ten amendments to the Constitution, ratified in 1791).
- The power of the national government is limited by granting state governments their own legal and political power and authority by the terms of Article IV of the Constitution and the Tenth Amendment.
- The Constitution contains provisions by which it can be formally amended (see below).

In these interlocking ways, the Constitution has patterned the structure of government and politics from 1787 to the present.

Limiting but 'Energizing' Government

The 'Founding Fathers' who designed the Constitution (no 'mothers' were present at the birth) had what the first female Supreme Court Justice, Sandra Day O'Connor, termed 'an array of intentions'. At the heart of the design, however, was a desire to establish a democratic system and strengthen the organs of national government while simultaneously limiting its power.

To achieve these goals, certain innovations were built into the federal government's architecture that reflected James Madison's conviction that 'ambition must be made to counter ambition'. Not only was the personnel of government separated so that no individual could sit in more than any one branch at a time, but the powers of individual branches of government – the executive, legislative and judicial branches – were both specified and shared. Each branch was granted particular powers and each also had a check on the others, thereby balancing the exercise of any one power by making this a shared matter. No *branch* of government could monopolize the exercise of its appropriate *power* of government so that, for example, although Congress was the legislature (the lawmaking branch of government), it did not possess complete lawmaking powers. American government, then, is a 'separated system': a system of separated institutions sharing powers.

But the Founding Fathers feared that federalism, the separation of powers, and checks and balances between the branches of government were still insufficient guarantees of the rights and liberties of individual citizens. To protect these, the system of elections that they established fragmented an already decentralized government even further. Elected offices of the federal government were given different constituencies, terms of office and modes of election:

- The president is the only figure in American government elected by a national constituency, for a fixed, four-year term (and, since passage of the Twenty-Second Amendment in 1951, may serve a maximum of two terms). But the president is not elected directly by the people. Instead of a popular vote, an Electoral College votes for the president.
- Members of the Senate serve a fixed, six-year term. They were originally selected by their state legislatures (two per state), but since passage of the Seventeenth Amendment in 1913, senators are elected directly by the people. But these elections are staggered so that only one-third of the total number of senators is up for election

every two years. Each state, no matter how few or many persons live there, is accorded two members of the Senate.

- The (currently) 435 members of the House of Representatives serve fixed, two-year terms, and all of them are up for election every two years. Unlike the Senate, the number of seats a state is entitled to in the House is decided every ten years – after the decennial census – on a population basis. From 2002, California – America's most populous state – therefore has 53 members of the House while Wyoming has just one (even though both states have two senators).

The cumulative result of these distinct constituency bases, terms, and timings of elections is shown in Exhibit 2.3.

This introduces further powerful disincentives to collective, purposeful and efficient action in government. Not only is the power of government fragmented rather than concentrated, but those who staff the government face markedly different political pressures and incentives. As Chapters 3 and 4 explain, this makes election campaigns individualistic, candidate-centred and personalized, and thereby renders political parties weak institutions, broad coalitions of remarkably diverse, often dissimilar, and even

Exhibit 2.2   Separation of powers and checks and balances

BRANCHES OF GOVERNMENT			
	The legislature can	*The executive can:*	*The judiciary can:*
LEGISLATIVE		Veto laws	
	Make laws	Recommend laws	Review laws
EXECUTIVE	Confirm executive appointments (Senate)	Enforce the laws	Review executive acts
	Impeach	Grant pardons	Issue injunctions
JUDICIAL	Create and eliminate courts	Nominate judges	Interpret laws

POWERS OF GOVERNMENT

Exhibit 2.3 The elected branches of the federal government

Different *constituencies* elect different *candidates* to different *offices* at different *times* to serve different *terms*:

Constituency	Office	Length of term
Nation	President	4 years
State	Senator	6 years
District	Representative	2 years

diametrically opposed interests (such as when both blacks and southern segregationists co-existed in the Democratic Party from 1932 to 1968). To sceptical observers such as Daniel Lazare (1996), the many divisions of power makes the federal government not only inefficient but also 'frozen' – not so much unlikely to pass new measures rapidly but unable to do so. Whether that is too strong a claim remains to be seen, but at the very least, the incentives for politicians to work together are fewer, and the sanctions for failing to do so weaker, than in most democracies – even if the need to cooperate is at least as great.

As if these institutional divisions were not enough, however, the Anti-Federalists desired further protections against arbitrary government. To this end they proposed, and the Federalists acquiesced in, ten amendments to the 1787 Constitution that were ratified in 1791, known collectively as 'The Bill of Rights' (Exhibit 2.4). The objective of these amendments was to protect further individual citizens' liberties and rights against the newly strengthened federal government. Their goal was to place certain spheres of private life entirely beyond the scope of federal government interference. Protections against the government were hence as important as protections to be secured through the government. Americans were thereby to be provided with a 'double security'. If the government passed a law that infringed one of these constitutional protections, the Bill of

Rights would 'trump' the government's right to legislate what it wished.

Many of the provisions of the Bill of Rights – terms such as 'freedom of speech' and 'cruel and unusual punishment' – are well known outside America (partly, in the UK, since it was the English who bequeathed Americans terms such as the 'right to bear arms'). Even the particular numbers of some of the amendments are known outside America, such as the First and 'taking the Fifth' (not incriminating oneself in a legal proceeding).

The Bill of Rights is as important to politics today as the governing institutions established by the Constitution. No public policy is unaffected by its provisions. Moreover, the Bill of Rights has been crucial in 'constitutionalizing' politics: seeking support for a policy requires more than popular or legislative majorities, it also requires constitutional validity. What this means is that while Americans disagree vociferously on many political issues, they share a notion of how to disagree: by reference to the Constitution. Whether or not a proposal is rational or reasonable – gun control, prohibition of alcohol, allowing same-sex marriages – is not essentially the point. Rather, one question informs policy debates constantly: is the proposal constitutional? In no European nation is everyday political discourse so pervaded by the language of constitutional law. Nor is any nation comparable in the readiness with which ordinary Americans invariably invoke

Exhibit 2.4   The Bill of Rights: what the federal government may not do

The First Amendment: no infringement of freedom of speech, religion, press, assembly or petitioning the government.

The Second Amendment: no infringement of the 'right to keep and bear arms'.

The Third Amendment: no quartering of troops in private property during peacetime.

The Fourth Amendment: no unreasonable searches and seizures of private property.

The Fifth Amendment: no double jeopardy (standing trial twice for the same crime) or self-incrimination; rights in criminal cases.

The Sixth Amendment: rights to a fair trial.

The Seventh Amendment: rights in civil cases.

The Eighth Amendment: no cruel and unusual punishments.

The Ninth Amendment: rights not specified ('enumerated') in the Constitution are retained by the people.

The Tenth Amendment: powers not listed in the Constitution are retained by the states and the people.

their constitutional rights to justify their actions (or to rule actions they dislike impermissible).

As Exhibit 2.5 notes, only 17 amendments have been ratified in the more than 200 years that have passed since the Bill of Rights was enacted, and only 12 during the twentieth century. Most have been concerned with advancing equal rights and, secondarily, reforming government structures. Only two have been concerned with the content of public policy, namely, the establishment and repeal of Prohibition of alcohol. The relative lack of formal amendments has reinforced the conception of the Constitution as an especially sacred and far-sighted work of genius among successive generations of Americans.

Ultimately, then, the combination of a remarkably heterogeneous society, a federal system of specific and limited government powers, a complex set of governing institutions with different officers elected by different constituencies at different times for different terms, equipped with countervailing powers and a Bill of Rights preventing government infringing certain rights and

liberties, together make American politics competitive and complex. The struggle to achieve the cooperation necessary to overcome the many conflict points built into the system occurs against a background of complex constitutional arrangements, competing interpretations of the Constitution's provisions, and a constant election campaign. American democracy is thereby rendered very much alive to its citizens' policy priorities and preferences, but not necessarily always healthy in terms of meeting them fully, promptly or clearly.

WHY HAS THE CONSTITUTION ENDURED SO LONG AND CHANGED SO LITTLE?

As the prior section emphasized, the constitutional settlement of 1787 was very much a compromise. But many important issues also went unresolved at the Philadelphia convention, including whether or not the United States should have a central bank, the basis on which the coinage should be established

Exhibit 2.5 Formal constitutional amendments after the Bill of Rights (numbers 11–27)

Number	Proposed	Ratified	Area of concern*
11	1794	1795	G
Prohibits an individual from suing a state in a federal court without the state's consent			
12	1803	1804	G
Requires the Electoral College to vote separately for president and vice president			
13	1865	1865	E
Prohibits slavery			
14	1866	1868	E
Gives citizenship to all persons born or naturalized in the US (former slaves); prevents states from depriving any 'person of life, liberty, or property, without due process of law'.			
15	1869	1870	E
Guarantees that citizens' rights to vote cannot be denied 'on account of race, colour or previous condition of servitude'.			
16	1909	1913	E
Gives Congress power to collect an income tax.			
17	1912	1913	E
Provides for popular election of senators			
18	1917	1919	P
Bans making/selling intoxicating liquors			
19	1919	1920	E
Gives women the right to vote			
20	1932	1933	G
Changes presidential inauguration from March 4 to January 20			
21	1933	1933	P
Repeals Eighteenth Amendment			
22	1947	1951	G
Limits a president to two terms			
23	1960	1961	E
Gives DC citizens the right to vote for a president			
24	1962	1964	E
Prohibits charging a poll tax to vote			
25	1965	1967	G
Provides for presidential succession, disability, and vice presidential vacancy			
26	1971	1971	E
Lowers voting age to 18			
27	1789	1992	G
Bars immediate pay increases to members of Congress until an intervening election has occurred.			

*P: Amendment legislating public policy; G: Amendment remedying perceived deficiencies in government; E: Amendment advancing equality.

(gold or silver) and the appropriate level of taxation to be transferred to the federal government. Disagreements over these issues raged throughout the nineteenth century – albeit not as fiercely as that over slavery – and were not fully resolved until 1913 (125 years after the convention) when the Sixteenth Amendment allowed a federal income tax to be approved, the Federal Reserve Board was established and both main political parties accepted the Gold Standard, rules which then had to be rewritten in the 1930s.

Yet since relatively few amendments have been ratified, does this suggest that Americans are universally happy with their Constitution? In part, this is the case. With the important exception of the white South during the Civil War, Americans have never wanted to overhaul the entire Constitution and the structure of government that it established. By comparison, the French have endured five changes of regime, each necessitating the design of a new constitutional order, dividing and polarizing French society. Only now, with the Fifth Republic (since 1958), has France enjoyed genuine and lasting political stability.

But American contentment with the Constitution is not the whole story to the nation's remarkable political stability and the respect in which the Constitution is held. Three factors make the Constitution the object of universal reverence in America:

- *Association with the nation-state.* The Constitution is intimately and inextricably bound to the founding of the United States as a new nation. In this sense, to challenge the Constitution as a whole is to challenge the nation itself, and American national identity. Since Americans adhere so tenaciously and intensely to the values contained in the Constitution, to act in an unconstitutional way is to be 'un-American.' National crises such as the Civil War and Vietnam are therefore also constitutional crises. Conversely, constitutional crises such as Watergate and Monicagate are crises of national proportions.
- *Longevity.* The Constitution is the oldest codified constitution in existence. America's survival through a civil war, rapid industrialization, a major economic depression, world wars, the Cold War, massive waves of immigration and internal convulsions over civil rights and Vietnam has occurred under the auspices of the same document. The Constitution has provided a stable fixture in a changing nation and world. In this sense, the simple fact of continuity has invested the document with a symbolic and substantive importance that is difficult to comprehend for many outside America. With each successive year, the sagacity and foresight of the Founding Fathers is reaffirmed, and the remarkable character of the Constitution – formally 'rigid' yet simultaneously adaptive to new political, social and economic circumstances – is embedded still further in the national American psyche.
- *Adaptation and changelessness.* Part of the apparent genius of the Constitution arises from the paradox of change being combined with fundamental continuity. The document seems, at one level, to comprise a series of fixed and eternal truths about the human condition, political values and government. Yet simultaneously, the ambiguity and vagueness of many of its provisions allow the meaning of its clauses to alter in substance – though not form – over time. The relative lack of formal amendments reinforces the combination of stability in governing arrangements with change in the meaning and practical application of the Constitution's various clauses.

These factors have together made the Constitution the venerated source of American pride that it is today. The British Prime Minister William Gladstone even referred to it as 'the most wonderful work struck off at a given time by the brains and purpose of men'. The genius of the Constitution refers not so much to who authored the document (though it is difficult not to admire the innovative and methodical way that they brought into being an entirely new – and still unique – design of government in 1787), but more in the content of the blueprint that they designed. As Isaac Kramnick put it:

Along with the flag, the Constitution stands

alone as a symbol of national unity. America has no royal family, no heritage of timeless and integrative state institutions or symbols, no national church. Add to that America's history of being peopled by diverse religious, national and racial stocks, many of whom came long after the founding, and one can see how the Constitution could become such a focus of national identity and loyalty. There is precious little else to compete with it as an integrative symbol and evocation of America. To this day, in fact, to become an American citizen it is traditional for immigrants to have to pass a test on the Constitution. Unlike the flag, however, which has changed dramatically over the years, with the constantly expanding number of states, the Constitution has endured virtually unchanged for two hundred years. This is, surely, another important source of its status as the focus of American identity, its stability and unchanging quality. (Kramnick, 1987: 12)

CONSTITUTIONAL AMENDMENT AND JUDICIAL ADAPTATION

There are two additional reasons why so few amendments to the document have been passed. One is the difficult amendment mechanism that was established at the time the Constitution was ratified. To achieve this, an amendment must be proposed either by both houses of Congress (two-thirds of the members of each must vote for it) or by a constitutional convention by Congress held at the request of three-quarters of the states. If proposed by either method, the amendment must then be ratified either by three-fourths of state legislatures or by constitutional conventions held in three-fourths of the states (see Exhibit 2.6). In formal language, this means that the Constitution is 'rigid', not 'flexible': it is difficult to muster sufficient popular support to get an amendment through, the two-stage conditions for so doing each being very demanding.

Perhaps the best illustration of this occurred in 1972, when Congress proposed an Equal Rights Amendment (ERA), designed to entrench equality for American women. The passage of the amendment through Congress reflected the substantial – but nevertheless partial – success of women's movements for equal rights during the 1960s and the extension of the black civil rights agenda beyond racial and ethnic minorities. But not enough states then endorsed the amendment for it to be successfully ratified. Congress granted an extension to the time available to ratify in 1978 but by the end of that extension – in 1982 – ERA supporters had not obtained the approval of the 38 states required for ratification. Since such broad public backing is fundamental to amendment politics, successful formal alterations to the document are few and rare.

The second explanation for the lack of amendments is that despite its 'rigidity' the Constitution can be updated and adapted in another way: through the interpretations of federal and state courts. To describe this as an

Exhibit 2.6   Amending the US Constitution

PROPOSAL STAGE Two-thirds vote of members present in both houses of Congress (34 amendments proposed)	*RATIFICATION STAGE* Three-fourths of state legislatures (26 amendments ratified)
or	or
National convention by Congress at the request of two-thirds of state legislatures (no amendments proposed)	Constitutional conventions in three-fourths of the states (one amendment – the 21st – ratified)

'informal' amendment mechanism is a little misleading. Judicial interpretation of the Constitution's clauses is crucial, as is the way that judges reconcile laws with particular constitutional provisions. Law – inherently a matter of form and procedure – is central to this process. Nonetheless, decisions handed down by an independent judiciary – what Supreme Court Chief Justice William Rehnquist termed 'the crown jewel of the Constitution' – can change the practical meaning of the document without altering the actual words. In this way, the rulings that courts give have a profound effect on everyday American life.

Take the Bill of Rights, for example. The first ten amendments of the Constitution were designed to protect individual citizens from the government. But when they were ratified in 1791, the government in question was the federal/national government. The Bill of Rights said nothing about protections for individuals against the governments of the individual states. Over time, however, the Supreme Court 'incorporated' several of the provisions through the 'due process' and 'equal protection' clauses of the Fourteenth Amendment and applied them to the states. For example, the protections for free expression in the First Amendment made against the federal government ('Congress shall make no law . . .') were also applied to state governments in cases dating from *Gitlow v. New York* (1925) to the present.

In a sense, then, the fact that so few formal amendments have occurred gives a misleading impression of the extent to which the 'living Constitution' (the practical meaning rather than its formal façade) has altered dramatically since 1787. The Constitution is not a self-executing document and judicial interpretations have changed its meaning and the reality of American life in profound ways. For its defenders, the Constitution's vagueness is a supreme virtue, allowing it to be adapted over time to apply to new and changing conditions. The deliberate ambiguity of its words and phrases ('due process', 'equal protection') lends itself to versatility in application to a changing real world. But for its detractors, the essence of law is procedure and process. Sticking to the letter of the law and not creatively reading into the law is what judges should be doing in a liberal democracy whose key principle is electoral accountability. To change the real world meaning without formally amending the document is a licence for unelected judges to place their own values and views ahead of the people who wrote the Constitution. This amounts to judicial legislating or 'raw judicial power'. (One reason why this is perceived as problematic is because a definitive judgment by the US Supreme Court on a constitutional issue requires a formal amendment of the Constitution to be overturned (see Chapter 8). Only five amendments to the Constitution have been ratified that overturned a judicial ruling by the Supreme Court.)

Short, ambiguous and imprecise, the Constitution's apparent weaknesses turn out to be its enduring strengths, the 'efficient secret' of its lasting claim to universal American respect. The oldest in the world, with every passing year the genius of its designers seems only more potent to those Americans contemplating the Founding Fathers in 1787 constructing a new and novel constitutional order that still operates in the twenty-first century. And while no other nation has sought to emulate the Constitution in its entirety (in particular, remarkably few have sought to emulate the fragmented system of government set up by the Constitution), the document has proven to be a model from which selective features (the Bill of Rights, especially) have emerged over time as some of America's more successful and important exports.

INTERPRETING THE CONSTITUTION

Since the document is so ambiguous, how should judges go about interpreting it in concrete cases? What, if any, principles should guide their deliberations? These questions are far from abstract or arcane since the answers condition the real world results for millions of Americans. From whether Americans have a right to own firearms, through whether government can prohibit a woman from procuring an abortion, to whether states can allow physician-assisted suicide, all hinge on how one interprets the document. What the document means is literally a matter of life and death for millions of Americans today.

Two basic questions inform the interpretation problem:

- Should courts defer to the will of elected representatives or assert their independence in striking laws down as unconstitutional?
- Should judges read the clauses of the Constitution narrowly or broadly?

The more courts are willing to strike laws down and read the Constitution's provisions broadly (whether for liberal or conservative ends), the more 'activist' courts appear. This can be problematic since, as unelected bodies, to deny elected legislators the fruits of their victories is controversial in a democracy. But the less willing courts are to strike laws down and the more they read constitutional clauses

Exhibit 2.7 Supreme Court cases incorporating (applying to the states) provisions of the Bill of Rights through the due process and equal protection clauses of the Fourteenth Amendment

Provision	Case
First Amendment	
• Freedom of speech and press	*Gitlow v. New York* (1925)
• Freedom of assembly	*Dejonge v. Oregon* (1937)
• Free exercise of religion	*Cantwell v. Connecticut* (1940)
• Establishment of religion	*Everson v. Board of Education* (1947)
Fourth Amendment	
• Unreasonable search and seizure	*Wolf v. Colorado* (1949)
• Exclusionary rule	*Mapp v. Ohio* (1961)
Fifth Amendment	
• Payment of compensation for the taking of private property	*Chicago, Burlington and Quincy R. Co. v. Chicago* (1897)
• Self-incrimination	*Malloy v. Hogan* (1964)
• Double jeopardy	*Benton v. Maryland* (1969)
• When jeopardy attaches	*Crist v. Bretz* (1978)
Sixth Amendment	
• Public trial	*In re Oliver* (1948)
• Right to counsel	*Gideon v. Wainwright* (1963)
• Confrontation and cross-examination of adverse witnesses	*Pointer v. Texas* (1965)
• Speedy trial	*Klopfer v. North Carolina* (1967)
• Compulsory process to obtain witnesses	*Washington v. Texas* (1967)
• Jury trial	*Duncan v. Louisiana* (1968)
Eighth Amendment	
• Cruel and unusual punishment	*Louisiana ex rel. Francis v. Resweber* (1947)

narrowly, the more the decisions of elected bodies will dominate. If this occurs, the rights of individuals and minorities may be abused and 'civilized' values go unprotected.

Although distinctions within the approaches to matters of constitutional interpretation are many and complex, two broad schools of thought have developed on this matter:

- *Interpretivism*. Adherents to interpretivism hold that the only manner in which justices can decide cases of constitutionality is with reference to the Constitution itself. If the words of the document cannot reasonably be read to apply to a case, judges must not intervene. The stricter version of this is sometimes termed 'historical originalism' or 'textualism' – these mean, respectively, that either the original understanding at the time clauses were written or the 'plain meaning' of the text must guide interpretation.

- *Non-interpretivism*. Upholders of non-interpretivism believe in a 'living Constitution'. They see interpretivists as too narrow. Political values inform the Constitution – civil rights, democracy, liberty, minority rights – and need to be defended and promoted. Too zealous an adherence to the Constitution's original or plain meaning would yield policy results that are repugnant to civilized values in today's world. On this view, the appropriate question is not so much *how* to interpret the Constitution but *whether* to do so at all through originalist methods.

The issues raised by constitutional interpretation are complex and important ones. This is not only a matter of the individual laws or policies that they affect but also the entire design of constitutional government. The Bill of Rights was intended to protect the

Exhibit 2.8   Originalism in the dock of time and civilization

The method of interpreting the Constitution according to the literal intentions of its authors is known as 'original intent'. Advocates of this method of constitutional interpretation claim that judges are obligated to find out what the Framers intended by the words they used in writing the Constitution (and its amendments).

But critics of original intent argue that most of the Framers did not expect those who came after them to be bound strictly by their work in perpetuity, regardless of changing social conditions or values. Rather, they expected that the basic principles of the Constitution would be retained but details would be adapted to meet the changing and unforeseen circumstances of the future. Justice William Brennan commented in 1985 that:

We current Justices read the Constitution in the only way we can: as Twentieth Century Americans. We look to the history of the time of framing and to the intervening history of interpretation. But the ultimate question must be, what do the words of the text mean in our time? For the genius of the Constitution rests not in any static meaning it might have had in a world that is dead and gone, but in the adaptability of its great principles to cope with current problems and current needs. (Brennan, 1985: 19)

Originalists reply, however, that the rule of law cannot be maintained unless judges apply the Constitution to current controversies as the Framers intended it to be applied. As Ronald Reagan's Attorney General, Edwin Meese III, put it, the problem with Brennan's 'living Constitution' approach '. . . is not that it is bad constitutional law, but that it is not constitutional law in any meaningful sense at all'. If original intent is ignored, judges become lawmakers not law-interpreters, forsaking their duty to maintain an unbroken continuity of constitutional meaning from the founding era to today.

Exhibit 2.9   Original intent v. A 'living Constitution': a case study

A good but difficult example of the complex questions raised by the interpretation debate occurred in *Maryland v. Craig* (1990), a case concerning the prosecution of an adult accused of sexually abusing a young child. The key question raised was whether a child could testify in court with only the prosecutor and defence counsel present (the defendant [her alleged abuser], judge and jury watching over closed-circuit television). The trial court had found that the child was too frightened to testify with the defendant physically present in the courtroom. The Supreme Court upheld the constitutionality of Maryland's state law that permitted her to testify with only the two counsels present.

But Justice Antonin Scalia dissented from the majority ruling in the case because the Sixth Amendment to the Constitution states that: '[I]n all criminal prosecutions the accused shall enjoy the right . . . to be confronted with the witnesses against him.' When originally written by the Framers, confrontation meant face-to-face confrontation, the intention being to make it more difficult for witnesses to lie to someone's face. The plain language seems clear: the term 'all' is unequivocal. But many today feel unease at forcing a child to be confronted by an alleged abuser in court.

Scalia subsequently argued:

Now no extrinsic factors have changed since that provision was adopted in 1791. Sexual abuse existed then, as it does now; little children were more easily upset than adults, then as now; a means of placing the defendant out of sight of the witness existed then as now (a screen could easily have been erected that would enable the defendant to see the witness, but not the witness the defendant). But the Sixth Amendment nonetheless gave *all* criminal defendants the right to *confront* the witnesses against them, because that was thought to be an important protection. The only significant things that *have* changed . . . are society's sensitivity to so-called psychic trauma . . . and the society's assessment of where the proper balance ought to be struck between the two extremes of a procedure that assures convicting 100 percent of all child abusers, and a procedure that assures acquitting 100 percent of those falsely accused of child abuse. I have no doubt that the society is, as a whole, happy and pleased with what my Court decided. But we should not pretend that the decision did not *eliminate* a liberty that previously existed. (Scalia, 1997: 44)

individual against the government and minorities against the majority – including, as in Exhibit 2.9, the rights of criminal defendants. If its meaning becomes dependent on what judges believe either they or a majority of the public desire, then this will reverse the entire purpose of the document: what should be a restraint on majoritarianism instead becomes an expression thereof. The debate over how to interpret the Constitution's provisions, then, goes to the very heart of the design of American democracy and the character of contemporary life. We will return to this when we examine how courts have gone about deciding cases involving the Constitution in Chapter 8.

AN AID TO SOCIAL CHANGE OR A BARRIER?

If Americans disagree over whether and how to interpret the Constitution, one of the relatively few features of the document about which most concur is that its provisions are vague and ambiguous. That ambiguity has permitted the Constitution to 'evolve' through interpretation over time but critics disagree over whether that ambiguity has either helped to hinder necessary social change or assisted in bringing it about. It is partly because American history has been replete with instances of illiberalism (slavery,

segregation, anti-Semitism, Japanese internment during the Second World War, repression, McCarthyism, 'political correctness')
that the issue of social change is so important.
And, despite their supposed role as protec-
tors of minorities against majority tyranny,
even Supreme Court decisions have upheld
(only later to strike down) some of these
practices – such as slavery, segregation, and
Japanese internment – on the basis of the US
Constitution.

Three main lines of criticism have been
particularly prominent in both academic and
popular writings on the Constitution.

The Constitution is elitist

The Founding Fathers had many differences
in their political views but shared a common
status as white, propertied men (many of
whom owned slaves). The document they
wrote protected their own economic interests
through the governmental structures it established and excluded both women and blacks
from American citizenship. Slaves – though
not mentioned by that term – were specifically included in Article I, Section 2, to count
as 'three fifths of all other Persons' for purposes of calculating state representation in
Congress and taxation levels. It was not until
the ratification of the Nineteenth Amendment
in 1920 that women were granted the right to
vote. As Thurgood Marshall, the first of only
two black Supreme Court justices, caustically
observed on its bicentennial, the Constitution
was 'defective from the start'.

But while the document of 1787 clearly did
not yield a democratic regime and slavery
and segregation are indictments on American
history, the difficulty here is assessing the
Constitution in today's terms. No constitution written in the eighteenth century was
likely to be fully democratic and representative in the terms familiar to the democratic
world of 2003 (the American one was remarkably enlightened for its particular time in
many respects). Moreover, the fact that
women and blacks have been able to use its
provisions to achieve political and civil

equality has demonstrated its political utility.
In the case of women, the use of the term
'persons' rather than men suggested that the
Constitution was intended to be inclusive.
While the absence of equality for blacks
meant America could only be considered a
full democracy from 1965, African Americans
appealed to the Constitution's own provisions to achieve social change. Most nations
have experienced internal and violent
upheavals, and several regime changes and
constitutions. Not only does America owe its
relative political stability to the Constitution,
but the Constitution has been remarkably
successful in allowing for its own democratization, encouraging its transformation while
preserving its core values and government
structures.

The Constitution is outmoded and inappropriate

Is the Constitution simply outmoded and ill-
suited to today's America? Exactly why current generations of Americans should be
bound in the Internet age to the quill-written
views of their ancestors is unclear. Take two
examples: much of the debate about gun control today still revolves around what the Second Amendment to the Constitution means –
does it give an individual citizenship right of
gun ownership, or is this a right limited to
service in a state militia? For many advocates
of gun control, the notion that a primary barrier to rational firearms laws is a provision
written in 1791 is ludicrous. Similarly, on
abortion, much of the debate has focused on
whether the Supreme Court was correct to
create a constitutional right to legalized abortion, in 1973, on the basis of a woman's 'right
to privacy'. Some argue that because the term
'right to privacy' does not explicitly exist
anywhere in the document, the Court was
wrong to invent it. Again, for many Americans, to debate the rights and wrongs of
important social policies – whether guns,
abortion, capital punishment or gay rights –
in terms of an eighteenth-century document
of 7,000 words seems absurd.

But this is arguably a misplaced criticism. The 'problem' about firearms or abortion or capital punishment is not so much the Constitution as the society. That is, Americans possess different beliefs about, for example, the importance of private legal access to guns. Many Americans are also strongly divided over these issues (though less so than often imagined). If Americans in a particular state, or all states, want to outlaw the death penalty, they can, and 12 states have done so. The Constitution does not require Americans to impose capital punishment or to use guns. It simply allows this to occur if sufficient numbers so wish. On this interpretation, then, the Constitution has not locked Americans into some eighteenth-century time warp. Rather, the evolving preferences of the public have led to policies and practices sanctioned by the Constitution, some of which non-Americans may dislike but many of which receive substantial support in the United States.

The Constitution is inefficient

Far from facilitating adaptation to a changed America, some critics, such as Lazare (1996) and Putley (1997), see the Constitution as a barrier to social change and a force for governmental inefficiency. They note that no other modern democracies have modelled their designs for government on that of America, the reason being that the American design appears a recipe for 'gridlock'. With so many veto points and checks and balances, it is tremendously difficult to achieve policy changes, especially at the federal level. For some, this means that government simply fails to deliver needed policy solutions to pressing problems that were not envisaged in the eighteenth century: environmental decay, industrial failure or health care provision. For others, the main deficiency of government is that the laws it produces are invariably compromises – lowest common denominator deals that partially satisfy multiple American constituencies (sufficient to muster legislative

majorities) but fully satisfy none and fail to resolve policy problems.

For many Americans, the Constitution has prevented, or at least slowed down, the likelihood of far-reaching social, economic and political change. On this interpretation, the Constitution is a fundamentally conservative force. This is partly due to the fragmented system of government it established, which makes it easier to stop than start innovative policies. It is also because some constitutional provisions suggest powerful entrenched barriers to change, for example with regard to gun control. And the courts' ability to strike down laws as unconstitutional means that even if Congress passes an innovative bill that the president signs into law, this is not the last word in whether or not it is implemented. Compromise is the watchword of American politics but this is rarely easy to achieve and typically requires a lengthy process. As a result, for example, black Americans had to endure decades of devastating deprivation and unequal treatment before gaining even formally equal political and civil rights to whites, while even today women – to some feminists – remain denied in practice the constitutionally guaranteed equality rights to which they are entitled in theory.

From an alternative perspective, however, a constitution that did not succeed in providing a substantial measure of political stability would be an odd and ineffective document. Constitutions are invariably designed, at least in part, to be conservative devices, ensuring that change can occur but only within an overall framework of fundamental continuity of political arrangements. In many cases, the reason for an absence of change has not been so much the constitutional design of American institutions, as it has been the policy priorities and preferences of the American people. That is, Americans have either been opposed, divided or indifferent to change.

Most Americans, for example, consistently favour stronger federal gun controls, but they tend not to mobilize in sufficient numbers, or vote on this basis, to overcome the intense minority opposition that exists to tougher federal gun control. To attribute weak firearms regulation to the Second Amendment is, on this interpretation, misplaced. Similarly, while the constitutional design allows for Americans to vote for tax-cutting presidents and members of Congress intent on raising social spending, it does not require them to do so. Apportioning the blame for the trillion dollar budget deficits of the 1980s on the Constitution, rather than on the conflicting preferences of the people as expressed in the elections returning divided party control of the federal government, again seems mistaken.

The Constitution does not prevent change from occurring – quite the contrary. Its design provides for many different possible agents of change: the presidency, Congress and the Supreme Court at the federal level, the various branches of the 50 individual states (governors, state legislatures, state courts, mayors, city councils) and provisions for state-wide referendums on measures from same-sex marriage to legalizing cannabis. What the Constitution most emphatically does do is to make change dependent on broad-based public support. Where that is lacking, change is unlikely to occur. But to indict a constitutional order on these grounds is, if not perverse, at least demonstrably lacking sensitivity to the imperative of majority support. Measures in the UK that are passed by a party with a majority of seats at the Westminster parliament elected on a minority of the popular vote – as was invariably the case with the Thatcher and Blair governments – simply cannot get through so easily in the American system. As Morris Fiorina (1992) has argued, this may prevent society from gaining through government action, but it also prevents society from losing through government action.

This is not to suggest that Americans may sometimes press for changes that they later come to view as mistaken. The exemplar of this was Prohibition. From the nineteenth century, a diverse coalition of interests (religious groups, feminists, and labour unions) sought a formal constitutional amendment to prohibit the sale or distribution of alcohol, a drive finally realized in 1919 with ratification of the Eighteenth Amendment. The result was disastrous, fuelling corruption and crime while simply driving up the cost of booze on the vast black market. In 1933, the ratification of the Twenty-First Amendment, to reverse its predecessor, ended the fiction of America as a 'dry' nation after 24 years of social upheaval and political turmoil.

Ultimately, as the Declaration of Independence and the Constitution make clear, the right of the government to govern rests on the consent of the people. But what the government does or does not do also hinges on what the people support or oppose. To attribute America's ills to the Constitution is, on this view, to miss the point about the system of democratic and limited government that it established.

Moreover, while America has clearly failed to live up to its constitutional guarantees fully at points in its history, the existence of those guarantees remains important. In October 1999, for example, when Chinese President Jiang Zemin paid a state visit to the UK, British police invoked a long-dormant law against protesting in 'royal parks' to stop people in London protesting (defined as unfurling flags and banners) against Jiang's visit. The notion that the freedoms of speech, association and expression could be so easily quashed is one entirely alien to America, where even the right of neo-Nazis to stage marches through Jewish communities and white supremacists to burn crosses has been defended under the First Amendment. However imperfect America's history, the record of extending democratic rights under the Constitution has been remarkable. Even groups which one might imagine would be least enamoured of the document, such as African Americans, have been among its most dedicated defenders.

At one level, then, the Constitution inhibits American political life by requiring those seeking political change to muster not only majority endorsement but also constitutional legitimacy. The desirability of change or new laws is secondary to whether or not they are constitutional. That can be a lengthy, frustrating, and even troubling requirement. But simultaneously, the need to achieve constitutional legitimacy subjects all citizens, decision-makers and government to a higher law – it holds government to account for its actions. Thereby, it shapes and stabilizes the context in which political conflict occurs and establishes settled, routinized mechanisms by which disputes can be resolved. The dangers of arbitrary rule that have plagued most of the world are thereby minimized, if not eliminated.

CONCLUSION

Tenacious adherence to a document designed by eighteenth-century gentlemen for an entirely different type of society might seem ludicrous, but the Constitution has endured through adapting to immense changes in American life while retaining its fundamental structure essentially intact. The readiness of many outside America to criticize the Constitution frequently co-exists with a reluctance to acknowledge its achievements. Moreover, many of those who deride Americans' faithful adherence to the Constitution and its values themselves continue to believe in values and ideas far older: the Bible, Torah and Koran, for example. The mere fact of age need not, of necessity, make particular claims or protections any less relevant today, or particular values less worthy of special

protection, than when they were first pronounced.

American identity is built centrally upon political values and the Constitution is the real fount of those values. In a sense, the Constitution – far more than the president or any public official, legislative assembly or court – is America. Precisely because it has proven to be the unshakeable foundation of American democracy, challenging – much less violating – its cherished wisdom is sacrosanct. The Constitution guarantees the consistent rule of law, not the arbitrary whim of individuals, and promises fairness in place of arbitrary decisions. All citizens are subject to its provisions, and none are above the law (one reason why the allegations of perjury and obstruction of justice against President Clinton proved so serious in 1998–99).

This common frame of reference has ensured that Americans may not always agree on the substance of political or policy debates, but they know how to disagree. In so doing, citizens can affirm their common bond as Americans and assert their participation in the continuing dialogue that is America. Even one the key Framers of the document, James Madison, was not fully satisfied with the Constitution and held it to be flawed. But to the extent that no constitution is perfect, the US Constitution has nonetheless provided a powerful basis for continuity as well as change in America. Ironically, it has been an institution that the Framers feared would damage the new constitutional democracy that has largely been responsible for making the Constitution work: political parties, to which we turn in the next chapter.

FURTHER READING

The Constitution of the United States of America is the only constitution that can be read from start to finish in less than an hour and that still structures government over 200 years since it was written.

Robert Bork, *The Tempting of America: The Political Seduction of the Law* (1990) is an argument strongly in favour of a limited judicial role and judges who strictly adhere to the actual text of the Constitution when making their rulings.

Michael Foley, *American Political Ideas* (1991) is an elegantly written discussion of the key ideas that underpin Americanism, with a concise chapter on 'constitutionalism'.

Mary Ann Glendon, *Rights Talk: The Impoverishment of Political Discourse* (1991) is an argument that Americans have become so obsessed by rights that this preoccupation has hindered attempts to deal with many public problems in America.

Alexander Hamilton, James Madison and John Jay, *The Federalist Papers* is the classic exposition of the rationale of the Constitution at the time of the ratification debates and a leading contribution to the political theory of democratic governance.

Daniel Lazare, *The Frozen Republic: How the Constitution is Paralyzing Democracy* (1996) is a strong critique of the Constitution's effects on contemporary American democracy.

Antonin Scalia, *A Matter of Interpretation: Federal Courts and the Law* (1997) is a set of essays for and against an originalist interpretation of the Constitution, with a leading essay by the Supreme Court's most influential proponent of this approach.

WEB LINKS

US Constitution, *The Federalist Papers*, historical speeches
www.santacruz.k12.ca.us/vft/constitution.html

The Federalist Papers
http://lcweb2.loc.gov/const/fed/fedpapers.html
www.findlaw.com/11stategov/indexconst.html

State constitutions
www.iwc.com/entropy/marks/stcon.html

National Conference of State Legislators (materials on how federal policies affect the states)
www.ncsl.org/statfed/afipolicy.html

Federalism debated
www.voxpop.org:80/jefferson

QUESTIONS

- Has the Constitution effectively reconciled the need for an effective national government with the protection of individual civil rights and liberties?

- 'There exist few, if any, compelling reasons why Americans today should be bound by a document written for the society of 1787.' Discuss.

- Why do Americans attach such importance to the Constitution?

- 'The Constitution needs fundamental overhaul.' Does it?

- To what extent, and why, is the Constitution too difficult to amend?

3 Political Parties and the Party System

In America democracy is unthinkable save in terms of a two-party system, because no collection of ambitious politicians has long been able to think of a way to achieve their goals in this democracy save in terms of political parties.

John H. Aldrich (1995: 296)

Partisanship does not define eras; ideology does. Just as Richard Nixon was the last New Deal president, it is very likely that Bill Clinton will be the last Republican-era president.

Theodore Lowi (1995: xi)

- The US Constitution
- What do the Democrats and Republicans Stand for?
- How Healthy? Decline, Adaptation and Revival
- Conclusion

Chapter Summary

Political parties are central to American government and politics but are highly distinctive compared to parties in other liberal democracies. Parties in liberal democracies can generally be seen to perform certain important functions along three key dimensions: providing sources of allegiance, information and voting cues for the electorate; recruiting candidates for office, financing and running their campaigns; and providing the personnel to staff the elected branches of government. But the extent to which this is the case in

America is unclear. Because of federalism, the separation of powers, checks and balances and different terms of office, political parties have always been weak and decentralized institutions. Without mass memberships, lacking clear ideological differences, and unable either to devise or implement a party programme or manifesto, American parties have never performed the strong roles characteristic of European ones. Moreover, proponents of 'party decline' argue that American parties have weakened even further since 1952 as new sources of information (especially the mass media) and alternative forms of political participation (interest groups, social movements, litigation) have emerged to challenge parties. Others have responded that the parties have adapted to changed conditions and, in some areas (such as Congress), revived strongly since the 1980s. In particular, although they remain broad coalitions of distinct interests, American parties today are more ideologically distinct and distant from each other than at any point since the early twentieth century. Partisan differences – especially during an era of divided party control of the White House and Congress – have therefore become a key feature of American politics. The party is by no means over, although its role and importance remains in flux in a democracy where political parties are relatively unloved and weak institutions.

In May 2001, Senator James Jeffords (Republican, Vermont) decided to call it quits. Frustrated by the Republican Party's conservatism, he announced that he was becoming an Independent but would caucus with Senate Democrats. With the 2000 election having yielded a 50–50 split in the Senate (in the event of ties, Vice President Dick Cheney would cast the deciding vote as president of the Senate), the decision was profoundly consequential. As a result, the following month, the Democrats took charge of the Senate for the first time in six years. The brief period of undivided Republican control of the White House and Capitol Hill – the first since 1953–54 – was brought to a dramatic end after just five months. It was also the first time in American history that control of the Senate changed between elections.

But Jeffords' example was not unprecedented. In 1983, Phil Gramm, a conservative Texan Democrat in the House of Representatives, was disciplined by his congressional party for disloyalty. Gramm had been a key ally of the Reagan White House and congressional Republicans during crucial budget negotiations over the previous two years, negotiations that ultimately resulted in a landmark budget for the president that substantially increased defence spending while cutting taxes and social programmes. As a result of his getting too close to their Republican opponents for comfort, the Democrats removed Gramm from chairing a subcommittee of the influential House Budget Committee, as a punishment. In a typically direct response, Gramm then resigned his congressional seat, but ran in the special election (similar to a British by-election) to fill it – as a Republican. He won, telling his voters that 'I had to choose between Tip O'Neill (Democratic Speaker of the House) and y'all. And I chose y'all.' The following year he won a statewide race as a Republican candidate for the Senate. In 1996, Gramm ran for the Republican Party's presidential nomination (this time losing to Bob Dole) before retiring from politics in 2002.

To non-Americans, such behaviour often seems peculiar, even baffling. We are typically used to party meaning something substantial in politics and party loyalty being a key condition of political success. But the Gramm example paradoxically indicates not only the weakness of American parties, but also their strength and tenacity. Although he switched parties, Gramm did not run for re-election as an 'Independent'. Nor did he form another political party to get back into office. He simply joined the other main political party to the Democrats: the Republicans. Party ties clearly matter in America, then, but in markedly different and more subtle ways from other democracies.

To understand the distinctive context of American party politics it is necessary to take an imaginative leap. Imagine a Member of Parliament at Westminster running for re-election without even mentioning which party she belongs to in her campaign advertisements; refusing to let the head of her government, the head of state or the leader of her party appear in her constituency since this could be detrimental to her chances of victory; publicizing votes on which she defied her party as virtues of her legislative record; raising her own campaign funds, through staff whose primary loyalty is to her, not to the party to which she nominally belongs; allowing professional 'hired guns' – independent political consultants – to run her campaign, from producing television ads to advising which issues to stress and even what clothes to wear. This is the contemporary American context of party politics: a profoundly decentralized and fragmented system where elections are centred relentlessly on the individual candidate, not a collective party organization.

In some respects, this picture is not new. Historically, American parties have usually been described as decentralized, weak, fragmented and incoherent, as broad coalitions with little in the way of obvious ideological content or clear programmes of government. But the same two parties, the Democrats and Republicans, have dominated American politics since the Civil War, respectively the oldest and third oldest parties in the world (the British Conservative Party squeezing in at number two). No third party has seriously challenged their dominance of the party system, though several have tried. All but two of the 535 voting members of Congress, and all but two of the 50 state governors, belonged to

either the Democratic or Republican parties in 1999–2000. So, if American parties are weak institutions, they are nonetheless remarkably resilient ones that have endured over time in the face of tremendous social, economic and political change, and they continue to command widespread loyalty today.

Just as elections provide the lifeblood of democracy, so democracy during the twentieth and twenty-first centuries has been inconceivable without the institution of political parties. Parties of all stripes played a crucial role in consolidating liberal democracies around the world and in providing citizens with a sense of representation in government deliberations. Competition between parties has been viewed as the necessary – but insufficient – condition of a genuinely democratic regime. But to understand American parties, it is important to look again at that pervasively influential force, the Constitution, and then to think about parties in each of three distinct, albeit related, arenas:

- in the electorate
- as organizations
- in government.

In this way, we can achieve a more rounded idea of the relative 'health' of American parties and whether they are declining or reviving in their ability to perform the functions traditionally associated with parties in liberal democracies.

THE US CONSTITUTION

In marked contrast to the German and Italian constitutions (among others) political parties are not specifically mentioned anywhere in the US Constitution. This is partly because the Founding Fathers, having seen the dangers posed by political division within the English government under King George III, feared the consequences of 'faction'. Parties, in this view, were inherently divisive, self-interested and narrow institutions more likely to endanger democracy than preserve it and more likely to pursue sectional goals than the national interest.

But from the 1830s parties did develop and, ironically, it is only parties that have made the Constitution work effectively. We saw earlier how the Constitution deliberately sets up multiple points of conflict within and between different levels and branches of government. Parties have traditionally been the key instruments by which these points of conflict are overcome. If American politics works despite, not because of its Constitution, political parties have a lot to do with this. In theory, at least, they constitute the bridge that overcomes the separations built into the structural architecture of government, the mechanisms by which competing political actors can be induced to share interests and resolve conflicts.

But the way in which parties achieve this resolution is distinctive primarily because their structure and functioning reflect the constitutional design of the Founding Fathers. First, and most significantly, the parties are affected by federalism. Unlike the European model of relatively centralized and hierarchical parties, American parties are decentralized – their base is local and state, not national. Partly because, as the next chapter explains, 'all politics is local' in a system that disperses rather than concentrates power, there is little sense among Americans of parties as national institutions. This has been compounded by American history and political culture, so that no tradition of strongly ideological or class-based parties has existed in the fashion familiar to Europe.

Traditionally, then, America's national parties only came together every four years, at a national convention in the summer of a presidential election year, to select a presidential candidate. After that, they effectively disappeared again. The notion of having permanently organized national parties, with mass memberships, identifiable ideologies, clear programmes of government, and conducting activities on a continual basis with a permanent national headquarters, has traditionally been alien to America (it was not until the 1970s, for instance, that the two main parties established permanent national headquarters in Washington, DC).

The second way in which parties are directly affected by the Constitution concerns the separation of powers and checks and balances within the federal government. This means that presidential and congressional parties co-exist, as do the Democrats and Republicans. In effect, then, four parties exist at federal level: the Democratic presidential and congressional parties, and the Republican presidential and congressional parties. The president cannot dissolve Congress and Congress cannot dismiss the president (short of impeachment). Members of Congress are therefore far less beholden to the president than a Member of Parliament at Westminster is to his or her party leader (whether prime minister or leader of the opposition). American lawmakers possess an independent base of political authority, and their electoral fortunes depend less on what the president does than on what they themselves do for their constituents. That independence offers both opportunities and constraints for their legislative behaviour.

The cumulative result is that American parties are broad and weakly-knit coalitions. In a sense, of course, all parties are coalitions. In the UK, although parties have conventionally been viewed as relatively strong and programmatic, all major parties have experienced substantial internal divisions, both within and outside government. In systems with more proportional electoral systems, in which the prospects for one party gaining a majority of seats in the legislature are less strong, most governments are formal coalitions of two or more parties, dividing up the spoils of office between themselves and forging compromises among divergent interests in order to get legislation passed and implemented. In this sense, then, the fact that American parties are coalitions of different interests and factions is not so remarkable in comparative terms. What is different is that coalitional politics occurs as much within as between the parties.

Exhibit 3.1 Party structures

Democratic National Committee	Republican National Committee
Democratic Congressional Campaign Committee	Republican Congressional Campaign Committee
Democratic Senatorial Campaign Committee	Republican Senatorial Campaign Committee
Democratic State Parties	Republican State Parties
Local parties	Local parties

One consequence, and also one of the baffling aspects, of American federalism is to allow so many different elements to co-exist within one or other main party. This is largely because the American social base is so diverse and heterogeneous. A Democrat from Alabama (with a large black population and substantial numbers of fundamentalist Christians) can therefore be a very different creature from one from Alaska (with relatively few blacks or fundamentalists). Even party officials from the same state can represent very different constituencies (rural, urban, suburban; densely or sparsely populated; ethnically diverse or homogeneous; agricultural, industrial, or post-industrial in economic base) and, partly as a result, profess different beliefs and values. It has even been suggested that rather than speaking of a two-party system, it makes more sense to think of a 100-party system (two parties for each of the 50 states).

For non-Americans, this often seems odd – an uncomfortable contrast to our usual conception of what parties are, and should be, about. But there is nothing inconsistent about such diversity existing within a party. The officeholders are elected by different constituencies, at different times, to different offices, for different terms. The social base is sufficiently heterogeneous that the decentralized parties consistently reflect the range of views of the diverse populations in their own ranks, making parties broad coalitions of interests.

WHAT DO THE DEMOCRATS AND REPUBLICANS STAND FOR?

Since the parties are broad coalitions and since American politics has proceeded within relatively narrow ideological confines dominated by the tenets of classical liberalism, it can sometimes appear unclear as to what the Republicans and Democrats stand for and what divides them. Traditionally, the two main parties were not seen by analysts as particularly different – both were self-consciously capitalist, democratic (with the important exception of the 'Dixiecrats' – the white southern segregationist wing of the Democratic Party) and anti-communist, and to Europeans both occupied markedly similar ideological ground (what the critic Gore Vidal once dubbed 'two right wings').

But that traditional picture now looks rather dated. The two main parties have not become the type of ideological and programmatic parties that were major features of European politics for most of the twentieth century. They have, nevertheless, become quite distinct, assuming different positions on a range of economic, social and political issues – one reason why a substantial proportion of Americans now classify themselves as 'Independents' rather than as partisans when asked about their party allegiance. Inter-party differences now matter at least as much as intra-party ones in American politics.

As Exhibit 3.2 shows clearly, the Democratic and Republicans have distinct messages on policies such as abortion, taxes,

Exhibit 3.2 Contrasting positions in the 1996 party platforms

DEMOCRATS	REPUBLICANS
Abortion	
The Democratic Party stands behind the right of every woman to choose, consistent with *Roe v. Wade*, and regardless of ability to pay. . . . We respect the individual conscience of each American on this difficult issue, and we welcome all our members to participate at every level of our party.	The unborn child has a fundamental individual right to life which cannot be infringed. We support a human life amendment to the Constitition and we endorse legislation to make clear that the Fourteenth Amendment's protections apply to unborn children
Budget	
President Clinton has put forward a plan to balance the budget by 2002 while living up to our commitments to our elderly and our children and maintaining strong economic growth. . . . The President's plan reflects America's values. The Republican plan does not.	Republicans support a Balanced Budget Amendment to the Constitution, phased in over a short period and with appropriate safeguards for national emergencies.
Crime	
We support the President's call for a constitutional amendment to protect the rights of victims.	Because liberal jurists keep expanding the rights of the accused, Republicans propose a constitutional amendment to protect victims' rights . . . [and] reform the Supreme Court's fanciful exclusionary rule.
Discrimination	
The Democratic Party has always supported the Equal Rights Amendment, . . . and to vigorously enforce the Americans with Disabilities Act. . . . When it comes to affirmative action, we should mend it, not end it.	We oppose discrimination based on sex, race, age, creed, or national origin and will vigorously enforce anti-discrimination laws. We reject the distortion of those laws to cover sexual preference and endorse the Defense of Marriage Act. . . . Because we believe rights inhere in individuals, not in groups, we will attain our nation's goals of equal rights without quotas or other preferential treatment.
Education	
Today's Democratic Party will stand firmly against the Republican assault on education. Cutting education as we move into the twenty-first century would be like cutting defense spending at the height of the Cold War. We must do more to expand educational opportunity – not less.	The federal government has no Constitutional authority to be involved in school curricula or to control jobs in the workplace. That is why we will abolish The Department of Education, end federal meddling in our schools, and promote family choice at all levels of learning.

Exhibit 3.2   Contrasting positions in the 1996 party platforms *continued*

DEMOCRATS	REPUBLICANS
Foreign Policy	
We are committed to promoting democracy in regions and countries important to America's security, and to standing with all those willing to take risks for peace . . . our allies, willing partners, the UN and other security organizations.	We oppose the commitment of American troops to UN 'peacekeeping' operations under foreign commanders and will never compel American servicemen to wear foreign uniforms or insignia.
Guns	
Today's Democratic Party stands with America's police officers. We are proud to tell them that . . . any attempt to repeal the Brady Bill or assault weapons ban will be met with a veto.	We defend the constitutional right to keep and bear arms.
Immigration	
As we work to stop illegal immigration, we call on all Americans to avoid the temptation to use this issue to divide people from each other . . . to bar the children of illegal immigrants from school . . . is wrong, and forcing children onto the streets is an invitation for them to join gangs and turn to crime.	Illegal aliens should not receive public benefits other than emergency aid, and those who become parents while illegally in the United States should not be qualified to claim benefits for their offspring. Legal immigrants should depend for assistance on their sponsors . . . not the American taxpayers.
Language	
We believe everyone in America should learn English so they can fully share in our daily life, but we strongly oppose divisive efforts like English-only legislation.	We support the official recognition of English as the nation's common language.
Taxes	
Today's Democratic Party is committed to targeted tax cuts that help working Americans invest in their future, and we insist that any tax cuts are completely paid for, because we are determined to balance the budget.	American families are suffering from the twin burdens of stagnant incomes and near-record taxes. . . . In response to this unprecedented burden, we support an across-the-board 15 percent tax cut to marginal tax rates. Fifteen percent represents that total tax increase in the federal tax burden since Bill Clinton took office.
Welfare	
We know the new bill passed by Congress is far from perfect – parts of it should be fixed because they go too far and have nothing to do with welfare reform. . . . Our job now is to make sure this welfare reform plan succeeds.	Because illegitimacy is the most serious cause of child poverty, we will encourage the states to stop cash payments to unmarried teens and set a family cap on payments for additional children.

Source: Democratic National Committee and Republican National Committee.

firearms and immigration. Broadly speaking, the Democrats seek to promote equality: they see a positive role for the federal government in intervening in the market to protect the environment, increase social equality, protect minorities (racial, ethnic, religious and sexual) and promote 'social justice'. The Republicans tend to support fiscal prudence, limited government intervention, and oppose proactive governmental measures designed to improve the position of collectivities like women, blacks, gays and immigrants. This is why the Democrats are generally referred to in popular commentary as the more liberal party, the Republicans as the more conservative (although, as we saw in Chapter 1, these terms are rather misleading descriptions since they conflate different dimensions of political conflict – social, economic and foreign policy).

Given a vast nation and diverse social base, neither party is uniformly consistent on these matters. It is always possible to find some Democrats who are relatively 'conservative' and some Republicans who are relatively 'liberal'. The marked diversity in local conditions precludes total party unity and factionalism is endemic in party politics. Both parties have been made up of internal factions whose views have frequently been very different, even diametrically opposed. Factions – groups that are self-consciously organized and possess some discipline and cohesion – tend to take one of two forms:

- *Clientelistic*. These groups are oriented towards particular constituencies or regional interests and seek to maximize some material gain for their adherents, such as money, jobs or political offices. They tend not to be especially concerned by questions of ideology or political purity, and are geared towards bargaining and striking compromises to secure desired benefits.
- *Ideological*. Ideological factions tend to emphasize the ideology of the party and seek to put it into practice, and are typically opposed by a faction that is pre-

pared to modify or disregard ideology in favour of electoral success. Such factions tend to be concerned with a particular vision of the good society, and are less occupied with the 'retail politics' of securing distributive benefits. Their adherents are often described as 'purists' or 'absolutists'.

What the two main parties stand for is therefore inextricably linked to where they sit – their political views are heavily conditioned by the particular groups that make up their respective electoral bases. These inevitably change over time. Since the 1960s, for example, several forces have combined to alter the internal make-up of the two parties dramatically, reducing the intense factional conflict in the Democratic Party while increasing the factionalism within the Republican Party and – simultaneously – making the two parties more dissimilar, such that they now offer more of a choice to voters than an echo:

- *Civil rights*. Heavily lobbied for by President Lyndon Johnson, the Voting Rights Act of 1965 enfranchised southern blacks, allowed them to register to vote with federal (rather than local) registrars, and helped to solidify blacks as the heart of the Democratic Party. Previously, black southerners (and some working-class whites) had been confronted by racist local registrars administering quasi-legal procedures such as literacy tests and questions ostensibly designed to test a citizen's fitness to vote ('how many bubbles are there in a bar of soap?'). These were supplemented by intimidation and violence, by official (sheriffs, courts, state legislatures) and unofficial (white supremacist groups like the Ku Klux Klan) upholders of the segregationist order. Although other factors have also played a role – not least economic conditions, foreign policy and social issues such as abortion and gun control – it was not coincidental that the last time a Democratic candidate for president (whether successful or not) won a majority of the national white vote was LBJ in 1964.

- *The South.* The white southern portion of the congressional Democratic Party declined after 1965 as some southern states and districts were won by Republicans (partly through new immigration and partly through the transference of traditional party loyalties) and most remaining Democrats found themselves having to cultivate mixed-race constituencies, thereby voting more like their non-southern, 'national' Democratic colleagues. As a result, although the party remained very much a coalition of distinct interests and groups (see Exhibit 3.3), con-

gressional Democrats since the 1980s have been less ideologically divided than at any time since the 1930s.

- *Cultural value conflicts.* Prompted into political action by federal intervention on questions such as abortion, school prayer, pornography and gay rights during the 1950s and 1960s, the activism of Christian evangelicals (especially in the Midwest and South) and so-called 'New Right' groups since the 1970s has helped to solidify the Republicans as a predominantly conservative (but, as Exhibit 3.4 notes, internally divided) party in which opposition to abortion rights, support for gun ownership and belief in the 'traditional

Exhibit 3.3   Democratic Party factions, 1990–2000

	Neoliberals	Radical Minorities
Issues	Free trade Downsizing government Cultural liberalism Environmentalism Multilateral foreign policy Balanced budget Pro-immigration	'Fair trade'/protection Extending government Cultural liberalism Environmentalism Multilateral foreign policy Help for disadvantaged Pro-immigration
Electoral support	Suburban voters Upper-middle-class whites Women	Urban voters Blacks and Latinos Gays and lesbians
Interest group support	National media Trial lawyers Banking/finance Entertainment industry Teachers' unions	Labour National minority organizations Feminist organizations National gay organizations Public interest groups
Party power base	Presidential primary voters Governors	Caucus participants Congress State/local parties
Leaders	Bill Clinton Al Gore Tom Daschle	Jesse Jackson Jerry Brown Dick Gephardt

Source: Nicol Rae (1998: 65).

Exhibit 3.4   Republican Party factions, 1990–2000

	Traditional Republicans	Supply-side Libertarians	Religious Right	Populist Conservatives
Issues	Balanced budget Free trade	Tax cuts/flat tax Free trade	Family tax cut Values-based trade policy	Workers' tax breaks Protectionism
	Cultural conservatism	Cultural moderation	Cultural conservatism	Cultural conservatism
	Unilateralism	Multilateralism	Values-based diplomacy	Nationalism
	Downsizing government	Downsizing government	Ending government secularism	Reducing federal intrusion
	Empowering states	Empowering individuals	Empowering families	Empowering workers
	Curbing immigration	Encouraging immigration	Pro-immigration	Anti-immigration
Electoral support	Small city/ suburbs Mainline Protestants	Wealthy suburbs Mainline Protestants	Middle-class whites Fundamentalists/ Evangelicals	Blue-collar workers Fundamentalists/ Catholics
	Midwest	Northeast/ Southwest	South Midwest/ West	Industrial Midwest/ Northeast
Interest group support	Chambers of Commerce Small business	Wall Street Banking/finance	Christian Coalition Anti-abortionists	Term-limiters Citizen militias
Party power base	Congress State/local parties	Northeast governors National media	State/local parties Party caucuses	Presidential primary voters 'Flash' movements
Leaders	Bob Dole George W. Bush	Jack Kemp Steve Forbes	Pat Robertson Dan Quayle	Pat Buchanan Jesse Helms

Source: Adapted from Nicol Rae (1998: 64).

family' are prerequisites of political success for most aspirant politicians.

Given such pronounced diversity in values, opinions and beliefs in contemporary America, it may appear odd that there has not been a serious challenge to this two-party hegemony. So many factions exist that some must necessarily be disappointed by not securing their political objectives, either fully or in part. It would surely make sense for a particular social group or faction that felt discontented or alienated by a particular party to break away and form its own (environmentalists, blacks, or Christian evangelicals, for example). Yet this has rarely occurred.

Exhibit 3.5 Celebrity political careers

American politics has been blessed (or cursed, depending on the viewpoint) by several individuals who forged political careers after pursuing paths not normally associated with a passion (or aptitude) for public life.

Jerry Springer. The host of the down-market but popular eponymous TV show was elected to the Cincinnati City Council in Ohio in 1971, became mayor, and ran unsuccessfully in the state's Democratic primary for Governor in 1982.

Ben Jones. The actor who played the reliably astute mechanic 'Cooter' in the down-home and intellectually challenging 1970s series, *The Dukes of Hazzard*, was elected to the House of Representatives from the 3rd District of Georgia the following decade.

Sonny Bono. The less surgically-enhanced half of the duo Sonny and Cher was elected as a Republican to the House of Representatives from California in the 1990s. A sixties 'flower-child', his views subsequently shifted sharply to the right. Asked for directions to Bono's office by Jay Leno on *The Tonight Show*, former Senate Republican leader Bob Dole once replied: 'He's in the right wing of the Capitol, but to get there you gotta take a right, then you take another far right, and then you go to the extreme right, and he should be right there.'

John Glenn. One of the astronauts whom Tom Wolfe famously described as having 'the right stuff' was elected from Ohio to the US Senate and ran unsuccessfully for the Democrats' presidential nomination in 1984.

Fred Thompson. A lawyer and actor who had supporting roles in several popular movies such as *In the Line of Fire* and *Cape Fear* was elected as a US senator for the Republicans in Tennessee in 1994 and was widely seen as a 'rising star' and potential presidential aspirant in the Grand Old Party until his retirement in 2002.

Ronald Reagan. The most successful former actor of all, the former star of B-movies such as *Bedtime for Bonzo* was elected Governor of California in 1966 and then president of the United States from 1981 to 1989.

Instead, most Americans (including, as Exhibit 3.5 notes, most American celebrities) have maintained an allegiance of sorts to one or other main party.

To this conundrum of pronounced two-party stability we can offer three explanations. First, the electoral system plays a decisive role in perpetuating the two-party system. Like the UK, America uses the plurality electoral system with single-member constituencies in national – and most state and local – elections. Often erroneously termed 'first-past-the-post' (the 'post' is in fact moveable rather than fixed, since winning demands only beating the nearest rival rather than securing an absolute majority of votes),

the plurality electoral system penalizes parties whose support is dispersed rather than concentrated in a particular constituency. By contrast, proportional representation systems encourage even small and extremist parties to field candidates, even if they regularly come fourth or fifth in national elections.

Second, another important set of institutional and legal barriers to third party success are ballot access requirements, which typically make it difficult even to run in elections in some states. Third party candidates for the US Senate in Florida, for example, need to gather almost 200,000 signatures simply to qualify to be listed on the ballot, whereas their counterparts in New Jersey need to

Exhibit 3.6 Against third parties: the case of Charles Evers

Having secured the right to vote with the passage of the Voting Rights Act of 1965, black Mississippians registered, turned out and supported the Democratic Party in large numbers subsequently. But after a decade of loyal support, many were deeply disenchanted with the party not delivering the socio-economic advances for which they had hoped. Knowing that black voters would not vote Republican (the party of Barry Goldwater, who had voted against the 1964 Civil Rights Act) the Democratic Party could more or less take black votes for granted. In an effort to rectify the situation, a black activist, Charles Evers, ran as a third party candidate for a Senate seat in 1978, when the incumbent conservative Democrat (and former segregationist), John Stennis, retired. But the result could not have been worse for many black Mississippians. Not only did Evers lose, but in splitting the Democratic vote, the Evers candidacy allowed the Republican, Thad Cochran, to win. Cochran remained in office, along with (from 1988) fellow Republican Trent Lott (indeed, Lott beat Cochran in a two-man all-Mississippi race to succeed Bob Dole as Majority Leader in the Senate from 1996 to 2001). The lesson for students of the party system: third parties rarely achieve electoral success and can end up contributing to the least favoured outcome for their erstwhile supporters.

gather only 800. Campaign finance laws that favour incumbents, the overwhelming majority of whom belong to one of the two main parties, also strongly work against the prospects of third party candidates. Contribution limits are especially harmful to third party candidates because they lack the type of established and large donor pools – common to the two main parties – from which to raise significant funds.

Third, an additional problem is the mass media, which is often hostile to third party and Independent candidates. In a self-fulfilling – albeit understandable – process, television and press coverage invariably focuses on the most 'electable' candidates (invariably Republicans and Democrats), to the detriment of all others. When minor party candidates attract media coverage, it is usually distorted, dismissive and even contemptuous. During the 1996 presidential election, for example, the *Washington Post* featured a story titled 'Here's the Ticket . . . A Selection of Running Mates for Ross Perot', that listed Binti the gorilla (who had recently rescued a toddler that had fallen into her cage) as first choice, followed by other exotic notables such as the UK's Prince Charles and

the physician-assisted suicide advocate, Jack 'Dr Death' Kevorkian. Many voters accept at face value the media-propagated idea that minor candidates are inconsequential or represent at best a 'wasted' vote.

Barriers, then, are one important consideration in perpetuating the two-party system. But incentives also play a key role in political life. Politically concerned individuals and groups must engage in a cost-benefit analysis of their possible actions to identify the most effective method to secure their goals. In this sense, the permeability of the two main parties helps to ensure their continued vitality. Why, for example, should a particular candidate (like Phil Gramm) leave one of the main parties to set up another party when he can capture the nomination of one of the existing ones?

To illustrate this point, consider the infamous figure of David Duke in Louisiana during the 1980s and 1990s. The ex-Grand Wizard of the Ku Klux Klan – who turned into a sharp-suited and blow-dried politico by the end of the 1980s – Duke could have set up his own political party (the 'Bigoted Hatred Party', say) and tried to run against the Democrats or Republicans. But, in the event, why bother? Instead, he could – and did – try to capture the nomination of one of the existing parties (he tried his luck in both at different points during the 1980s). In 1989, Duke was elected as a Republican to the state legislature to represent a suburban New Orleans district. Despite profound misgivings, the Republican Party could not stop him since, equipped with enough funds and a message that appealed to a sufficiently large number of primary voters, the nomination was not theirs either to grant or withhold. Capturing the nomination this way not only avoids the costs of setting up a new party, but has the added benefit that a whole segment of the electorate who identify, strongly or weakly, with the existing party is immediately predisposed towards you. (Although Duke lost his bids for the Senate in 1990 and

the governorship of Louisiana in 1991, a majority of the state's white voters supported him in both elections.) Party therefore provides a basic set of indicators about an individual, however limited and imperfect, that is simply absent if he or she runs as an Independent.

One final factor that is particularly influential in maintaining a two-party system concerns the institutional (rather than the electoral) sources of party strength. Whether in Congress or state legislatures, legislative life is organized according to which party holds a majority of seats in the particular assembly. Conventionally, the majority party in an assembly possesses majorities on all committees that write the laws and has special privileges in terms of timetabling debate and scheduling legislative action and

Exhibit 3.7   Switching parties I: too many extremists, too many moderates

In July 1999, Representative Michael P. Forbes (Republican, New York) switched parties to join the Democrats. Having voted to impeach President Clinton, he also became the only Democrat in Congress who had been a supporter of George W. Bush for president. The Democrats assured Forbes that if he switched parties he would retain his seniority on the key Appropriations Committee and the party would oppose a primary challenge to him in 2000. Forbes blamed the Republican congressional leadership for his change of partisan heart, claiming the party had become dominated by extremists:

> Because the national Republican Party in Congress no longer speaks for Suffolk County Republicans, because it no longer speaks to the concerns of my friends and neighbors, because the House Republicans have stood in the way of my efforts to improve the lives of Long Island families, today I am announcing . . . that I will be joining the House Democratic Caucus.

Ironically, 14 months later, Forbes was defeated for renomination in his district's September 2000 Democratic primary election. The national party could do nothing to stop disaffected local Democrats ousting him in a popular intra-party election – a far cry from the party-dominated politics in the UK where a candidate who runs against his party (such as Ken Livingstone's bid for the Mayoralty of London in May 2000) is typically expelled.

But party-switching was not confined to Republicans wary of their party's purported extremism. In July 1999, Senator Bob Smith (Republican, New Hampshire), who had begun to campaign for the 2000 Republican presidential nomination, also left his party to become an Independent, accusing the party of becoming too moderate. Curiously enough, Smith returned to the Republican Party shortly after Senator John Chafee of Rhode Island died in the autumn of 1999. Smith, as the next most senior-ranking Republican, was in line to take over as chairman of the influential Science Committee in the Senate. Although he denied that it had anything to do with this fortuitous promotion, the Republican Party had not become more obviously conservative in the brief time that he had been away.

Exhibit 3.8   Switching parties II: party-switching since 1900

Between 1902 and 1954, no member of Congress jumped from one of the major parties to the other. (The numbers below do not include independents or minor parties.

Congress	House of Representatives	Senate
106th	RD	
104th	DR (3)	
103rd		DR
101st	DR (2)	
98th	DR (2)	
97th	DR	
94th	DR	
93rd	RD	
92nd	RD	
89th	DR	
88th		DR
85th	RD	
84th		RD
57th	RD	RD

RD – Republican switches to Democrat
DR – Democrat switches to Republican

Source: *CQ Weekly*, July 24, 1999, p. 1768.

amendments. It makes little sense for an individual to run formally as an Independent or third party candidate if, in doing so, that candidate will be excluded from such benefits when elected. It is far more sensible to join one or other party that may form a majority. Perhaps the most shameless example of this influence occurred in November 1994 when, the day after the Republicans won the mid-term elections, Senator Richard Shelby of Alabama announced that he was switching his life-long allegiance from the Democrats to the Republicans. Although Shelby had been a dissident Democrat and a constant irritant to President Clinton, regularly voting with the Grand Old Party rather than his fellow Democrats, the timing of his party switch was hardly coincidental. In return, Shelby gained influential committee and subcommittee chairs that enabled him to exploit his incumbency – and deliver distributive benefits back to Alabama – to advantageous effect: Shelby's re-election as a Republican – and the most popular politician in his state – in 1998 was never in doubt.

What this means is the picture of American parties is a rather fluid one in which the individuals are as important as the collective entities. For those societal and economic interests seeking to influence decision-makers, a degree of pragmatism is the order of the day. Since neither party can guarantee its members' re-election, much less compel them to vote a particular way, Americans – individually and collectively – wanting to influence the policy process generally steer a course that deals with members of both parties. As Exhibit 3.10 notes, such pragmatic dexterity is no guarantee of political success but can yield rewards.

Exhibit 3.9   The bees of American politics: third parties

Historians of American third parties conventionally compare them to bees: they sting temporarily and die. Although America is the purest two-party system in the democratic world, third parties have intermittently broken the duopoly for brief but consequential moments. In 1968, the American Independence Party of former Democratic segregationist governor of Alabama, George Wallace, proved extremely influential, winning 13 million votes and splitting the vote three ways in one of America's closest presidential elections. In 1992, the Texas billionaire, Ross Perot, won 19 per cent of the national vote against Bill Clinton and George H.W. Bush. In 2000, although Green Party candidate Ralph Nader won few votes, he took enough in sufficient key states to cost Al Gore the presidential election.

But third parties generally face three formidable difficulties:

- *Electoral laws.* Getting on the ballot is not straightforward. Some states require large numbers of signatures, beyond the means of most insurgent movements.
- *The electoral system.* The plurality system penalizes parties whose votes are dispersed and rewards those whose votes are concentrated.
- *Major party marginalization.* If a third party does make inroads in an election by exploiting an issue that the two parties have either neglected or been divided over, one or both parties is likely to co-opt that issue in the following election. The result is invariably that the original motivation for supporting a challenge is undermined. With both Clinton and the Republicans agreeing to deficit reduction after 1992, Perot found his electoral appeal undercut by 1996. Also, the two main parties often seek to marginalize minor party opponents, excluding candidates from debates, ridiculing them or treating them as sideshows.

Faced by so many obstacles, third parties have their greatest impact when a major party splits. In 1860, Abraham Lincoln won after the Democrats and the Whigs split over slavery. In 1912, Woodrow Wilson won, becoming the first Democrat elected in 20 years, when the Republican Party split between incumbent President William Howard Taft and former president Theodore Roosevelt.

After 1968, the GOP employed a 'Southern Strategy' to co-opt the Wallace vote by targeting disgruntled white southerners, who traditionally voted Democratic, to support Republicans. During the 1990s, the Reform Party drew substantial media attention, and in 1999–2000 figures as varied as Pat Buchanan, Jesse 'the Body' Ventura (Governor of Minnesota from 1998 to 2002), entrepreneur Donald Trump, and film star Warren Beatty all toyed with trying to win the party's presidential nomination. A variety of concerns – campaign finance, trade and America's global role – prompted interest in the Reform nomination but Buchanan's controversial success ultimately helped to condemn the party to a rapid and decisive demise.

The American two-party system is imperfect. Candidates with 'fringe' or controversial appeals are discouraged from campaigning, each party is set on seeking political advantage over the other in an adversarial fashion and – though corrupt practices such as patronage and the awarding of government contracts to party insiders have waned – both parties regularly face strong public criticism for questionable fundraising practices. Against this, however, the parties help to clarify the issues and simplify the choices for American voters, enable politicians to form coalitions to get things done in government, and help candidates by providing an existing base of public support and mobilizing voters and party supporters behind a candidacy.

Exhibit 3.10   Mickey Mouse politics

During the summer of 1998, Michael D. Eisner, chairman of the Walt Disney Corporation, faced a major problem. The expiration of Disney's 75-year copyright on Mickey Mouse was looming and the company was unwilling to cede the rights and revenue from its flagship character. On June 9, 1998, Eisner flew to Washington to meet Trent Lott, the Majority Leader of the Republican Senate. One week later, Disney contributed $10,000 to Lott's campaign committee and, on that day, June 16, the Senator signed on as a co-sponsor to the Copyright Term Extension Act of 1998, which proposed to add 20 years to the copyright lives of not only Mickey but also Donald Duck, Goofy and other Disney cartoon stars.

But Mississippi's Lott was not the only beneficiary of Disney's generosity. Ten co-sponsors of the bill in the House of Representatives received money from Disney's Political Action Committee, including Howard Coble (Republican, North Carolina), chair of the House Judiciary Courts and Intellectual Property Subcommittee, and Howard Berman (Democrat, California) – $5,000 each. Senate Judiciary Committee chairman Orrin Hatch (Republican, Utah) received $6,000 and Senator Barbara Boxer (Democrat, California) $8,000. (The Judiciary Committees in the two chambers had jurisdiction over extending copyright legislation.)

Less than four months after Eisner's visit, on October 7, 1998, the copyright extension bill passed both houses. There were no public hearings or floor debates on the measure in Congress. President Clinton signed the act into law later that month and, with the nation deep in the 'Monicagate' morass, the copyright legislation received little media coverage. Evidently, Disney was as skilled in playing the corridors of Capitol Hill as in crafting movies to achieve a broad popular appeal.

How Healthy? Decline, Adaptation, and Revival

The central debate in American political science about parties since at least 1950 has concerned their relative strength. Have they been in terminal decline ('the party's over' thesis)? Or have they experienced a revival, adapting to changed patterns of electioneering and new media ('the party's just begun' thesis)? To assess this, it is necessary to look at parties at the three distinct (though related) levels at which they perform important functions: the party in the electorate; the party as organization; and the party in government.

The party in the electorate

For voters, the traditional strength of parties is that they simplify political life immeasurably. They offer a source of emotional or psychological attachment and provide structures and cues (or guides) for voting decisions. Knowing that a candidate is a Democrat immediately yields information about where that particular individual stands on a range of issues. Without party, a voter has to expend precious resources, time and energy on finding these things out. Knowing a candidate's party affiliation provides a basic set of information – however limited – about his or her core values and beliefs.

Many political scientists argue that the party in the electorate has declined, since at least 1968. What this means is that voters no longer identify with parties so much. Not only has the volume or scope of voter identification decreased, but so has the strength of identification among those who still identify with a party. That is, fewer Americans identify with either the Republicans or Democrats, and those who do, identify only weakly

TABLE 3.1   Party identification in America, 1964–96

Year	Democrats (%)	Republicans (%)	Independents (%)
1964	52.3	24.8	23.0
1968	46.0	24.5	29.5
1972	41.0	23.8	35.2
1976	40.2	23.0	36.8
1980	41.7	23.0	35.3
1984	37.7	27.6	34.8
1988	35.7	28.0	36.3
1992	35.8	25.5	38.7
1996	39.3	27.8	32.9

Source: National Election Studies, University of Michigan.

rather than strongly. Partly as a result, elections are less predictable, voters more volatile. Knowing that citizens identify with the Democratic Party no longer suggests that they will automatically vote for that party's candidates in federal, state or local elections. Instead, Americans vote less on party than on individual candidates, important issues and economic performance.

Is this true? Certainly, lots of evidence supports the 'declinist' case. Table 3.1, for example, records the extent of party identification between 1964 and 1996. Over half of all Americans identified with the Democratic Party in 1964, but this has undergone a clear decline to under 40 per cent of the electorate

by 1996. But the Republicans did not make up the difference, not reaching 30 per cent at any stage during this 22-year cycle. Instead, the real growth came with those identifying as 'Independents', up from just over one-fifth of the electorate in 1964 to well over one-third by 1992. This suggests that millions of Americans have come loose from their traditional party moorings.

But let's look again. As Table 3.2 shows, if we take the proportion of voters who describe themselves as 'pure' or 'independent Independents', this is a very small pool. Most Americans still identify with one or other party but the strength of identification varies significantly within the sample (though most

TABLE 3.2   Party identification, 1980–2000

	1980	1982	1984	1986	1988	1990	1992	1994	1996	1998	2000
Strong Democrat	18	20	17	18	17	20	18	15	18	19	19
Weak Democrat	23	24	20	22	18	19	18	19	19	18	15
Independent Democrat	11	11	11	10	12	12	14	13	14	14	15
Independent Independent	13	11	11	12	11	10	12	11	9	11	12
Independent Republican	10	8	12	11	13	12	12	12	12	11	13
Weak Republican	14	14	15	15	14	15	14	15	15	16	12
Strong Republican	9	10	12	10	14	10	11	15	12	10	12
Apolitical	2	2	2	2	2	2	1	1	1	2	1

Source: National Election Studies, University of Michigan.

show stability from 1980 to 2000). The surprising fact about parties is not so much that they have weakened in their hold on voter loyalties, but rather that they have remained so strong in the face of such intense pressures and the many competing sources of political affiliation and mobilization: interest lobbies, the mass media, litigation in the courts and social movements.

Another important qualification occurs when we consider state, as well as federal, elections. As of 1999, there were 7,424 state legislative seats in America. These represent critical political and policy battlegrounds, and many who win these seats ultimately move on to higher offices, such as Congress, governor, and other statewide posts. At state level, where television coverage is less significant in election campaigning, campaigns are less well funded, and the issues are even more locally focused than in congressional contests, party labels matter even more than in national races. A survey of 364 state legislative candidates by *Campaigns and Elections* magazine in 1999, for example, found that the top two factors that candidates rated as most important to their election prospects were voters' traditional party loyalties and incumbency.

Another aspect that reinforces the argument that parties still matter concerns the continued allegiance of candidates to one of the main parties. For while Independents have increased among the electorate, and many candidates run in a manner that suggests their independence from party ties (not mentioning their party label in campaign advertising, for example), few candidates run as Independents. This suggests that party still means something, not only to voters but also to aspirant public officeholders.

Parties 'in the electorate' have declined but they are still important and it would be wrong to dismiss the notion that a revival of identification is possible. The party here isn't over, though it has slowly been stagnating. Voters no longer treat parties in terms of 'brand loyalty', consistently turning out to support the brand that they have always identified with, like the infamous 'yellow dog Democrats' (Democratic identifiers who used to say that they would vote for a yellow dog as long as he was a Democrat). Equally, however, voters have not become consumers who merely decide between individual products anew on each voting occasion. Most voters retain some basic attachment to one or other main party, albeit a weak one.

The party as organization

Traditionally, strong parties did not just provide information and cues to voters when deciding on their ballot choice. They also provided the personnel in everyday politics. Parties select candidates to run in elections; develop issue positions and rival programmes for government to offer voters a choice; raise money to fund those election campaigns; and organize or run the campaigns of their candidates for public office. 'Declinists' point to parties declining in their ability to perform these traditional functions and, again, they have a powerful case.

The first point to note is that, unlike European parties, American parties do not select their own candidates. This often strikes students of American politics as absurd but for many Americans this party openness is the essence of a truly democratic and participatory system. If primaries choose candidates, it is voters not party officials, who register to participate in those primaries that select nominees. There is hence no need to go through the laborious process of working for a party for years, delivering party literature through letterboxes, accumulating political CV points, impressing senior party officials and finally winning the votes of party selection committees to stand as a party candidate. In America, since a party apprenticeship is not required to win the nomination, the incentive to run on a party-centred platform, much less to work diligently for a party if elected, is substantially diminished. It is not a candidate's party peers who will select him or her, but the voters at large.

Formally, an elected American politician has to overcome two constituencies or hurdles to get into office:

• *The primary election.* Here, the candidate faces a contest against one or more competitors for the privilege of winning the party's nomination as the official (Democratic or Republican Party) candidate. The focus here is on the internal party electorate and the divisions within the party coalition (although candidates also run on a basis that they are the most likely to defeat the other party's nominee). Candidates of the same party must therefore do battle with each other to achieve the nomination, in the glare of public and media attention.

• *The general election.* Having won the primary contest, the two parties' nominees square off against each other. Attention now focuses on mobilizing the party's base to turn out in large numbers and/or trying to persuade swing voters, nonvoters, and even to convert the other party's voters to switch allegiance. In some cases, independent or third party candidates may also run in the general election against the main party candidates.

What this means in practice, however, is that an incumbent politician faces not two, but a multiplicity, of re-election constituencies. As Exhibit 3.11 reveals, not everyone in a constituency registers to vote, or turns out to do so. Similarly, of those who are registered and turn out, some ('strong partisans') will rarely vote for the candidates of the rival political party. The difficulty – especially for incumbents – is to judge how to deal with each of these important constituencies. A particular vote cast in Congress may pacify one constituency while simultaneously antagonizing another.

For example, suppose a Democratic Senator from Georgia faces a vote on the floor of the Senate on a civil rights bill (often attacked by opponents of affirmative action as a 'quota bill'). To vote for the bill would help to reinforce the Senator's prospects of getting renominated as the Democrats' choice for the next election, since it would please several important groups that participate in Democratic Party primaries (African Americans, Latinos, women's groups). But simultaneously, to vote for the bill would alienate or antagonize many Republican voters and moderate or swing voters, and could therefore lose support for the Senator in the general election among groups who dislike affirmative action. Conversely, to vote against the bill might well make the Senator more attractive to moderate or conservative voters in a general election. Yet at the same time, it would probably provoke a challenge from more progressive Democrats in a party primary angered by a Democrat voting against a civil rights measure.

Because of the participatory element that primaries create, the people, not the politician's peers, choose who the parties' candidates will be. One important result is that elected officials are made still more attentive to what their constituents – in particular, what their crucial re-election constituencies – want. Richard Fenno (1978) argues that elected politicians pursue two strategies in this regard: a 'protectionist' approach that seeks to consolidate existing support and an 'expansionist' approach that seeks to build wider support. Whichever strategy is pursued, the overall picture is different from that of European politics, where parties have an internal life that is insulated from the priorities and preferences of ordinary voters (nonparty members).

The second aspect that makes party politics so different is money. Money does not so much talk in American politics as shout. The traditional picture – until the early 1970s – was of 'fat cat' donors like business companies and labour unions giving vast sums of money directly to parties, often in return for favours if the party was in government. What happened during the 1970s, prompted in large part by revelations of illegal donations to Nixon's Committee to Re-Elect the President (CREEP) in 1972, was that the fat cats

Exhibit 3.11   The re-election calculation: one constituency or several for a Democratic Party candidate?

Personal

Those voters who will stick by you through thick and thin. This may consist of family, friends, business associates, and so on. Personally loyal, this is the slimmest section of the multiple constituencies you face.

Primary

Those voters whom you can normally rely on to support you, even against another candidate from the same party in a primary election.

Democratic voters

The mass of party voters who may – or may not – vote for you in a primary and general election, depending on your recent record and achievements.

Swing/marginal voters

Voter whose allegiance to either party is weak or non-existent, and whose judgement on whether to vote for you rests exclusively on their assessment of your record.

Republican voters

Voters with some attachment to the Republicans, who are generally unlikely to vote for you no matter what your efforts.

Non-voters

Registered voters who do not turn out to cast ballots, whether from disillusionment, alienation, satisfaction or ignorance.

Eligible voters

Voters who meet the criteria of eligibility to vote but have not actually registered, and hence cannot cast a ballot.

Constituents

All those legal citizens within the particular district or state.

were replaced by two main sources of funding:

- *Political action committees (PACs)*. Corporate, labour and ideological (or 'cause') groups can form their own political action committees under the terms of the 1974 Federal Election Campaign Act and its subsequent amendments. These PACs can raise and distribute campaign funds, subject to certain specified regulations and limits.

- *Individual contributors*. Like corporate entities, individual Americans are able to donate large sums of money to candidates, PACs and parties, again subject to certain prescribed limits. Contrary to popular imagination, individual contributions are the largest source of campaign monies for candidates, greater even than corporate (PAC) donations.

The result is the triumph of political individualism. Not only do candidates *not* need to serve an apprenticeship in order to get nominated by a party, but the candidates have to raise their own funds from individuals, PACs and others. This does not norm-

ally make successful candidates feel that they owe their party a political debt if elected to office. As a result, elected officials traditionally have been as likely to part company as to

Exhibit 3.12   The money-go-round: campaign finance regulations

There are four main types of campaign expenditure categories that affect who may donate contributions, to whom, how much, and for what purposes.

'Hard' money

This category consists of those contributions made directly to candidates under the terms of the federal campaign laws. Individuals may give up to $1,000 per candidate per election, but are subject to a total annual limit of $25,000 of contributions. PACs may donate up to $5,000 per candidate per election and are not subject to a cumulative annual limit. Parties may also donate to candidates, again without total limits. The federal campaign finance reform of 2002 elevated the importance of hard money, encouraging groups such as law firms to 'bundle' individual donations of $1,000–$25,000 together to give to parties and candidates.

'Soft' money

This comprises contributions by individuals and groups to political parties. Although in theory these donations are limited to being used only for 'party-building' activities (such as voter registration, get out-the-vote drives, and generic party advertising), in practice these activities can – and are – used by parties to help individual candidates. This is important, since the amount of money that individuals and PACs can donate for party building was unlimited until 2002, when soft money donations were effectively prohibited by new campaign finance legislation.

Independent expenditures

This category consists of money that is spent by individuals or groups on issue-ads that do not focus on particular candidates or parties and that are uncoordinated with official candidate or party campaign organizations. Again, while in theory there exists a wall between these monies and official activities, in practice the two can powerfully complement each other. An official ad may buy time to praise an incumbent's record, for example, while an independent expenditure ad – say a National Rifle Association ad attacking the challenger's votes on gun control – may reinforce the other ads. Under the McCain–Feingold/Shays–Meehan campaign finance law, signed by President Bush in March 2002, any broadcast ads after November 2002 that refer to a specific candidate and run 60 days before a general election or 30 days before a primary must be paid for by 'hard money' contributions.

Personal spending

Since the decision of the Supreme Court in *Buckley v. Valeo* (1976), there exists no limit on how much candidates may spend of their own money on their campaign. This is because the Court held that to place limits on such expenditure would violate the First Amendment to the Constitution, since spending money was an expression of freedom of speech. As a result, presidential candidates such as Ross Perot and Steve Forbes, and congressional candidates such as Michael Huffington, have been able to spend millions of dollars of their personal fortunes on federal election contests.

vote with their parties when voting on new laws or being asked to support their party leaders or the president.

In addition to these two important sources of private funds for aspirant elected officials, an element of public funding is available in

Exhibit 3.13 Selected campaign finance laws

Federal regulation. The Federal Election Commission (FEC) is the federal agency responsible for enforcement of campaign laws (1976).

Presidential candidates must file regular reports listing campaign contributions and expenditures (1971). Donors of $200 or more must be listed on the reports (1979). Any organization spending more than $5,000 on campaigns must establish a formal political committee (1979 amendments). Those reports must be filed with the FEC (1976 amendments). Candidates must establish a single organization for their campaigns (1974). The name of the candidate must be listed on campaign materials (1979).

Local party expenses. Certain expenses of local party organizations, such as get-out-the-vote drives and voter education activities, do not have to be reported (1979). Up to $1,000 in voluntary services, such as lending a home for meetings and lodging, do not have to be reported as contributions (1979).

Independent expenditures. Independent spending of $250 or more must be reported to the FEC (1979). Organizations without formal ties to campaign organizations do not have to adhere to spending limitations (1974).

'Lowest-unit' rule. To prevent unfair pricing and keep campaign costs down, broadcasters can charge campaigns only as much as they charge other advertising clients for spot commercials (1971).

Political action committees. Corporations and labour unions may establish separate units to promote political ends and not be in violation of federal prohibitions on direct contributions (1971).

Taxpayer check-off. Citizens may indicate on their tax forms that they would like tax money to be put into the Presidential Election Campaign Fund. This fund has been used to help finance nomination and general election campaigns (1971).

Matching funds during primaries. Candidates may receive federal matching funds if they raise at least $100,000 in 20 or more states. Each of those states must contribute a total of $5,000 to the candidate in individual donations of $250 or less (1974).

Limits on contributions. Citizens may contribute only $1,000 to each primary or general election campaign, a total of $25,000 to federal candidates overall, and $20,000 to committees of national parties (1976). Candidates may spend only $50,000 of their own or their family's money on their campaigns if they accept federal funding (1976).

Multi-candidate committees. Multi-candidate committees – mostly PACs – may contribute only $5,000 per candidate and $15,000 to committees of the national parties (1976).

Federal funding of national conventions. The parties receive public funding to help cover the cost of their summer conventions (1979).

Spending limits. Candidates receiving federal matching funds may spend limited amounts during the nomination season and other limited amounts in each of the states (state limits are determined by population). The limit is adjusted between elections to account for inflation (1974).

Federal funding of general election campaigns. The federal government offers the nominees of the major parties equal sums of money for the general election campaign. Candidates who accept the money may not raise or use additional campaign funds. The amount of the grant is adjusted each election year according to the inflation rate (1974).

Note: Year in parentheses is the year that the particular law was enacted.

presidential elections. This occurs when candidates who raise at least $5,000 in individual contributions of $250 or less, in each of at least 20 states, become eligible for public funds that match these individual contributions (but not PAC/party money). However, to receive these matching funds, candidates must agree to abide by Federal Election Campaign spending limits on total expenditures.

Although the sums involved seem extraordinary, the importance of money to parties – and American politics more broadly – is contested. Popular coverage tends to convey an image of politicians awash with cash, preoccupied by the search for campaign funds, and dominated in their legislative and governing activities by moneyed interests. Political scientists offer some limited evidence to support this view but generally qualify the significance by noting many exceptions to the general rule. One of the most important is that, per capita, American elections are not especially expensive. Even presidential contests work out to just over one dollar per

voter – hardly an exorbitant price to pay for the race to occupy the world's most powerful political office.

The third feature that distinguishes party politics is related to the first two. Since parties are so marginal to most candidates' electoral fortunes, individual candidates tend to have to organize their own campaigns. More precisely, they purchase professional hired guns to do so, and pay them well. Political consultants, who earn their living as paid professionals by running campaigns, have boomed since the early 1970s, and now constitute a lucrative industry – with its own trade publications like *Campaigns and Elections* – in America. Consultants take opinion polls and surveys, make advertisements, advise on everything from what suit to wear to which pop star to avoid being seen with. These individuals and firms are not entirely mercenary 'dogs of war'. Most have a preference for a particular party, a tendency within it (moderate, liberal, conservative, populist, anti-establishment) or a type of candidate.

TABLE 3.3   Top 'soft money' donors, 1995–96

To Democrats:	
Joseph Seagram & Sons (alcohol/entertainment)	$1.171m
Communication Workers of America (labour)	$1,132m
Walt Disney Co. (media/entertainment)	£997,000
American Federation of State, County and Municipal Employees (labour)	$993.000
United Food & Commercial Workers (labour)	$714,550
Revlon Group MacAndrews & Forbes Holdings (cosmetics/holding company)	$673,250
MCI Worldcom (telecommunications)	$650,203
Lazard Freres & Co. (finance)	$637,000
To Republicans:	
Philip Morris Cos. Inc. (tobacco/food/beer)	$2.538m
RJR Nabisco Inc. (tobacco/food/beer)	£1,189m
American Financial Group (insurance)	$794,000
Atlantic Richfield Co. (energy)	£766,506
News Corporation (media)	$774,700
Union Pacific Corporation (transportation)	$707,393
Joseph Seagram & Sons (alcohol/entertainament)	$685,145
Bell Atlantic Corp. (telecommunications)	$649,854

Source: Center for Responsive Politics.

Nevertheless, the fact remains that their job is related to individual candidates, not the collective party. Like the consumer market, consultants face the task of selling a particular product, and their experience provides ample evidence and theories on how best to market an individual candidate in a given market segment.

Against this picture of decline, however, several important contrary developments have occurred which muddy the water. These suggest a rather different picture of parties, in which the institutions have adjusted to a new political context.

The most important is that the national parties have become institutionalized. That is, they possess permanent headquarters in Washington, DC, with large staffs and formidable budgets. Equipped with banks of computers, video production facilities and state-of-the-art technology, the national committees offer a sophisticated and slick operation. As a result, they have been able to play an active role in both presidential and congressional campaigns, especially in recruiting 'quality' candidates to run for Congress (those with some prior experience of public office and elections), assisting their political

Exhibit 3.14   Parties as coalitions: the Republicans and the Christian Right

The emergence of a conservative wing of the Republican Party inspired by fundamentalist Christian values and abortion politics is a relatively new phenomenon. Abortion entered the political sphere as a partisan issue only in the early 1970s, but as late as the 1980 election evangelical Christians gave large numbers of votes to Jimmy Carter and congressional Democrats. In 1980, religious organizations began supporting Reagan, whose campaign centred on family values rather than religion as such. By 1984, about 80 per cent of fundamentalist Christians voted for Reagan.

But by 1988, Republican leaders began to perceive the costs. With primaries historically seeing very low turnout, highly mobilized Christians began to dominate many selection processes. Such intensity led one Texas leader to accuse the Christian Right of having 'unwavering ideas. They won't accept you if you have one little doubt about anything.' Another noted: 'When you get a three-martini Episcopalian in a room with a tee-totaling Baptist . . . you got a problem. One is telling dirty jokes and the other is there in prayer. It is like mixing oil and water.'

On the Christian Right side, however, they perceived a party establishment that failed to reward the party's most loyal voters. In 1988, when Pat Robertson came second in the Iowa caucus, pushing Bush into third place, party leaders began to engage in tough battles over delegate selections, to try to exclude Robertson supporters. A political consultant for Pat Robertson argued that the 'Republican establishment want us to sleep with them on election night, but they won't respect us in the morning. . . . What happened in South Carolina, [including] the description of a Robertson meeting as a Nazi rally, is the worst sort of bigotry I've seen in a long time' (Frymer, 1999: 193–5).

In 1996, the Christian Right in South Carolina and Texas won the majority of those states' delegates to the Republican national convention. South Carolina governor, Carroll Campbell, finished twelfth in the balloting to represent the state's Republicans at the party's national convention behind eleven unknown Christian Right activists. Texas Senator Kay Bailey Hutchinson barely held on as a pro-choice delegate in her state's selection process. However, although influential, the Christian wing has never been able to select 'one of its own' as the GOP presidential nominee. Partly as a result, Pat Buchanan ran for the Reform Party rather than the Republicans in 1999/2000. John McCain even described two of the most prominent leaders, Falwell and Robertson, as 'agents of intolerance' during the 2000 primaries. But George W. Bush benefited strongly from evangelical support.

'grooming', and donating funds to state parties and candidates in close election races.

The revival, however, has been limited. Parties still aim not to promote public policy or legislative programmes, but simply to elect the maximum number of candidates. Similarly, offering candidates assistance with media appearances and advertising is important, but strongly resembles the role that consultants already provide.

The overall verdict? Parties that were always comparatively weak as organizations have declined still further, and even the rise of national and state organizations has not really halted this. But parties have adapted to developments that have partially displaced them from American politics, and remain crucial to how government operates at state and federal levels.

The party in government: the return of 'party government'?

The final third of our party puzzle is what is often termed the party in government. Two aspects here are key: the president's administration and the parties in Congress.

Once a presidential candidate has finished celebrating his victory, he confronts a daunting task: filling the thousands of posts in his administration. To do so, he must rely on assistance. The traditional, and obvious, source of assistance was the president's own party. Party officials could advise on whom the president should appoint to be his Defense Secretary, Chief of Staff, CIA Director, and so on. They would normally have worked with these individuals, know their strengths and weaknesses, and assess their potential to fill the given role effectively. The peer group review that existed at the level of selecting presidential candidates was replicated once the president acceded to office.

The 'declinist' case rests partly on the basis that this too has changed. In the new electoral environment, presidents obtained their party nominations through an organization that they had created, staffed by individuals loyal to the candidate. Once ensconced in the

Oval Office, it became simple and appealing to rely on this organization once again, not the party, as a source of advice and personnel to staff the government. Successive presidents then surround themselves with their own home state 'mafias': Jimmy Carter's Georgia appointees, Reagan relying on contacts from California, and Clinton on a cadre of 'Friends of Bill' from Arkansas.

There is some strength to this view but it rather oversimplifies the case. Presidents since 1968 have still relied on their party to assist appointments. Clinton, for example, appointed Lloyd Bentsen as his first Treasury Secretary and Mike Espy as his Agriculture Secretary. Before him, George H.W. Bush had assembled a highly experienced and impressive set of administration officials with strong party links, such as James Baker (Secretary of State) and Dick Cheney (Secretary of Defense). George W. Bush in 2001 appointed many Republicans from his father's era and even well before then (Cheney, Rumsfeld, Powell). Moreover, presidents before 1968 also made appointments that did not stem exclusively from party sources, but were personal and non-party decisions. One might also question how desirable it is to staff an administration with party figures. In the case of Kennedy and Johnson, after all, a highly regarded group of officials – the so-called 'best and the brightest' – were responsible for the decisions that led to America's disastrous involvement in the Bay of Pigs invasion of Cuba and the war in Vietnam.

In Congress (as Chapter 7 explains in more detail) party organizes legislative life: determining the composition of committees, the legislative agenda, the scheduling of votes and much more besides. The party here has not only persisted but also gained important dimensions of strength since the mid-1980s. The declinist logic, taken to its extreme, would suggest that it no longer matters whether the White House and Congress are controlled by the same party, or whether divided party control exists. But, as was apparent from the two ends of Pennsylvania Avenue being unable to agree a budget in

1995 and passing trade promotion authority ('fast track') in December 2001 by just one vote in the House of Representatives, party differences are extremely important.

In particular, if one considers the number of votes in which a majority of voting Democrats voted against a majority of voting Republicans, 'party unity' scores in the 1990s reached unprecedented levels (Chapter 7 discusses this phenomenon in more detail). Admittedly, this is a very weak measure when compared to European legislatures, but in the American context, the growth in party voting is substantial. The reasons for this are several. Most significant has been the erosion of the conservative faction in the Democratic Party and the liberal faction in the Republican Party. This has meant that both parties have become more ideologically coherent and homogeneous internally. At the same time, this has ensured that the distance between the two parties has increased. Voters have more of a choice, and less of an echo, between the two parties than has existed in the postwar period.

To some extent, the traditional picture remains true. Where British MPs voting against their party is seen as a relatively rare and notable act of rebellion, such votes remain routine in America for members of both parties. 'Voting the district' is still paramount, whether the assembly is the Senate, the House of Representatives, or a state legislature, but the levels of party cohesion that congressional Democrats and Republicans currently exhibit are quite unlike the politics of the 1950s or 1960s. Party has become more important in the corridors of Congress, to such an extent that many critics now identify unbridled partisanship as a substantial obstacle to effective government – ironically, a criticism which the Founding Fathers shared.

CONCLUSION

That American political parties are weak and may have become weaker in selective

respects does not mean that they are any less important to the conduct and content of contemporary politics. Few analysts could convince Bill Clinton and Newt Gingrich that the party differences that separated them did not matter. Instead, as Alan Ware (1987) argues, political parties are rather like the smile of the Cheshire Cat in Lewis Carroll's *Alice in Wonderland.* Just as the smile persisted after the body had disappeared, so party remains central to American politics despite the atrophy of party organization and the (relative) decline of the party in the electorate. Organizationally weak parties are simultaneously ideologically robust and basic sources of information to the electorate.

American parties remain remarkably broad coalitions of interests, beliefs and values. They could hardly be otherwise when a Republican national convention sees evangelists from Alabama alongside Wall Street billionaires, or the Democratic convention sees gay suburbanite teachers from San Francisco alongside blue-collar steel union representatives from Pittsburgh. But the breadth of these coalitions is less than a generation ago. The divisions within the parties, while remaining substantial, are fewer than those between the parties. In particular, the decline and 'nationalization' of the southern presence in the Democratic Party and the development of the Republican Party as a genuinely conservative force has provided a more coherent logic to party politics, which has itself been 'nationalized'. This amounts to nothing less than a transformation of American party politics.

How parties are faring is crucial, because they provide one of the very few channels of accountability in a democracy. Parties, despite their defects, are the only devices that can generate collective power on behalf of the many individually powerless against the relatively few who are individually, organizationally, politically or economically powerful. The health of parties therefore matters immensely, not only to whether government works effectively, but also for whom government works – not least whether government works accountably to the majority of American citizens.

FURTHER READING

John H. Aldrich, *Why Parties? The Origin and Transformation of Party Politics in America* (1995) is an excellent analysis that focuses on the individual motives of politicians in sustaining America's two-party system.

Alexander Lamis, *The Two-Party South* (1990) is a fascinating historical analysis of the transition of diverse Southern states from a one-party region to one where Democrats and Republicans are in intense competition.

Nicol Rae, *Southern Democrats* (1994) is a superb analysis of the declining presence of a once-dominant party faction.

Byron Shafer (ed.), *Partisan Approaches to Postwar American Politics* (1998) is a set of detailed essays on how parties' role and importance in the American political system has altered during the post-Second World War era.

Alan Ware, *Political Parties and the Party System* (1996) is a detailed and comprehensive comparative analysis of the organization and functions of political parties.

WEB LINKS

Democratic Party
www.democrats.org

Republican Party
www.rnc.org

Reform Party
www.reformparty.org

Ross Perot official site
www.perot.org

Libertarian Party
www.lp.org

Socialist Party USA
www.socialist.org

US Taxpayers Party
www.ustaxpayer.org

QUESTIONS

- Is America as close to a party-less democracy as it is possible to be?

- If parties in America are so weak, why is partisan conflict so strong?

- If individuals, not parties, are the key players in American politics, why does the United States still possess such a solid two-party system?

- 'Sometimes it makes sense for a conservative Democrat to stay in a predominantly liberal Democratic Party and a liberal Republican to remain in a predominantly conservative Republican Party.' Discuss.

- In what ways, if any, do parties matter in American politics today?

4 Elections and Voting Behaviour

Voting is simply a way of determining which side is the stronger without putting it to the test of fighting.

> H.L. Mencken, 1956

The only way I won't get re-elected is if they catch me in bed with a dead girl or a live boy.

> Louisiana Governor Edwin Edwards (Democrat), 1983

- Voting and Non-voting: rationality and ignorance
- The Electoral System and the Electoral College
- The Features of American Elections
- Explaining American Voting Behaviour
- Conclusion

Chapter Summary

Elections are the lifeblood of American democracy, offering citizens regular opportunities to reward successful public officials and, for the less successful, to 'throw the rascals out.' But American elections are distinctive in five respects: local issues tend to dominate; campaigning is heavily individualistic, centred on the candidate rather than the party; incumbents tend to win re-election; money is crucially important, with a substantial campaign budget a necessary (though insufficient) condition of success; and, for elections to the House of Representatives, a redistricting process occurs every ten years that redraws congressional boundaries roughly in line with population shifts. Although electoral turnout has been steadily declining since 1960 and millions of Americans do not register to vote, explaining how and why Americans vote the way that they do is not easy. For many years, political scientists used the notion of alignment and 'realignment' to explain the patterns of stability and instability that existed in federal elections. Traditionally, Americans formed a sense of identification with a political party, and only major events such as the 1930s Depression shifted that identification, resulting in a new pattern of electoral outcomes. But with the decline in party identification since the 1950s and the steady atrophy of party organization, other theorists have posited a 'de-aligned' party system and volatile electorate voting on individual issues, candidates and assessments of past performance, not parties. Still other research has sought to portray American history in terms of 'electoral orders' in which government offices, issue clusters and candidates' positions are integrated to explain the post-1968 pattern of divided party control of the federal government. Which of these approaches best explains results since 1968 is unclear, but with the decline of political parties and the crucial informational role of television and the Internet, it seems unlikely that the old patterns of partisan alignment can return. This does not mean, however, that elections (and the analysis of voting behaviour) cannot tell us important facts about the quality of American democracy – both in relation to those who vote and the many millions who do not.

Every four years, America engages in a ritual bout of national navel-gazing required by the Constitution: a presidential election. Presidential elections provide much of the excitement in American politics, capturing national attentions in ways unlike other regular political events. But elections are a constant and pervasive part of American life: from president, senator, and state governor to dog-catcher and school board member (even high school students cast votes for their 'homecoming' or 'Prom queen' and 'most likely to succeed' students). Thirty-eight states currently elect the judges who sit on their state Supreme Courts. More elections are held in America than any other nation, yet fewer citizens who are eligible to vote turn out to exercise that right than in most industrialized democracies. While in Eastern Europe and South Africa millions fought for the privilege of casting a ballot in the late 1980s and early 1990s, American turnout declined to 49 per cent of eligible voters in 1996.

Liberal democracies depend heavily on free and fair elections that allow citizens to have their say about those who govern them. For the electorate, such elections provide the key mechanisms by which those in power can be held accountable. Provided they are competitive and fairly administered, elections offer voters a choice of personnel to staff government and competing directions in which to take public policy. The people's will can therefore be expressed with greater clarity at election time than between elections, when interest groups, lobbying, donating campaign funds, letter-writing and direct action assume the key means of reaching those in government.

For elected officials, too, campaigns are central to their political lives. Whatever goals a politician wants to accomplish – forging a long career, achieving certain public policy goals or acquiring political influence – they are subject to a simple but fundamental requirement: getting (re)elected. The prospects for securing these goals will also be strongly influenced by the composition of the elected branches of government that elections determine.

Despite the apparent ease with which many members of Congress and state legislators get re-elected, however, elections are anything but a straightforward matter in America. Rather, elections are generally expensive, media-driven, focused on the individual candidate rather than the party, and highly mixed in terms of the quantity and quality of political information they convey to those both in and outside government. In this chapter, we first assess the nature of American elections, and then examine the main approaches that have sought to explain recent federal election outcomes. Although elections form only one part of a liberal democratic regime, the problems that surround them in America are formidable and partly undermine the nation's democratic credentials and the political legitimacy of public policies.

VOTING AND NON-VOTING: RATIONALITY AND IGNORANCE

A vexing question confronts democratic theorists: Is it rational for an individual to bother to vote? And if so, under what, if any, conditions is it rational for an individual to vote? Assuming that we behave in terms of acting in our self-interest (which is not the same as acting selfishly), can we ever say that voting is a rational activity?

Some Americans become indignant at the suggestion that it may be irrational to vote. Hundreds have died to obtain the right to vote in America (as elsewhere). Women required nothing less than a constitutional amendment – the Nineteenth – to give them universal adult suffrage. Even then, many black women could not vote, since most southern blacks were prevented by white segregationists from voting until passage of the Voting Rights Act in 1965. Not to vote today seems simultaneously to insult the collective memory of huge numbers who struggled to secure the right to the franchise and to squander an important part of citizenship. Yet, as Table 4.1 demonstrates, voter turnout – recorded as the proportion of those citizens who are eligible to vote – has shown a steady decline in presidential elections since 1960 (with an exceptional upward blip in 1992). (In midterm congressional elections,

Exhibit 4.1   Constitutional amendments expanding the right to vote

Amendment XV, Section 1. The right of citizens of the United States to vote shall not be denied or abridged by the United States or by any State on account of race, color, or previous condition of servitude. [Ratified in 1870.]

Amendment XIX, Section 1. The right of citizens of the United States to vote shall not be denied or abridged by the United States or by any State on account of sex. [Ratified in 1920. Although some states had enfranchised women earlier, this amendment ensured that white women and those African American women outside the South had the right to vote as a matter of American citizenship.]

Amendment XXIV, Section 1. The right of citizens of the United States to vote in any primary or other election for President or Vice President, for electors for President or Vice President, or for Senator or Representative in Congress, shall not be denied or abridged by the United States or any State by reason of failure to pay any poll tax or other tax. [Ratified in 1964.]

Amendment XXVI, Section 1. The right of citizens of the United States, who are eighteen years of age or older, to vote shall not be denied or abridged by the United States or by any State on account of age. [Ratified in 1971.]

turnout is even lower, with about one-third of eligible voters typically casting ballots.)

Rationally, however, it only makes sense to vote if individuals believe that they can truly make a difference and affect the result of an election – and the chances of this occurring are generally minimal. That is, few state or federal elections are decided by very close margins. For the individual voter, casting a ballot when the prospects that the ballot will make a difference to the outcome are minimal is therefore a rather perverse act. Nevertheless, voting appears to millions of Americans to be at minimum a chance to express their political views, and thereby – perhaps – to influence government.

Current levels of relative voter apathy are striking – but not unprecedented – in historical perspective. Voter turnout in the late nineteenth century was extraordinarily high by today's standards, routinely over 70 per cent in presidential elections (free whiskey, money and patronage jobs played a role in the political enthusiasm of Americans at the time). For most of this period, parties distributed at the polls their own 'tickets', listing only their own candidates for office. A voter

TABLE 4.1 Voter turnout in presidential elections, 1960–2000

Year	Percentage of voting age population
1960	63
1964	62
1968	61
1972	55
1976	54
1980	53
1984	53
1988	50
1992	55
1996	49
2000	51

TABLE 4.2 Tuning out the news?

In 1998 a Gallup poll asked American respondents about the sources of their news and information about public life. The result suggested a rather unenlightened, or at least politically disinterested, electorate. Another indicator of a rather disinterested public was that daily newspaper circulation declined from 62 million in 1970 to 56 million in 1999.

Source	Frequency			
	Every day	Several times per week	Occasionally	Never
Local newspapers	53	15	22	10
National newspapers	4	11	26	59
Nightly network news	55	19	19	7
CNN	21	16	33	29
C-SPAN	3	4	25	65
National public radio	15	12	25	47
Radio talk shows	12	9	21	58
Discussions with family and friends	27	26	41	6
On-line news	7	6	17	70
Weekly news magazines	15	6	27	52

Source: The Gallup Organization, cited in Schudson (2000: 20).

simply took a ticket from a party worker and deposited it in the ballot box, without needing to read it or mark it in any way. Voting was therefore a public act of party affiliation.

Beginning in 1888, however, and spreading across the nation by 1896, this system was replaced with government-printed ballots that listed all the candidates from each eligible party. The voter marked the ballot in secret, as is the case today, in an act that affirmed voting as an individual private choice rather than a social act of party loyalty. Political parades and other public spectacles increasingly gave way to pamphlets in what reformers dubbed 'educational' political campaigns. Leading newspapers, once little more than organs of the parties, declared their independence and portrayed themselves as non-partisan commercial institutions of public enlightenment and criticism. Public secondary education also began to spread.

These and other reforms enshrined the notion of the informed citizen as the foundation of democracy but at the cost of voter turnout plummeting. In the presidential election of 1920 turnout dropped to 49 per cent, its lowest point in the twentieth century, until it was matched in 1996 (but the contemporary context has a much expanded voter base, making current levels of voter disaffection even more striking). To many observers of American history it seems baffling that so many citizens, knowing so little, and voting in such small numbers, have built a democracy that appears to be so successful. But critics who are more sanguine about electoral participation note several important influences on American voters that depress turnout rates:

- *Complexity.* A certain amount of ignorance about politics is a by-product of a uniquely complex political system. No nation has as many elections, as many elected officials and as complicated a maze of overlapping governmental jurisdictions as America. It is simply harder to 'read' American politics and to act

through the electoral process to achieve clear and comprehensive policy changes.
- *Lack of ideological intensity and coherence.* The traditional ideological inconsistencies of parties compound the problem. Unlike the British context of parliamentary government, a voter casting a ballot for a Democrat or Republican has no assurance that a candidate will follow a collective party line in office, nor any guarantee of a clear programme being implemented in the fragmented system.
- *Relative insularity.* The fact of America's political, military and cultural 'megapower' status limits the political awareness of its citizenry. America possesses no monopoly on a relatively de-politicized citizenry. But with a vast domestic market, bordered by only two other countries, many American producers have relatively few dealings with customers in other countries ('globalization' notwithstanding). Most Americans do not travel abroad (only one-sixth own passports). The combination of an inward-looking focus – other than in times of war – with marked prosperity has compounded the tendency not to look to government for innovation and change, and hence not to emphasize politics as a key element of American life.
- *Voter fatigue.* The steady drop in presidential election turnout starting in 1960 coincided with the beginning of a broad expansion of non-electoral politics that may have drained American political energies away from the polling places into other forms of political participation: the civil rights movement, the anti-war demonstrations of the Vietnam years, the women's and gay rights movements, environmental groups, gun rights and gun control lobbies, and the emergence of the Religious Right. The decline in turnout may partly signify disengagement from public life but it may also (or alternatively) suggest that Americans judge electoral politics to be relatively peripheral to the public issues that concern

them and government to be marginal to solving key social problems.

- *Voluntary registration.* Unlike nations such as Italy and Australia, American voters must register before they can cast a ballot. High levels of geographic mobility pose a disincentive to registration. When the proportion of voters who cast a ballot is compared to those who are registered, voter turnout is at least as high as in nations such as the UK. The perennial problem, however, is that a large proportion of Americans who are eligible to register do not do so. The passage of the National Voter Registration Act in 1993 did increase the number of registered voters from 133.8 million in 1992 to 149.8 million by 1996 (increasing the proportion of registered voters from 70.6 per cent of the voting age population to 76.25 per cent, an all-time high). This so-called 'motor-voter' law allowed citizens to apply to register to vote when they received their driving licences, and required states to offer mail-in voter registration and registration at offices offering public assistance and military recruitment (catering to supposedly Democratic and Republican constituencies, respectively). But the relative voter turnout decreased in 1996 and almost a quarter of the eligible electorate remained unregistered.

Should such a relative lack of enthusiasm for the electoral process concern us? Low as American levels of political knowledge may be, a generally effective political democracy survives. This may be because a low level of political information provides sufficient material to act rationally. Voters can still rely on party affiliation as a rudimentary voting cue, along with endorsements by other party officials. Voters also process information without necessarily retaining it, but frequently maintain a reasonable basis on which to judge competing candidates (or recall previous judgements). Finally, voting is only one part (though an important one) of a broader concept of democratic citizenship in which

other forms of political participation – from joining civic groups through donating funds to interest lobbies and candidates to litigating in the courts – also figure strongly. While it would be foolish to be complacent about the sources or consequences of non-voting, the extent to which the phenomenon discredits or undermines democracy needs to be qualified.

Nevertheless, for the world's premier democracy regularly to see approximately half of its eligible electorate not bothering to register or vote is an indictment. Moreover, the tendency to stay at home is especially pronounced among the more disadvantaged sections of society: the jobless, racial and ethnic minorities, and the poor. The combination of these facts suggests strongly that, in terms of the political equality of its citizens, America suffers something of a 'democratic deficit' in which the key groups participating in elections (thereby determining the composition of government) are the relatively affluent.

THE ELECTORAL SYSTEM AND THE ELECTORAL COLLEGE

The electoral system used in America for most elections is the plurality system in single-member constituencies: a candidate who wins more votes than any other candidate – even if he or she fails to secure an absolute majority of voters – wins election. This system distinguishes America from most other liberal democracies.

American elected officials are directly elected by the people and put into office to represent particular geographic constituencies. But unlike the UK, they are much more akin to delegates than representatives. American officials are expected to follow their constituents' policy priorities and preferences closely in their legislative behaviour, not to speculate about the national interest and vote 'against' their district or state. Although many elected politicians display biases in their legislative behaviour that are independent of their constituents, they are mostly tied

TABLE 4.3   A sample of electoral systems in liberal democracies

Nation	Type of electoral system	Single or multi-member districts
Austria	PR-list system	Multi-member
Belgium	PR-list system	Multi-member
Canada	Plurality	Single-member
Finland	PR-list system	Multi-member
France	Mixed PR/Plurality	Single-member
Germany	Mixed PR/Plurality	Mixed single-member/multi-member
Ireland	PR–STV* system	Multi-member
Italy	Mixed PR/Plurality	Mixed single-member/multi-member
Portugal	PR-list system	Multi-member
Spain	PR-list system	Multi-member
UK	Plurality	Single-member
USA	Plurality	Single-member

* Single Transferable Vote

closely to the voters who put them in office. Their prospects for re-election rest with their own efforts, not the popularity of the party to which they belong.

The key exception to direct election in the elected branches of the federal government is the presidency (the Seventeenth Amendment making senators directly elected from 1913). Under the Constitution, the president is elected indirectly by an Electoral College. States' votes in the Electoral College are calculated by adding the House and Senate seats together. These are recalculated and adjusted every ten years after the decennial census has identified which states have gained and lost population (for example, after the 2000 census, eight states gained additional votes while ten lost seats). As Table 4.4 notes, in the 2004 election 53 House seats and two senators will give California fifty-five Electoral College votes, four House seats and two Senators will give Mississippi six. Since all of a state's Electoral College votes go to the winning candidate, even if the popular vote margin is just one vote, the calculation for presidential candidates is not about winning the most votes nationwide (the popular vote), but winning the necessary states to pass the 270 Electoral College vote landmark (Wash-

ington, DC has three Electoral College votes, making a total of 538).

What this means, in turn, is that presidential campaign strategies focus on states rather than individual voters. For example, Republican presidential candidates from 1972 to 2000 have mostly been able to rely on southern states voting for them (the exceptions were 1976, 1992 and 1996). A 'solid South' (Alabama, Arkansas, Florida, Georgia, Kentucky, Louisiana, Mississippi, North Carolina, Oklahoma, South Carolina, Texas and Virginia) provides a total Electoral College vote of 152. Prior to the civil rights revolution of the 1960s, that 'solid South' was the backbone of the Democrats' New Deal coalition and assisted Franklin D. Roosevelt, Truman and Kennedy to reach the White House. Since then, the 152 votes have tended to go to candidates such as Nixon, Reagan and the Bushes, meaning that GOP presidential aspirants needed to find only another 118 votes from across the nation, allowing them to concentrate their resources on large Electoral College states such as California and New York and medium-size states such as Michigan, Missouri, Illinois, Ohio and Pennsylvania. By contrast, Democrats have typically been forced to fight for as many states as

TABLE 4.4 The Electoral College, 2004*

California	55	(54)	South Carolina	8	(8)
Texas	34	(32)	Connecticut	7	(8)
New York	31	(33)	Iowa	7	(7)
Florida	27	(25)	Oklahoma	7	(8)
Illinois	21	(22)	Oregon	7	(7)
Pennsylvania	21	(25)	Arkansas	6	(6)
Ohio	20	(21)	Kansas	6	(6)
Michigan	17	(18)	Mississippi	6	(7)
New Jersey	15	(15)	Nebraska	5	(5)
North Carolina	15	(14)	Nevada	5	(4)
Georgia	15	(13)	New Mexico	5	(5)
Virginia	13	(13)	Utah	5	(5)
Indiana	11	(12)	West Virginia	5	(5)
Massachusetts	12	(12)	Hawaii	4	(4)
Missouri	11	(11)	Idaho	4	(4)
Tennessee	11	(11)	Maine	4	(4)
Washington	11	(11)	New Hampshire	4	(4)
Arizona	10	(8)	Rhode Island	4	(4)
Maryland	10	(10)	Alaska	3	(3)
Minnesota	10	(10)	Delaware	3	(3)
Wisconsin	10	(11)	District of Columbia	3	(3)
Alabama	9	(9)	Montana	3	(3)
Colorado	9	(8)	North Dakota	3	(3)
Louisiana	9	(9)	South Dakota	3	(3)
Kentucky	8	(8)	Vermont	3	(3)
			Wyoming	3	(3)

Total votes: 538   Needed to win: 270

* The distribution of votes from 1990 to 2000 – prior to the redistribution after the 2000 census – are in brackets.

Source: National Archives and Records Administration.

possible to compensate for their lack of an equally reliable base of votes.

The Electoral College is a curious eighteenth-century relic. The elite who framed the Constitution neither anticipated nor would have approved of the arrival of mass democracy. The Founding Fathers devised a system by which the president would be chosen by a set of wise and worthy individuals (much like themselves) who would be nominated by their states. This mechanism worked exactly as planned for the election and re-election of George Washington but has provoked concern ever since.

On the plus side, the Electoral College has mostly functioned without a problem or serious popular complaints through two world wars, a major economic depression and several periods of intense civil unrest. Its 'winner-take-all' system generally means that third party and Independent candidates receive few Electoral College votes, inhibiting splinter and extremist parties from securing an enduring presence in national politics. It typically also translates narrow popular vote margins into much larger Electoral College vote victories, helping to unite the nation behind a new president. Since a relatively

TABLE 4.5 Presidential election results, 1932–2000

Year	Name	Party	Popular vote	Electoral College vote
1932	Franklin D. Roosevelt	Democrat	22,809,638	472
	Herbert Hoover	Republican	15,758,901	59
1936	Franklin D. Roosevelt	Democrat	27,752,869	449
	Alfred Landon	Republican	16,674,665	8
1940	Franklin D. Roosevelt	Democrat	27,307,819	449
	Wendell Wilkie	Republican	22,321,018	82
1944	Franklin D. Roosevelt	Democrat	25,606,585	432
	Thomas Dewey	Republican	22,014,745	99
1948	Harry S. Truman	Democrat	24,179,345	303
	Thomas Dewey	Republican	21,991,291	189
	Strom Thurmond	Dixiecrat	1,176,125	39
	Henry Wallace	Progressive	1,157,326	–
1952	Dwight D. Eisenhower	Republican	33,936,234	442
	Adlai Stevenson	Democrat	27,314,992	89
1956	Dwight D. Eisenhower	Republican	35,590,472	457
	Adlai Stevenson	Democrat	26,022,752	73
1960	John F. Kennedy	Democrat	34,226,731	303
	Richard M. Nixon	Republican	34,108,157	219
1964	Lyndon B. Johnson	Democrat	43,129,566	486
	Barry Goldwater	Republican	27,178,188	52
1968	Richard M. Nixon	Republican	31,785,480	301
	Hubert Humphrey	Democrat	31,275,166	191
	George Wallace	American Independent	9,906,473	46
1972	Richard M. Nixon	Republican	47,170,179	520
	George McGovern	Democrat	29,171,791	17
1976	Jimmy Carter	Democrat	40,830,763	297
	Gerald R. Ford	Republican	39,147,793	240
1980	Ronald Reagan	Republican	43,904,153	489
	Jimmy Carter	Democrat	35,483,883	49
	John Anderson	Independent	5,719,437	–
1984	Ronald Reagan	Republican	54,455,074	525
	Walter Mondale	Democrat	37,577,137	13
1988	George H.W. Bush	Republican	48,881,278	426
	Michael Dukakis	Democrat	41,805,374	111
1992	Bill Clinton	Democrat	43,727,625	370
	George H.W. Bush	Republican	38,165,180	168
	Ross Perot	Independent	19,236,411	–
1996	Bill Clinton	Democrat	45,628,667	379
	Bob Dole	Republican	37,869,435	159
	Ross Perot	Independent	7,874,283	–
2000	George W. Bush	Republican	50,456,600	271
	Al Gore	Democrat	50,997,100	267

Exhibit 4.2 A stolen election? 2000's 'perfect tie'

The 2000 presidential election was the closest since 1960. Al Gore won the popular vote, with 48.3 per cent to George W. Bush's 48 per cent (Green Party candidate Ralph Nader picked up just over 3 per cent). But the Electoral College vote handed Bush victory by a 271:267 margin, the closest margin since 1876 and the first time since 1888 that the identity of the popular and electoral vote winners differed. With the Senate split 50–50 and the House of Representatives with a narrow Republican majority, the elections were a 'perfect tie'. Some commentators claimed that Bush had 'stolen' the election. But the Constitution explicitly requires a majority in the Electoral College, not the popular vote, to win the presidency. Moreover, the Supreme Court's intervention was designed to prevent an egregious intervention by Florida state courts – also staffed by political appointees – from determining the result. When the votes were counted again by media-sponsored groups in 2001, they suggested that Gore had won the total statewide vote (but he had not requested a statewide recount). The selective counties that Gore litigated to get recounted had indeed given Bush a narrow majority. Whether or not the 25 votes of Florida should have gone to Bush remains heavily disputed, but Richard Posner, one of the most dispassionate observers of American politics, argues persuasively that there can be little doubt that Bush was indeed the correct victor of the 2000 presidential election (Posner, 2001a).

small number of votes in a state can determine which candidate wins that state's votes, it also affords well-organized minorities a chance to influence the result (for example, black votes were crucial to the narrow successes of Carter in 1976 and Clinton in 1992 in several key Electoral College states such as Ohio and Georgia). Finally, the Electoral College reflects and reinforces federalism, making states rather than individuals the key functional units.

Against this, the Electoral College ignores the national popular vote and has the potential to produce a constitutional crisis. Most notably, it is possible for a presidential candidate to win the popular vote but lose the election in the Electoral College. George W. Bush in 2000, Rutherford B. Hayes in 1876 and Benjamin Harrison in 1888 were elected president without winning the nationwide popular vote. This almost happened in 1960 when JFK was elected and in 1976 (had fewer than 9,000 electors in Ohio and Hawaii voted differently, the incumbent Gerald Ford would have 'beaten' Jimmy Carter despite trailing him by more than 1.5 million votes nationally). The College may also discourage

turnout since the election is indirect and many states are invariably uncompetitive (for example, Utah for the Republicans). Like the composition of the Senate, the College privileges smaller states, giving them a disproportionate influence. If neither candidate wins a majority of the 538 Electoral College votes, the House of Representatives selects the president (two elections in 1800 and 1824 were decided in the House of Representatives, where each state delegation has one vote regardless of its size). Finally, there exists a danger that Electoral College delegates from each state (chosen by each candidate) are not legally obliged to vote for the candidate they had originally supported – some could switch sides.

THE FEATURES OF AMERICAN ELECTIONS

Five features mark American elections as comparatively distinctive: localism; individualism; the power of incumbency; the role of money; and redistricting.

Localism

Thomas ('Tip') O'Neill, the Democratic Party's Speaker of the House of Representatives from 1977 to 1985, summed up American political life: 'All politics is local.' The dictum remains the single, best guide to American politics for its tens of thousands of elected officials.

Localism is important for several reasons. As a federal and separated system, candidates elected to the Congress are sent to Capitol Hill – like those to the 50 state legislatures – to protect, defend and advance the interests of their particular constituencies. They are not sent by their voters primarily to serve a national interest, political party, president, ideology or programme of government. These other interests may, or may not, be accomplished as a by-product of serving the constituency, but they are not the main reason for being in office and nor are they the key factors in seeing an incumbent returned to office.

The populist nature of American democracy reinforces the local focus. Since elections are held so often (thousands of elections occur annually), elected officials are regularly called to account for their records as executive officers (presidents and governors) or legislators (federal, state and local). Even members of the US Senate – with six-year terms – must effectively be looking to the next election as soon as they get into office. The choice of committees and subcommittees that they sit on, the bills they sponsor and the votes they cast must all be considered with a view to how these will play in the next election. No more damning political indictment exists than the accusation that members of Congress have 'gone Washington', finding the excitement and glamour of life in the capital (let alone abroad on taxpayer-funded trips) more compelling than serving their constituency's needs. Elected officials cannot forget their constituents in favour of working on public policy or travelling abroad. Those who do, do so at their electoral peril.

The final factor making for localist politics is the mass media. Most Americans get their information about politics mainly from local sources (the Internet may alter this but only in the long run). Although some newspapers exist that have a wide circulation beyond their home bases (the *Washington Post*, *New York Times*, *Wall Street Journal*) and one national paper exists (the middle-brow *USA Today*), these are exceptional. As Table 4.2 above noted, most Americans receive their political information from nightly newscasts on CBS, NBC, ABC, Fox and CNN in brief news programmes with relatively little detailed discussion of politics. What this means is that most Americans receive relatively little national news coverage and even national news and events are frequently approached through a local lens that focuses on distinctly parochial concerns ('what does a cut in federal price supports to wheat growers mean for farmers in Kansas?').

Individualism

Localism reinforces another important dimension of electoral life: individualism. Just as American political culture prizes individualism, so America's politicians are heavily self-selected, self-driven and self-reliant. Like their compatriots' approach to social and economic success, politicians tend to see their individual fate as being largely within their own hands to determine.

Candidates for elective office outside America typically rely on their political party for workers, money, advice and, most importantly, determining their chances of election. That is, whether or not given candidates win an election tends to depend not on what they do, but on how popular their party is among voters in the particular constituency. A 'personal vote' exists in the UK (one that is independent of party attachments as a result of good constituency service) of about 500–1,000 votes maximum. A British candidate for Parliament in Birmingham knows that, whatever party he or she belongs to, the chances of victory or defeat are tied to how popular his or her national party is within the particular constituency, something that, as a backbench MP or even a minister, he or she will have little ability to influence directly.

American elections are different. True, most candidates run with a party label – as Democrats or Republicans, not as Independents or members of a third party – but elections are individualistic contests where what matters most are the candidates. It is common for candidates not even to mention which party they belong to in campaign literature and advertisements. A candidate in Birmingham, Alabama can largely insulate him or herself from his or her national party by emphasizing what he or she has done – or will do – for the particular district and how he or she has consistently acted in the interests of Birmingham in Washington, DC. What is more, the candidate genuinely has the opportunity in Congress (or a state legislature) to secure material benefits for the constituency in ways that are usually alien to strongly party-dominated governments. Even if the Democratic president or Congress is despised, Democrats who distance themselves from them and work effectively can prosper in their own constituencies.

The political context is therefore one in which the central question that voters typically pose – 'What have you done for the district/state lately?' – dominates candidates' behaviour in office. Their party may be riding high or low in the national polls, but re-election hinges more on how voters in their districts or states evaluate the candidates' particular performance. Since voters cannot elect a government, only a collection of individual officeholders, it is entirely rational for electors and candidates to focus overwhelmingly (though not necessarily exclusively) on individual performance in the service of the constituency – not support for a president, party, or government programme.

Politics is therefore often described as 'personalized'. Insofar as the emphasis in elections tends to be on concrete individuals rather than abstract entities such as parties or programmes, this is true. But this does not mean that elections turn on 'personality'

rather than issues, records in office or ideological biases. Questions of personal 'character', such as trust, integrity, experience and honesty, partly inform election campaigns, and candidates frequently exploit these traits (in 2000 Gore sought to exploit his experience of government, Bush his personal integrity and trustworthiness). Personality does not, though, determine election outcomes any more than sharp suits or good looks. However much the focus of campaigns is centred on the individual, American voters behave much like those elsewhere: voting on the issues important to them (taxes, social programmes, health, education, international affairs) and selecting between the different political positions and approaches of rival candidates.

Incumbency

The most striking, distinctive and persistent fact about elections is this: incumbents win. That is, those politicians in office who seek re-election rarely fail. Turnover in Congress is due more to retirement than defeat at the polls. Such has been the 'incumbent advantage' over recent decades that President Reagan once quipped that there had been more turnover in the Soviet Union's (famously geriatric) Politburo than in the US Congress during the 1980s. He was not far wrong, though it was ironic that some of the most constant features in Congress, such as Strom Thurmond and Jesse Helms, who were elected to the Senate in 1964 from South Carolina and in 1970 from North Carolina, respectively, and were re-elected every six years thereafter until retiring in 2002, were among Reagan's most reliable supporters.

In the worst of recent election years for incumbents, the House of Representatives re-election rate has dropped to a 'low' of 87 per cent; in the best (1988, 1998 and 2000), it has soared to 98 per cent, that is, 98 per cent of all those incumbents who ran for re-election were successful. The average incumbent re-election rate from 1980 to 1998 was 94 per cent. The Senate has been less reliable, the average re-election rate for incumbents being 'only' in the high 80 per cent region (Senate elections, being statewide, fewer and more prestigious, tend to attract more competitive and well-financed challengers than House contests). Even seriously endangered incumbents often manage to win re-election, sometimes after pundits and their own party have all but given them up for dead.

The reasons for this success are several, but there is nothing automatic about it. Incumbents are well aware of the localist and individualist character of elections and consistently tailor their behaviour to suit these needs. As Anthony King (1997) has argued, American politicians are unusually 'vulnerable' compared to those in other democracies: they face re-election more often, possess little party cover, must compete in primaries to win nomination as the party's candidate and must raise their own campaign funds and run their own campaigns. Hence, incumbents behave in a manner akin to workers in a nuclear power plant: they may know that 'objectively' they are safe in that few are ever beaten – provided that they work hard – but they must take every possible precaution to ensure that this is the case. Incumbents therefore invest inordinate resources – time, energy and money – to ensure their re-election.

Of course, not all districts have an incumbent running for re-election, and these 'open seat' districts are invariably the most competitive races. They provide a more 'level playing field' for candidates since none has the formidable advantages of incumbency. But even in open-seat contests, the job of recruiting candidates to run is often difficult. Prospective candidates must weigh the possibility of rigorous and adversarial news coverage; loss of privacy; invasive research by opponents for damaging personal and financial information; and a personal toll in the event of losing (and sometimes if successful). Promising potential candidates often become convinced that a candidacy will cost more than the office and public service will

be worth – emotionally, psychologically, physically and financially.

One of the most important aspects of such pronounced incumbent advantages is that relatively small shifts in voting patterns can result in substantial changes in the control of Congress. In 1980, for example, when the Republicans gained 12 Senate seats to take control of the chamber, some commentators interpreted this as a mandate for President Reagan's brand of conservatism. In 1994, when not one Republican incumbent member of the House, Senate or governor lost his re-election bid, and the party took control of both houses of Congress for the first time in 40 years, this was again widely seen – not least by many congressional Republicans – as firm evidence of a decisive rejection of the Clinton administration by the voters and an embrace of an assertive conservatism. In both cases, the reality was more complicated.

Money

It was once said that 'money is the mother's milk' of politics. The incumbent advantage rests heavily, though not exclusively, on a large campaign chest. Money is a necessary, if not sufficient, condition of winning elections because elections are an expensive business. This is especially so in the larger states, such as California, Texas and Florida, where vast sums are necessary merely to wage a competitive race in a populous and multi-media market. Even in relatively sparsely-populated states, federal elections typically command expenditures well in excess of $1 million. In 2000, former Goldman Sachs investment banker Jon Corzine spent $60 million as a Democratic candidate to win a Senate seat representing New Jersey, against a Republican opponent who spent $2 million. (Surprisingly enough, Corzine won.)

Incumbents have a two-fold advantage: a direct and an indirect effect. The direct effect stems from the large sums that incumbents typically raise. Most money comes from small individual contributions, listed by computer in the incumbents' Washington,

TABLE 4.6   Party control of the Senate

Year	Before election D	Before election R	Incumbents lost by D	Incumbents lost by R	Open seats lost by D	Open seats lost by R	After election D	After election R
1954	47	49	2	4	1	1	49	47
1956	49	47	1	3	3	1	49	47
1958	51	47	0	11	0	2	64	34
1960	66	34	1	0	1	0	64	36
1962	64	36	2	3	0	3	68	32
1964	66	34	1	3	0	0	68	32
1966	67	33	1	0	2	0	64	36
1968	63	37	4	0	3	2	58	42
1970	57	43	3	2	1	0	55	45
1972	55	45	1	4	3	2	57	43
1974	58	42	0	2	1	3	62	38
1976	62	38	5	2	3	3	59	41
1978	62	38	5	2	3	3	59	41
1980	59	41	9	0	3	0	47	53
1982	46	54	1	1	1	1	46	54
1984	45	55	1	2	0	1	47	53
1986	47	53	0	7	1	2	55	45
1988	54	46	1	3	2	1	55	45
1990	55	45	0	1	0	0	56	44
1992	57	43	2	2	0	0	57	43
1994	56	44	2	0	6	0	47	53
1996	47	53	0	1	3	0	45	55
1998	45	55	1	2	2	1	45	55
2000	46	54	1	5	1	1	50	50*

* The balance altered in June 2001 to 50 Democrats, 49 Republicans and one Independent, when James Jeffords of Vermont left the Republican Party and became an Independent, thereby giving control of the Senate to the Democrats.

DC and state/district offices. Secondly, large sums are raised from PACs, the conduits for corporations, labour unions and advocacy groups seeking access to incumbents on Capitol Hill. Thirdly, but of least significance, the incumbent often receives campaign funds from his political party. Taken together, these three sources amount to formidable campaign budgets (often exceeding those of national parties outside America). Incumbents benefit disproportionately since they sit on the congressional committees that write the legislation that corporate, labour and other interests are directly affected by; their challengers do not. But other 'perquisites'

(benefits) that accrue to congressional incumbents supplement this direct effect:

* *Offices and staff.* Incumbents have allocated to them, at public expense, large numbers of staff. These can be apportioned in both Washington and the incumbent's home district or state (about 40 and 30 per cent of House and Senate personal staff, respectively, are assigned to district or state offices). These staffers handle much of the day-to-day business of serving constituent demands: answering letters, arranging meetings, seeking intervention with the bureaucracy. They help

the incumbent to know what concerns constituents (their priorities) and also what their views are (their preferences).

- *Subsidized travel*. In order to keep in contact with constituents, members of Congress receive subsidized travel back to their home districts and states. This assists the impression of officials who are assiduously keeping in touch with local concerns, which are part of their representative and legislative job. But it simultaneously helps to craft a consistently positive image ripe for exploitation in subsequent election campaigns.
- *Subsidized mailings*. The incumbents have, again at taxpayers' expense, a budget with which to keep in touch with constituents. Although this 'frank' is intended to let constituents know what their officials are doing on their behalf on the Hill, it is simultaneously a means by which the incumbents can create a highly favourable impression. Information about their lack of activity, ignorance of policy issues, and ethical lapses is left for political opponents and the media to uncover.

Taken together, these benefits have been estimated to amount to approximately $3 million per House member (over two years) and as much as $20 million for a six-year Senate term – a substantial sum for many incumbents and almost all challengers.

In addition to this direct effect, incumbents can exploit an 'indirect effect': effectively pricing their opponents out of the electoral marketplace. By raising so much money long in advance of an up-coming election through a 'war chest', the costs of even competing against an incumbent can become prohibitive for a prospective challenger. Every federal election sees dozens of incumbents re-elected without even facing a challenger in either their primary or their general elections. In 1988, for example, Mike Espy (Democrat, Mississippi) spent over $800,000 on his re-election campaign in one of the poorest districts in the nation in the Mississippi Delta. The chance that any challenger could raise sufficient funds to wage a competitive race here were minimal.

The problems challengers face are exacerbated by the campaign finance regime (authored, coincidentally, by incumbents). As Table 4.7 documents, several different categories of contributions to candidates, interest lobbies and parties in federal elections exist, some with strict limits, some with none whatsoever.

But incumbents need not actively chase these sources of money. For party leaders and chairs of influential congressional committees, especially, money invariably finds them. Outside groups want access to members of Congress, and hence pro-actively donate to influential lawmakers. Lawmakers can themselves form PACs to donate funds to fellow colleagues. Those wanting to influence government must consider where the power lies in a political system before choosing to whom

---

TABLE 4.7   How money enters federal elections, 1974–2002

Category of donation	Legal limits
Independent expenditures for or against candidates	unlimited
Individual donation to PACs	$5,000
Individual donation to interest group for issue advocacy	unlimited
Individual donation to a candidate	$1,000
Individual donations to political parties for issue advocacy	unlimited
Individual donation to political parties in 'hard money'	$20,000
Individual donation to political parties in 'soft money'	unlimited

Exhibit 4.3   Celebrity donors

In the 2000 election, many Americans exercised their legal rights to donate. Robert De Niro, Harrison Ford, Gwyneth Paltrow and Sharon Stone contributed the maximum legal donation of $1,000 to Al Gore's Democratic Party presidential campaign. De Niro, Ted Danson, Robin Williams, Tom Cruise and Nicole Kidman also gave $5,000 to Hillary Clinton's New York Senate campaign, and Jerry Springer donated $10,000. Such are Hollywood's predominantly liberal political leanings that in the summer of 2000, that prominent political observer, actress Bo Derek, even complained of 'witch-hunts' against Republican-minded thespians such as herself, Chuck Norris and Arnold Schwarzenegger. (As partial compensation Bo, along with World Wrestling Federation star 'The Rock', at least got to address the Republican national convention in Philadelphia in July 2000.)

to donate. In centralized systems such as the UK, where a party normally wins a majority of seats in the House of Commons and the prime minister can implement his or her programme more or less unimpeded by political actors outside government, the incentive generally favours giving to the party closest to a donor's views. In decentralized systems, there is more reason to give to the array of particular individuals – party leaders, influential committee or subcommittee chairs, policy entrepreneurs – who matter on the policy area(s) affecting a potential donor directly.

But it is crucial to challenge the idea – popular within and outside America – that money is the only thing that counts in elections. The importance of finance needs to be qualified. Money is not the whole story. No matter how much money a senator for Alabama may have in his campaign chest, if he or she votes in favour of gay rights, abortion 'on demand' and stringent gun controls, or against the death penalty, prayer in school and curbs on 'obscenity', he or she is unlikely to stay in office long. Financial clout has a direct and frequently powerful effect on politics but cannot substitute for politics. Michael Huffington, for example, spent $25 million in 1994 running as the Republican nominee for a Senate seat in California but was defeated.

As Exhibit 4.4 notes, several factors combine to affect a candidate's vote in a given election. No matter how much money a

conservative Republican may have, if he or she is running for election in a heavily Democratic district, he or she will lose, and vice versa (black Republicans running in mostly black districts regularly suffer defeat because most blacks are solid Democrats). A combination of influences condition who enters election races and who succeeds, but a candidate who lacks funds is also one, ultimately, who ends up lacking votes. Money is a necessary but insufficient condition of electoral success.

Redistricting

The final influence to note is election boundaries. Political parties are 'quasi-public' institutions regulated by the state. Every decade, after the decennial census has been taken, some states gain and others lose seats in the

Exhibit 4.4   Factors affecting the candidate's vote

- Incumbency
- Campaign receipts and expenditures
- Opponent's spending
- Media coverage and endorsements
- Partisanship of the electorate
- Trends in support of the candidate's party

Exhibit 4.5   Racial gerrymandering: affirmative electoral action

Not until 1965 and passage of the Voting Rights Act (VRA) could most southern blacks vote. Even then, black representation in Congress and other legislative assemblies remained low. Partly, this was the result of ideological factors. Blacks are the most consistently liberal social group on issues of socio-economic policy and hence many voters would simply not support a black candidate who was 'too liberal' for them. But race also played a role. With blacks a demographic minority in every state and racially polarized voting the norm in states where they made up a substantial minority (such as Mississippi, Louisiana and Alabama), electing blacks to state or federal office was rare.

Using provisions that amended the VRA in 1975 and 1982, federal and state courts during the 1980s mandated the redrawing of congressional district boundaries so that a district contained a majority of voting age population from the black community: so-called 'majority–minority' districts. Not only did this overcome the historic problem of racially polarized voting (which the courts argued deprived minorities of their right to voting equality), but it also resulted in an expanded Congressional Black Caucus after 1992, increasing from 26 to 39, almost the same proportion as that of blacks in the population (11 per cent).

Against this, however, critics argued that not only was the practice questionable on grounds of resegregating America politically (though not socially), but also that it was counterproductive for minorities. By taking the most solid Democratic voters, dispersed across several districts, and packing them into one, remaining districts became 'lily-white' and more competitive for Republicans. The result: an expanded black delegation, but a greater Republican presence. This is what happened in 1994, when the Republicans took both houses of Congress and, simultaneously, won a majority of southern congressional seats for the first time in their history. The larger black delegation found itself out of power, a larger minority of a minority party – a heavy policy price to pay for the representational benefits of electing more blacks and Latinos to Congress.

House of Representatives, reflecting the population flows of the previous decade. Districts are redrawn to take account of this, some states gaining and others losing seats. Redistricting is messy and politically controversial, creating new political careers, extinguishing others, and fuelling ambition among state and local officials. State legislatures draw up the districts, meaning that each party has a powerful incentive to control the state legislature after each decennial year election (1980, 1990, 2000). Redistricting is also one of the few times when, in cases where a state loses House seats, incumbents may be forced to run against each other in a newly-drawn district. Finally, as Exhibit 4.5 notes, many states are subject to the provisions of the Voting Rights Act of 1965 regarding racial and ethnic minorities, making the redistricting task even more controversial and partisan.

EXPLAINING AMERICAN VOTING BEHAVIOUR

Although they live and work in very different districts and states, Americans share markedly similar values and experience many shared events collectively. Few, regardless of region, race or religion, were immune from the effects of anti-communism, the Vietnam War, OPEC oil shocks, increasing budget deficits, crime or 9/11. Political scientists have therefore been keen to examine the sources of voting behaviour and explain what election results – particularly federal ones – signify.

The most striking aspect to recent election

results has been a shift from the New Deal era to the era of divided party control of the federal government. As Table 4.8 reveals, the electoral norm from 1932 to 1968 was for the Democratic Party to control the White House and Congress. There were exceptions but these were few and unusual. When Truman declined to run in 1952, the way was paved

TABLE 4.8   The New Deal era and the era of divided government, 1932–2000

Year	Presidency	House of Representatives	Senate	Undivided or divided government
1932	D	D	D	Undivided
1934	D	D	D	Undivided
1936	D	D	D	Undivided
1938	D	D	D	Undivided
1940	D	D	D	Undivided
1942	D	D	D	Undivided
1944	D	D	D	Undivided
1946	D	R	R	Divided
1948	D	D	D	Undivided
1950	D	D	D	Undivided
1952	R	R	R	Undivided
1954	R	D	D	Divided
1956	R	D	D	Divided
1958	R	D	D	Divided
1960	D	D	D	Undivided
1962	D	D	D	Undivided
1964	D	D	D	Undivided
1966	D	D	D	Undivided
1968	R	D	D	Divided
1970	R	D	D	Divided
1972	R	D	D	Divided
1974	R	D	D	Divided
1976	D	D	D	Undivided
1978	D	D	D	Undivided
1980	R	D	R	Divided
1982	R	D	R	Divided
1984	R	D	R	Divided
1986	R	D	D	Divided
1988	R	D	D	Divided
1990	R	D	D	Divided
1992	D	D	D	Undivided
1994	D	R	R	Divided
1996	D	R	R	Divided
1998	D	R	R	Divided
2000*	R	R	R/D	Un/Divided

* Although the Senate in the 107th Congress was initially split 50–50, the Republicans controlled the Senate thanks to Vice President Cheney's casting vote. With Jeffords' defection, the Democrats took a 50–49–1 majority in June 2001.

for Eisenhower, the war hero, to win the presidency as a Republican. But his successes in 1952 and 1956 did not translate into legislative victories for his party (Ike's victories cemented the triumph of the New Deal through confirming Republican acceptance of the new government role). The Republicans captured Congress in 1946 and 1954, only to lose control two years later in both cases. As the majority party since 1932, the Democrats dominated federal, state and local election results.

From 1968, however, this pattern changes dramatically. The norm becomes one of divided party control of the federal government. From 1968 to 1988, the Republicans won five of the six presidential elections. Only in the aftermath of Watergate and Nixon's resignation did Jimmy Carter win the presidency for the Democrats. But Republican presidential triumphs again did not translate into congressional successes. With the exception of winning the Senate in 1980 (which they lost in 1986), the Democrats dominated Congress. Moreover, apart from a brief period of undivided Democratic control from 1993 to 1994, the norm of different parties controlling the White House and Capitol Hill continued – albeit in a different pattern – under Bill Clinton. Although he was the first Democratic president since FDR to win re-election twice, he also saw the Republicans capture Congress for the first time in 40 years – in 1994 – and hold on to control in 1996, 1998 and (briefly) 2000.

What makes the era of divided government perplexing is that the White House/Congress splits occur at presidential elections. Nixon, Reagan, George H.W. Bush and Clinton (in 1996) all won presidential elections at the same time as the other main party won control of one or both houses of Congress. Although two instances (1986 and 1994) saw the presidential party lose control through midterm defeats, divided government in the post-1968 era has primarily been a product of presidential election years.

The shift to the divided party era has been an important and enduring change. So too

has the occasion on which this occurs. Prior to 1968, if divided party control occurred at the national level it normally did so as the result of a midterm loss by the president's party in midterm elections. As Table 4.9 shows, the party that controls the White House normally loses seats in midterm elections. Occasionally, as in 1986, the losses transfer control of one and sometimes (1946, 1954 and 1994) of both houses of Congress to the other party.

This phenomenon provides two distinct, but related problems for analysis:

- How to account for post-1968 patterns of election results and to explain why no 'classical realignment' has occurred?
- How to explain the shift from (mostly) undivided to divided party control of the federal government?

Realignment theory

The 'father' of realignment theory was V.O. Key, who argued that:

- Certain elections are of special importance to partisan change.
- These 'critical elections' occur periodically (every 32–36 years).
- With realignment, a unidirectional shift takes place in partisan control over agencies of government and partisan allegiance among the electorate – a new 'majority party' appears at all levels of the political system.

What this means is that the way that individuals and groups look at politics alters dramatically. In a stable alignment, groups form a lasting identification with a particular political party. This psychological state is then typically replicated in their voting behaviour. Not only do voters identify with, say, the Republican Party, but at election time, they consistently vote for its candidates. A realigning election disturbs this stability, eroding the identification of some groups with one party, shifting it to that of the other. These elections are 'critical' since they disrupt traditional

TABLE 4.9   Losses by the White House party in midterm elections, 1946–98

Year	White House party	Losses	
		House	Senate
1946	D	55	12
1950	D	29	6
1954	R	18	1
1958	R	48	13
1962	D	4	+3
1966	D	47	4
1970	R	12	+2
1974	R	48	5
1978	D	15	3
1982	R	26	1
1986	R	5	8
1990	R	9	1
1994	D	52	8
1998	D	+5	–

patterns of division among the electorate, creating a new 'majority party' at federal, state and local levels.

Key's approach was subsequently refined by other analysts, most notably, Walter Dean Burnham (1970) who identified six features of 'critical elections':

- Short-lived but intense disruption to traditional voting patterns.
- Abnormally high political intensity (e.g. in the presidential nomination process).
- An increase in ideological polarization (both intra- and inter-party).
- Higher than normal voter participation.
- Recurrence of realigning elections at 36-year intervals.
- Realigning elections preceded by third-party revolts.

For realignment theorists, the last clear example of a realignment prompted by a critical election was that of the New Deal. In 1932, FDR won 472 Electoral College votes against Herbert Hoover's 59. Faced by the Depression, millions voted for Roosevelt (despite the fact that he ran on a promise to balance the budget). FDR's New Deal measures then consolidated that coalition in 1936, when Roosevelt won re-election in one of the greatest landslides ever known in American history.

The realignment was clear: the issue division prompting the new alignment was economic. The social divisions were based on class. The vehicle for the new alignment was the Democratic Party, which brought together a new coalition of identifiers – urban dwellers, northern blacks, Catholics, white southerners, Jews and working-class voters. Whatever their many differences, all were united behind the federal government intervening to combat the social and economic dislocation caused by the Depression. Commonality of economic interest took precedence over other cleavages: cultural, racial, religious and regional. The New Deal relegated the Republicans to being the minority party, left primarily with voters in the Northeast, Midwest and farmers as their base. Faced by an overwhelming Democratic Party majority, it was not until 1996 that the Republicans would control both houses of Congress for more than two years. But for Eisenhower, it was not until 1968 that a Republican would win the presidency.

1968 then assumed a special importance. For if realignment theory was correct, a new alignment should emerge every 32–36 years. (The periodicity relied on the waning of the salience of the issue that prompted the initial critical election, the changing composition of the electorate, as the older voters died and new voters entered the electorate, and the development of new issues commanding voter attentions.) Whether one took 1932 or 1936 as the key realigning election, 1968 should have seen another critical election.

In many respects, the conditions seemed right for realignment to occur. If one takes Burnham's six conditions, all applied. Traditional voting patterns were disrupted by intense conflict over Vietnam, urban race riots, increasing inflation and the 'counter-culture'. That intensity manifested itself in bitter conflict over the two main parties' presidential nominations. In the Republican Party, Richard Nixon fought off challenges from both the liberal (Nelson Rockefeller) and conservative wings (Ronald Reagan) to win the nomination. In the Democratic Party, President Johnson refused to run for renomination in March 1968, Minnesota Senator Eugene McCarthy's anti-Vietnam campaign was bested by New York Senator Robert Kennedy before Kennedy was assassinated in June 1968, and ultimately the incumbent Vice President, Hubert Humphrey, was imposed on the party as its nominee at a tumultuous national convention in Chicago. Both parties appeared polarized, the election campaign prompted widespread interest among Americans and featured a third party revolt by Alabama governor George Wallace on a reactionary 'American Independence Party' ticket.

But the results yielded the norm that was to follow for 20 years: a Republican in the White House confronted by a Democratic Congress. No classical realignment occurred.

Moreover, it was not to do so subsequently. Republican presidential candidates could not export their success to Congress. When the GOP finally took Congress, in 1994, it had lost the presidency. Despite reading the tea leaves of each election to discern whether a new alignment had arisen, political scientists found the enterprise increasingly akin to 'waiting for Godot'; the realignment stubbornly refused to arrive.

This has not rendered the notion of realignment redundant. Some observers wrote of, from 1968 to 1988, a 'split-level' realignment, the Republicans holding the presidency, Democrats holding a lock on the Congress. But this split-level explanation was then reversed with the results from 1994–98 (a Democrat winning the White House, the GOP taking Congress). Others responded that a 'no majority realignment' had occurred, in which the nation had shifted to embrace conservative policy positions but where the Republican Party had failed – due to internal factional divisions and post-Reagan leadership failings – to become a new majority party. The most prominent exponent of this view, Everett Carl Ladd (1997), pointed to opinion surveys such as that of Gallup on election night in 1996 (see Table 4.10) which demonstrated the growing, though incomplete, conservatism of the electorate.

As Table 4.10 shows, the electorate was not uniformly conservative. On some questions, such as raising the minimum wage, banning assault rifles and banning abortions, most voters endorsed liberal positions. What is clear, however, is that on most issues, the electorate embraced conservative positions by decisive margins. This powerfully supported Ladd's case for a steady shift towards Republicanism in terms of public philosophy but not electoral outcomes. Even as they embraced conservative stances, Americans sent Clinton back to the White House for a second term.

The difficulty here, however, is that the 'no majority' realignment is, by definition, not a classical realignment. In the writings of Key

TABLE 4.10   The 1996 Gallup Opinion Survey

Question: *Suppose that on election day this year you could vote on key issues as well as candidates. Please tell me whether you would vote for or against each one of the following propositions?*

Balanced Budget Amendment	83% FOR	(14% against)
Racial preferences in jobs/schools	83% AGAINST	(14% for)
English as the official language	82% FOR	(16% against)
Life sentences for drug dealers	80% FOR	(17% against)
Death penalty for murder	79% FOR	(18% against)
Congressional term limits	74% FOR	(23% against)
Legalization of marijuana	73% AGAINST	(24% for)
Prayer in School Amendment	73% FOR	(25% against)
Reducing all government agencies	71% FOR	(23% against)
Two-year cut-off for welfare without work	71% FOR	(24% against)
Legalization of gay marriages	67% AGAINST	(28% for)
School busing for racial balance	62% AGAINST	(34% for)
School choice	59% FOR	(37% against)
Ban on partial birth abortions	57% FOR	(39% against)
Ban on assault rifles	57% FOR	(42% against)
Reduce defense spending	54% AGAINST	(42% for)
Federal flat tax system	49% FOR	(39% against)
Reduce social spending	42% FOR	(54% against)
Ban on all abortions except for life of mother	42% FOR	(56% against)
Raising the minimum wage	15% AGAINST	(83% for)

Source: Ladd (1997: 11).

and Burnham, this requires the existence of a majority party (whether by means of one critical or several) commanding majority control of government and the attachment of most Americans – a status that has tenaciously eluded the GOP for decades. While increasing numbers of Americans have come to feel an attachment to the Republican Party, and to share its core conservative values, this has not represented a clear or stable majority.

Dealignment

Proponents of dealignment, such as Martin Wattenberg (1996), see the quest for discovering realignments as futile. This is largely because the foundations of electoral politics have altered profoundly in the post-1952 context of televised campaigns, weakening parties, and the breakdown of traditional social allegiances. What was seen by realignment theorists as a temporary condition of dealignment – a period when the old electoral coalition no longer retains public loyalties but a new one has yet to be born – is now a permanent state of affairs. The watchwords of dealignment emphasize aspects of modern politics alien to eras of stable alignments: weak identification, ticket-splitting, defections, issue-based and retrospective voting. In this unstable environment, voters can be viewed as consumers, selecting between rival packages or products but not reliably adhering to brand names.

The evidence for dealignment is powerful. Most obviously, in just 12 years from 1988 to 2000, every possible outcome at the federal level occurred: undivided Democratic control of the White House and Congress (1993–94); undivided Republican control (2001); a

Republican president facing a Democratic Congress (1989–93); and a Democratic president facing a Republican Congress (1995–2001). Beyond this:

- *Political parties have weakened.* As Chapter 3 recorded, parties have declined in their ability to structure the vote, convey political information, organize, finance and run campaigns, and even select party candidates. Since any search for a realignment relies on parties as its vehicles, their decline is of the utmost significance.
- *Attitudes to parties have altered.* The link between identification and voting behaviour has weakened. Knowing that voters identified as Democrats used to be a fairly reliable guide to their behaviour in 1960. An identifier would also vote for Democratic Party candidates. In 2000, knowing voters' affiliations is no longer as reliable a guide to how the voters cast their ballots.
- *The growth in 'Independents' among the electorate.* Since 1952, there has been a steady growth in voters who do not identify with either of the main two parties but see themselves as Independent. Although this has not seen a great increase in the number of self-proclaimed 'Independent' candidates running for office or in government, it has had an important effect on encouraging candidates to downplay their party ties.
- *Weak partisans have increased, strong partisans declined.* Even if the proportion of 'pure' Independents remains relatively low, there has also been a growth in the volume of weak partisans and party 'leaners': those who identify with a party but whose strength of affiliation is relatively weak. When weak partisans and leaners are combined with pure Independents, over one-third of the electorate in the 1990s fell into this category (compared to less than one-fifth in 1958).
- *Ticket-splitting and defections.* Even among those voters who still identify with a party – strongly or weakly – the propensity for these voters to abandon their traditional affiliation when casting votes has increased substantially since 1968. These voters (such as 'Reagan Democrats' in the 1980s, and 'Clinton Republicans' in the 1990s) retain a basic psychological attachment to one of the main parties, but because they feel that the party's candidate does not consistently reflect their values and beliefs, they vote for the candidate closer to their priorities and preferences. Reagan Democrats felt abandoned by the Democratic Party nominating excessively liberal presidential candidates. Clinton Republicans, conversely, felt that the GOP had become too intolerant and conservative on issues such as abortion rights and race.

Taken together, these features suggest a campaigning environment of marked volatility and unpredictability.

But this interpretation requires qualification. First, the dealignment approach suggests that partisan success should be completely individualized, with outcomes depending on the particular circumstances of individual races and the results hinging on individual offices, constituencies and the circumstances of a given year. What one would not expect from such volatile and unpredictable conditions is a stable pattern of electoral outcomes. Yet that is exactly what has occurred: Republicans in the White House from 1968 to 1992 (Carter the exception), with Democrats in the Congress (except the GOP Senate from 1981 to 1987); a Democrat in the White House from 1993 to 2001, with Republicans controlling Congress for all but two of these years.

Another criticism is that were dealignment to be correct, the break-up of the New Deal coalition must filter down to lower offices. But this has not happened. The Democrats remain competitive in congressional elections and at the state level. Although the Republicans made strong advances among whites, men, and the wealthy (see Table 4.12 below), as well as in certain regions and states – especially the South – this was not a national phenomenon. Going into the 2002 midterm elections, the GOP possessed no majority in the Senate and only a six-seat majority in the House. This suggests that there must be some deeper forces at work in America's electoral geography to account for recent results.

Electoral order approaches

The third approach to analysing election results is Byron Shafer's 'electoral orders' (1991). This offers a sophisticated yet intuitively convincing interpretation that incorporates the key aspects of elections: government offices; public preferences on particular sets of issues; and candidate and party positions on those issues (Table 4.11).

In essence, Shafer's argument is that certain types of issue are associated with particular governmental offices. The presidency is particularly associated with foreign policy (as Commander-in-Chief, chief diplomat and, from 1945 to 1991 and perhaps 2001 onwards, 'leader of the free world' equipped with a nuclear arsenal) and cultural values (as Head of State and Government, the only nationally elected official and nominator of Supreme Court justices). The House and Senate are mostly associated with issues of social welfare and service provision (the Constitution giving them the power to raise and spend

money, and the extension of the federal government in the New Deal and subsequently creating many new federal programmes and regulations subject to congressional approval). But since the Senate has a role in ratifying treaties and confirming executive appointments, foreign policy and cultural issues sometimes affect senatorial elections.

On these issues, the public has clear preferences: nationalism on foreign policy (a strong Americanism); traditionalism on cultural values (favouring capital punishment, opposing same-sex marriages); and liberalism on social welfare and service provision (supporting the minimum wage, social security, Medicare and Medicaid). The key determinant of election results is therefore whether the parties offer the right candidates on the right side of the issues that count in the elections to particular government offices.

The results of the New Deal and divided government eras can be explained fairly simply. In 1932, economic issues – the Depression – intruded on the presidential election, assisting Roosevelt's victory. Thereafter, Democrats offered presidential candidates who were nationalist on foreign policy and traditionalist on cultural values: FDR, Truman, Kennedy and Johnson. The Republicans did also, but Eisenhower's exceptional victories (while

TABLE 4.11 Changing electoral orders, 1932–2002

Offices	Issue clusters	Majority preferences	Electoral Outcomes*				
			1932–68	1968–92	1992	1994–00	2000–02
Presidency	Foreign Policy Cultural Values	Nationalist Traditionalist	D	R	D	D	R
US Senate	Social Welfare Service Provision	[Liberal]	D	D	D	R	R/D
US House	Social Welfare Service Provision	[Liberal]	D	D	D	R	R

* The exceptions here were: Eisenhower's presidency (1953–61); Republican control of Congress (1947–49 and 1953–55); Carter's presidency (1977–81); and Republican control of the Senate (1981–87).

America was at war in Korea) aside, the New Deal coalition propelled Democrats to the White House. At the same time, in congressional elections, Democrats were pro social welfare and service provision. Although most Republicans reconciled themselves to the New Deal by 1952, they mostly opposed extending the federal government's role substantially, hence leaving the Democrats controlling Congress and supporting the creation of measures such as social security, minimum wage laws, and Medicare and Medicaid.

What altered in 1968 was that the Democrats began to nominate as their presidential candidates individuals who were 'accommodationist' (not nationalist) on foreign policy and progressive (not traditionalist) on cultural values. These two types of issue now entered presidential elections in ways that cut across the New Deal economic agenda. For millions of traditional Democrats, no choice existed but to vote for Nixon over McGovern in 1972, Reagan over Carter in 1980, Reagan over Mondale in 1984, and Bush over Dukakis in 1988. In all these cases, traditional Democrats felt not that they had left the Democratic Party but that – at the presidential level – the Democratic Party had left them by shifting decisively to the left on matters of national security and cultural values.

Crucial here was the democratization of party procedures for selecting presidential candidates. By expanding the role of primaries and caucuses, the Democratic Party allowed a variety of special interest lobbies, such as women's groups, civil rights activists, labour unions, environmentalists, consumer activists and gay rights groups, a crucial role in selecting its presidential candidate. The result was that while many relatively conservative and moderate Democrats still existed in the House and Senate, their prospects for winning the nomination in the new process grew increasingly slender. Gradually but inexorably, the party drifted away not only from the median voter, but also from its own Democratic Party identifiers, who saw themselves as much more 'middle-of-the-

road' than the new issue activists and 'purists'.

The result, then, was that the Democratic Party nominated candidates on the wrong side of the issues that counted in presidential elections, while the Republican Party offered candidates on the wrong side of the issues that counted in congressional elections. For many voters, they had no alternative to 'splitting their ticket': voting for one party's candidate for the presidency, the other party's candidate for Congress. The consequence: a fairly consistent pattern of divided party control of the federal government from 1968 to the present.

Two important problems confront the 'electoral order' schema. First, how can the model explain Clinton's victories in 1992 and 1996? Secondly, how can it explain the Republicans capturing and retaining Congress from 1994 to 2000?

Clinton's presidential victories are explicable in relation to three factors. First, foreign policy was no longer so salient in the presidential elections after the end of the Cold War and the collapse of the Soviet Union in 1991. Republican charges that Democrats were 'soft on communism', so powerful from 1948 to 1988, were now irrelevant. Although, according to exit poll data on election day in 1992, in excess of 80 per cent of those voters who considered foreign policy important in casting their vote supported George Bush, only 8 per cent of the electorate thought foreign policy was important (despite the successful Desert Storm operation in the Gulf in 1991).

Second, in the midst of a (relatively mild) economic downturn in 1992, economic issues – the traditional strength of the Democratic Party coalition – intruded on the presidential contest to Clinton's benefit. With many Americans suffering, the type of cross-cutting issues – race, abortion, national security, crime, immigration – that had hampered the Democrats since 1972 now took a secondary place to the 'meat and drink' of jobs and growth.

Thirdly, it was difficult to cast Clinton in

the same mould as previous Democratic nominees as being 'soft' on both communism and crime. Not only did he run to the right of Bush on foreign policy by pledging an air war on Bosnia (the first time a Democrat had run on a more conservative international platform than the Republican presidential candidate since Kennedy in 1960), but Clinton and Gore promoted themselves as 'New Democrats': pro capital punishment, wanting to put 100,000 new cops on the streets, and seeking an 'end to welfare as we know it'. This made traditional GOP charges that Democrats were 'soft on crime' hard to stick in the face of a governor who even flew back to Arkansas in 1992 to refuse to grant clemency to a mentally retarded black death row inmate.

Explaining Republican successes in 1994 is less straightforward, but a couple of related factors are significant. The first is that, despite the self-consciously 'New Democrat' image in 1992, Clinton's behaviour as president during 1993–94 instead suggested an 'old-style' Democrat: pushing for the admission of gays to the armed forces, abandoning a pledged middle-class tax cut, seeking a Keynesian-style job stimulus package, rejecting a bi-partisan approach to budget negotiations, promoting new federal gun control measures and sponsoring a government-orchestrated national health care plan. At the first opportunity, in 1994, the voters imposed a crushing defeat on the Democrats, giving control of Congress to the Republicans for the first time in 40 years.

The second aspect to this remarkable embrace of a new form of divided government goes back to Ladd's thesis of an increasingly – but not uniformly – conservative electorate. One part of Shafer's matrix, public preferences, necessarily allows for changes in public attitudes. Here, not only did the public embrace increasingly conservative views on a range of important issues by the early 1990s, but they also reaffirmed their faith in a basic government interventionism to temper the market with regard to issues such as social security and minimum wage laws. When the

Gingrich-led 'Republican revolution' mistook a rejection of Clinton for an embrace of a robust conservatism, the electorate punished the GOP by according it only narrow congressional majorities from 1996 to 2000. Shafer's approach can therefore be criticized, but it has a great advantage over competing theories in that it possesses a genuine predictive capacity. Providing we identify which party provides candidates on the right side of the issues that matter to the particular office at a given time, we should be able to anticipate election outcomes fairly well.

Ultimately, the three approaches to analysing election returns are not mutually exclusive. The empirical data supports the notion that voters continue to exhibit a basic attachment to the Democratic and Republican parties that has endured, but one that is less strong than a generation ago. Rather than simply automatically endorsing their favoured brand product, they are more apt to be fairly selective, to choose on the basis of the individual candidates and on the issues about which they care in a given election contest. To that extent, American voters are acting as 'rational' consumers and, as Table 4.12 illustrates, selecting between candidates on the basis of where they stand on the issues that matter to them.

CONCLUSION

As the controversy over the 2000 presidential race demonstrated, elections are the lifeblood of liberal democracy. They provide one of the few regular opportunities for ordinary citizens to express their views about government, politics and politicians. By choosing between candidates and parties, and by the margins of victory and defeat that voter choices yield political parties, election results send messages – sometimes muddy, misinterpreted, but always sought – to government decision-makers. Elections offer a means of ensuring at least some accountability of the governing class to the governed, and they

TABLE 4.12 The 2000 presidential vote: electoral geography and issues (%)

Category	All	Gore	Bush	Buchanan	Nader
Sex and race					
Men	48	42	53	0	3
Women	52	54	43	0	2
White men	48	36	60	0	3
White women	52	48	49	0	2
White	81	42	54	0	3
Black	10	90	9	0	1
Latino	7	62	35	1	2
Asian	2	55	41	1	3
Age					
18–29	17	48	46	1	5
30–44	33	48	49	0	2
45–59	28	48	49	1	2
60+	22	51	47	0	2
Income ($)					
Under 15,000	7	57	37	1	4
15,000–29,999	16	54	41	1	3
30,000–49,999	24	49	48	0	2
50,000–74,999	25	46	51	0	2
75,000–100,000	13	45	52	0	2
100,000+	15	43	54	0	2
Region					
East	23	56	39	0	3
Midwest	26	48	49	1	2
South	31	43	55	0	1
West	21	48	46	0	4
Political ideology					
Liberal	20	80	13	1	6
Moderate	50	52	44	0	2
Conservative	29	17	81	0	1
Condition of the economy					
Excellent	28	53	46	0	1
Good	12	38	53	2	6
Not good	57	47	49	0	3
Most important issues and qualities					
World affairs	12	40	54	1	4
Medicare/PX drugs	7	60	39	0	1
Health care	8	64	33	0	3
Economy/jobs	18	59	37	0	2
Taxes	14	17	80	0	2
Education	15	52	44	0	3
Social Security	14	58	40	1	1

Note: For 'all', percentages read down; for individuals, percentages read across. A zero for Buchanan voters indicates less than 0.5 per cent.

Source: CNN exit poll data (www.cnn.com/ELECTION/2000).

help, however partially and indirectly, to induce responsible and representative behaviour by elected officials fearful of future defeat. Liberal democracy is as unthinkable without regular elections as it is without political parties.

Ironically, for all the discontent that Americans express regarding government and politicians, one way of looking at recent elections is that Americans are basically happy with their particular elected officials. A 98 per cent re-election rate for members of the House suggests that they are doing a good job and serving their constituents well. (Whether they are simultaneously serving America well as a whole, however, is a matter we will return to later.) A crucial tenet of democratic theory is that those elections should also be free and fair. Many dispute that this is – and, arguably, ever was – the case in America. Money is crucial (and often decisive), parties take a back seat to individual candidates, important social issues can be neglected, and genuine choice for voters between rival packages of ideas or programmes of government can be elusive. In the balance between political freedom and political equality, liberty has won out – but to the extent that money plays a vital role in American elections, political competition, meaningful choice, and the legitimacy of government all suffer somewhat as a result.

FURTHER READING

Richard Fenno, *Home Style* (1978) is a classic study of 18 members of the House of Representatives, showing how their particular districts affected their behaviour in Congress and vice versa.

Paul Herrnson, *Congressional Elections: Campaigning at Home and in Washington* (1995) is an excellent analysis of the nature of modern elections for Congress.

Gary Jacobson, *The Politics of Congressional Elections* (1983) is a classic analysis of all aspects of elections to Congress.

Richard Posner, *Breaking the Deadlock: The 2000 Election, the Constitution and the Courts* (2001a) is an excellent and supremely balanced interpretation of the 2000 presidential election and its aftermath.

Byron Shafer (ed.), *The End of Realignment? Interpreting American Electoral Eras* (1991) is a set of important and competing interpretations of the concept of realignment in a supposedly 'dealigned' era.

WEB LINKS

Federal Election Commission
www.fec.gov

Democratic National Committee
www.democrats.org

Republican National Committee
www.rnc.org

The Democracy Network, comprehensive coverage of elections and campaigns
www.dnet.org

NBC politics section
www.msnbc.com/news/politics_front.asp

Project Vote Smart offers non-partisan election and candidate information
www.vote-smart.org

C-SPAN
www.c-span.org

Cable News Network
www.cnn.com

PollingReport.com offers non-partisan polling on elections and public policy
www.pollingreport.com

League of Women Voters, a non-partisan site covering lots of information about elections and policies
www.lwv.org

Rock the Vote (includes 'youth-oriented' information on elections)
www.rockthevote.org

QUESTIONS

- Is the American party system dealigned, realigning or in a new 'electoral order'?

- What are the key features of American electoral politics?

- Why is incumbency such a powerful factor in American elections?

- 'Money determines who wins and loses elections in the United States.' Discuss.

- How important are elections in American politics?

5 Presidential Selection

When he was a quarterback he played without a helmet.

Bob Dole on Jack Kemp

When his library burned down, it destroyed both books. Dole hadn't finished coloring in the second.

Jack Kemp on Bob Dole

It is the greatest honor of my life to have been asked to run by the greatest American hero.

Jack Kemp accepts Bob Dole's invitation to be his vice presidential running mate in 1996

- The Traditional Picture
- The Breakdown of the Established System
- The Post-Reform Process
- Evaluating the Criticisms
- Conclusion

Chapter Summary

Since the US presidency is the single most important office in American government, the process by which candidates for the White House are selected assumes a particular political significance. For many years, the presidential selection system seemed to work well, with ideologically moderate, politically experienced and popular candidates – such as FDR, Truman, Eisenhower and Kennedy – winning their parties' nominations. But the old party, elite-dominated 'mixed system' altered after 1968 to a 'post-reform' system dominated by primary elections and party caucuses. In effect, control over the nominations was taken away from party elites and given to ordinary voters who registered as partisans. Many critics see this system as profoundly deficient – too lengthy, too dominated by ideological or 'purist' groups and money, giving too much influence to unrepresentative small states, and encouraging relatively unknown, inexperienced 'outsiders', candidates who are well suited to campaigning but not to governing. More recently, the post-1988 process has been seen as being too favourable to well-funded 'establishment' candidates, preventing the achievement of sufficient choice for American voters in the nomination process and yielding relatively uninspiring nominees such as Al Gore and George W. Bush. Overall, the process works reasonably well and history shows that no obvious apprenticeship is available for the most singular and isolated political job in the world. But the need for a balance of choice and continuity is one that remains consistently difficult to achieve and some reform of the process – short of returning to the old mixed system – is hence recommended regularly.

In the late nineteenth century, Lord Bryce, a noted English observer of American politics, penned a chapter of a lengthy book on American government and politics that was entitled 'Why Great Men Do Not Become President'. In many respects, and especially after the 2000 presidential election, much of the contemporary debate on the presidency still reflects such a decidedly negative conviction. When the genuinely 'great' presidents of the past are invoked, few (if any) of the modern incumbents of the White House seem to stand comparison with the likes of Washington, Jefferson or Lincoln. Instead, recent presidents have either refused to run for re-election in the midst of national disaster (Johnson), resigned from office in disgrace (Nixon), been denied re-election by a disenchanted public after only one term or less (Ford, Carter and George H.W. Bush), or ended up completing second-terms as 'lame-duck' presidents mired in scandal and sleaze (Reagan and Clinton).

Some of the reasons cited for this apparently recurring legacy of presidential failure attribute the recent difficulties of successive presidents to the nature of the presidency as an institution. As the next chapter explains, some commentators view American politics as having become so fragmented, polarized and conflict-ridden since the late 1960s that it

is extremely difficult – even impossible – for any president now to be truly successful as a leader, much less 'great'. The presidency has increasingly become 'all things to all men' – an office burdened by wildly unrealistic public expectations of what the occupant of the White House can achieve in domestic policy and international affairs. But some explanations of presidential 'failure' since 1972 focus not on the office of the presidency but instead on the way that the main two political parties select their presidential candidates. The implicit argument is that a deficient selection system has produced national leaders who are not quite up to this most demanding of political jobs.

As the exceptionally close and controversial results of the 2000 election demonstrated, choosing a president is often a difficult enterprise for American voters. Equally, choosing which candidates to offer those voters has become a problematic, time-consuming and expensive task for the main political parties. To an extent, the dilemma is as old as the republic, and intrinsic to all democratic political systems with popularly elected presidencies: there exists no obvious apprenticeship for a unique job. No other position – governor, senator, representative, mayor – can adequately prepare a politician for life in the White House. (Even the vice presidency is conventionally seen, as John Nance Gardner, one of FDR's vice-presidents put it, as 'not worth a pitcherful of warm spit'.) In parliamentary systems, it is normally the case that whoever becomes Head of the Government has previously served in the great offices of state, is well known to his or her peers in party and government, and is selected by the party officials with whom he or she will subsequently have to work closely in office, not by the public at large (John Major, for example, had been Chief Secretary to the Treasury, Chancellor of the Exchequer and Foreign Secretary (albeit briefly) before becoming Prime Minister of the UK in 1990; Jacques Chirac had been Mayor of Paris, a member of the National Assembly and Prime Minister before becoming President in 1995). In presidential systems, however, there is no other government job that can fully prepare a potential president for the experience of the highest office.

That need not matter tremendously where the powers and responsibilities of the office are few and weak as, for the most part, they had been in the case of the US presidency during the nineteenth century (though even then, having a president of the quality of Abraham Lincoln was immensely important in times of national crisis). Not having 'great' presidents in the Oval Office since 1932, however, has been far more worrying for America and the world. With America the most powerful military, diplomatic and economic force on the planet, who sits in the White House is a matter of grave international, as well as domestic, concern. Precisely because the office is so important, the methods by which presidents are selected therefore assume a crucial political significance. The four-yearly presidential election provides the single greatest opportunity for national dialogue and democratic decision-making in the American system (whether this is seized or not is another matter).

In this chapter, we review how the presidential selection process has altered in the modern era and the arguments concerning its alleged deficiencies. Underpinning many of the criticisms is a sense that, were Lincoln or Jefferson to try to run for the presidency today, they would be no-hopers. The obstacles are so substantial that 'good-quality' or 'qualified' candidates either fail or, in many cases, do not even bother to run. On some accounts, this can become an even more extreme claim: that a process which once yielded men of integrity and self-sacrifice dedicated to public service now encourages self-started millionaire egomaniacs whose willingness to court publicity knows few bounds and whose principal reasons for getting to the White House are money and personal charm, not coherent policy programmes or suitable qualifications for the job. The task for students of the process is to assess how valid the criticisms advanced are in the light of the available evidence.

THE TRADITIONAL PICTURE

Until the late 1960s, the features of the presidential selection process were fairly clear and stable. For both Democrats and Republicans, the nomination battle was centred on their particular party, not the public. The four-yearly national convention of each party performed the critical role in actually determining who the nominee would be, with a role of brokerage between distinct state party delegations. Party bosses largely controlled these delegations and had a clear interest in sustaining an open and flexible system, switching their delegate votes when necessary to support the eventual winner (often in return for promises of patronage rewards such as federal funds or jobs). Candidates with established party ties were strongly advantaged. The convention was the key site of bargaining, with outcomes uncertain, frequent ballots common until a consensus nominee was chosen, and candidates did not need substantial personal financial resources for a successful campaign. It was this process that produced nominees such as Roosevelt, Truman, Kennedy and Johnson, individuals who had served in government office,

Exhibit 5.1   Protecting the presidential candidates

The US Secret Service assumed full-time responsibility for protection of the president after the assassination of President William McKinley in 1901. Presidential aspirants were not offered this security option until 67 years later, when Senator Robert Kennedy of New York was shot while campaigning for the Democratic Party's presidential nomination in California. After this, President Lyndon Johnson issued an executive order calling for protection of all announced candidates for the presidency. LBJ's order later became law, with the provision that candidates could decline protection if they wished.

A five-person advisory committee now determines whether prospective candidates meet the criteria for Secret Service protection. To qualify, a candidate must:

- Be a declared candidate.
- Have received financial contributions and be likely to qualify for federal matching funds.
- Conduct an active campaign.

But the Secret Service has been known to make exceptions to these criteria. In 1979, for example, Senator Edward Kennedy was given Secret Service protection even though he had not formally declared his candidacy for president.

became well known to their fellow party officials, and generally knew the complex highways and byways of the US Congress. Selected by individuals who knew them, and with whom they would subsequently have to work effectively once in the White House, the process was seen as encouraging moderation and responsibility.

THE BREAKDOWN OF THE ESTABLISHED SYSTEM

The old picture of presidential selection collapsed in the face of three important developments: social change, an increased resort to candidate primary elections, and a

Exhibit 5.2   Chicago: 1968's turbulent year

Rarely has a national party convention been so controversial in its proceedings, and so far-reaching in its legacy, as that of the Democrats in Chicago, Illinois, in 1968. In March of that year, President Lyndon Johnson decided not to run for re-election, his presidency battered by the war in Vietnam, protests against it and urban riots. Senator Eugene McCarthy had run Johnson a close second in New Hampshire's primary, but his campaign then ebbed against that of Senator Robert Kennedy. Assassinated in June after he had won the California Democratic primary, the convention then selected Johnson's vice president, Hubert Humphrey, as its candidate, despite Humphrey having failed to run in a single party primary. Outside the convention, Chicago police assaulted anti-war protestors, while inside turmoil engulfed proceedings and Chicago boss Mayor Richard Daley hurled anti-Semitic abuse at Senator Abraham Ribicoff (Democrat, Conecticut). No more eloquent a lesson in how not to present a party's image to a nationwide audience has ever been offered by one of the main American political parties. Never again would one of the main parties allow its nominee to be selected by a party elite. Instead, ordinary American voters would gain the decisive say in choosing presidential candidates.

democratization of party procedures. The development of a basic welfare state, professionalization of the civil service and increased suburbanization together removed the basis for old-style party patronage and 'machine' politics. The steady erosion of the 'mixed system' that these developments brought about reached its zenith in 1968 when the Democrats selected Hubert Humphrey to be their presidential nominee (see Exhibit 5.2). Subsequent reforms altered the manner in which nominees were selected for both parties. The cumulative result was, as Byron Shafer put it, 'the diminution, the constriction, at times the elimination of the regular party in the politics of presidential selection' (1983: 525). The post-1968 national party convention was very different in composition, role and influence.

THE POST-REFORM PROCESS

The process after 1972 was drastically altered by the recommendations of the McGovern–Fraser Commission, set up to examine the Democratic Party's 1968 convention débâcle and make recommendations for reform. Its results were dramatic for both parties and, ultimately, for America.

Keen to loosen the hold of elite party barons over candidate selection, the Commission's recommendations had two, conflicting, results. Its first concern was to make the selection process more democratic and participatory. Although it did not specify primary elections, many states adopted these selection mechanisms, with the result that a decentralization of control occurred, away

Exhibit 5.3   Major changes in rules effected by reform

Pre-reform	Post-reform
Majority of delegates selected through non-primary process.	Majority of delegates selected in or bound by primaries.
In some states non-primary process confined to party officials.	Non-primary process open to voters.
Delegate selection process spread over several years.	Delegate selection process confined to the election year.
Racial discrimination in selection; under-representation of women and the young.	Positive discrimination programmes to increase participation of racial minorities, women and youth.
Participants unable to express candidate preferences in many states.	Participants able to express candidate preferences.
Winner-take-all primaries; unit rule in Democratic Party.	Proportional representation in the distribution of delegates.
Rules often absent; party officials exercise discretion.	Rules provided.
Campaigns financed from private sources.	Federal matching funds available.
No limits on size of donations.	Limits on size of donations.
No federal limits on spending.	Federal limits on expenditure for candidates accepting matching funds.

Source: Adapted from Dean McSweeney (1995: 199).

Exhibit 5.4   Primary colours: the party nominations

- *Closed primary.* A closed primary is the most common type in America, with participation restricted to voters who have registered with the party that is sponsoring the election.
- *Open primary.* In an open primary, voters show up at the polls and at that time can choose which party's primary they want to vote in. Party leaders do not favour these types of primary because they allow voters outside the party to influence the selection of a nominee.
- *Direct presidential preference primary.* Here, all candidates for a party's presidential nomination are listed on the party ballot. The voters' preferences among the candidates then drive the selection of delegates to the party convention.
- *Indirect presidential preference primary.* Here voters are asked to choose not among candidates but among prospective convention delegates. Delegates are identified on the ballots as preferring certain candidates or as uncommitted.
- *Binding primary.* Here, delegates who are elected by the voters to go to the national convention agree to support the candidates they are pledged to – at least until it becomes clear that those candidates cannot win the nomination.
- *Proportional representation primary.* National convention delegates are selected on the basis of the proportion of the vote won by the various candidates. These are now much more common than winner-take-all primaries.
- *Winner-take-all primary.* Some of the Republican Party presidential primaries are binding, winner-take-all events, meaning that all of a state's convention delegates must support the presidential candidate who receives the most primary votes in the state. The Democrats have outlawed winner-take-all primaries, preferring proportional representation primaries instead.

from party officials and towards the party's registered voters. At the same time, a second reform gave unprecedented powers to the Democratic National Committee to set conditions by which state parties had to abide if they wanted to see their delegations represented at the national party's convention. In particular, state delegations needed broadly to reflect their particular state's population in terms of gender, race and age profile. This, then, centralized power at the national level in an unprecedented way.

Key to the new system was the mass participation of American voters in choosing the parties' nominees. Primaries are internal party elections to choose a nominee; caucuses are meetings that must be attended before a vote is finally cast. State laws govern what types of primary and caucus exist, but in most states voters must register with the party sponsoring the election in order to

participate in so-called 'closed primaries' (see Exhibit 5.4). This means that millions of ordinary Americans get to choose which candidate they want as their favoured party's nominee. From 1972, the number of states using primaries increased dramatically. By 1996, fully 90 per cent of delegates to the Republican Party's national convention were selected in this way (see Table 5.1).

Partly as a result of the transformation that this critical expansion of primaries brought about, the selection process has been regularly criticized on several important grounds: length; money; the media; unrepresentativeness; activist influence; outsider nominees; and negative campaigning.

Length

Some critics of the modern selection process view it as excessively lengthy. Formally, the process commences with the first caucuses

TABLE 5.1 Number of presidential primaries and percentage of convention delegates from primary states by party, 1912–96

Year	Democratic Party		Republican Party	
	Number of primaries	Percentage of delegates from primary states	Number of primaries	Percentage of delegates from primary states
1912	12	32.9	13	41.7
1916	20	53.5	20	58.9
1920	16	44.6	20	57.8
1924	14	35.5	17	45.3
1928	17	42.2	16	44.9
1932	16	40.0	14	37.7
1936	14	36.5	12	37.5
1940	13	35.8	13	38.8
1944	14	36.7	13	38.7
1948	14	36.3	12	36.0
1952	15	38.7	13	39.0
1956	19	42.7	19	44.8
1960	16	38.3	15	38.6
1964	17	45.7	17	45.6
1968	17	37.5	16	34.3
1972	23	60.5	22	52.7
1976	29	72.6	28	67.9
1980	31	74.7	35	74.3
1984	26	62.9	30	68.2
1988	34	66.6	35	76.9
1992	39	78.8	38	80.4
1996	34	62.6	43	90.0

Source: Wayne (2000: 12).

and primary elections at the beginning of the presidential election year in late January and February. For most of the period from 1972 to 1992, these occurred with the Iowa caucus and the New Hampshire primary in the first two weeks of February. The last states to convene these contests did so in June, making the process a five-month haul. But campaigning in these states actually pre-dates the official calendar by many months and, frequently, several years. Long before the official elections, aspirant presidential candidates face an 'invisible primary' to gain money and media attention in the months before the election year proper, and most candidates accord-

ingly plan their campaigns from two to as many as four or six years in advance.

The fact of such an extended schedule also has several by-products, which critics tend to view in decidedly negative fashion: one is the unusual mix of resources that successful candidates must develop to run competitive national races: physical stamina; a thick skin to endure personal attacks and intense media scrutiny of private and public lives; a willingness to raise vast sums of money; the ability to withstand extensive travel and deal with the mass media. Some critics suggest that what the process tests is not presidential quality but sheer physical and mental endurance – not the governing capabilities of a

TABLE 5.2   2000 Republican presidential nominating calendar

State	Date	Delegates	Method
Louisiana	1/15	21	caucus/convention
Alaska	1/24	23	caucus/convention
Iowa	1/24	25	caucus/convention
New Hampshire	2/1	17	primary
Delaware	2/8	12	primary
Hawaii	2/7–13	14	caucus/convention
South Carolina	2/19	37	primary
Arizona	2/22	30	primary
Michigan	2/22	58	primary
Am. Samoa	2/26	4	caucus/executive committee
Guam	2/26	4	caucus/convention
Virgin Islands	2/26	4	caucus/convention
Puerto Rico	2/27	14	primary
North Dakota	2/29	19	caucus/convention
Virginia	2/29	55	primary
Washington	2/29	12	primary
California	3/7	162	primary
Connecticut	3/7	25	primary
Georgia	3/7	54	primary
Maine	3/7	14	primary
Maryland	3/7	31	primary
Massachusetts	3/7	37	primary
Minnesota	3/7	34	caucus/convention
Missouri	3/7	35	primary
New York	3/7	101	primary
Ohio	3/7	69	primary
Rhode Island	3/7	14	primary
Vermont	3/7	12	primary
Washington	3/7	25	caucus/convention
Colorado	3/10	40	primary
Utah	3/10	29	primary
Wyoming	3/10	22	county conventions
Florida	3/14	80	primary
Louisiana	3/14	7	primary
Mississippi	3/14	33	primary
Oklahoma	3/14	38	primary
Tennessee	3/14	37	primary
Texas	3/14	124	primary
Illinois	3/21	74	primary
Nevada	3/21	17	caucus/convention
Kansas	4/4	35	primary
Wisconsin	4/4	37	primary
Pennsylvania	4/25	80	primary
DC	5/2	15	primary
Indiana	5/2	55	primary
North Carolina	5/2	62	primary

TABLE 5.2 *continued*

State	Date	Delegates	Method
Nebraska	5/9	30	primary
West Virginia	5/9	18	primary
Oregon	5/16	24	primary
Arkansas	5/23	24	primary
Idaho	5/23	28	primary
Kentucky	5/23	31	primary
Alabama	6/6	44	primary
Montana	6/6	23	primary
New Jersey	6/6	54	primary
New Mexico	6/6	21	primary
South Dakota	6/6	22	primary

prospective president but simply the campaigning skills of a good candidate. This can be sufficiently unappealing to discourage serious and respected politicians from even entering the race. In 1976, for example, Senator Walter Mondale withdrew from the Democratic contest, stating that he simply did not possess 'the overwhelming desire to be president' required to go through the process (though he subsequently developed that desire by 1984, when he gained his party's nomination to run – unsuccessfully – against President Reagan).

The length question is inseparable from the sheer physical strain imposed by campaigning across as vast a landmass as the United States, with its three time zones. While candidates need not visit all 50 states, in practice, candidates tend to cross the nation seeking votes in key Electoral College states. The stamina necessary, and the relentless nature of modern campaigning, makes this a thankless task to many politicians (during the 2000 campaign, for example, Governor George W. Bush complained to journalists about missing his home in Texas and its creature comforts as he was forced to jet back and forth across the nation during the Republican Party's presidential primaries and caucuses).

One vitally important result has also been that the national party convention no longer has a meaningful role in actually choosing the nominee, since this is known well before it convenes. Primaries and caucuses have wrapped up sufficient delegates for a candidate to win well in advance of the convention. Instead, the convention has become a site for intra-party wrangling over the party manifesto (the 'platform') and a symbolic opportunity to rally the party around the nominee at the start of the presidential election proper.

Money

In order to run competitive races, money is an essential requirement for prospective presidential candidates – and lots of it. This is seen by some critics as further deterring good-quality candidates, exacerbating the preoccupation of elected officials with raising funds and undermining – if not precluding – a level playing field of elections that are fair as well as free.

For example, George W. Bush had amassed $36 million (£22.7m) in just four months of campaigning from April to July 1999, more than any presidential candidate had ever raised for the primary election season. By the end of October 1999, fully one year before the general election, more declared GOP candidates (six) had dropped out of contention for their party's nomination before any votes were cast than actually remained in the race

Exhibit 5.5 National party conventions: the 'bounce'

Conventions no longer decide the nominee nor do they play a genuinely important role in policy formulation for either main party. Their viewing figures have also declined substantially since the 1960s. But millions of people still tune in to the conventions, virtually guaranteeing the nominees a 'bounce' in the polls.

Television ratings

Year	Democratic		Republican	
	Rating	Households	Rating	Households
1988	19.8	17.4 million	18.3	16.2 million
1992	22.0	20.5 million	20.5	20.0 million
1996	17.2	16.4 million	16.5	15.8 million

Poll effect

Voters were asked: If the election were held today, for whom would you vote?

Year	Before convention (%)	After first convention (%)*	Early September (%)	Election result (%)
1988				
Bush	41	37	50	53.4
Dukakis	47	54	44	45.7
1992				
Clinton	28	50	49	43.0
Bush	35	30	35	37.5
Perot	30	2	1	18.9
1996				
Clinton	49	48	51	49.2
Dole	30	41	33	40.9
Perot	11	7	4	8.5

In the 2000 election, having trailed his opponent for months in opinion surveys, Vice President Al Gore finally managed to achieve a clear lead in the opinion polls over Governor George W. Bush in the week following the Democratic Party national convention in Los Angeles, in August 2000.

* The party that controls the White House normally holds its convention last: in 1988 and 1992, Democrats went first; in 1996 and 2000, Republicans went first.
Sources: Nielsen Media research; Gallup Organization.

(five). Among the vanquished were a former vice president (Dan Quayle), a former governor of Tennessee (Lamar Alexander), a former Cabinet Secretary (Elizabeth Dole), a House member (John Kasich), a senator (Bob Smith) and a former television commentator (Pat Buchanan). After just the first two months of elections in the spring of 2000,

Bush had spent over $60 million and had accumulated so much funding that he felt able to refuse federal matching funds (and the limits that these imposed on total spending) for his campaign.

Possessing a solid war chest cannot guarantee a victory on its own. And not having a personal fortune does not preclude success, since millions of dollars can be raised from individuals and PACs. However, though not a sufficient condition of electoral success, a large campaign fund is a necessary one and, arguably, one of the most important factors in a candidate's prospects. Put simply, no candidate lacking the ability to raise substantial financial resources in the tens of millions of dollars can currently hope to become president of the United States.

Media

Often the brunt of blame for the ills of modern American politics, the mass media offer an especially inviting target for critics of the presidential selection process. This critique takes several forms. Journalists are seen as concentrating on the frivolous and symbolic at the expense of the serious and substantive. The media focus on personalities, personal issues and the horse race – who's ahead, who's behind – rather than what candidates stand for in terms of policy positions. Journalists also exercise an interpretative function that sometimes distorts election results. That is, they not only report what share of a vote candidates have received, but also put this in the context of what they were expected to receive. As such, candidates who 'win' a contest can be portrayed as losers, and candidates coming second or third can be seen as 'winning' against what they were expected to achieve.

For example, Bill Clinton came second in the New Hampshire Democratic primary of 1992, behind the former senator for Massachusetts, Paul Tsongas, but because the election took place shortly after a series of scandals about Clinton – an affair with Gennifer Flowers, allegations of dodging the draft over Vietnam, and drugs (the claim that Clinton had smoked cannabis but 'didn't inhale') – the fact that Clinton had done so well was interpreted by the media as a victory. In 1996, when Pat Buchanan narrowly topped the New Hampshire primary for the Republicans, this was interpreted less as a win for him than as a defeat for Bob Dole because Dole had been expected, as the front-runner, to win the primary easily.

Another dimension to media influence is the dominance of television. This is seen as encouraging candidates to pay for slick, short advertisements that often gloss over policy or make 'negative' attacks on others. Adverts can appeal not to policy or principles but to base fears and frustrations and symbolism over substance. As Exhibit 5.6 notes, the images conveyed on television can reinforce voter perceptions even to the point of clouding out adverse media commentary.

Finally, the media stand accused of trivializing and personalizing American elections by concentrating on personality issues at the expense of policies and programmes. In 1987, for example, Senator Gary Hart of Colorado was seen as the front-runner for the Democratic Party's presidential nomination. But after rumours arose of Hart having extramarital affairs, the media confronted the senator. Hart denied the allegations, challenging journalists to tail him. Journalists from the *Miami Herald* duly did so, and found a woman leaving Hart's Washington residence after spending a weekend with him. When photos emerged of the woman – a former model called Donna Rice – sitting on Hart's lap on a yacht called 'Monkey Business', the senator's political career lay in ruins. In 2000, concerns over George W. Bush's problems as a young man with drink and – allegedly – drugs were briefly raised by journalists, but how far these personal issues are relevant to the business of being president is, at best, unclear.

Exhibit 5.6 'Morning in America': the triumph of symbol over substance?

President Ronald Reagan's re-election campaign of 1984 was one of the most slickly packaged and tightly organized in recent decades. Designed with a view to creating maximum positive exposure during the year of the Olympics held in Los Angeles, it regularly set the president against patriotic backdrops of flags and cheering young Americans. In a television report that sought to expose how the campaign was virtually bereft of actual policy commitments, the CBS journalist Lesley Stahl showed footage of Reagan's 'feel-good' campaigning with a highly critical voice-over targeting the lack of policy substance. The result: the Reagan campaign team telephoned Stahl to offer their congratulations. Their polling showed that most viewers had watched the positive images and neglected to pay attention to the negative voice-over, reinforcing their pro-Reagan sentiments.

Unrepresentativeness

All men may be created equal in America, according to the Declaration of Independence, but the 50 states are a rather different matter. In the presidential selection process especially, some states are considerably more equal than others, but contrary to logical inference (the more populous the state, the more influential), the more influential states in selecting nominees have until recently tended to be the smaller and more unrepresentative ones. The relative influence of states has been largely a matter of timing. For many years, candidates would be obliged to devote their resources to small and (socially and politically) unrepresentative states such as Iowa and New Hampshire while effectively relegating large and populous states such as California, Texas and New York to the sidelines.

As Table 5.3 illustrates, not only did this accord a disproportionate role to early states but it also compounded the 'horse race' nature of media coverage of the campaigns. Rather than focusing on what specific candidates were proposing in terms of public policies, media attention instead dwelt on issues of personal character and who was ahead or behind in the race. As such, the amount of information on substantive policy issues that Americans received was comparatively limited, not only during the primaries but also in the general election.

Activist influence

Those critics and politicians who yearn for the pre-1972 selection system often see the current system as irresponsible. A large part of this lies at the hands of issue or cause activists. Whereas previously state delegations, dominated by elected public officials, chose the candidates at the national conventions, these forces are now marginalized. Instead, mass participation allows organized groups which have little or no concern for the party collectively to influence the selection of the presidential candidate(s). Their motivation is typically to advance a particular cause rather than the victory of the party as such: abortion rights, affirmative action, prayer in school, opposition to gun control, environmentalism. What matters to such activists is that individuals are chosen as nominees who profess the 'right' position on these issues: 'purity' is the key. Questions of who is likely to have the broadest voter appeal are decidedly secondary, if not entirely irrelevant, to the choice.

The ironic result of democratizing presidential selection procedures has therefore been the selection of candidates who are not only unrepresentative of the ordinary, median voter, but who are also unrepresentative of those voters who traditionally identified with the particular party. Both parties have therefore selected nominees more ideologically extreme than their own party's

TABLE 5.3   Focus of television news coverage, 1988 presidential election

Period	Horse race (%)	Campaign issues (%)	Policy issues (%)	Number of stories
Primaries and Caucuses				
1987 (2/8–12/31)	33	48	19	258
Iowa (1/1–2/8)	39	38	22	238
New Hampshire (2/9–2/16)	70	22	7	108
Super Tuesday (2/17–3/8)	58	23	18	130
Midwest (3/9–4/5)	82	8	10	148
New York (4/6–4/18)	56	22	22	59
California	41	15	43	123
Total	50	29	20	1,064
General election				
Pre-convention (6/8–7/21)	11	55	33	248
Conventions (7/22–8/18)	18	43	38	200
First debate (8/19–9/25)	11	51	38	296
Second debate (9/26–10/13)	18	45	37	184
Final 25 days (10/14–11/7)	33	35	33	309
Total	19	46	36	1,237
Combined total	**33**	**38**	**29**	**2,301**

Note: 'Horse race' coverage focuses on the contests – who's ahead, who's behind; 'campaign issues' concern candidate character; 'policy issues' concern actual public policy questions.
Source: Stanley and Niemi (1990: 57).

electorates, much less the median American voter. The ultimate consequence has been the unravelling of the parties' electoral and governing coalitions. That is, those individuals and groups to whom an aspirant presidential nominee must appeal in order to win the party nomination are no longer the same as those individuals and groups with whom – should he succeed in his quest for the White House – he will need to work once in the White House.

The most glaring example of this was the Democrats' selection of George McGovern as the party's nominee in 1972. A senator from the small state of South Dakota, McGovern was one of the most liberal members of Congress. His presidential campaign focused on progressive causes, in particular withdrawal from Vietnam, and appealed to ethnic minorities, feminists, labour unions and youth.

Although such groups strongly assisted his winning the nomination, McGovern was easily derided in the general election campaign as the candidate of 'acid, amnesty and abortion' and was trounced by President Nixon – one of the few presidential candidates even to lose his home state (until Al Gore repeated the feat in 2000).

Outsider nominees

The cumulative result of these changes has, for some, been the selection of candidates who have little or no practical experience of what political life in Washington, DC is like. 'Outsider' candidates who have been chosen by the parties run for the White House by running against what they portray as a Washington establishment in need of fundamental change.

Exhibit 5.7   Two ways of choosing a leader

In 1990, John Major was elected leader of the Conservative Party by the Tory Members of Parliament at Westminster. Two years later, George Bush, the incumbent president, was required to submit himself to voters in Republican primaries and caucuses. Ultimately, 12 million Americans participated. Which process is more sensible? Major had served in the House of Commons since 1979, had been a member of the Cabinet, and had held – albeit briefly – the posts of Chancellor and Foreign Secretary. He knew his colleagues and the system of government well. Bush had been a member of the House of Representatives, chairman of the Republican National Committee, US Ambassador to China, Director of the CIA and Vice President. Ultimately, neither proved particularly successful leaders at home (though both claimed important achievements in the international arena). Defenders of the distinct selection processes point to relatively inexperienced figures proving broadly competent leaders as proof of their suitability for the particular British and American systems. For example, Tony Blair entered 10 Downing Street in May 1997 never having served in government before, while Ronald Reagan and George W. Bush had never served in Washington in any official capacity before entering the White House in 1981 and 2001, respectively.

The most obvious example of such a candidate was James Earl Carter in 1976. A peanut farmer and former two-time governor of Georgia (a southern state, heavily dominated by Democrats until the later 1980s), Jimmy Carter ran a populist nomination campaign which drew heavily on the fact that he had never been part of Washington. In the aftermath of Vietnam, the Watergate scandal, Nixon's resignation and President Ford's pardon of Nixon's criminal wrong-doing, Carter offered Americans a promise of truthfulness and integrity, along with a commitment to get Washington to address the nation's many pressing problems.

What appeared a shrewd electoral strategy was less positive once Carter reached the Oval Office. With few established links to the Democratic members of Congress, Carter felt he owed Democratic public officials little in terms of his nomination and electoral success and acted accordingly. As a president selected in a plebiscitary manner by the people at large, he initially alienated and antagonized crucial sections of his governing coalition in the congressional Democratic Party. Critics laid much of the responsibility at the process that had given him the nomination. Unencumbered by a need to cultivate his peers in Congress, Carter subsequently proved poorly equipped at persuading them once in office.

But even candidates who have extensive experience in Washington are now encouraged to engage in 'anti-Washington' politics. Bob Dole resigned his position as Majority Leader in the US Senate in the summer of 1996 so that he could run more effectively for president. Vice President Al Gore, his campaign stalling in the autumn of 1999, relocated his headquarters from Washington to Nashville, Tennessee. Despite having served many years in Congress and the administration, respectively, both candidates felt the need to distance themselves from Washington as a means of returning there. For Gore, this was an especially acute problem, since his campaign message equivocated between consolidating the Clinton years and pushing for change, saying, in effect, 'we have unprecedented peace and prosperity, and I'm angry as hell about it'.

Negative campaigning

Finally, the primary-dominated process has been criticized as encouraging intra-party disagreements and 'negative campaigning'.

Exhibit 5.8 The 'invisible primary'

One important source of concern for analysts has been the phenomenon of the 'invisible primary'. By this they mean the process which occurs before any actual voting takes place, in which certain individuals are singled out as likely presidential contenders. Two factors are crucial here: the media and money. The media is important because it is primarily journalists – print and broadcast – who do the naming. Acting as 'gatekeepers' to information, these journalists can screen out candidates who may or may not be viable. But they do so, of course, according to what they themselves judge to be the key criteria for viability, and more often than not, a crucial condition for their deeming a candidate to be viable is cash. That might not be problematic in and of itself. But the difficulty here is that those candidates who are mentioned as viable thereby become more attractive to potential donors, who swell their war chests; and who therefore, in turn, become even more viable in the eyes of the media. A self-fulfilling prophecy is hence at work. The first task of an aspirant president, then, is to get interviewed, mentioned, and to receive approving stories from television and print media – to shed one's invisibility on the national stage and finally be recognized as a serious contender. (Hence Bob Dole's sardonic quip in 1995 concerning another contender for the Republican nomination the following year. Dole observed that the most dangerous place to be in Washington was 'between [Senator] Phil Gramm and a television camera'.)

Candidates who share much in common politically are forced to highlight their differences and magnify minor disagreements, which can then be exploited by the other party in the general election. To some extent, this tradition is a very old one in American politics. In 1800, candidate John Adams was described as a 'fool, hypocrite, criminal tyrant'. In the same year, Thomas Jefferson's opponents argued that electing the Virginian would ensure that 'murder, robbery, rape, adultery and incest will be openly taught and practiced'. In 1844, candidate Henry Clay was described as spending 'his days at the gambling table and his nights in a brothel'. The great American journalist H.L. Mencken described Franklin D. Roosevelt as such a political opportunist that: 'If he became convinced cannibalism would win him votes, FDR would fatten a missionary at the White House immediately.' Negative campaigning, then, has a long history. Critics fear, however, that the sheer scale and intensity of the negative, anti-Washington campaigns in the television and Internet age compounds the public's distrustful and cynical view of government, politics and politicians.

EVALUATING THE CRITICISMS

Clearly, the criticisms of the post-reform process are several and, if valid, individually and collectively powerful. But how do they fare when tested against the evidence?

Length

It remains the case that potential candidates tend to declare their candidacies long in advance of the actual election year. Moreover, they campaign actively even prior to any formal declaration. But the length criticism has altered over time, away from one of excessive duration to one of insufficient length. The central contention here is that the process in 1996 and 2000 became unduly 'front-loaded': a spate of primary and caucus states holding their contests within a very compressed calendar. Not only this, but some larger states altered the dates of their primaries to hold them much earlier in the process (in March, in California's case).

The dangers here were seen as twofold: (i) candidates with established party ties were accorded a premium, even though ordinary voters were largely unimpressed by them; and (ii) the importance of a large financial war chest was further reinforced, encouraging not only established figures but also outsiders who had never been elected to any office (such as billionaire Steve Forbes) to enter the race in the hope of 'buying' the nomination. As a result, Al Gore and George W. Bush took commanding leads in opinion surveys as front-runners that, despite hiccups, neither relinquished in 2000.

Money

Finance is clearly crucial to success, but it is not the whole story. Without money, a national campaign is possible but unlikely to succeed in securing victory. With money, a campaign has a great boost but no guarantee of success. Both Phil Gramm in 1996, and Steve Forbes in 1996 and 2000, demonstrated that far more than cash was necessary for electoral success in the Republican Party primaries. Former Senator Bill Bradley also amassed a substantial campaign chest in 2000 but never came close to threatening Gore's nomination for the Democrats. In absolute terms, the money spent in presidential campaigns is indeed substantial, but per capita, they amount to relatively little (approximately $1 to $1.50 per American), and offer a relatively inexpensive way of conducting a nationwide search for a suitable set of nominees to contest an election for the most powerful political office in the world.

Conversely, it is possible for candidates who have a distinctive message or base of support to wage serious campaigns despite a relative lack of funds. The black preacher Jesse Jackson, for example, ran second to Michael Dukakis in the Democratic Party contest of 1988, having mounted a campaign with a clear progressive programme and a strong appeal to blacks, labour unions and the more radical elements within the party. The Christian evangelical preacher Pat Robertson in 1988 and Pat Buchanan in 1992 and 1996 both posed challenges to the mainstream Republican candidates on the basis of socially conservative platforms. Concerted appeals to key groups in the parties' respective electoral coalitions can therefore partially ameliorate the money problem, though they cannot eliminate it altogether.

Nevertheless, the overall significance of money cannot be denied. Considerations of hard cash condition how many television advertisements can be bought, how professionally they are produced, and can hence affect the name recognition of candidates (crucial, since most are normally unknown outsiders in the states where they must campaign), support for their favoured issue positions, and the agenda of elections (what the election issues are about and therefore which candidates the election favours). The need to raise money also demands that candidates and their staff expend substantial amounts of time and energy on the basic job of acquiring dollars. A large war chest is not a sufficient condition of a victorious campaign, but it is a necessary, and more often than not, a very effective one.

The media

The media exert a crucial influence on the outcomes of presidential primaries and caucuses. To suggest that journalists merely report what is going on in a consistently and clearly 'objective' fashion is naive. Not only do they cover news, they create news and determine what is and is not considered 'news'. Without casting votes, television and print journalists are active participants in the selection process as much as neutral observers. They decide what information reaches potential voters, how much, and what kind.

Again, though, criticisms of the media's role need to be qualified. In some respects, the criticism is not so much one of the media but of the American public. That is, if American television viewers turn off from stories on detailed public policy, television journalists are likely to concentrate on the horse race and character aspects of the campaign instead. It is not at all clear that extensive discussions of policy issues on television would attract significant viewers, even in the unlikely event that television corporations allowed these to be aired in prime time. Admittedly, Ross Perot's half-hour, prime-time 'infomercials' in 1992 did attract millions of viewers, but this was as much a function of their novelty value as a reflection of a genuine thirst for policy analysis among American voters.

Also, the media's role has ebbed and flowed over time. After 1988, for example, many journalists lamented what they saw as an especially negative campaign, and their own role in ignoring or fuelling that negativity. In 1992, 1996 and 2000, journalists therefore began to evaluate the accuracy of campaign advertisements, which themselves now tended to include references to policy proposals so that the charge of vacuous, personalized, issue-less campaigns was less easy to sustain.

It is also worth noting that in politics today, governing comprises, in an important respect, a continuation of campaigning. In America, in particular, the changes that have affected parties have meant that persuading other political actors to go along with the president – particularly Congress – requires what amounts to a series of distinct campaigns. The old levers of power centred in the parties have ebbed away. It is not, therefore, inappropriate that a politician's skill at using the media – especially television – should be rigorously tested in the election campaign. An inability to communicate effectively is likely to hamper a president substantially in office. After losing in 1984, Walter Mondale graciously conceded that he had never been able to master the use of television in the way that his opponent, Ronald Reagan, so clearly had. Without that mastery, effective political leadership is likely to prove difficult to sustain.

Ultimately, both politicians and journalists know that they are locked in an unbreakable embrace. Politicians need journalists to get their message or responses out to the public; journos need politicians to be able to get a story. Both are aware that they have their own agenda(s), and the process is one in which manipulating news is inherent in the business.

Unrepresentative states

Despite the efforts of Louisiana to pre-empt them in 1996 and 2000, the Iowa caucus and New Hampshire primary remain the first important tests of a presidential campaign. But both states also remain rather unlike the rest of America in terms of race, ethnicity, urban centres and socio-economic indices. To this extent, the process begins in an odd and unrepresentative fashion. But the charge that these states predetermine the eventual outcomes of the nomination process cannot be sustained. Bill Clinton in 1992, Bob Dole in 1996, and George W. Bush in 2000 lost the New Hampshire primary but went on to win their respective parties' presidential nominations. Conversely, as Table 5.4 records, many successful early victors went on to lose the election battles. Whilst Iowa and New Hampshire therefore remain influential, as any states that commenced the season would necessarily be, they are hardly reliable predictors of the eventual nominees.

Activist influence

How far the activist criticism is valid is a matter of much conjecture. It is incontrovertible that activists have achieved an influential role in the nomination process in a way that (with the important exception of Barry Goldwater's hard-line conservative triumph in 1964) had not previously been the case. Party platforms have been crafted with a view not only to appealing to the broadest swathe of voters, but also to placating internal party factions. For example, the Democratic Party's strong plank against the apartheid government of South Africa in 1988 and the Republican Party's strongly pro-life platform on abortion in 1992 were both directed more at appeasing internal factions than attracting large numbers of undecided voters.

TABLE 5.4 Peaking too early

Year	Candidate	What happened
2000	John McCain	The Arizona senator scored a dramatic victory over George W. Bush in the New Hampshire primary, but the Texan came back hard in South Carolina and then walked away with the nomination.
1996	Pat Buchanan	The crusading conservative won an upset victory over Bob Dole in New Hampshire, but it was Dole who then powered his way to the Republican Party nomination.
1992	Paul Tsongas	The former senator for neighbouring Massachusetts bested a scandal-plagued Bill Clinton in the Democratic New Hampshire primary only to see the 'Comeback Kid' anointed the real winner by the media.
1988	Richard Gephardt	The Missouri congressman placed first in the Iowa caucuses but rapidly lost the Democratic nomination to Michael Dukakis.
1980	George H.W. Bush	The future president beat Ronald Reagan in the Republican Iowa caucuses but had to settle for the vice presidency after Reagan won the party's nomination.

But activist influence can be exaggerated. The most obvious examples of 'purity' candidates have never come close to being selected by either main party. Buchanan, Robertson and Jesse Jackson have caused formidable difficulties to established candidates and front-runners, but mostly in rare and unusual circumstances. Indeed, given the dominant features of the contemporary selection process – length, national campaigning, large war chests, intense media scrutiny and popular participation – it is difficult (though not impossible) for 'extremists' to achieve a strong showing. So dominant were the moderate candidates in the two parties in 1999/2000 (George W. Bush and John McCain in the Republican Party, Al Gore and Bill Bradley in the Democratic Party) that those on the more extreme wings of the parties ended up contemplating running for another party's nomination: Buchanan, Bob Smith and, in the Democratic Party, film actor Warren Beatty.

Party platforms have also remained far from the clear statements of ideological principle and the manifesto-style setting out of programmes of government characteristic of European politics for most of the twentieth century. Attention often focuses on the more hard-line examples of intra-party conflict, such as abortion for the Republicans, which are deemed 'newsworthy'. But most of the commitments in the platforms of the two main parties remain rather vague, imprecise and general statements of values and beliefs rather than precise policy commitments.

Outsider candidates

Linked to the previous point, the issue of outsider candidates is more complex than the conventional example of the Carter candidacy suggests. While it is certainly the case that governors have become increasingly important in the pool of selection, along with other non-Washingtonians (such as talk-show hosts, priests and billionaire businessmen), most of the fields remain dominated by elected officials, mostly (current or former) senators and representatives. Admittedly, it is also true that even these individuals tend to adopt 'anti-Washington' appeals as strategically sensible campaigning postures. But it is hardly the case that established figures do not enter the race.

Exhibit 5.9 Presidential life begins at 40?

The constant exposure of candidates to media scrutiny is a genuine consideration for prospective participants in the selection process. Who among us really desires his or her private life and personal history to be scrutinized in the minutest detail by adversarial journalists eager for a career-advancing scoop? But this exposure can also be considered a positive virtue of the American system. It means that Americans know an awful lot about their president, and may well screen out drunks, crooks, psychopaths and other undesirables from the Oval Office. That transparency also means that a candidate's entire personal history is up for grabs. A successful presidential candidacy essentially requires three features: political clout, a clear message, and a positive biography. Political endorsements, money and favourable opinion polls can yield the first, but the message is a matter for the candidate to identify, and the biography is effectively out of his or her hands by the time a presidential contest is under way. In that crucial respect, a candidate may only run for the office in middle age (the Constitution prohibits anyone under the age of 35 from becoming president). But life definitely does not begin at 40 in terms of the scrutiny that the media will display. From the town of birth through youthful indiscretions to choice of marriage partner (it remains virtually inconceivable that a single person can become president), a candidate's entire history and personality are legitimate matters of public interest, at least as far as American journalists are concerned. As Clinton's troubles over extra-marital affairs, draft-dodging and drugs in 1992 graphically revealed, what may appear to some as entirely irrelevant details can assume significance in suggesting broader 'truths' about what kind of character a prospective president possesses. But politics nevertheless evolves with the times so that, for example, both Al Gore and George W. Bush were able mostly to avoid close scrutiny of their alleged dabbling in marijuana and cocaine, respectively.

For critics such as William Mayer (1996), the evidence of recent elections in fact points in the opposite direction: party regulars, rather than outsiders, now have an advantage in achieving nomination. For the Republicans, George H.W. Bush in 1988 and 1992 and Bob Dole in 1996 were quintessential Washington insiders, with a long pedigree of jobs in the Beltway. Even in 2000, George W. Bush may have been a twice-elected Governor of Texas, but he was so clearly the overwhelming choice of Republican elected officials that he was effectively an 'insider' figure, not a party insurgent. Gore and Bradley for the Democrats were, similarly, well-respected party figures who had served for many years in Washington as federal lawmakers.

The lesson seems to be that the process can yield either outsider or insider candidates, but a particular bias now tends to favour insider candidates who have been able to amass substantial sums of money and party contacts. In this context, it is extremely difficult for genuine outsiders or radicals – or even 'reformist' insiders with modest campaign budgets – to pose a remotely serious threat to established party figures. Whether that is a virtue or vice depends heavily, of course, on where one stands on the need for, or desirability of, fundamental change in today's America.

On balance, the post-reform process can therefore be defended against most of the charges levelled against it. Moreover, the process has also had two effects that are welcome in American politics. First, the primaries have encouraged candidates representing minority and underrepresented groups to contest presidential elections. Jackson's campaigns in 1984 and 1988, and Robertson's in 1988, brought new groups of voters into the

Exhibit 5.10   Choosing a 'Veep'

There are two reasons why the choice of vice presidential candidate is crucial to a presidential nominee. In a narrowly partisan sense, the presidential candidate wants to make his ticket as attractive as possible, albeit without eclipsing his own appeal, profile and dominance. But also, since the VP is next in line to the White House should the president die, resign, be incapacitated or impeached, the choice of number two on the ticket assumes a great political significance for the country as a whole. Some wags used to argue that Bush selected Dan Quayle in 1988 as his best guarantee against assassination attempts (the Dukakis campaign even aired a television advertisement making the point that several Veeps had succeeded to the presidency in times of crisis, with pictures of Truman and LBJ to illuminate the message). But when thinking of whom to select as a running mate, several political considerations weigh heavily on a nominee:

Ideological balance. Since the two main parties are such broad and heterogeneous coalitions, it is often the case that a successful nominee comes from a particular wing of the party. It is sensible, then, to shore up broad party support by choosing a VP candidate from the other wing. In 1988, for example, Michael Dukakis, widely seen as being on the moderate/progressive wing of the Democratic Party, selected Lloyd Bentsen, a well-respected and relatively conservative senator from Texas (famed for his 'Senator, you're no Jack Kennedy' put-down of Quayle in the vice presidential debate, and later Clinton's first Treasury Secretary) as his running-mate; George H.W. Bush, a relatively moderate Republican regarded with some unease by the right of his party, chose J. Danforth Quayle, a politician well liked by the conservative right of the party as a social and economic conservative. Similarly, in 1996, the relatively moderate and spendthrift Bob Dole chose the relatively conservative supply-sider Jack Kemp. In 2000, George W. Bush shored up his credentials with conservative Republicans by selecting former congressman and Defense Secretary Dick Cheney, while Al Gore balanced his liberal record in Congress with that of the more centrist Senator Joe Lieberman.

Regional balance. With 50 states in the Union, presidential aspirants typically need to demonstrate sensitivity to areas outside their own geographical base. Typically, then, Veeps are chosen who will add 'balance' to the ticket in geographic as well as ideological terms. For Massachusetts's Dukakis, Bentsen hailed from Texas. For the Georgian Carter, Mondale came from liberal and Midwest Minnesota. The exception that proved the rule here was Bill Clinton in 1992, selecting Al Gore from his neighbouring state of Tennessee. But this was as shrewd a political move as it was unusual. An all-southern ticket suggested a real shift away from traditional old-style Democratic politics towards 'New Democrat' themes. The 2000 election was unusual in that both candidates favoured VPs for reasons other than region (neither Cheney's Wyoming nor Lieberman's Connecticut were either swing states or states with many Electoral College votes).

Demographic appeal. Candidates may be chosen partly because they appeal to a particular social group or suggest a symbolic shift. Mondale selected Geraldine Ferraro, a congresswoman from New York, in 1984 partly to attract women voters. No ethnic or racial minority candidate has yet been selected, though how much this derives from fears of popular prejudice based on race rather than ideology – most black elected officials, for example, tend to be liberal Democrats – is unclear. (General Colin Powell was encouraged to run in the Republican primaries of 1996 but declined to enter the race.) Gore's choice of Lieberman in 2000, the first Jew on a national ticket, was partly due to demographics (a solid Jewish turnout could help in key states) but more to signify the Vice President's political courage and the moderation of his ticket (Lieberman was not only a Jew but also a practising one).

Exhibit 5.10   Choosing a 'Veep' *continued*

Age. How old a presidential contender is can affect his choice of running mate. For elderly candidates, a younger running mate is clearly a good counterpoint. Hence, Reagan selected the comparatively youthful Bush in 1980, and Dole chose Kemp in 1996. Equally, a relatively youthful candidate can benefit from an older VP, such as Kennedy's choice of Johnson in 1960 and Dukakis's of Bentsen in 1988. Again, though, this factor can play out in different ways. Clinton's choice of Gore in 1992 reinforced their desire to emphasize change and the onset of a generational shift in the Democratic Party. Bush's choice of the experienced Cheney in 2000 sought to reassure voters of his gravitas and electability to the highest office.

Compatibility. A final consideration – often neglected – is a straightforward one: can the two running mates get along personally? The chemistry between Gore and Clinton in 1992, and for both parties' tickets in 2000, was notoriously excellent; that between Kennedy and Johnson in 1960 was famously fraught. Bush chose Cheney in 2000 partly because he simply got on so well with the man who had been given the task of shortlisting prospective VP candidates for the Texan governor.

Ultimately, the key to VP selection is to find someone who is able to add to the ticket without detracting from the 'star': the candidate for president. If, in the process, some compromises have to be made with former opponents, the old and typically colourful advice of Lyndon Johnson is always on hand: better to have your enemies 'inside the tent pissing out than outside the tent pissing in'.

parties' selectorates in large numbers. Secondly, the broader base of participation, combined with the influence of activists, has partly led to the creation of more meaningful party platforms and, as a result, a clearer choice between the parties for voters. To the extent that this has occurred, it has facilitated a greater level of accountability in national politics.

Perhaps the most important counter to critics of the process, however, is their lack of historical perspective. There never existed a 'golden age' of presidential selection. Prior to the 1968 reforms, the process had itself thrown up 'outsider' candidates with little or no experience of Washington politics, such as Eisenhower. Even at the time, insider experience was no guarantee of legislative success (the records of Truman and Kennedy were meagre in this regard) and other presidents selected through the 'mixed system', such as Harding and Coolidge, were regarded poorly. Conversely, the post-1968 process has yielded 'insider' candidates with impeccable governing credentials, whose records as president were not particularly distinguished, such as George H.W. Bush. It may well be that the importance of prior political socialization depends on factors like the size of the state. The experiences of Reagan and George W. Bush in California and Texas, respectively – states where as Republican governors they faced Democratic state legislatures and enjoyed few powers over them – were surely better preparations for DC politics than Carter's or Clinton's in small one-party southern states.

But what initially appears to be an intrinsic problem of the American presidency – the absence of an appropriate apprenticeship – may also be a virtue. The singularity of the office means that whoever arrives at the White House must adapt quickly to the distinctive demands of the job and seek sound advisors across the policy spectrum. As the next chapter explains, the reasons for the relative lack of success of many recent presidents has more to do with the profound changes in many other areas of American political, economic and social life than with a faulty selection system.

CONCLUSION

When American voters decided between Al Gore and George W. Bush in 2000, one question that many considered was which candidate was 'ready' to be president. Millions reached diametrically opposed conclusions. For some, being experienced in Washington, DC, having a clear and strong command of policy details, and being obviously intelligent pointed to Gore. For others, not being part of the DC 'establishment', not being too bogged down in policy minutiae, and being a 'regular guy' pointed equally clearly to Bush. That so many Americans could split over such matters – in addition to the core issue concerns animating their partisan choices – indicated strongly that the most powerful office in the world is not one that makes particular character attributes absolute essentials for most voters.

Quite what qualities an effective presidential selection process should test is, in itself, a difficult question to resolve. It begs the equally difficult question of what type of individual is 'best-suited' to being president. Some would argue that skilful use of television is an essential quality today. If insufficient to guarantee legislative success, it may nevertheless be a necessary condition of persuading lawmakers. The president is, *de jure* and *de facto*, centre-stage – 'acting' skill is hence not inappropriate for what amounts to, as Lou Cannon described Reagan's tenure, 'the role of a lifetime'. But the office is quite different from Congress and the Supreme Court, where experience as a state legislator or as a state or lower federal court judge can serve as good preparation. Because the presidential office is unique, neither an obvious

nor a single appropriate training ground exists for it. As the experiences of Johnson, Nixon and Bush showed, even occupying the vice presidency is no assurance of presidential success.

But while it is true that the nature of the office is such that no other job can serve as a good apprenticeship, this should not lead us to abandon a search for the right credentials in potential presidents. Nor should it induce complacency about the system that screens such candidates. Sheer intelligence is no guarantee of political success (Carter, Clinton), while a relative lack of intellect (Reagan, George W. Bush) or even physical frailty (FDR, JFK) give no assurance of failure. On balance, though, most would surely argue that the process should encourage candidates who are more intelligent than modestly intellectually equipped, more honest than dishonest, more emotionally and psychologically balanced than unbalanced, unstable or prone to uncontrollable urges. Americans conventionally want a president who embodies the more admirable human characteristics but who is neither so special nor so different as to be distant from the values, beliefs and behaviours of ordinary citizens.

With this in mind, few observers of the current process are satisfied with it, but then equally few proposals have arisen which convincingly suggest that a satisfactory process is achievable. The need to involve all 50 states is unavoidable. Once granted mass participation, Americans are unlikely to look favourably on proposals to return the nomination of major party candidates to party elites. The existing process has yielded self-conscious outsiders and consummate insiders, politicians with no experience of Washington who were successful presidents, and politicians with extensive experience in DC who were relative failures. While popular conceptions of the process as some kind of grotesque American beauty contest massively oversimplify its nature, it is probably true that the Lincolns and Roosevelts would have been unlikely to have secured their respective parties' nominations through the contemporary process (Lincoln's modern advisors would no doubt have been deeply concerned by that sorrowful face, lengthy beard and long black coats). But perhaps a process that demands that those seeking the nominations possess an 'overwhelming desire' to be president is one which, given the nature of the president's job, is desirable after all. An imperfect system has, for all its deficiencies, nevertheless yielded effective chief executives and, in the absence of compelling alternatives, 'if it ain't broke, don't fix it'.

FURTHER READING

Stephen Wayne, *The Road to the White House 2000: The Politics of Presidential Elections* (2000) is an excellent, comprehensive analysis of the politics of presidential selection that deals with everything from the Electoral College and primary process to advertising strategies.

James Ceaser and Andrew Busch, *The Perfect Tie: The True Story of the 2000 Presidential Election* (2001) is an excellent account of the 2000 elections, from the primaries through to the eventual results.

William Mayer (ed.), *In Pursuit of the White House: How We Choose Our Presidential Nominees* (1996) is a collection of readable essays on presidential selection politics, focusing on the key aspects of the presidential election of 1996.

Nelson Polsby and Aaron Wildavsky, *Presidential Elections* (1988) is a classic study by two of America's foremost political scientists of the nature of the presidential election contest.

WEB LINKS

Campaigns & Elections journal
www.campaignline.com

Republican Party
www.rnc.org

Democratic Party
www.democrats.org

Federal Election Commission
www.fec.gov

QUESTIONS

- 'The current presidential selection system deters the best-qualified candidates from even entering the race.' Discuss.

- What qualities should a presidential selection system test in contemporary America?

- Is the post-reform presidential selection system too democratic or not democratic enough?

- 'Since the US presidency is a unique job, there exists no particular apprenticeship that is a better preparation than any other.' Discuss.

6 The Presidency

My choice early in life was either to be a piano-player in a whorehouse or a politician. And to tell the truth, there's hardly any difference.

President Harry Truman

The essence of a President's persuasive task, with congressmen and everybody else, is to induce them to believe that what he wants of them is what their own appraisal of their own responsibilities requires them to do in their interest, not his.

Richard Neustadt (1990: 40)

- The US Constitution
- Presidential Leadership
- Presidential Success
- From Imperial to Impotent and back again?
- After the Postmodern Presidency
- Conclusion

Chapter Summary

The US presidency is the most important position in American government. But the presidency was never intended by the Founding Fathers to play the central and powerful role that it now does in both domestic and world affairs. At once the most powerful office in the world in virtue of the growth of America's global influence and the reach of the federal government at home, and also an inherently weak one in terms of its few and checked formal constitutional powers, presidential effectiveness in America's separated system of government depends heavily on what Richard Neustadt (1990) termed the 'power to persuade'. But while the president's formal powers have remained unchanged since 1787, the informal resources that presidents possess to persuade have ebbed and flowed in strength. Weak party ties, divided party control of the federal government, a more adversarial and fragmented mass media, a vast executive bureaucracy and a post-Cold War international system in flux have together posed substantial problems to successive presidents of both main parties. Since no other officeholder possesses a national constituency, with the unique legitimacy and prestige that this affords, presidential leadership remains crucial to American socio-economic fortunes and national security, but it is only rarely present in domestic politics for a sustained period. Only in the most exceptional conditions, such as war or economic depression, is the presidency as powerful as the popular image of influential presidents such as Washington, Lincoln or FDR suggests. Even then, this power relies on active congressional approval or passive acquiescence. The president is part of a co-equal system of government, sharing powers with other branches of government at the federal level as well as with state and local governments. However, as the response of George W. Bush to September 11 vividly showed, no other figure in American politics possesses the capacity – and faces the public and international expectation – to lead the nation to economic prosperity and national security.

Contrary to President Truman's assertion, most brothel pianists rarely enjoy the opportunity to wage global war with the world's most powerful military forces, launch nuclear weapons at their enemies, and speak both to and for the American nation. The president of the United States occupies a uniquely powerful but isolated office, at once the most important, prized and problematic position in American government.

A favourite exercise of American historians is therefore to 'rate' presidents and identify the four or five 'greatest' politicians to occupy the White House. Typically, George Washington, Thomas Jefferson, Abraham Lincoln and Franklin D. Roosevelt are found at the top of these presidential 'greatest hits' lists. Conspicuous by their absence from 'America's Most Presidential' are individuals such as Gerald Ford, Jimmy Carter, George H.W. Bush and Bill Clinton. The scholarly message – sometimes implicit, often explicit – is that recent chief executives have been relative failures. That can also occasion claims that the reasons for this lack of success lie beyond the individuals themselves – that the presidency as an institution has shifted from being an 'imperial' office to being an 'impotent' or even 'imperilled' one, no matter who occupies the White House.

The view from the White House itself has rarely shown individuals revelling in

awesome power. In one of the most famous remarks about the presidency, Truman declared that his Republican successor, Dwight Eisenhower, would enter the White House and 'sit here and say "do this", "do that", and nothing will happen'. It would all be very different from the world Ike had been used to in the army during the Second World War, where an order from a senior official would be implemented by a clear hierarchy of authority and with military precision, care and efficiency. Instead, the president could only cajole, nudge and pressure others into acting as he wished. At once an office burdened by massive public expectations and the heaviest political responsibilities, the presidency is simultaneously an inherently weak institution and the president an unusually isolated leader. Such is the perplexing nature of the most powerful political office in the modern world.

But whatever the burdens of the office and constraints on political leadership, the presidency remains the ultimate prize in American politics. Even so, few presidents in recent decades have left the Oval Office without expressing regret and frustration at the many formidable difficulties they encountered in trying to exercise leadership. As Table 6.1 shows, of the 11 presidents who served from 1933 to 2001, only four (FDR, Eisenhower, Reagan and Clinton) managed to complete

TABLE 6.1   US presidents in the era of the modern presidency (post–1933)

President	Party	In Office	Reason for Leaving Office
Franklin D. Roosevelt	Democrat	1933–45	Died in office
Harry S. Truman	Democrat	1945–53	Decided not to run again
Dwight D. Eisenhower	Republican	1953–61	Completed two full terms
John F. Kennedy	Democrat	1961–63	Assassinated
Lyndon B. Johnson	Democrat	1963–69	Decided not to run again
Richard M. Nixon	Republican	1969–74	Resigned after scandal
Gerald Ford	Republican	1974–77	Defeated at election
Jimmy Carter	Democrat	1977–81	Defeated at election
Ronald Reagan	Republican	1981–89	Completed two full terms
George H.W. Bush	Republican	1989–93	Defeated at election
Bill Clinton	Democrat	1993–2001	Completed two full terms
George W. Bush	Republican	2001–	

two or more terms. The rest were defeated, assassinated, decided not to run again, or resigned in disgrace. That some presidents manage to get re-elected and accomplish their goals – whether through personal skill and intelligence, favourable conditions, or luck – only casts those who do not in an even more unfavourable light.

In this chapter, we focus on the president's powers and role, the nature of presidential leadership, and the transition of the office from one of almost 'imperial' grandeur during the period from 1960 to 1973 to one of relative weakness in the three subsequent decades.

THE US CONSTITUTION

In designing the presidency, the Framers of the Constitution consciously constructed an office with limited formal powers. The president was never intended to occupy the central and dominant role in political life. Not only did Congress occupy Article I of the Constitution (symbolically relegating the president to a secondary place), but also the second article dealing with the presidency is much shorter and less detailed than that dealing with the legislature. The Framers did not want to create a despotic, monarchical or dynastic figure dominating public life.

Article II nevertheless confers on the president several formal powers. He is Commander-in-Chief of the armed forces, may negotiate treaties with foreign governments, nominate Cabinet members, Supreme Court justices and ambassadors, make recommendations to Congress for legislative action, and veto laws that Congress has passed. In theory, at least, the president is Chief Diplomat, Chief Legislator, Chief Administrator and Chief of the Military – a potentially formidable set of governing roles not possessed by any other figure in the federal government. Moreover, as Table 6.2 notes, the president is relatively unusual in liberal democracies in being both the Head of State

Exhibit 6.1   Qualifications for the office of the presidency

Under the US Constitution, a president must be:

- A natural-born US citizen.
- At least 35 years old.
- A US resident for at least 14 years.

TABLE 6.2   Executive arrangements in 15 democracies

Nation	Head of Government	Head of State
Brazil	President	President
Canada	Prime Minister	Governor-General
France	Prime Minister and President	President
Germany	Chancellor	President
India	Prime Minister	President
Ireland	Prime Minister	President
Israel	Prime Minister	President
Italy	Prime Minister	President
Japan	Prime Minister	Monarch
Portugal	Prime Minister and President	President
Russia	President	President
Spain	Prime Minister	Monarch
Sweden	Prime Minister	Monarch
UK	Prime Minister	Monarch
USA	President	President

and the Head of Government – a combination that makes for a potentially powerful national figurehead.

But this impressive, if limited, array of formal constitutional powers is subject to powerful countervailing 'checks and balances' that strongly limit the president's political authority. As Commander-in-Chief, for example, the president faces a Congress that possesses the exclusive responsibility to declare war and fund the armed forces. The Senate must ratify treaties that the president negotiates and confirm presidential nominations. Although the president can recommend new legislative measures, Congress need not act on presidential recommendations and may even overturn a presidential veto of newly passed bills if two-thirds of both the House and Senate so vote.

The Constitution, then, gives the president relatively few formal powers, other branches being accorded partial vetoes that limit even those it does confer. Although the president possesses important informal resources (professional staff, partisan supporters, a unique focus by the mass media, international contacts, and the so-called 'bully pulpit' of the White House from which – with the advent of radio, television and the Internet – he can address the nation and the world), we will

Exhibit 6.2   The formal and informal resources of the presidency

Formal Powers	Informal Resources
• Veto	• Staff in the executive branch
• Executive orders	• Party ties
• Nominations	• Mass media
• Recommendations	• International contacts
• Commander-in-Chief	• The 'bully pulpit'
• Head of State and Head of Government	

TABLE 6.3   Presidential pardons, 1944–2000

President	Presidential pardons*	Months in office	Pardons per months in office
Clinton	146	85	1.71
Bush	77	48	1.60
Reagan	406	96	4.23
Carter	566	48	11.79
Ford	409	29	14.10
Nixon	926	67	13.82
Johnson	1187	62	19.15
Kennedy	575	34	16.91
Eisenhower	1157	96	12.05
Truman	2044	93	21.98

* Includes full pardons, commutation of sentences and remissions of fines. In 1946 President Truman issued an amnesty covering 1,500 draft resisters in the Second World War, and in 1952 he granted amnesty to 9,000 individuals who had deserted from the military during the Korean War. Presidents Ford and Carter also used the amnesty power for more than 10,000 individuals who had resisted the draft during the Vietnam War.

Source: Office of the Pardon Attorney, Department of Justice.

see later in this chapter that these can offer obstacles to, as well as opportunities for, presidential leadership.

The only power totally at the discretion of the president is that of granting pardons to individuals convicted of criminal or other misdeeds. Although these are exercised quite often (see Table 6.3), the most notorious incidence of this power occurred in relation to a disgraced president, when President Ford pardoned his predecessor and former boss, Richard Nixon, for his involvement in the Watergate burglary and cover-up. (Ford later argued that had he not pardoned Nixon, the ensuing legal proceedings would have perpetuated the constitutional crisis into the second half of the 1970s.)

But even though these formal constitutional powers remain fundamentally unaltered, historical developments have accorded the presidency immense power and prestige both at home and abroad. The vast growth of the federal government during the New Deal and the Second World War, together with the assumption of an extensive international role by America after 1945, accorded the president immense power as the head of the federal government and the one officeholder empowered to order nuclear strikes (a power exercised by Truman in 1945 against Japan but contemplated by most of his successors). Congress, and most members of both political parties, acquiesced in an expansion of presidential power in order to fight the Cold War against communism. Such was the presidency's new found authority in international affairs that the American political scientist Aaron Wildavsky even described the office as 'two presidencies' in 1966: one largely dominant presidency in foreign policy, another much-hampered and frustrated presidency in domestic policy where Congress assumed a much larger role. Although the end of the Cold War seemingly ushered in a new era of more limited and contested presidential dominance in foreign affairs, the terrorist strikes of September 11, 2001 again demonstrated the power of the president to use the variety of resources at his disposal (see Exhibit 6.3).

Exhibit 6.3   Presidential powers: George W. Bush and the war presidency

Both before and after September 11, 2001 President Bush demonstrated the vast range of powers that a president can use to influence policy from the environment to war. Among these were:

Commander-in-Chief. Bush personally ordered US military forces into battle in Afghanistan and called up the armed forces reserves. Although he stated that America was at war against terrorism, he did not seek a congressional declaration of war. Congress instead passed resolutions ceding authority to, and supporting, presidential action.

Military tribunals. The president issued a military order setting up tribunals for alleged terrorists, to be presided over by military officers. The tribunals' rulings and recommendations went to the Secretary of Defense but Bush held final authority over verdicts and sentences, including capital punishment. He also approved the decision to declare suspected Al Qaeda and Taliban captives on Guantanamo Bay, Cuba, as detainees rather than prisoners of war.

Executive orders. Bush revoked or nullified several Clinton-era pro-organized labour executive orders; ordered the impoundment of American assets of any person or institution suspected of providing financial help to Al Qaeda and its direct supporters; banned federal funding for any research on new embryonic stem-cell lines; imposed new process requirements on the release of papers of previous presidents, including his father's; and created a President's Council on Bioethics.

Presidential instructions. The president initially limited classified war briefings to eight senior members of Congress and renamed the Justice Department in honour of former Attorney General Robert Kennedy.

Regulations. Bush reversed Clinton's environmental policies by easing wetlands rules affecting developers, reducing energy-saving standards for air conditioners, allowing more road-building and power lines in national forests, delaying a ban on snowmobiles in national parks, and easing restrictions on mining on public lands.

Secrecy. Bush denied congressional committee and General Accounting Office requests for information about energy policy deliberations with industry and environmental policy decisions. He also denied a request for Justice Department documents and invoked executive privilege over the collapse of the energy firm Enron.

Staff. Bush created the offices of Faith-Based and Community Initiatives in the White House, and also the Office of Homeland Security. He intially rejected the idea of a Department of Homeland Security which would have been subject to congressional oversight, but proposed such a Department to Congress in June 2002.

Appointments. Bush circumvented Senate confirmation by placing ten judicial and executive appointees in posts when the 107th Congress was not in session.

Even before September 11, President Bush – like all his predecessors in the White House – resorted to a number of ways to circumvent the powerful obstacles to presidential autonomy posed by Congress and the courts. In particular, presidents frequently use executive powers by issuing executive orders that alter or introduce new regulations that the federal bureaucracy must implement (see Chapter 10). As Table 6.4 shows, even in his first year in office Bush was among the more active presidents in using these powers.

TABLE 6.4 Average number of executive orders per year

President	Executive orders	President	Executive orders
Eisenhower I	66	Carter	80
Eisenhower II	55	Reagan I	53
Kennedy	71	Reagan II	42
Johnson	65	G.H.W. Bush	40
Nixon I	62	Clinton I	49
Nixon II	59	Clinton II	41
Ford	72	G.W. Bush	55

Source: *National Journal*, January 26, 2002.

But even here, presidents who make law using these powers can find themselves reined in by Congress or the courts. The Supreme Court declared President Truman's seizure of US steel mills in 1952 unconstitutional, for example, and a federal appeals court struck down Clinton's 1995 executive order prohibiting federal contractors from doing business with employers that permanently replaced striking workers. War conditions can, however, encourage other branches to support the president. For example, in 1942, Congress passed legislation supporting President Roosevelt's executive order imprisoning over 100,000 Americans of Japanese descent in 'relocation centres', an action ruled constitutional by the Supreme Court in 1944.

Ironically, popular usage of the term 'presidential-style leadership' is therefore a little inaccurate. As Exhibit 6.4 notes, when British prime ministers such as Margaret Thatcher and Tony Blair are commonly said to have been 'presidential', they have in fact been acting in ways quite unlike those familiar to American presidents.

The confusion over presidentialism reflects a broader debate on the nature of American

Exhibit 6.4 Presidents and prime ministers: 'presidentialism'?

In the UK, it has become common for popular, and even academic, commentaries to refer to certain prime ministers behaving in 'presidential' styles. Margaret Thatcher (1979–90) and Tony Blair (1997–) were strongly criticized for behaving in autocratic, even authoritarian, ways, ignoring their Cabinets, party and Parliament, essentially crafting policy with a select band of loyal personal supporters in Downing Street that was then imposed on the remainder of the government machine, rammed through Westminster and established as law. (The poll tax in the late 1980s was perhaps the most infamous example.) But on reflection, this is exactly what American-style presidential leadership is not: no president can hope to achieve a new policy in this way, since the barriers – formal and informal – are so many and formidable. Conversely, when prime ministers were said to be acting in the conventional 'first-among-equals' fashion – bargaining with ministers and party members, striking compromises, offering concessions to win political support – this type of behaviour was much more in the conventional American presidential style of brokerage, compromise and consensus-building. Ironically, then, when defenders of Thatcher and Blair deny they are acting 'presidentially' by pointing to all the conciliatory measures the prime ministers struck, they support the claim that they seek to deny.

Exhibit 6.5   The line of succession to the presidency

In the event that the president dies or is unable to serve out his or her term in office, Congress established a line of succession to the presidency as follows: the vice president; Speaker of the House of Representatives; president *pro tempore* of the Senate; and the president's Cabinet members in the order in which their departments were created, starting with the Secretary of State. Thus far the line of succession has not passed below the vice president. Some observers speculated (with a mixture of horror and fascination) that had Clinton, Gore and Gingrich all been simultaneously incapacitated in 1998, the presidency would have fallen to the then 95-year-old Republican senator from South Carolina, Strom Thurmond – the then president *pro tempore* of the Senate – a scenario revisited two years on in the deadlocked aftermath of the November 2000 presidential election.

government. It is conventional to refer to America as a 'presidential democracy', but the influential scholar Charles Jones (1994) argues that this is profoundly misleading. While the president occupies an important role, American government is a 'separated system' in which the branches of the federal government are co-equal. However understandable the contemporary preoccupation with the presidency in a television age, a presidency-centred view of government leads to highly erroneous ideas about what a president can and should achieve, and the role of Congress and other institutions in relation to the president. But while Jones is right to emphasize the co-equality of the branches, it remains the case that only the president can lead.

PRESIDENTIAL LEADERSHIP

As the last section stressed, the president faces an awesome responsibility and expectation to lead but occupies an office that is institutionally isolated and constitutionally constrained. As the sign on Harry Truman's desk famously put it, the buck stops with the president. (Truman candidly advised potential presidents that if they wanted to find a genuine friend in Washington, 'get a dog' – advice that was taken literally by the three most recent presidents.)

Since FDR, the American public has consistently looked to the president to provide national and international leadership. The only figure elected by a national constituency (albeit indirectly), the president possesses a unique legitimacy to speak to and for the American people. Only the president can articulate a clear agenda for action, prioritize the most important issues facing the nation, and mobilize political support behind that agenda and policy proposals to tackle key issues (Congress, with 535 voting members, is too fragmented while the unelected Supreme Court lacks democratic legitimacy). In terms of the key features of presidential leadership – the strategic ability to set an agenda and the tactical ability to persuade the necessary political figures within and outside Washington to support it – the president faces many competitors but no equal.

Achieving success, however, is a highly complex matter. One of the most skilled political operators, Lyndon Johnson, advised that a president must take advantage of his initial 'honeymoon' period to get his key priorities accomplished. Thereafter, the many competitors for political power tend to make the president's task increasingly difficult, and the tendency of the president's party to lose seats in Congress in midterm elections compounds the problem. But presidential success – judged on a rounded basis of a president's overall achievements – frequently requires

Exhibit 6.6   The State of the Union

The Constitution provides that the president can make recommendations to Congress for action. Over time, the prime focus for such presidency-centred advocacy has been the State of the Union address, usually delivered in late January or early February by the president to both houses of Congress (physically from the podium of the House of Representatives) with the Cabinet, Supreme Court and other dignitaries present.

1790   The first presidential 'Annual Message' is delivered in Federal Hall in New York City on January 8.
1800   After John Adams gives his annual message on November 22, presidents stop delivering the speeches in person. Instead, clerks in each chamber of Congress read the texts.
1913   Woodrow Wilson resumes the practice of appearing before a joint session of Congress on December 2.
1947   The address was re-titled the 'State of the Union' address. The January 6 speech by President Truman was the first carried live on American television.
1997   The address by President Clinton on February 4 was the first to be carried live on the Internet.

attending to more than merely the early months of a presidency, however key these may be.

PRESIDENTIAL SUCCESS

To assess how effective or successful presidents are as leaders is notoriously difficult. To begin with, the criteria for success are many and varied. Beyond this, the appropriate weight that should be given one criterion over another is not necessarily clear. For example, presidential success can be evaluated according to the following.

- *Achieving legislative priorities*. Presidential candidates normally run for office with a set of commitments (albeit vague and imprecise ones) to make policy changes if they get elected. In office, however, the constitutional limits on presidential power make the achievement of those goals dependent on the skills by which

Exhibit 6.7   Presidential honeymoons

The 'honeymoon' is the short period after a president is inaugurated when the opposition party refrains from partisan attacks. Congress is inclined to defer to the president's agenda, to support some of the president's initiatives and the president receives high public approval ratings. Within a month or two partisan attacks tend to resume and the honeymoon period ends. Most recent presidents have been unable to translate successful honeymoons into enduring marriages with Congress. While President Kennedy even extended the concept by calling on the Soviet Union to extend him a honeymoon period as a goodwill gesture (unsuccessfully), one of the shortest honeymoons was that of Gerald Ford, whose pardon of Richard Nixon for all Watergate crimes sparked public outrage and led to a 30-point drop in his popularity after his first month in office (he nevertheless almost won election in 1976).

the president can persuade others – especially members of Congress – to support his objectives. One of the most impressive aspects of a presidency is therefore the extent to which the president can set and achieve his priorities in terms of getting new laws passed (or old ones repealed). In this regard, for example, Ronald Reagan achieved some of his key commitments, such as increasing defence spending, reducing tax and cutting social programmes, in 1981, and others (such as renewing the autonomy of individual state governments) later on by staffing the federal judiciary with conservatives. By contrast, Bill Clinton failed to achieve some of his key commitments, such as a national health care system, a job stimulus package, and a tax cut for middle-income Americans, in 1993.

- *Getting re-elected.* Presidents since 1951 can serve a maximum of two full terms in office (the Twenty-second Amendment was ratified to prevent another FDR-figure winning four elections in succession). Having served four years in the White House, an unfavourable verdict by the electorate is a major blow to any president's reputation. Jimmy Carter and George H.W. Bush were both rejected by the voters after their first terms, and in the midst of the Vietnam War Lyndon Johnson so feared rejection that he did not run for re-nomination after March 1968. By contrast, however mixed their overall records as chief executives, Eisenhower, Nixon, Reagan and Clinton all succeeded in winning the endorsements of the electorate for two full terms (though Nixon was forced to resign in the face of impeachment proceedings).

- *Popular approval.* Winning and maintaining the approval of the public may seem a rather nebulous goal but popular approval can be vital for achieving other presidential objectives, especially gaining congressional support for new or important initiatives and avoiding hostile or negative results. Reagan's immense personal popularity strongly assisted his ability to withstand many policy failures, such as Iran–Contra. Clinton's high job approval ratings in his second term also contributed powerfully to his withstanding impeachment proceedings, even though many of the same Americans who approved of his job performance did not trust him or rate him highly in terms of ethics and integrity.

- *Foreign policy achievements.* Given America's pre-eminence in the world arena since 1945, no president can ignore foreign policy. For some, simply maintaining peace and prosperity is a crucial – and sufficient – legacy. For others, using American power to help to achieve peaceful settlements in other parts of the world, to promote democracy and human rights, and assist in spreading international co-operation on issues such as trade and the environment are landmark achievements. Although widely seen as uninterested and ineffective on domestic policy, for example, George H.W. Bush achieved several far-reaching successes in foreign policy, including defeating the Iraqi forces in Kuwait in 1991 and presiding over the end of the Cold War. By contrast, Carter is widely seen as a weak national leader whose presidency saw the Iranians hold Americans hostage in Tehran and the Soviets invade Afghanistan.

- *Economic success.* Although the president cannot control the national or international economy, arguably the most important basis on which Americans judge their Head of State is securing economic well-being. For those presidents who pass this criterion, history has tended to look favourably on them (Reagan, Clinton). For those who do not (Johnson, Carter, George H.W. Bush), the historical verdict has been less generous. Most Americans expect material success and that successive generations should prosper even more than their immediate predecessors. Presidents who fail to deliver often pay a high political price.

• *Use of the veto.* Although the Constitution does not mention the term 'veto' (from the Latin for 'I forbid') Article I, Section 7 provides that the president may return any legislation of which he disapproves to Congress with an explanation of his objections. (The only exceptions to measures requiring presidential signature to pass into law are resolutions to adjourn Congress and constitutional amendments.) Because the president possesses the power of vetoing laws, and since over- turning the veto is difficult, even the mere threat of using the veto can be a potent weapon. This is a 'negative' weapon to force concessions or delay passage of new measures, but it forms part of the president's arsenal of formal and informal resources and its skilful use can assist a president's reputation on Capitol Hill (an important asset in itself). As Exhibit 6.8 shows, although Republican presidents Gerald Ford and George H.W. Bush both faced a House and Senate controlled by

Exhibit 6.8   Presidential vetoes, 1933–2001

The president's veto authority is one of his most important weapons in legislative dealings with Congress. It is effective not only in preventing laws from passing, but also as a threat, sometimes compelling Congress to modify legislation before it is presented to the president. Experts on executive–legislative relations argue that Congress's strength resides in passing statutes, the president's in vetoing them. In the case of vetoed appropriation bills, the results can be the closure of federal agencies and the temporary dismissal of hundreds of thousands of federal employees, with accompanying disruptions to federal programmes and services. Congress faces four options when a veto is carried out: letting the veto stand, overriding the veto, meeting presidential objections in a new bill, or resubmitting the same provisions under a new bill number. Illustrative of the power of the veto is the fact that, from 1789 to 2001, presidents vetoed 1,485 bills and Congress overrode only 106 of these.

President	Regular vetoes	Vetoes overridden	Percentage overriden	Pocket vetoes	Total vetoes
Roosevelt	372	9	2.4	263	635
Truman	180	12	6.6	70	250
Eisenhower	73	2	2.7	108	181
Kennedy	12	0	0.0	9	21
Johnson	16	0	0.0	14	30
Nixon	24	7	29.1	17	41
Ford	48	12	25.0	18	66
Carter	13	2	15.3	18	31
Reagan	39	9	23.0	39	78
Bush	29	1	3.4	17	46
Clinton	37	2	5.4	1	38
Total	843	56	6.6	574	1,417

Note: unlike regular vetoes, Congress cannot override 'pocket vetoes'. With these, the president effectively places a bill in his pocket by refusing either to sign or return it to Congress. If Congress has adjourned or is in recess for more than ten days, the absence of the signature kills the bill. When Congress returns to session, it must begin all over again of it wishes to revive the bill.
Source: Congressional Research Service.

Exhibit 6.9 The rise and fall of the presidential line-item veto

Unlike most state governors, the president lacks a line-item veto. This means that he must approve or veto an entire appropriations bill and may not veto any single part of the bill. Reagan, Bush and Clinton all called for a constitutional amendment to give them a partial veto as a means of controlling spending and reducing the deficit. With it, they could disapprove of what they considered wasteful 'pork barrel' spending without having to reject many more worthy projects in the remainder of the bill. Lacking the two-thirds vote necessary for a constitutional amendment, Congress in 1995 passed a law providing for the line-item veto. President Clinton used the new power sparingly. But in 1998, the Supreme Court ruled the line-item veto an unconstitutional delegation of Congress's exclusive 'power of the purse'.

the Democrats, Bush saw just one, while Ford saw one-quarter, of his vetoes over-ridden by Congress.

Different criteria of success exist, then, for presidents. At a particular time, some of these take on greater importance than others. Most obviously when America is at war or deploys its military forces abroad, the issue of foreign policy weighs far more heavily in political significance than it does during times of relative peace and prosperity. The contributions of Reagan and Bush to ending the Cold War were arguably far more important than any domestic policy achievements accomplished by their (or any other post-Second World War) administrations. JFK's successful handling of the Cuban Missile Crisis in October 1962, when the world came close to nuclear annihilation, was more important than his relative lack of domestic policy successes. Equally, while re-election may not appear to be on a par with other categories of success for many observers of the presidency, presidents themselves typically devote substantial resources to securing that objective.

It should also be stressed that all of these criteria of presidential success are susceptible to factors outside any president's control: international crises, wars, natural disasters and economic recessions. Successfully steering the ship of state necessarily requires an element of good fortune in negotiating relatively calm rather than rough waters. Most presidents encounter at least a few waves that batter the vessel, but voters tend to be less forgiving of presidential failure than academics. The Cold War's end and victory in the Gulf War of 1991, for example, were not sufficient reasons for most voters to re-elect Bush in 1992 in the face of problematic economic conditions at home. In terms of assessing presidential success, it may therefore make more sense to follow Fred Greenstein (2000) and look to six broad qualities that affect the public performance of chief executives (see Exhibit 6.10).

When these conditions are considered, we can achieve a more rounded view of presidents and the skills and success that accompanies their highly demanding (but, as Exhibit 6.11 notes, financially unrewarding) job.

It is telling that in the comparative surveys of presidents that periodically appear, 'great' presidents have invariably been those who were accorded the most severe tests of national and international crises, not least war and economic dislocation: Washington, Jefferson, Lincoln and the Roosevelts (Theodore and Franklin). These figures loom over other presidents, not so much for their personal attributes as such (though these were impressive), but through leading America effectively during deeply troubled times of crisis, threats and profound socio-economic or political change. In a peculiar way, then, the relative lack of great presidents

Exhibit 6.10 The presidential difference: Eisenhower, Kennedy and George W. Bush

The six qualities that affect the public performance of presidents are:

Cognitive style. Ike and JFK had impressive intelligence, more so than the notoriously intellectually incurious Bush. As suits a military strategist, Ike had a gift for reducing complex issues to their basics and placing them in larger contexts – an invaluable ability as he framed national security policy in the Cold War. Kennedy's thinking was tactical in nature. A speed-reader who absorbed large quantities of information and easily mastered the specifics of issues, JFK was wary of theory and addressed emerging events on their own terms rather than assimilate them into an overall framework. Bush, though widely derided, has shown a careful ability to sift competing advice, make measured public statements and exercise final decision-making authority.

Emotional intelligence. Some presidents have been masters of their own psyches, productively channelling their feelings into their leadership. Others have been in thrall to their emotions, allowing them to undermine their public performance. (Nixon acted against real and perceived enemies in a way that ultimately destroyed his presidency; Clinton's affair with Monica Lewinsky was a serious error of judgement.) Neither Ike, JFK nor Bush was at the mercy of his emotions, although Kennedy's compulsive womanizing – encompassing not only Marilyn Monroe but also women with links to organized crime – might conceivably have undermined his presidency had it not been cut short by assassination. Bush manages to combine a focus on key priorities with an informality and the maintenance of a relatively 'normal' lifestyle, setting aside time for rest and relaxation.

Political skill. During his years in office, Ike was inaccurately perceived as a political innocent out of his depth in civilian office. He is now recognized as a political sophisticate who chose to exercise influence through intermediaries in order to maintain broad bipartisan public support. JFK was a more conventional practitioner of the art of the possible. When it became evident that Congress was dominated by a coalition of Republicans and conservative Southern Democrats, Kennedy backed off an election-year pledge to take action against racial discrimination. However, he was also prepared to play political 'hardball', as he did in 1962 in using the federal government's anti-trust powers to compel the steel industry to reverse a price increase. Bush not only persuaded Congress to enact his two key priorities – a tax cut and education reform – in his first year, but managed to link together the war on terrorism and economic security at home. The consistent underestimation of his political skills by his political opponents has often worked to his advantage.

Policy vision. Even the most politically skilled president can go astray if his goals are flawed, as were those of LBJ in 1965 when he embarked on an open-ended military involvement in Vietnam without establishing clear goals and probable troop requirements. One of Ike's great strengths was his policy vision. He agreed to run for president out of an interest in putting the nation's security policies on a firm footing, balancing long-term military effectiveness with the need to maintain a strong economy. Because of his broad public support and prestige as a military leader, he was able to resist the demands of hawks in both parties for massive military expenditures and to craft a national security programme to defeat the Soviets in the long run. Despite the lofty rhetoric of JFK's public addresses, he was a quintessential pragmatist. Lacking an overall conception of how to deal with the Soviet threat, he inadvertently alarmed the men in the Kremlin by engaging in an arms build-up and indulging in high-flown rhetoric that they viewed as bellicose. Although he would have preferred not to, Bush reacted to September 11 as if he now knew the overarching purpose that defined his presidency.

Exhibit 6.10   The presidential difference: Eisenhower, Kennedy and George W. Bush *continued*

Organizational capacity. No American chief executive has had a richer background in the organization of human endeavour than the architect of D-Day and the Allied victory in Europe. Ike organized his National Security Council in a manner that maximized his exposure to accurate intelligence and varied advice. JFK scrapped Ike's National Security Council (NSC) process without assessing its utility, seeing it as an unwise application of military staff procedures to the world of politics. Well before he had served 100 days, JFK agreed the ill-fated attempt to invade Cuba at the Bay of Pigs in 1961. He subsequently improved his decision-making procedures but as late as the final month of his life his national security team authorized an ill-considered coup in South Vietnam that destabilized that regime, leaving his successor LBJ with a far more dangerous Southeast Asian problem than Kennedy had inherited from Ike. Bush assembled a mature and experienced team – Cheney and Rumsfeld had served in the Ford administration in the mid-1970s – but ensured that the final decision was always his on foreign policy.

Public communication. Ike, JFK and Bush achieved the highest levels of public support of the 11 chief executives who have been the subject of regular public approval polls. The popularity of the likeable Ike resulted from his wartime prestige, attractive persona and steadiness of leadership, not his public speeches. JFK's popularity was a function of his rhetorical brilliance and his incisive and witty performances in his regular televised news conferences. Only FDR, Reagan and Clinton possessed comparable gifts. But Kennedy was insufficiently attentive to the message conveyed by his speeches. The soaring rhetoric about paying any price and bearing any burden to preserve liberty that played so well at home sat poorly with Nikita Khrushchev, escalating the Cold War to a potentially lethal level in the Cuban Missile Crisis of October 1962. Bush's approval ratings not only achieved record highs post-9/11, but he also sustained them in the 80–90 per cent range for several months. Like Truman in 1945–53, he managed to turn his lack of adeptness with words into an asset, as a testimony of his sincerity and seriousness at a time of crisis.

Exhibit 6.11   Presidential pay: value for money?

1789 $25,000 *1873* $50,000 *1909* $75,000 *1949* $100,000 *1969* $200,000 *2001* $400,000	In 1999, Congress voted the next president an annual salary of $400,000. This was only the fifth time since George Washington (the first American president) that the chief executive's salary had been increased. Had Washington's salary been adjusted for inflation, George W. Bush would have earned $4 million per year for his job. But, in addition to using Air Force One, the president receives $50,000 in expenses (taxable), $100,000 for travel and entertainment (tax free), and retirement benefits. As head of the executive branch of the federal government, charged with implementing national laws and regulations, the president is in charge of approximately three million civilian employees.

Source: *CQ Weekly,* November 20, 1999, p. 2760.

in the modern era can be seen as a mixed blessing, a function partly of the lack of towering personalities or inspiring leaders, but more of the absence of genuinely disturbing national or global crises. (Whether 9/11 will lead to calls for Bush's visage to be carved on to Mount Rushmore remains to be seen.)

Finally, it is worth noting that presidential reputations can alter dramatically with the passage of time, when historical judgement gains the powerful analytic benefit of hindsight. Truman, for example, was never a particularly popular president when he was in the White House and was widely despised by the American public on leaving office in 1953 (he was perceived as having 'lost' China and committed the US to a deadlocked war in Korea). Yet in subsequent years, and especially with the end of the Cold War, Truman has been elevated to 'near great' stature in many surveys for rallying the nation to the banner of anti-communism and setting up the institutional machinery – the National Security Council, Central Intelligence Agency and Department of Defense – to implement containment. Similarly, LBJ was seen as a failure for many years after the end of his term in office in 1969 (having escalated US involvement in Vietnam and seen widespread urban riots and crime at home), yet history has seen some reassessment from liberal analysts. As Lewis Gould puts it:

> Only one post-LBJ president has come close to matching Johnson's ambition, and his failures have played a significant role in raising LBJ's standing. In Bill Clinton the nation found a southern politician whose appetites exceeded Johnson's – and then some. The Lewinsky scandal and Clinton's impeachment made Johnson's personal peccadilloes, from summoning staff members to confer while he was seated on the john to careening around the LBJ ranch in his limousine with a beer in hand, seem almost quaint in their relative innocence and discretion. The Texas twang and Hill Country manner that made Johnson seem boorish and vulgar now seem at least to have the virtue of not being slick. Far more important, the thirty-sixth president

Exhibit 6.12   Presidential greatness

GREAT
Lincoln
Washington
F.D. Roosevelt

NEAR GREAT
Jefferson
Jackson
T. Roosevelt
Wilson
Truman
Polk

HIGH AVERAGE
Eisenhower
John Adams
Kennedy
Cleveland
L.B. Johnson
Monroe
McKinley

AVERAGE
Madison
John Quincy Adams
Harrison
Clinton
Van Buren
Taft
Hayes
George H.W. Bush
Reagan
Arthur
Carter
Ford

BELOW AVERAGE
Taylor
Coolidge
Fillmore
Tyler

FAILURE
Pierce
Grant
Hoover
Nixon
Andrew Johnson
Buchanan
Harding

Source: Schlesinger (1997: 189).

Exhibit 6.13   The modern presidents: a rough guide

Truman. Although he was never popular at the time, Truman's presidency is now regarded as a major, even a 'near great' one. He ended the Second World War, sanctioned the use of the atom bomb in Hiroshima and Nagasaki, and helped to create the Cold War and the public and institutional support for containing international communism. Although, like Democrats before and after him, he was frustrated in domestic politics by the 'Conservative Coalition' of conservative Southern Democrats and Republicans, who opposed his attempts at extending social welfare and civil rights measures, his presidency marked a defining moment in America's postwar history.

Eisenhower. Ike's presidency was not noted for major accomplishments at the time but many now regard it as a notably successful one. Ike presided over a generally prosperous economy, ended the Korean War, and crafted a largely successful national security policy. Some see the 1950s as a time of complacency, others as one when, with the vitally important exception of the civil rights movement, America was at peace with itself before the turbulent 1960s opened up major domestic divisions and conflicts.

Kennedy. Arguably the most overrated and under-achieving president of modern times. Unable to pass significant domestic measures, Kennedy oversaw the disastrous Bay of Pigs invasion of Cuba in 1961 and increased American involvement in Vietnam (where, Oliver Stone's *JFK* notwithstanding, there is little evidence to suggest he would have done anything differently from his successor). Kennedy's great achievement in the Cuban Missile Crisis in October 1962 was significant, but averting a nuclear war whose advent he had partly precipitated hardly amounted to a positive resumé. Revered more after his death than during his life, the perception of the Kennedy presidency as one of great achievement is more about the 'Camelot' myth (invented by Jacqueline Kennedy and then deliberately popularized by sympathetic journalists after JFK's assassination) than policy substance or positive achievements.

Johnson. A landslide victory in 1964 helped Johnson to persuade a compliant (and overwhelmingly Democratic) Congress to enact major pieces of 'Great Society' legislation. The Civil Rights Act and Voting Rights Act were the great victories of the civil rights movement. But Johnson's disastrous escalation of war in Vietnam not only contributed to America's first military defeat, but also stoked fires of inflation and social disquiet at home. Beset by urban unrest, race riots and anti-war demonstrations, LBJ's presidency ended in a shattered fashion when he announced in March 1968 that he would neither seek nor accept the Democratic Party's (re)nomination for president.

Nixon. For all of Nixon's political skills and achievements, the two great scandals of modern American politics – Vietnam, and the disgrace of Watergate and the first and only presidential resignation – overshadowed all else that he achieved. Nixon was a pragmatic conservative who nevertheless signed into law a remarkable raft of liberal measures from health and safety laws to environmental protection and affirmative action programmes (albeit partly to divide his Democratic opponents). Recognition of China, the end of the Vietnam War, and détente with the Soviets amounted to a set of innovative foreign policy achievements. Although few would have agreed at the time, Nixon proved surprisingly effective at bringing the country together at a time of intense domestic controversy and international instability.

Ford. Selected by Nixon as his vice president and then succeeding to the White House when Nixon resigned, Ford's brief two years in office occurred with America in the midst of domestic and international upheaval. Faced by an overwhelmingly Democratic Congress elected in the Watergate-backlash 1974 midterm elections, Ford had little opportunity to craft a meaningful policy agenda, but he nevertheless restored a measure of dignity to the office and only narrowly lost the 1976 election.

Exhibit 6.13   The modern presidents: a rough guide *continued*

Carter. Although some analysts have sought to 're-evaluate' Carter's presidency in a positive light, few such attempts have been convincing. Despite – or perhaps partly because of – his formidable intellect, Carter's presidency was the epitome of a naive and arrogant chief executive, totally inexperienced in the ways of Washington, inept in his handling of the media and obtuse in his understanding of how to appeal either to Congress or the public. Although his presidency saw some political successes (the Panama Canal Treaty, Middle East peace agreements), it is remembered more for galloping inflation and unemployment, the energy crisis, the Soviets invading Afghanistan, and the Iranian hostage crisis. Carter's personal foibles (declaring how, while rafting, his boat was attacked by 'killer rabbits') left him as one of the least presidential chief executives of modern times. Much as his successor was to prove that lack of intellectual gifts was no barrier to presidential success, so Carter demonstrated that intelligence alone was no guarantee of effective leadership.

Reagan. Celebrated by many, demonized by others, Reagan's greatest achievement as president was to restore America's national self-confidence. Reagan's economic policies would have shamed a Keynesian in increasing the budget deficit to $4 trillion by the end of his two terms. His presidency was also marked, after 1981, by decreasing congressional support and increasing bitterness between the White House and Capitol Hill. However, many commentators (some enthusiastically, others reluctantly) credit Reagan with playing the key role in bringing about the beginning of the end of the Cold War. For his admirers, Reagan's defence build-up, sponsorship of the Strategic Defense Initiative (or 'Star Wars'), and implacable anti-communism convinced the Soviets finally to negotiate serious arms reductions. Reagan's sincere hatred of nuclear weapons, his pragmatism and political skill made him open to Mikhail Gorbachev's overtures and able to convince the sceptical Republican Right to accept meaningful reductions in the nuclear arsenal. His presidency has become as much a reverential historic example for conservatives as FDR's is for liberals.

George H.W. Bush. Arguably one of the most talented foreign policy presidents of modern times and the least interested or successful domestic chief executive, Bush was 'an American Tory'. The spiritual opposite of Groucho Marx, he never met a club he didn't want to belong to and his patrician sense of *noblesse oblige* contributed to the lack of empathy many Americans felt towards him by the end of his first term in office. Bush antagonized conservative Republicans by agreeing to tax increases in 1990, despite his 1988 'read my lips: no new taxes' election pledge, and displeased Democrats by a lack of domestic policy initiatives. Yet his foreign policy achievements – assembling and leading an effective coalition against Iraqi forces in Kuwait in 1990–91, presiding over the revolutions in Eastern Europe, the reunification of Germany and the break-up of the USSR (without exploiting them or harming the transformations) – are among the most impressive of postwar US presidents.

Clinton. At least as politically talented as Reagan, and far more intellectually gifted, Clinton remained an enigmatic figure during his two terms as president. Elected as a New Democrat, he governed as an Old Democrat for his first two years in office, only to revert to type in the face of Republican control of Congress from January 1995. His strategy of 'triangulation' helped to win him re-election easily in 1996, but the impeachment proceedings against him in 1998–99 – though unsuccessful – cast him as the lamest of lame duck presidents. His achievements were relatively few and were clouded by his affair with Monica Lewinsky and impeachment. Ironically, he completed the 'Reagan Revolution' with a far-reaching reform of welfare, devolution of responsibilities to the states, and a balanced budget agreement. For progressives, Clinton's greatest failure was his inability to achieve some form of universal health coverage for Americans. Yet to many his lack of clear doctrinal belief – pragmatism to some, absence of principle to others – matched an era of remarkable peace and prosperity in America, the first era of such prolonged good times since the 1920s.

looks like a much larger political leader when measured against the forty-second. Where Johnson risked a great deal to pursue great purposes such as the War on Poverty, the Great Society, and civil rights, knowingly jeopardizing not only his own political welfare but the future of his party, Clinton and his adviser Dick Morris used their political capital for small causes and petty political advantage. (2000: 83)

Reagan, similarly, was not the subject of widespread scholarly admiration when he left office in 1989, his tenure as president having been tarnished by trillion-dollar budget deficits, bitter partisanship with Democrats on Capitol Hill, and the Iran–Contra affair. Yet by the late 1990s, with the end of the Cold War and the succession of tawdry scandals that plagued Clinton, Reagan's reputation underwent something of a critical revival as the re-builder of American self-confidence and the architect of – or, at minimum, an important contributor to – the collapse of the USSR. Clinton's reputation will, no doubt, also undergo a reassessment as the passage of time allows scholars to balance his achievements (not least economic growth and prosperity) alongside his more obvious failures.

FROM IMPERIAL TO IMPOTENT AND BACK AGAIN?

The focus of much contemporary debate about the presidency is not simply the relative lack of 'great' presidents or the changing historical reputations of individual chief executives, but also the possibility that presidential leadership is increasingly vital but now virtually impossible to achieve on a sustained basis. On this view, the presidency has been in steady 'decline' since the era of LBJ and Nixon (and partly because of the experience of those two ill-fated presidencies). Much as the weakening of political parties adversely affected the operations of constitutional government (as we saw in Chapter 3), so challenges to presidential leadership have

arguably caused chronic problems for the policy process.

Conceptions of the relative strength of the presidency have undergone rapid and sometimes dramatic changes. Notions that the presidency was impotent and imperilled in the later 1970s succeeded the publication of Arthur Schlesinger's *The Imperial Presidency* (1974). Schlesinger, a liberal Democrat of the Kennedy era, scolded LBJ and Nixon for their steady centralization and unconstitutional accumulation of personal power in the White House. Yet the subsequent presidencies of Ford and Carter appeared weak and vacillating, Carter even speaking publicly of a crippling 'malaise' in American society. While the Reagan presidency suggested that these conceptions of presidential weakness were fanciful, neither the Reagan, Bush nor the Clinton administrations quelled fears about the many constraints – some legal and formal, others informal, some international, others domestic – that now exist on presidential power.

The concern of many critics remains that, while presidential power amounts to 'the power to persuade', the resources by which to persuade – the incentives that presidents can offer and the sanctions they can impose – are few in number and weak in nature. Scholars have hence discussed phenomena such as the 'fettered presidency', the 'tethered presidency' and even the 'no-win presidency'. The implication is that the 'bully pulpit' is now a bullied pulpit and that a good dose of political Viagra is necessary to allow the presidency to regain its old potency.

But how far does the evidence suggest that presidential leadership is close to impossible to achieve and sustain? Moreover, how far is a strong president either necessary or desirable? While these are difficult and complex questions, a few comparative points are clear.

First, party is immensely important to a president's prospects for successful leadership. Other things being equal, a president with his own party controlling both houses of Congress occupies a much better position than one facing one or both houses in control of the other party. This does not mean that same-party control is a guarantee of presidential success. As Carter and Clinton demonstrated, having the president's party in control of Congress is not a sufficient condition for legislative success. Reagan, conversely, showed that it might not even be a necessary condition if political conditions are favourable and the president's skills are good.

David Mayhew (1991) has even argued that, in terms of major pieces of legislation, divided or undivided control of the federal government does not matter very much at all. Others, however, strongly dispute that argument. Not only does Mayhew's measure not take account of legislation that failed to pass because of split partisan control, but also his approach says little about the content or quality of legislation that was enacted. In many instances, divided party control causes lengthy delays to the passage of new laws and dilutes the content of those that do manage to pass. The compromises necessary to enact new measures may often gut them of any real substance, thereby inhibiting their effectiveness.

The conventional measure of presidential effectiveness in crude legislative terms is *Congressional Quarterly*'s 'presidential success' ratings. This measure is often invoked in efforts to provide 'scientific' evaluations based on measurable data, but it is imperfect. It addresses only those votes where the president has taken a stand in favour or against, without weighting votes according to their relative importance. But while imperfect, many academics use the *CQ* data since they provide a rough indication of a president's success in relation to Congress (see Table 6.5).

What is clear is that the chances of presidential success with Congress hinge partly on the party in control on Capitol Hill. Other things being equal, having the same party in control of the White House and one or both houses of Congress is more likely to assist than impede presidential leadership. LBJ's successes in 1964–65 were strongly assisted by large Democratic majorities. However, this does not guarantee success (Carter

notoriously alienated Congress). Equally, the absence of same-party control does not guarantee failure. In 1980, for example, the fact that the Republicans captured the Senate for the first time since 1954 provided a strong boost to Reagan's claims of a 'mandate' for enacting conservative policies. His success rating of 82.4 was impressive, especially with the Democrats still controlling the House of Representatives. When one Republican gave up his seat and became an Independent in May 2001, thereby giving control of the Senate to the Democrats, the change posed serious obstacles to President George W. Bush's legislative agenda. But Bush nevertheless achieved a rating of 87 per cent success, the highest since LBJ in 1965.

A second factor is the size of the party's majority in Congress. For example, Johnson enjoyed huge Democratic majorities in the House and Senate that facilitated the passage of his Great Society legislation, while Clinton's majorities in 1993–94 were slim and he could not rely – although he tried – on his own party pushing his legislative proposals through. Large partisan majorities are rarely sufficient on their own, as Carter discovered, but they often provide strong ballast to presidents steering the ship of state on new courses.

Moreover, the Clinton presidency provided very clear examples of what occurs when a president's party loses control of Congress. In Clinton's first term, some notable pieces of legislation were enacted with most congressional Democrats opposing their president, the most important example being the passage of the North American Free Trade Agreement (NAFTA) and the General Agreement on Tariffs and Trade (GATT). Clinton relied on a majority of Republicans and a minority of Democrats to push this landmark legislation through. Other than such exceptional examples, the Democratic Party in Congress frequently supported Clinton by decisive margins. Once the GOP won control of Congress in 1995, the president's success ratings dropped precipitously to the lowest ever recorded (at 36.2 per cent). Although

TABLE 6.5 *Congressional Quarterly's* presidential success rate history

President	Year	Success rate	President	Year	Success rate
Eisenhower	1953	89.0	Carter	1977	75.4
	1954	82.8		1978	78.3
	1955	75.0		1979	76.8
	1956	70.0		1980	75.1
	1957	68.0	Median		76.4
	1958	76.0			
	1959	52.0	Reagan	1981	82.4
	1960	65.0		1982	72.4
Median		72.2		1983	67.1
				1984	65.8
Kennedy	1961	81.0		1985	59.9
	1962	85.4		1986	56.1
	1963	87.1		1987	43.5
Median		84.5		1988	47.4
			Median		61.8
Johnson	1964	88.0			
	1965	93.0	Bush	1989	62.6
	1966	79.0		1990	46.8
	1967	79.0		1991	54.2
	1968	75.0		1992	43.0
Median		82.8	Median		51.6
Nixon	1969	74.0	Clinton	1993	86.4
	1970	77.0		1994	86.4
	1971	75.0		1995	36.2
	1972	66.0		1996	55.1
	1973	50.6		1997	53.6
	1974	59.6		1998	50.6
Median		67.0		1999	37.8
				2000	55.0
Ford	1974	58.2	Median		57.6
	1975	61.0			
	1976	53.8			
Median		57.6	Bush (W.)	2001	87.0

Source: *Congressional Quarterly Weekly Report*, January 12, 2002, p. 112.

they recovered significantly thereafter, the president was reduced to claiming that he was 'still relevant'. In the aftermath of his impeachment, the success rate again plummeted to 37.8 per cent in 1999.

A third concern is the internal structure of Congress. As the next chapter argues, Congress is a highly dynamic institution, prone to constant change in its structures and procedures. These changes can both hinder and assist presidents. Growth in the executive branch of government and the vast federal bureaucracy occurred precisely because Congress willed it. But the 1970s saw Congress undergo a process of internal reform – democratization and decentralization – and external reassertion of its constitutional powers against the executive.

The internal reforms saw a variety of changes, the overall effect of which was to undermine the authority of committee chairs and enhance the power of party leaders. With Congress frequently controlled by the party other than that of the president, the White House confronted a supposed partner in government whose approach was often more competitive than cooperative. From 1981 to 1993, for example, Democratic leaders regularly placed the blame for the budget deficit on Republican presidents, demanding that taxes be raised and social programmes protected. With a more partisan approach – and the parties themselves increasingly polarizing – congressional leaders used their independent base of authority to challenge and often change administration policy.

The main external changes occurred with respect to the two key constitutional powers of the purse and sword. In the former, the Budget and Impoundment Control Act of 1974 established two budget committees and the Congressional Budget Office, by which Congress provided itself with an independent base from which to assess economic issues and draw up the federal budget. In essence, presidents no longer controlled the resources that the executive branch could command, with their own requested budgets often 'dead on arrival'. The latter change occurred in 1973 with passage of the War Powers Resolution over President Nixon's veto. This sought to prevent presidents from abusing their war powers while, paradoxically, ceding presidents the legal authority to wage war for 90 days. These reforms, among others, saw Congress attempt to reassert its role in the policy process, albeit with far more success on domestic than foreign policy.

A fourth important consideration is popular approval and presidential 'coat-tails'. Popular approval assists a president by making it harder for legislators to oppose his proposals. In extreme cases, such as Iran–Contra and Monicagate, popularity can even insulate presidents from the threat of impeachment proceedings. Presidential popularity encourages members of Congress to look at presidential proposals in a positive light, since it is in their own interests to do so. This is even more likely to occur if the president has demonstrated strong 'coat-tails' which have helped members of Congress win election.

If, for example, congressman X is elected with 56 per cent of the vote and, in his district, the vote for President Y is 60 per cent, he can safely assume that his re-election will benefit from supporting the president. Similarly, while a popular president cannot assure a member of Congress of re-election, he can assist. The president is still the most prestigious single political actor in America. In this respect, Clinton could hardly command much loyalty or fear among most members of Congress, who had won election with more than the 43 per cent of the vote that Clinton achieved. Similarly, Bush in 2000 failed to win the popular vote, and the majorities in Congress were so close that few lawmakers owed the president a political debt. By contrast, Reagan ran ahead of many members, both Republican and Democrat, in their own districts and states in 1980 and 1984. Given his popularity among their constituents, it made sense for these members to support – at least selectively – the key elements in Reagan's legislative programme. This was not only productive of good relations with the White House, but also good for politics back home too. Reagan, however, was a notable exception. It is rare nowadays for presidents to possess coat-tails of consequence and, as Table 6.6 notes, American history has seen 17 presidents who failed to win a majority of the popular vote entering the White House.

Fifth and finally, the president's own definition of his role is important. In their public pronouncements, their organization of the executive branch, and the key aspects of their legislative programmes, presidents set out what their presidency is intended to be

TABLE 6.6 Minority presidents by popular vote

Year	Candidate	Percentage of popular vote
2000	Bush	48.00
1996	Clinton	49.24
1992	Clinton	43.01
1968	Nixon	43.42
1960	Kennedy	49.72
1948	Truman	49.52
1916	Wilson	49.24
1912	Wilson	41.84
1892	Cleveland	46.05
1888	Harrison	47.82
1884	Cleveland	48.50
1880	Garfield	48.27
1876	Hayes	47.95
1860	Lincoln	39.82
1856	Buchanan	45.28
1848	Taylor	47.28
1844	Polk	49.54
1824	Adams	30.92

'about'. Eisenhower, for instance, adopted a non-partisan image, one crafted to the general management of economic and national security rather than the achievement of specific goals. Carter was notoriously prone to personal involvement in the minutest details of proposed laws. When laws failed to be enacted, or events took a downturn, Carter was hence perceived by many Americans to be personally to blame. By contrast, Reagan consistently projected an image of being concerned by fundamental principles, not details, which should be left to subordinates to determine and implement. When things went pear-shaped, as in Iran–Contra, Reagan's denial of knowledge was plausible to many Americans precisely because he had crafted an image in which total command by the chief executive was not expected to be the case. Hence Reagan was seen as not being culpable for policy failures rather than, like Carter, incapable of political leadership.

AFTER THE POSTMODERN PRESIDENCY

Richard Rose (1988) coined the term 'the postmodern president' to describe the new nature of presidential leadership in the 1990s and the three strategies – going Washington, going public, and going international – available for presidents to seek political success. Yet more than a decade on from Rose's work, the American presidency has changed still further. In some respects, there is no reason why we should not expect the dynamism inherent in American politics not to encompass the presidency also. But in virtue of its unique position, the changes that shape the presidency have an especially profound importance.

Expectations of presidential leadership – often encouraged by candidates who inflate the public's sense of what the institution can achieve if only placed in the right hands – remain remarkably, and often unrealistically,

Exhibit 6.14   Should President Clinton have been impeached?

Unlike the UK's prime minister, an American president enjoys a fixed term of office and can only be removed by an exceptional process. The Constitution confers on Congress the power to remove a president by impeachment. The House must draw up and present the charges; the Senate then conducts the trial and votes on guilt or innocence. Only two presidents have faced impeachment proceedings by Congress: Andrew Johnson and Bill Clinton (Nixon resigned before the entire House formally voted on these). Both were narrowly acquitted after a trial by the Senate. However, some observers argue that Clinton should have been impeached. Much of the debate turns on how much weight was accorded the substantive scandal (Clinton's affair) versus the procedural scandal (the alleged attempts to cover up, obstruct justice and commit perjury). Just as in Watergate, and as is often the case, the real political problem stemmed from the procedural rather than the substantive scandal.

YES. The issue in the impeachment was not, as was popularly thought, sex or adultery. Rather, it was the obstruction of justice and perjury that followed the affair with Lewinsky. Clinton deliberately lied on oath in his deposition in the Paula Jones case and in his testimony to the Starr Grand Jury. Were ordinary citizens found guilty of these very grave charges, they would go to jail. For a republic founded on the equality before the law of every citizen, making an exemption is not legitimate. Moreover, not only is the president – like each citizen – bound by the rule of law, but he also takes an oath under the Constitution faithfully to execute (implement) the laws. (He also takes an oath to uphold the dignity of the office of president.) Not to impeach him sent a message that presidents could lie, obstruct justice and prevent investigations and are above the law. Comparing Monicagate to Watergate or Iran–Contra was irrelevant, since the issue in impeachment is not 'was it worse than case X?' but simply 'does the action merit impeachment?' As Clinton himself conceded on his last day in office, his testimony had 'failed to walk the fine line' between not being forthcoming and telling outright lies.

NO. The case against fell into two broad themes. One was that even if Clinton had committed the alleged offences, they were not impeachable. This was either because they were relatively unimportant in absolute terms or because they were far less important in relative terms than the Watergate episode (and, arguably, the Iran–Contra scandal that engulfed Reagan in 1986–87). A second case was that Clinton was the victim of a politically motivated vendetta or 'vast right-wing conspiracy' to overturn the election results of 1992 and 1996. In fact, the results could not be 'overturned' since, even had Clinton been removed from office, his replacement would not have been George H.W. Bush or Bob Dole but his twice-elected vice president, Albert Gore. However, the fact that the Senate could not muster a majority for either the perjury or obstruction of justice charge suggested that the case against Clinton was not considered sufficiently serious – either by the Senate or the public – to remove him from office.

high. Each presidential election reinforces the perception that the White House, if occupied wisely, can solve America's problems. Presidents are expected to make America safe and secure militarily, to keep the United States as the pre-eminent world power, to avoid unnecessary wars but wage just interven-tions, to ensure economic prosperity, rising standards of living, to set a shining example as the 'first family' for all other Americans, to provide moral leads, and to speak eloquently for and to the nation at times of national crisis or mourning (be it the Challenger space shuttle disaster in 1986, the bombing of the federal building in Oklahoma City in 1995, or the attacks of September 11). No other political office in the world labours under such heavy burdens. It is hardly surprising that the anticipation of so many positive results often occasions much disappointed soul-searching when presidents fail to match up to a singularly demanding set of expectations.

CONCLUSION

Evaluating presidents may seem a subjective and futile matter. The point of such exercises is not so much to 'grade' them but to learn from them. An understanding of past presidents provides voters with benchmarks for assessing future aspirants to the Oval Office. It also provides a reservoir of institutional memory, making it less likely that new chief executives will repeat their predecessors' errors and more likely that they will profit from their successes. What we are concerned with here is not the content of their programmes or policies (liberal, conservative or otherwise) but simply whether, how and why they managed to achieve their main policy goals in a supremely difficult political and institutional environment.

As Jones (1995) notes, American government is a 'separated system', not a presidential one. But within that separated system, the president's pre-eminence remains a key fact of political life. However much the presidency may resemble an elected monarchy, the president can abdicate neither his political responsibilities nor his unique position in the governmental system. The occupant of the White House cannot compel others whose support he requires to do what he wishes – in this sense, the office is the most difficult political job in the world. Even after September 11, President Bush had to persuade Congress to endorse his preferences on matters from trade policy to the environment, and he frequently found himself stymied by Democrats in the House and Senate during 2001–2. However, only the president can articulate and cajole sufficient political support among the key institutions that he cannot command – especially but not only Congress – to see urgent, desirable and necessary measures enacted and implemented effectively.

Woodrow Wilson wrote in 1907 that 'The President is at liberty, both in law and conscience, to be as big a man as he can.' But, as Lyndon Johnson noted in 1964, 'The presidency has made every man who occupied it, no matter how small, bigger than he was; and no matter how big, not big enough for its demands.' As the size of government has grown and the world responsibilities of the United States have increased, the president's task has become more burdensome and difficult to satisfy. But it is not thankless. Skilled and shrewd chief executives can exploit the array of formal and informal resources the president possesses to lead. The expenditure of political capital by a president can make the difference between success and failure on measures as varied as free trade, tax cuts and gun control. As the next chapter notes, however, the view from Capitol Hill is frequently one that sees America – and the world – through markedly different lenses than that of the White House.

FURTHER READING

Charles O. Jones, *Separate but Equal Branches: Congress and the Presidency* (1995) is an excellent collection of essays by the leading proponent of the idea that American government must be regarded as a separated system, not a presidential one.

Richard Neustadt, *Presidential Power and the Modern Presidents: The*

Politics of Leadership from Roosevelt to Reagan (1990) is the classic statement of the presidency's 'power to persuade'.

Colin Campbell and Bert Rockman (eds), *The Clinton Legacy* (2000) is an excellent collection of essays on most aspects of the presidency of Bill Clinton.

Fred Greenstein, *The Presidential Difference: Leadership Style from FDR to Clinton* (2000) is a chronological comparison of modern presidents, emphasizing the importance of the individual skills of the occupant of the White House.

Ernest May and Philip Zelikow, *The Kennedy Tapes: Inside the White House during the Cuban Missile Crisis* (1997) comprises edited White House conversations that show how JFK and his key advisors approached and resolved the greatest crisis of the twentieth century.

Robert Shogun, *The Double-Edged Sword: How Character Makes and Ruins Presidents, from Washington to Clinton* (2000) is a survey of several presidents that emphasizes the importance of 'character' in shaping presidential performance.

WEB LINKS

The White House
http://www.whitehouse.gov

Office of Management and the Budget
http://www.whitehouse.gov/WH/EOP/omb

General resources on the presidency
http://www.lib.umich.edu/govdocs/fedprs
http://www.theamericanpresidency.net
http://www.c-span.org/executive/links.asp
http://www.netcolony.com/news/presidents

Resources on the vice presidency
www.vicepresidents.com

Department of the Treasury
www.ustreas.gov

National Archives and Records Administration (links to presidential libraries)
www.nara.gov/1

QUESTIONS

- Can the president provide effective political leadership?

- Is successful leadership by a president more a matter of individual aptitudes and skills or institutional constraints?

- What are the main constraints on presidential leadership?

- Compare and contrast one presidential 'success' and one presidential 'failure.' What accounts for the difference?

- Has the presidency moved from being 'imperial' to 'impotent', or the reverse?

7 Congress

Reader, suppose you were an idiot; and suppose you were a member of Congress; but I repeat myself.

Mark Twain

It is widely believed in Washington that it would take Congress thirty days to make instant coffee.

David Brinkley (Harris, 1995: 1)

- The US Constitution
- Bicameralism: House and Senate
- Committees and Leadership
- Parties and Caucuses
- The Electoral Connection
- Three Eras of Congress
- In defence of Congress: a qualifying note
- Conclusion

Chapter Summary

Congress lies at the heart of the federal government. The national legislature was described in detail in Article I of the US Constitution and remains an extremely powerful assembly today – the most powerful national parliament of any liberal democracy. Divided into two co-equal chambers that have markedly different numbers of members, modes of composition, term lengths and internal procedures, as many as 50 veto points exist in Congress before a law can be passed and sent to the White House for signature. This means that Congress is often criticized for being slow, obstructive and conservative – easily prone to resisting but rarely able or eager to pass innovative new proposals. Federal lawmakers are frequently said to be parochial, invariably looking to their districts or states, prior and future financial contributors, and the next election to determine their legislative behaviour, not to the 'national interest' – thereby leading to compromises, deals and concessions that result in lowest common denominator fudges that may not produce the optimal public policies to address America's social and economic problems. But such criticisms need to be strongly qualified. Congress is both a lawmaking body and a representative one. In reflecting the priorities and preferences of a remarkably heterogeneous and diverse nation comprising many competing social and economic interests, conflicting public priorities and divergent preferences, Congress is necessarily forced to confront a system in which compromise, consensus and conciliation are the necessary order of the day in legislative politics. However much Congress can legitimately be criticized, its role in American government is vital to ensuring that as many social interests as possible are represented at the national level, forging broadly acceptable laws, legitimating public policies and maintaining America's political stability. In representing interests, legislating and overseeing the activities of the executive branch of government, Congress performs crucial functions that few legislative assemblies elsewhere now match.

How often do you get a recurring sense that those of us outside the United States do not celebrate the wonders of dairy goats often enough these days? Or that we have neglected the many joys of asparagus? Or forgotten the aesthetic beauty of tap-dancing? Americans are luckier than Europeans in this respect, since their national legislature, the United States Congress, displays a remarkably acute sensitivity to these matters. So much so, in fact, that fully one-quarter of all public bills enacted by the Congress during the 1980s were so-called 'commemorative resolutions', that is resolutions that specify a particular day, week or month for national celebrations of a specific activity, product or theme. These included: National Dairy Goat Awareness Week, National Asparagus Month, and National Tap-Dance Day. The 99th Congress (1985–86) passed 307 such commemorative bills and resolutions, 46 per cent of all public laws enacted in the two years that it sat. Small wonder, perhaps, that most Americans take a rather dim view of the collective behaviour of their national legislators: as Mark Twain once scathingly put it, America's 'only native criminal class'.

Curiously, however, those same Americans are extremely fond of sending back their particular representatives and senators to serve again on Capitol Hill, so much so that, in several recent congressional elections, the proportion of those incumbent members of the House of Representatives who wanted to be re-elected and successfully achieved re-election reached highs of 98 per cent in 1988, 1998 and 2000. In the Senate, the average figure for re-election was only slightly lower, in the high-80 per cent range.

In examining Congress, this chapter seeks to reconcile these seemingly incongruous facts – that individual lawmakers experience pervasive unease about their re-election chances yet win re-election regularly by large margins, and that in doing so the public's mostly negative view of Congress as a whole is confirmed. Along the way, we encounter an incredibly parochial legislature whose members sometimes appear congenitally unable to look beyond the preferences of their particular constituents to the national interest, as well as an institution that seeks persistently to articulate as accurately and fully as possible the prevailing sentiments of a heterogeneous American people.

As Table 7.1 notes, Congress is not only perennially unpopular among the public (even in wartime), but it is also a reliable beast of burden to all presidents, regardless of party. Occupants of the White House typically begin their term approaching relations with Congress as a labour of love, often to

TABLE 7.1 Public confidence in American institutions (2000 v. 2002)

2000		2002	
Institution	**(%)**	**Institution**	**(%)**
The military	64	The military	71
Organized religion	56	The White House	50
The police	54	The Supreme Court	41
The Supreme Court	47	The executive branch	33
Banks	46	Colleges and universities	33
The presidency	42	Medicine	29
The medical system	40	Television news	24
Public schools	37	Organized religion	23
Newspapers	37	**Congress**	**22**
Television news	36	Wall Street	19
Big business	29	Major companies	16
Organized labour	25	The press	16
Congress	**24**	Law firms	13
The criminal justice system	24	Organized labour	11
Health maintenance organizations	16		

Note: the 2000 column is the percentage of respondents expressing 'a great deal' or 'a lot' of confidence; the 2002 column is the percentage expressing 'a great deal'.

N = 1,021 (2000); 1,011 (2002)

Sources: Gallup Poll, June 25, 2000; *National Journal*, July 15, 2000, p. 2329; Harris Interactive poll, January 21, 2002; *National Journal*, February 9, 2002, p. 403.

end up seething at a once-blossoming relationship that has broken down irretrievably. For Congress possesses a distinctive political constituency that affords the national legislature an independence and power shared by no other parliament or assembly in liberal democratic regimes. In legislating and making (rather than simply influencing) public policy, overseeing the executive and judicial branches of government, and representing citizens' views (in all their diversity), Congress functions as a genuinely multifunctional parliament in ways that are true of no other western assembly today – for both better and worse for American democracy.

THE US CONSTITUTION

The symbolism of dedicating the first article of the Constitution to Congress offers an important indication of the significance the

Founding Fathers placed on the position of the national legislature within America's federal government. As noted in Chapter 2, Congress possesses the two crucial powers of 'the purse' (to raise and spend money) and 'the sword' (to declare – and fund – wars and regulate the armed forces of the United States). Other formal powers are also parcelled out to one or other chamber exclusively, most notably the Senate's particular power to confirm executive appointments to the Supreme Court, the Cabinet and ambassadors, and to ratify international treaties negotiated by the executive branch.

None of these powers would amount to much, however, were Congress dominated by a disciplined political party holding a majority of legislative seats, in the manner typical of the UK. In this respect, Congress remains a remarkable exception to the general pattern of relative legislative weakness in industrialized democracies. The twentieth century saw a remarkable eclipse of the power of national parliaments in most democracies, in large part owing to the development of organized and disciplined political parties that could compel their members to vote together in support of particular programmes, policies and leaders. With a majority of seats in the legislative assembly, either as a single-party or – as typically occurs in continental Europe and Israel – a coalition government of two or more parties, parliamentary government in the western world has mostly become 'party government'.

This is much less the case in America. First, Congress possesses a constitutionally-mandated independent base of political authority. The decentralized and fragmented system of government established by the Constitution has helped strongly to augment the specific congressional powers conferred by it to Congress. Secondly, since members of Congress run for election as individuals, relatively little in the way of a common programme can be imposed on them by political leaders – either by congressional leaders or the White House. Thirdly, jealously guarding their rights and privileges as individual lawmakers, Congress is collectively difficult to control – for congressional leaders almost as much as the president and regardless of which party possesses the Oval Office or commands majorities in the House of Representatives and Senate. With neither the president nor party leaders able to dissolve Congress and call for new elections (in the manner that a British prime minister can dissolve the House of Commons and a French president can dissolve the National Assembly), members of Congress enjoy an enviable, enduring and powerful political independence.

Such is the strength and complexity of Congress that scholars such as Roger Davidson (1992) argue that, conceptually, rather than one institution, 'two Congresses' exist. One is the Congress that acts collectively, as a lawmaking body for the entire nation. The laws that it makes – provided the president

signs them or Congress overrides his vetoes – are applicable nationwide and enforceable by the executive branch (albeit open to constitutional challenge in state and federal courts). Another Congress, though, is the representative one – the collection of 535 voting members who reach the two houses of Congress by very different routes, serve different constituencies for different term lengths, possess distinct political ambitions, and whose legislative careers ultimately rest less on what Congress does collectively in terms of lawmaking than on how well they serve their particular districts and states. Each legislator is recruited and elected separately, faces distinct incentives and pursues political goals that are largely independent of the institution as a whole.

This profound and inherent tension between the collective institution and the individuals who serve there is a constant, complex and, for presidents, congressional leaders and the American public, a deeply problematic one. It is also one that is exacerbated by Congress being composed of two co-equal houses.

AMERICAN BICAMERALISM: HOUSE AND SENATE

Like the Westminster parliament, Congress is a bicameral legislature, divided into two chambers: the House of Representatives and the Senate. Unlike Westminster, however, where the House of Commons clearly dominates the House of Lords, these national American chambers are co-equal in their status and authority. Strictly speaking, there is no 'upper' or 'lower' chamber, although the Senate is undoubtedly the more prestigious of the two (hence it is common for members of the House to seek election to the Senate, but the opposite almost never occurs). As Table 7.2 notes, such co-equality is comparatively unusual among bicameral democratic legislatures today, where the lower house typically possesses more political influence than its 'upper' counterpart.

TABLE 7.2 A sample of liberal democracies using different legislative arrangements

Nation	Number of houses	House with more power?
Brazil	2	Roughly equal powers between the two houses
Canada	2	Lower house dominates
France	2	Lower house dominates
Germany	2	Lower house dominates
India	2	Lower house dominates
Italy	2	Roughly equal powers between the two houses
Japan	2	Lower house dominates
Portugal	1	Only one house
Spain	2	Lower house dominates
Sweden	1	Only one house
UK	2	Lower house dominates
USA	2	Roughly equal powers between the two houses

Although co-equal, however, the two chambers differ dramatically in crucial respects:

- *Composition.* The House is made up of 435 voting representatives. The Senate currently comprises 100 members, two for each of the 50 American states. This means that the need for collective mechanisms and extensive rules is much greater in the House than the Senate, which traditionally has had a more 'clubbish', exclusive and individualist feel to its composition, procedures and operating norms.
- *Basis of representation.* House seats are apportioned on a population basis and reapportioned after every ten-yearly census. Although, since the Supreme Court apportionment rulings of the 1960s, House seats are roughly equal in population (approximately 550,000 each), states with larger populations are accorded more House seats. Hence, as of 2003, the relatively unpopulous Mississippi has four congressional seats, while populous California has 53. By contrast, Senate seats are apportioned on a strictly territorial basis that pays no attention to population levels or shifts therein: all states, no matter how large or small their populations

or geographic area, and no matter what population changes occur (in- and out-migration) are given two senators each. Thus Wyoming, with approximately half a million people, and California, with over 30 million (approximately 12 per cent of the total US population), both have two senators each. The result is that, in terms of representation, smaller states are significantly overrepresented in the Senate (see Table 7.3).

- *Term length.* House terms are two years, with all 435 members running for re-election at the same time. Senate terms are six years in length, but the elections are staggered, so that only one-third of the senators (33 or 34 of them) are running for election in a given two-year cycle. In theory, though not necessarily in practice these days, this means that, compared to House members, senators can devote more time to policymaking and legislative work free from the constraints of constantly thinking about re-election.
- *Special provisions.* Only the Senate has the constitutional right to confirm executive appointments and judicial nominations and to ratify treaties. Combined with the

TABLE 7.3   State representation in the Senate

Overrepresented states (N = 31)	States represented approximately according to one person, one vote (N = 5)	Underrepresented states (N = 14)
Wyoming	Maryland	Indiana
Alaska	Washington	Massachusetts
Vermont	Tennessee	Virginia
North Dakota	Wisconsin	Georgia
Delaware	Missouri	North Carolina
South Dakota		New Jersey
Montana		Michigan
Rhode Island		Ohio
Idaho		Illinois
Hawaii		Pennsylvania
New Hampshire		Florida
Nevada		Texas
Maine		New York
New Mexico		California
Nebraska		
Utah		
West Virginia		
Arkansas		
Kansas		
Mississippi		
Iowa		
Oregon		
Oklahoma		
Connecticut		
Colorado		
South Carolina		
Arizona		
Kentucky		
Alabama		
Louisiana		
Minnesota		

Source: Lee and Oppenheimer (1999: 162).

other factors above, this makes the Senate a more prestigious body, and a Senate seat more desirable, than the House. It also means that Senate elections tend to be more competitive than House elections. More politicians want to get there, more funds are required to win election campaigns, and a small partisan change in seats (such as six or seven) can alter which party has a majority in the Senate. In the House, by contrast, a larger shift in seats is typically required to shift party control in an environment where, given the entrenched advantages of incumbency, it is relatively unusual to see many election upsets at all.

The House of Representatives

Traditionally, the House of Representatives has been viewed as the populist body in national American government, displaying more sensitivity to the public mood – and swings in it – than the Senate. With all of its members subject to re-election every two years, the Framers of the Constitution deliberately intended that the House be close to popular opinion. Contrary to the Framers' intentions, however, the House has also been the chamber where party plays a crucial role in organizing national legislative life. With 435 members, the need to formulate rules, procedures and norms by which the House can go about its legislative business is greater than in the Senate. Without some type of central direction, the House would simply be unable to coordinate its legislative business, and would thereby adversely affect the interests of all its members. The cost of some centralized control is therefore bearable for most House members most of the time, given the much higher price of legislative anarchy.

But this does not mean that legislative life proceeds smoothly. Because House members reflect very diverse constituencies (compare the one seat for Montana, of 147,046 square miles with a seat encompassing just ten square miles in Harlem, for example) and face election every two years, the pressure to tend constantly and carefully to constituency business is immense. If a conflict arises between constituency priorities and preferences and party goals, the House member will conventionally 'vote the district' (likewise, senators invariably 'vote the state'). This means that although party discipline exists in the House, it is a more fragile and unreliable entity than is the case in, say, the UK House of Commons. Legislative parties must cajole and persuade their members to

Exhibit 7.1   The 'Contract with America', 1994

1. The Fiscal Responsibility Act had two parts, entailing amendments to the Constitution: the balanced budget amendment and the line-item veto.
2. The Taking Back Our Streets Act was also known as the anti-crime package, which eventually divided into several bills dealing with victim restitution, the exclusionary rule, prison construction and law enforcement.
3. The Personal Responsibility Act dealt with welfare reform, giving more discretion to the states and providing restrictions on eligibility.
4. The Family Reinforcement Act provided tax breaks for families and the elderly, child support enforcement and penalties for child pornography.
5. The American Dream Restoration Act repealed the marriage tax penalty (married couples paid more in taxes than they would if single and making two incomes) and established a tax credit for children.
6. The National Security Restoration Act prohibited foreign (UN) command of US troops and the use of defence cuts to finance social programmes; it also proposed developing an anti-ballistic missile (ABM) system.
7. The Senior Fairness Act raised the Social Security earnings limit, under which seniors who earn over a certain amount of money lose a percentage of their Social Security benefits, and also repealed the 1993 tax increases on Social Security benefits.
8. The Job Creation and Wage Enhancement Act gave incentives to small businesses, cut the capital gains tax, and eliminated 'unfunded mandates' (requiring states or businesses to engage in specified activities without reimbursing them).
9. The Common Sense Legal Reforms Act was designed to discourage litigation. It limited punitive damages, instituted 'loser pays' rules and limited product liability.
10. The Citizen Legislatures Act limited the terms of both senators and representatives.

support party positions and can do relatively little if they fail to do so. Only on rare occasions, such as following the Republican victories in 1994, in which most GOP candidates for the House signed up to party-style manifesto, 'The Contract with America' (see Exhibit 7.1), does a party seek the type of unified collective approach common in Europe.

The Senate

Compared to the House, the Senate is a much more individualistic body. Writers in the 1950s even referred to it as a 'citadel' or 'secret club' whose members were proud of their elevated position and jealously guarded their individual prerogatives. Party counted for less and the individual rights of senators were highly respected. The Senate was viewed – not least by its own members – as an 'incubator' for future presidents, where they would learn and refine their political skills and acquire the knowledge and expertise necessary for the highest office. Presidents Truman, Kennedy, Johnson and Nixon all served in the Senate before going on to the White House.

The Senate was also intended by the Framers to be a brake on the House. With longer terms, staggered elections, and (originally) an indirect method of election, the Senate was supposed to represent an American-style House of Lords. Senators of experience, wisdom and public spirit would act to cool the passions of the popular House.

Although, with ratification of the Seventeenth Amendment in 1913, senators have since been popularly elected, the basic notion of the Senate as a moderating influence has remained powerful. Not only do senators have longer term lengths but also, in virtue of representing entire states rather than districts, they generally need to consider wider sets of interests than House members (the important exceptions are those relatively lightly populated states that possess only one House member and two senators, such as Wyoming and Vermont).

COMMITTEES AND LEADERSHIP

In a notably, and perhaps mercifully, rare occurrence, a political scientist (at Princeton University) later became President of the United States. Woodrow Wilson wrote in his 1885 classic study, *Congressional Government*, that: 'Congress in session is Congress on public exhibition, whilst Congress in its committee rooms is Congress at work. Whatever is to be done must be done by, or through, the committee.'

Until recently, that description remained valid. Unlike many assemblies that lost their independence during the twentieth century as disciplined political parties developed, Congress genuinely makes its own laws. But the arena in which the details of their content is determined has traditionally been less the floor of the House than the committee

Exhibit 7.2 Categories of committees in the House of Representatives, 2001–02

- *Prestige Committees*: Appropriations, Budget, Rules, Ways and Means
- *Policy Committees*: Education and Workforce, Energy and Commerce, Financial Services, Government Reform, International Relations, Judiciary.
- *Constituency Committees*: Armed Services, Resources, Science, Small Business, Transportation and Infrastructure, Veterans' Affairs.
- *Miscellaneous Committees*: House Administration, Standards of Official Conduct, Select Intelligence.

system, comprising full standing committees and their various subcommittees, alongside ad hoc committees and special committees. In this sense, Congress is itself a highly decentralized legislature within a powerfully decentralized federal and separated system of government. Yet again, this creates still more barriers to efficient collective action in American government by fragmenting authority and creating competing power centres.

Most standing (or permanent) committees are divided on a basis similar to that of the overall chamber. Crucially, the majority party has majorities on the committees and can, if not too divided, therefore have a major say in what emerges. But the motivations for joining particular committees also varies with the district or state politics of the member concerned. Some committees, such as Agriculture and Armed Services, are regarded as 'constituency service' committees. Members join them typically to try to protect and promote their home constituency's interest. 'Prestige' committees, such as Appropriations, are attractive because of the power they wield within Congress. Still other 'policy committees', such as Education and Workforce, tend to attract lawmakers interested primarily in 'good public policy'.

The result is not only that all committees are different, but also that, depending on their focus and composition, they may be highly unrepresentative of the overall chamber in terms of ideological leanings and legislative approaches. For example, lawmakers from urban and financial centres tend to be attracted to the banking committees, while members representing constituencies with significant military interests (such as ports or army bases) tend to prefer the Armed Services committees and those from farming areas seek out the Agriculture committees. Since these committees conventionally draw up the laws that the chambers then vote on, the contents of bills can often comprise parochial rather than national imprints.

As Exhibit 7.3 illustrates, the process of enacting a bill into law is a lengthy and circuitous one that invariably demands compromises and concessions within committees, between committees, across the two main parties and between the two legislative chambers. Moreover, as Exhibit 7.4 demonstrates, even in the midst of crisis and war, the requirement for deals to be struck between competing interests and viewpoints is unavoidable if legislation is to be enacted.

Unlike the government-dominated committees at Westminster, the influence of congressional committees is substantial. They can:

- Identify and research public problems.
- Examine proposals introduced by individual lawmakers, party leaders and the president.
- Convene hearings at which concerned parties may testify.
- Publish reports of their findings.
- Draft legislation.
- Investigate executive actions and individuals.
- Recommend or reject executive branch nominees.

In sum, committees are key generators of laws from consumer protection to transport programmes. Committee action can jeopardize a president's prospective appointments (in 2002, for example, the Senate Judiciary Committee refused to vote to send President Bush's nomination of the conservative Mississippian Judge, Charles Pickering, to the floor of the Senate for confirmation). Committees also have the power to hold hearings, investigations and to subpoena witnesses. Some landmark moments in American history – from the Senate Judiciary Committee's investigation of Watergate in 1973–74 to the House Judiciary Committee's drawing up the charges of impeachment against President Clinton in 1998 – have featured witnesses testifying before congressional committees. Independent of party leaders and the executive branch, lawmakers can and do act on a myriad of issues and concerns that they deem worthy of investigation or reform. That many

Exhibit 7.3 How a bill becomes law

House	Senate
Bill introduced in House and assigned to committee(s).	Bill introduced in Senate and assigned to committee(s).
Committee refers bill to subcommittee(s).	Committee refers bill to subcommittee(s).
Subcommittee studies bill. If approved bill goes to full committee.	Subcommittee studies bill. If approved, bill goes to full committee.
Full committee considers bill. If approved it goes to the Rules Committee.	Full committee considers bill. If approved, it goes to the Senate floor.
Rules Committee issues rule to govern floor debate and sends to House floor.	
Full House votes on rules attached to the bill for debate.	
House debates and votes on passage.	Senate debates and votes on passage.
If approved and is different from the Senate version, bill goes to a House–Senate conference committee.	If approved and different from the House version, bill goes to House–Senate conference committee.

House–Senate conference committee reconciles two versions of bill and sends the identical compromise bill back to House and Senate.

House votes to approve bill.	Senate votes to approve bill.

President signs or vetoes bill. Congress can override veto by two-thirds majority vote in both houses.

Bill becomes law (subject to interpretation in case of private litigation in state and federal courts).

are lawyers themselves (see Table 7.4) assists that process.

PARTIES AND CAUCUSES

Committees and subcommittees are the key decentralizing forces in Congress that craft the details of legislation but they face a competing pressure towards more centralized action: the political parties and, especially, party leaders. The tension between what members do on their committees and subcommittees and what they seek as partisans is crucial to the functioning of Congress as a whole. For several reasons, as explained below, the traditional 'textbook' picture of committee dominance has recently been partially eroded. In particular, since 1981, as the parties have steadily become more ideologically coherent internally – and hence more opposed to each other more often (especially in the context of divided party control of the White House and Capitol Hill) – congressional party leaders have accrued heightened powers in the legislative system.

Although legislators sit on committees that occupy much of their legislative life, members of Congress have multiple loyalties. In particular, any federal legislator must balance four forces that can pull in different directions: constituency, committees, party and congressional caucuses.

Exhibit 7.4   Airport security: to federalize or not to federalize?

In the aftermath of September 11, 2001, the American aviation industry was hit hard by loss of business and forced to make substantial redundancies. However, a key issue also arose concerning the security of airports and, in particular, whether the private workers who screened passengers and baggage on to planes should now become government workers. Also, should all airports (no matter how big or small) be subject to the same standards? And should the standards and training be set by an existing agency or a new agency (and, if the latter, should this be within the law-enforcing Department of Justice or the Department of Transportation?). In October, the Democratic-controlled Senate unanimously voted to federalize airport screening staff, but the Republican-controlled House disagreed, preferring to keep them as private employees. Ultimately, in November 2001, both houses passed a compromise bill that:

- Federalized all airport passenger and baggage screening within one year, but allowed airports to choose private screeners after three years.
- Set uniform airport security standards and training standards for screeners.
- Created a Transportation Security Agency with the Transportation Department.

The measure demonstrated that Congress can move with rapidity, but that even then successful measures invariably demand compromise between conflicting groups of lawmakers within and between the House and the Senate.

Constituency considerations invariably come first in terms of priority, and often underpin the choice of a particular committee assignment. But party considerations are increasingly important, too. All members of Congress belong to one or other party caucus – the groups of all rank-and-file Democrats or Republicans. Since the later 1970s, party caucuses have become increasingly important forums for discussing party policy, strategies and tactics, for ratifying who gets to chair committees (if the party is in the majority in either chamber) and for holding party leaders to account. Party leaders, in turn, can assist rank-and-file members through providing contacts, information and assisting them in achieving desirable committee assignments. Although party leaders cannot compel legislators to toe a party line, they can and do encourage a modest but still significant level of party discipline and coherence in Congress.

Beyond party caucuses, all members of the legislature belong to at least a handful of (mostly, though not all, non- or bipartisan) congressional caucuses. These organizations are like-minded bodies of legislators that come together to serve a common purpose. Typically, they have both an interest group and a labour union role. As interest groups, caucuses try to promote certain causes within the legislature, such as arms control or trade protection for mushroom farmers. As labour unions, they often try to help to get their members on particular committees, to secure promotions and to be elected to party leadership positions. Achieving the latter personnel objective is one attractive method of furthering the former policy goal.

Caucuses vary in size, role and influence. None can be said to be consistently influential but several have achieved notable successes, particularly in getting Congress to consider particular issues. For example, the Black Caucus has had some effect on issues such as sanctions against South Africa in 1986 and Haiti in 1994 (Singh, 1998). The Caucus on Women's Issues has managed to get issues such as breast cancer, childcare and hate crimes on the agenda of Congress (even though its members have often then divided over the most appropriate solutions). The

TABLE 7.4   Lawmakers' occupations, 107th Congress, 2001–02

	House			Senate			
	D	**R**	**Total**	**D**	**R**	**Total**	**Total**
Actor/Entertainer		1	1		1	1	2
Aeronautics		1	1	1		1	2
Agriculture	8	17	25	1	5	6	31
Artistic/Creative		1	2*				2*
Business/Banking	56	103	159	8	16	24	183
Clergy	1	1	2		1	1	3
Education	53	38	92*	8	8	16	108*
Engineering	1	8	9				9
Health Care	3	1	4				4
Homemaker	1	1	2	1		1	3
Journalism	1	7	8	1	6	7	16*
Labour	1	1	2		1	1	3
Law	84	71	156**	28	25	53	210**
Law Enforcement	7	3	10				10
Medicine	6	8	14		3	3	17
Military		2	2		1	1	3
Professional Sports		3	3		1	1	4
Politics	70	56	126	18	10	28	154
Real Estate	2	22	24	2	2	4	28
Secretarial		2	2				2
Technical/Trade	1	2	3				3
Miscellaneous	1	5	6				6

* Total includes Independent Bernard Sanders of Vermont.
** Total includes Independent Virgil Goode of Virginia.
Note: Some members say they have more than one occupation.
Source: *CQ Weekly*, January 20, 2001, p. 181.

Arts Caucus has had some successes in defending federal grants to institutions such as the National Endowment for the Arts.

Taken together, then, each legislator has a complex set of loyalties, pressures and responsibilities. First and foremost, however, each federal lawmaker must attend assiduously to the district or state that sent him or her to Capitol Hill.

THE ELECTORAL CONNECTION

In Chapter 4, the importance of incumbency was noted. Here we return again to this cru-cial aspect of congressional life. The central fact of congressional elections is that turnover is mainly caused by voluntary retirement, not electoral defeat. With extensive staff, subsidized travel, heavy financial support from PACs, and an appropriate 'home style', most federal lawmakers tenaciously exploit their electoral connection to their home districts and states on an ongoing basis during their legislative terms. Indeed, such was public concern with this that 22 states passed laws limiting the terms of office of their elected officials, but these were ruled unconstitutional by the Supreme Court in *US Term Limits v. Thornton* (1995).

TABLE 7.5 The House of Representatives, 1960–2003

Year	Before election		Incumbents lost by		Open seats lost by		After election	
	D	**R**	**D**	**R**	**D**	**R**	**D**	**R**
1960	281	153	23	2	6	6	262	175
1962	263	174	9	5	2	3	259	176
1964	254	176	5	39	5	8	295	140
1966	294	139	39	1	4	3	248	187
1968	245	187	5	0	2	4	243	192
1970	243	187	2	9	6	8	255	180
1972	256	176	6	3	9	5	244	191
1974	248	187	4	36	2	13	291	144
1976	286	145	7	5	3	7	292	143
1978	285	146	14	5	8	6	277	158
1980	273	159	27	3	10	1	243	192
1982	241	192	1	22	4	6	269	166
1984	266	167	13	3	5	1	253	182
1986	253	180	1	5	7	8	258	177
1988	255	177	2	4	1	2	260	175
1990	258	175	6	9	0	6	267	167
1992	266	166	16	8	11	9	258	176
1994	256	178	34	0	22	4	204	230
1996	197	235	3	17	10	4	207	227
1998	206	228	1	5	5	6	211	223
2000	209	222	2	4	6	6	211	221

Tables 7.5 and 7.6 demonstrate how few lawmakers suffer defeat when seeking re-election. In 2000, for example, only three House incumbents lost their primaries and six House members and six senators lost the general election. Of 403 House members who sought re-election, 394 were successful.

However, the figures in Tables 7.5 and 7.6 are deceptive. As Anthony King (1997) has argued, American politicians are especially 'vulnerable' and 'run scared' – that is, compared to politicians in other industrialized democracies, they are particularly exposed to the vagaries of electoral politics:

- They face re-election more often than counterparts outside America.
- They face the prospect of contesting primary elections to be re-nominated.
- They receive little protective cover from strong political parties.

- They have to raise most of the money to finance their campaigns.

Some of these conditions exist outside America in particular national political systems, but nowhere else in the world do all four conditions apply simultaneously to national lawmakers.

The result is that, despite the high aggregate re-election figures, American politicians experience a pervasive unease about being returned to Congress. According to Richard Fenno (1978), members of Congress are apt to perceive electoral troubles where even the most imaginative observer could not conjure or hallucinate them. King, similarly, describes lawmakers as analogous to workers in a nuclear power plant. Although statistics suggest that the plants are 'objectively' safe, their workers have to go to extreme lengths to

TABLE 7.6   The Senate, 1960–2003

Year	Before election		Incumbents lost by		Open seats lost by		After election	
	D	R	D	R	D	R	D	R
1960	66	34	1	0	1	0	64	36
1962	64	36	2	3	0	3	68	32
1964	66	34	1	3	0	0	68	32
1966	67	33	1	0	2	0	64	36
1968	63	37	4	0	3	2	58	42
1970	57	43	3	2	1	0	55	45
1972	55	45	1	4	3	2	57	43
1974	58	42	0	2	1	3	62	38
1976	62	38	5	2	3	3	62	38
1978	62	38	5	2	3	3	59	41
1980	59	41	9	0	3	0	47	53
1982	46	54	1	1	1	1	46	54
1984	45	55	1	2	0	1	47	53
1986	47	53	0	7	1	2	55	45
1988	54	46	1	3	2	1	55	45
1990	55	45	0	1	0	0	56	44
1992	57	43	2	2	0	0	57	43
1994	56	44	2	0	6	0	47	53
1996	47	53	0	1	3	0	45	55
1998	45	55	1	2	2	1	45	55
2000	46	54	1	5	2	5	50	50

ensure that this is the case. Similarly, members of Congress may collectively win re-election with apparent ease, but this is only because most of them work extremely hard on a daily basis, year-in, year-out to achieve this.

How they go about this is also of tremendous political importance. In a landmark study, David Mayhew (1974) argued that members pursue three means of securing re-election:

• *Advertising*. Members seek to let constituents know what they are doing on Capitol Hill. This may concern laws they are supporting or opposing, meetings with the president, foreign leaders or business figures, or even meetings with constituents who have come to Washington. The message of these mailings is invariably about what the member is doing to defend and advance the interests of the district or state in DC and beyond. One happy coincidence is, of course, that such mailings offer an advantageous – and publicly subsidized – electoral weapon.

• *Position-taking*. Beyond informing constituents of congressional activism, members can also let them know of the positions they have taken on particular bills. Members representing rural districts or states may alert constituents to their opposition to a new gun control bill, for example, or members representing constituencies with a large Jewish population may notify them of their support for increased foreign aid to Israel.

• *Credit-claiming*. Whether or not they are responsible for them, members of Congress seek to take the credit for whatever

Exhibit 7.5   Factors affecting the decisions and activity of lawmakers

- *Constituency.* How will the decision affect the interests of the district/state?
- *Lawmakers' political ideology and beliefs.* Is the decision consistent with party or ideological allegiances?
- *Preferences of party leaders in Congress.* Is the decision one that the party leadership supports?
- *Interests of other lawmakers' states.* How are colleagues approaching the decision?
- *Other executive officials* (e.g. the president, governors). Does the president have a clear position on the issue to be decided?
- *The bureaucracy.* Are those public servants charged with implementing the decision favourable or unfavourable to it?
- *Contributors* (past and potential). How will concerned campaign contributors react?
- *Interest group activity* (lobbying, contributions, testimony at hearings). What do key organized lobbies prefer?

federal projects, monies or programmes come to the district or state.

Because members of Congress must be highly attentive to their particular constituents and contributors, many Americans think of Congress as a collective institution as ineffective. But when making decisions about what committees to sit on, what legislation to sponsor, and how to vote on bills, members of Congress have several considerations to take into account. Although constituency interests weigh heavily, they do not always take priority and, as Exhibit 7.5 notes, other factors may often play either a reinforcing or competing role.

One of the most important and enduring insights of Mayhew's work was that the organizational structure of Congress is

Exhibit 7.6   Constitutionalizing congressional pay

Year	Salary ($)	Year	Salary ($)
1979	60,663	1991	125,100
1982	69,800	1992	129,500
1984	72,600	1993	133,600
1985	75,100	1998	136,700
1987	89,500	2000	141,300
1990	96,600		

The Twenty-seventh Amendment to the US Constitution was about a subject many might find rather unworthy of constitutional dialogues: the pay of members of Congress. The measure requires that any pay raise that lawmakers award can only take effect after an election has intervened – thereby giving American voters a chance to 'throw the rascals out'. Members received a pay increase of $4,600 on January 1, 2000, the level being set automatically by a cost of living adjustment. Although the current salary may seem relatively high, it remains much less generous than the fees that most members could earn in the private sector in America. But whenever pay increases are proposed and passed it adds to regular bouts of 'Congress-bashing' by the many critics of the national assembly among the American media and the public.

designed to serve its members' electoral needs. When those needs alter, for whatever reason, there is a strong likelihood that the internal structure of Congress will also change in response. Utilizing this way of analysing Congress, it is possible to identify three distinct modern congressional eras.

THREE ERAS OF CONGRESS

Any organization, from Congress to the Boy Scouts, faces two general types of pressures: the external demands made on it and the internal pressures of its members. This general tension is exacerbated by the 'two Congresses' phenomenon that we noted earlier, with each lawmaker separately elected and facing distinct goals and incentives independent of the collective institution yet simultaneously needing the support of other legislators to realize key policy goals. The structure and procedures of Congress have therefore altered over time as a result of changing external and internal pressures. Congressional observers generally divide the

patterns of behaviour in the modern Congress into three distinct eras. This is not to suggest that no continuity existed between the three periods, but rather that Congress was subject to quite different external pressures and internal forces in each. With the shift in each, relations between parties and committees, the relative strength of congressional party leaders and the legislative focus, operations and productivity of successive Congresses altered dramatically.

1937–64: The textbook Congress – 'to get along, go along'

The traditional picture of Congress is often termed the 'textbook Congress' of 1937–64. This was an era in which power was centred on the chairs of full committees. Committees were the central arenas of legislative life and were dominated by their chairs, who controlled their budgets, determined the number of their subcommittees (and which members sat on and chaired them), and allocated staff and funds to the subcommittees. As Exhibit 7.7 explains, seniority determined who occupied the chair (and still largely does so

Exhibit 7.7   The seniority principle

The seniority principle determines which lawmakers chair committees. This does not mean – as is sometimes thought – that the oldest member chairs the committee (though age often correlates with seniority). Instead, the member of the majority party of the particular committee who has sat on the committee the longest automatically becomes its chairperson. What this meant during the middle of the twentieth century was that southern Democrats exercised disproportionate influence in Congress, (a) because the Democratic Party tended to have majorities in both houses and (b) since the South was effectively a one-party region (with minimal Republican competition), Southern Democrats were returned more easily than most others in America, thereby accumulating seniority on the committees on which they sat. This enabled them strongly to resist even considering, much less passing, the civil rights laws that presidents such as Truman advocated. Although seniority was strongly challenged in the 1970s, and committee chairs made subject to approval by their respective party caucuses (rank-and-file members as a whole), in practice the norm remains the key to who gains the chair. The reason is straightforward: seniority is a neutral means of selection. It ignores ideological leanings, region, race, ethnicity, gender and other divisions. Were seniority not applied, members, both of specific committees and party caucuses, would have to vote over chairs, causing major internal party divisions.

today), and junior members were expected to serve a long apprenticeship, defer to their more senior colleagues, and specialize in particular policy areas. In order to get on, the incentive structure was such that junior members would toe the line. Mavericks, grandstanders and generalists were unwanted and unloved. As the advice of one powerful Speaker of the House, Sam Rayburn (Democrat, Texas), put it, 'to get along, go along'.

Certain norms and 'folkways' dominated congressional life during these years. In particular:

- *Reciprocity.* A legislator would normally be expected to accept the recommendations of other committees, just as they should in turn accept those of his committee.
- *Specialization and division of labour.* Lawmakers at this time were expected to be specialists, not generalists. Their task was to develop expertise only on one or a handful of areas (tax policy, defence, energy), not to have views on subjects across the entire legislative spectrum (much less offer bills or amendments on subjects outside their specialism). As a result, Congress functioned according to a more or less clear-cut division of legislative labour among its members.
- *Apprenticeship.* In order to develop such expertise, lawmakers were expected to spend the early terms of their legislative lives learning about their particular areas of expertise. Only after a few years were they expected to offer their own bills for consideration, and only then on their specialized areas.

In addition to these structural dimensions, the other important aspect of this era was the partisan aspect and, in particular, the domination of Congress by a bipartisan 'conservative coalition' of Republicans and Southern Democrats. This period saw intra-party differences as at least as important as inter-party ones, with relatively low levels of party unity. Instead, large numbers of one party would typically join with the other party – most typically, Dixiecrats (Southern Democrats) would combine with conservative Republicans to prevent the passage of new federal legislation extending the interventionism of the New Deal or challenging southern segregation.

1965–78: The reform era Congress – from whales to minnows

The 'textbook Congress' was broken by a series of developments that saw Congress undergo a drastic change. Many of these occurred during the 1970s but the catalyst for change was the 1958 elections that ushered into Congress 16 new Democratic senators and 51 new Democratic representatives. Most of these were committed liberals eager to achieve major policy goals such as civil rights and medical insurance (see Chapter 11). Some were more directly concerned with re-election motives: more legislative influence could yield more 'pork-barrel' returns to districts and states. Others were concerned with the growing volume of complex and cross-cutting legislation that Congress had to consider. Taken together, and frustrated by conservative chairs of full committees acting in autocratic ways that denied them a meaningful influence on policy, the existing structure of power needed to be made flatter.

As Exhibit 7.8 notes, the cumulative result was a substantial challenge to the established ways of doing things in Congress. Congressional structures became much more open, participatory and transparent, with recorded votes, more use of an expanded and properly funded network of subcommittees, and lawmakers acting 'not as role players in a complex system of interactions in equilibrium but as individual entrepreneurs in a vast, open market place that rewarded self-interested competitiveness with little or no regard for the welfare of the whole' (Davidson, 1992: 12–13).

Exhibit 7.8   Key changes to the House of Representatives committee system in the 1970s

- Members were prohibited from chairing more than one subcommittee.
- The 'subcommittee bill of rights' was promulgated: powers were taken away from committee chairs, including the right to select subcommittee chairs, to define subcommittee jurisdictions and to determine subcommittee budgets.
- The 'sunshine reforms': committee hearings were opened up to the public, and hearings became televised.
- The 'seniority rule', by which committee chairs went to the senior serving member on the committee in the majority party, was weakened. This allowed for a turnover in committee chairs.
- All full committees with more than 20 members had to establish at least four subcommittees.
- Members were limited to serving on a maximum of five subcommittees.

Such a fragmented environment, however, altered once again as it proved too decentralized to permit the achievement of individual member goals. By the end of the 1970s, as America confronted enormous economic, social and foreign policy problems, the new structure appeared only to worsen rather than improve the federal government's capacities to resolve them. Established leadership structures had become so weakened, and legislative power so fragmented among a vastly expanded number of players, each of whom exercised strictly limited influence, that it had become tremendously difficult for lawmakers of either party to pass bills they favoured. At the same time, with the growing grass-roots activism of liberal groups in the Democratic Party and conservative ones in the Republican Party, differences between the parties were growing broader and deeper. As a result, Congress began to adapt to these changes and operate in a more modified style that facilitated more centralized, though still limited, party leadership, especially in the House.

1979– : The post-reform Congress: the return of 'party government'?

Even before the Republicans won control of Congress in the 1994 elections for the first

time in 40 years, a 'post-reform' Congress had emerged. The national context to this was a new era of 'deficit' or 'cut-back' politics that defined the 1980s and early 1990s. Massive annual budget deficits (and, as a result, a rapidly increasing national debt) strongly limited the room for new federal programmes to be passed. Partly as a result, five features distinguished post-reform congressional politics:

1   Individual legislators sponsored fewer bills. By the mid-1980s, on average, senators sponsored 41 (down from 55 in 1969–70), while members of the House sponsored just 17 (down from 56 in 1967–68).
2   Instead of claiming credit for new federal projects (as Mayhew (1974) noted, this was a common and effective political strategy), legislative life became dominated by 'blame avoidance'. Lawmakers employed techniques to protect themselves from adverse public reactions. For example, instead of voting on closures of military bases, Congress established an independent commission to recommend such closures, with members having to vote yes or no to the entire package.
3   Non-controversial resolutions, such as National Catfish Day, became increasingly popular, being both inexpensive and

targeted to particular parochial constituencies.

4 Driven by a combination of the growing nationalization of the two main parties, the centrality of budget votes to legislative life and the norm of divided party control of the federal government, party unity voting became more common.

5 Party leadership in the House and, to a lesser extent, the Senate, became stronger than at any time since 1910.

This saw two important changes from the era of flux during the 1970s. The first was the development of 'leadership by inclusion'. One aspect of this was that party leaders responded to the earlier fragmentation by expanding the ranks of the party leadership structures, involving more and more rank-and-file members in leadership positions. This process helped to develop a greater sense of collective identity and *esprit de corps*. For example, the whip system was expanded, so that many more individual lawmakers became whips. By 2002, the Republican whip organization in the House, headed by Tom 'The Hammer' DeLay (Republican, Texas), comprised 60 lawmakers: a Chief Deputy Whip, 15 Deputy Whips and 44 Assistant Deputy Whips. While this does not amount to a Westminster-style operation in which party whips can impose discipline on recalcitrant backbenchers, it does mean that more information on voter intentions is forthcoming and more lawmakers feel that they are involved in, and hence have a stake in, the party's leadership and its collective agenda.

Another aspect to the new state of American 'party government' involved increasing leadership coordination of the passage of bills through each chamber. With many laws now involving multiple considerations, party leaders used powers given them in the 1970s reforms to intrude more directly in legislative life. In 1995, for example, the Commerce Committee reported out a telecommunications bill by a 38–5 margin but its chair was forced by Speaker Newt Gingrich to sponsor an amendment that reversed its entire purpose. In July 2001, the Rules Committee, an important arm of the party leadership, refused to allow Mark Foley (Republican, Florida) to offer a floor amendment to President Bush's bill to expand the role of 'faith-based' (religious) charities, fearing that it would attract Democrats and thereby weaken the content of the bill.

This process of increasing leadership strength was driven by increasing partisan polarization. As Table 7.7 details, 'party unity' votes increased dramatically after 1981, partly driven by the centrality of budgetary issue concerns, partly by the norm of divided government, and partly by the presence of polarizing presidents such as Reagan and Clinton in the White House. As a result, the costs to individual rank-and-file lawmakers of strong party leadership in Congress – which had been prohibitively high in the two previous eras – began to decline significantly, especially in the House. Members of both parties wanted stronger leadership: its absence was leading to gridlock and frustration and the 'out party' (that did not possess the White

Exhibit 7.9 Referrals

Multiple referral. Instead of a bill being referred to a single committee to draw up its detailed provisions, a bill is referred to more than one committee. This frequently occurs when a bill encompasses more than one jurisdiction.

Joint referral. A bill is referred to more than one committee at the same time, with party leaders coordinating the delivery and reconciliation of the different committee's drafts.

Sequential referral. A bill is referred to a particular committee for action but with provisions that it then go on to another (or more) committee for scrutiny.

TABLE 7.7 Party unity: average scores, 1964–2000

'Party unity votes' are those recorded votes that split the parties, pitting a majority of Democrats who voted against a majority of Republicans who voted.

Year	Republicans	Democrats	Year	Republicans	Democrats
1965	70	69	1983	74	76
1966	67	61	1984	72	74
1967	71	66	1985	75	79
1968	63	57	1986	71	78
1969	62	62	1987	74	81
1970	59	57	1988	73	79
1971	66	62	1989	73	81
1972	64	57	1990	74	81
1973	68	68	1991	78	81
1974	62	63	1992	79	79
1975	70	69	1993	84	85
1976	66	65	1994	83	83
1977	70	67	1995	91	80
1978	67	64	1996	87	80
1979	72	69	1997	88	82
1980	70	68	1998	86	83
1981	76	69	1999	86	84
1982	74	76	2000	87	83

Source: *CQ Weekly*, January 6, 2001, p. 67.

Exhibit 7.10 Killing the bill: filibusters

The filibuster is a device that allows a senator to engage in extended debate without limit. The record is held by Strom Thurmond, who spoke for just under 24 hours straight against the 1957 civil rights bill (at one point reciting South Carolina cooking recipes on the Senate floor).

In the 1950s and 1960s, only senior senators used the filibuster, and only on important national legislation like civil rights. But under the electoral pressures that grew substantially from the end of the 1960s, even junior senators will now use it on minor, parochial legislation to win concessions favourable to their particular states. Some senators in both parties became especially notable – and disliked by many colleagues – for their ready willingness to use, or threaten to use, filibusters for their relatively narrow ends (Jesse Helms and Dan Quayle for the Republicans, Howard Metzenbaum and Paul Wellstone for the Democrats).

As Senate committees and leaders increasingly send party-driven legislation to the floor, opposition forces have mounted a growing number of filibusters. Many of these filibusters have succeeded in killing the bills, since Senate rules require 60 votes to invoke cloture and limit further debate. By the 1990s, the Senate's large workload, limited floor time and many contentious bills made threats to filibuster a potent weapon. Just as presidents have threatened to veto laws in order to extract concessions from Congress, individual senators increasingly employed such threats to win changes or state-related benefits.

TABLE 7.8   Filibusters and clotures, 1951–98

Years	Filibusters per Congress	Cloture votes per Congress
1951–60	1.0	0.4
1961–70	4.6	5.2
1971–80	11.2	22.4
1981–86	16.7	23.0
1987–92	26.7	39.0
1993–94	30.0	42.0
1995–96	25.0	50.0
1997–98	29.0	53.0

Source: *National Journal*, July 31, 1999, p. 2212.

House) required a clear leader to counter the president. As long as party leaders paid attention to their rank and file, they would be allowed a lot of autonomy to strike deals, negotiate on behalf of their members and craft legislative outcomes.

The cumulative result is that the post-reform Congress exhibits 'conditional party government'. This is not party government in a European sense, but parties have become the most significant organizational structures on Capitol Hill. Party is the best predictor of a member's vote, even though individual lawmakers frequently cast votes against most of their partisan colleagues. The recent narrowness of party majorities also accentuates the individualism inherent in Congress, especially so in the Senate. The emphasis in conditional party government is on the conditional aspect. As the failed budget negotiations of 1990 showed (when, having negotiated a budget deal on their behalf with the White House, party leaders found the deal they had agreed rejected by their rank-and-file lawmakers), dissident factions within both parties are quite willing and able to refuse to support the agreements that their leaders have brokered. The bottom line remains, for most members most of the time, that 'all politics is local'. As the Democratic Speaker Tip O'Neill observed:

You can be the most important congressman in the country, but you had better not forget the people back home. I wish I had a dime for every politician I've known who had to learn that lesson the hard way. I've seen so many good people come to Washington, where they get so worked up over important national issues that they lose the connection to their own constituents. Before they know it, some new guy comes along and sends them packing. (O'Neill with Novak, 1987: 26)

Nevertheless, parties – and party leaders – are more influential now than at any time since 1910 in the legislative life of Congress.

IN DEFENCE OF CONGRESS: A QUALIFYING NOTE

To put it mildly, the images presented above do not show Congress in an especially positive light. Many of the criticisms ventured of Congress – slow, negative, reactive, obstructive, parochial, introspected, irresponsible – have re-occurred with fairly reliable frequency. At times, such as in 1990, 1992 and 1994, congressional scandal and misdeeds can prompt the type of wholesale turnover – through retirements and resignations – that is otherwise rare in elections to the federal legislature. But it would be mistaken and misleading to end the discussion of Congress without some important qualifications.

One cautionary note concerns the society from which members of Congress are drawn, and which they must govern. Key here is the marked heterogeneity of America's distinctive social base. Compromise, conciliation and concession are often seen as negative terms of abuse in popular commentary on politics within and outside America. Why that is the case seems odd. In a society so rich in regional, religious, racial, ethnic and social diversity, the need to bargain and reach a broadly acceptable consensus is persistent and powerful. The alternative – a 'strong' party government able to implement its programme against the wishes of sizeable sections of American society – is deeply unpalatable to Americans, for good reason.

Another aspect, not unrelated to the first, is that members of Congress are sent to Washington to do two jobs: first, as delegates, to defend and advance the interests of their respective districts and states (few of which are internally homogeneous, much less when compared to neighbouring or distant ones); secondly, as national legislators, to craft federal policies that address America's various social, economic and political problems. The two roles are inextricably linked but also exist inherently in tension. Whatever the collective consequences, to castigate members for seeking to balance them appears rather a strange and, perhaps, unfair criticism. Most lawmakers work extremely hard, under the most demanding of conditions, at home and on Capitol Hill, to achieve their political goals. That so many of them succeed in gaining re-election is, at one level, a testament to the success rather than the failure of the American system. No matter how great their campaign budgets, legislators who let their constituents down would not be returned to Capitol Hill.

Moreover, whatever its successes or failures as a policymaking and executive-checking institution, Congress operates, for the most part, in the most transparent of fashions. For a non-American accustomed to having to request tickets or queue for hours merely to enter the Houses of Parliament at Westminster, it is a revelation to be able literally to walk off the streets into congressional offices, committee hearings, and related buildings in the two square miles that make up Capitol Hill. Going to the Federal Election Commission and requesting the documents can allow any citizen to access the campaign finances of a member: how much he or she raised, from where, and when. Compared to most other national parliaments around the world, there is a voluminous amount of information on Congress and an accessibility to federal lawmakers that is remarkable.

In short, Congress displays as many virtues as it does vices, and the two are frequently inseparable from the institutional design, constitutional powers and public pressures – on individual lawmakers and the legislature as a whole – that together shape how the assembly must work. Particularly when the two ends of Pennsylvania Avenue are occupied by different parties, the prospect of intense political conflict both within and between the Congress and the White House is great. But this should be regarded less as an indictment of a deliberately divided democratic system than an expression of competing interests and opinions.

CONCLUSION

Congress does not share in the marked affection that Americans bestow on their individual lawmakers, but the unpopularity of Congress and the popularity of individual members is inextricably linked. Congress is more often than not cumbersome, slow, negative and reactive. It is capable of innovative and rapid activity but it cannot move rapidly when proposals are contentious or controversial, public sentiment is divided, presidential leadership is either lacking or problematic, political parties are relatively weak and the myriad interest lobbies whom new laws and regulations will affect raise genuine and reasonable concerns about legislative proposals.

Compared to most other liberal democracies, legislative life in America is slow, cumbersome, obstructive and difficult. But it is also, arguably, more rewarding and consequential. Members of the Westminster parliament, much less that of the European Union, would barely recognize Congress, an independent institution where rank-and-file members play a genuine role in making policy and in scrutinizing the activities of the executive branch in detail, and enjoy a well-resourced, well-staffed and information-rich legislative body. Congressional committees and subcommittees genuinely write public laws and develop public policies rather than simply ratify drafts composed within the executive branch. Moreover, although Congress has a somewhat uneven record of exercising its oversight powers, few civil servants can treat congressional hearings, investigations or recommendations as those of a legislative paper tiger.

As for the parochialism manifest in commemorative resolutions and congressional caucuses, the fact remains that millions of Americans are employed in producing catfish, farming dairy livestock, and making and selling mushrooms, wine and asparagus. They expect their elected representatives in government to defend and advance policies that protect and benefit their material interests and their livelihoods. For elected members, this is not just good politics, but is precisely what their job requirements effectively specify. Whatever the effects on coherent national (and foreign) policy, deriding congressional parochialism is ultimately neglecting the pronounced diversity of the United States. The collective output of Congress can confirm the worst fears and prejudices of ordinary Americans both physically and psychologically distant from Washington, but the inherent tension exists because it is built into the design of the institution: the conflict between the national interest and the particular interest is never far from congressional politics.

FURTHER READING

David Mayhew, *Congress: The Electoral Connection* (1974) is one of the most widely cited works on Congress in which the author analyses how members of Congress go about seeking re-election and how this affects their actions in Congress.

Richard Fenno, *Home Style: House Members in their Districts* (1978) is a landmark study in which the author demonstrates how life at home and on Capitol Hill interact for different members of the House.

Roger Davidson (ed.), *The Postreform Congress* (1992) is an excellent collection of essays on the key aspects of how Congress operates in the 'post-reform' era.

Frances Lee and Bruce Oppenheimer, *Sizing Up the Senate: The Unequal Consequences of Equal Representation* (1999) is a seminal study of how allocating two Senators to each state affects politics and policy.

WEB LINKS

The Senate
http://www.senate.gov

The House of Representatives
http://www.house.gov

Congressional Quarterly, the most authoritative monitor of Congress
http://www.cq.com

Capitol Hill newspaper
htttp://www.rollcall.com

Cable network with much information on Congress
http://www.c-span.org

Congress's own web site:
http://www.thomas.loc.gov

Center for Responsive Politics
http://www.opensecrets.org

QUESTIONS

- 'Congress is extremely good at representation, much less so at lawmaking in the national interest.' Discuss.

- 'Powerful but obstructive.' Assess this view of Congress's role in the policy process.

- Can the high re-election rates of members of Congress be reconciled with their being 'vulnerable'?

- Is Congress too powerful a legislative assembly?

- What are the causes and consequences of Congress being divided into two co-equal chambers?

8 The Supreme Court

We live under a Constitution. But the Constitution is what the judges say it is.

> Chief Justice Hughes

For myself, it would be most irksome to be ruled by a bevy of Platonic Guardians, even if I knew how to choose them, which I assuredly do not.

> Judge Learned Hand

- The Role of the Courts
- The Structure of the Court System
- Denying Democracy? The Case of Flag-burning
- Appointing the Justices
- After the Appointment: Life Tenure and Judicial Independence
- Three Courts, Three Types of 'Activism'
- The Limits to Court Influence
- A Juridicized Politics and a Politicized Judiciary?
- Conclusion

Chapter Summary

Just as the Congress is the most powerful legislature in liberal democracies, so the US Supreme Court has no rival in influence among national judiciaries. Given the centrality of the Constitution to American political development, the importance of the judiciary is immense. Federal and state courts interpret, and thereby adapt, the Constitution to changing social, economic and political conditions. Most notably, through the power of constitutional judicial review, courts can strike down the laws passed by Congress and state legislatures as violating particular provisions of the Constitution. During the twentieth century, courts played crucial roles in striking down racial segregation, expanding the rights of women and minorities, and policing the boundaries between the presidency and the other branches of government. Landmark cases such as *Roe v. Wade* (establishing a woman's right to an abortion) demonstrated the ability of courts not simply to interpret law but also to initiate policies that elected branches of government had rejected. However, the growth of judicial power has led to the politicization of American courts, with prospective judicial appointments becoming key tests of political – and especially partisan – conflict between the White House and Congress. The intense battles over the nominations of Robert Bork and Clarence Thomas to the Supreme Court demonstrated how important the influence and composition of the Supreme Court is to Americans today. Despite the necessary myth that courts merely find rather than make the law, only by acting politically – as well as legally – can the judiciary safeguard its crucial position in the constitutional order and perform its necessary role in checking the elected branches of government, protecting individual liberties and rights, and maintaining the rule of law. The role of the courts is not only as important as that of the elected branches of government in making America a properly functioning liberal democracy but is also at least as controversial.

Writing in 1835, Alexis de Tocqueville famously observed that 'scarcely any political question arises in the United States that is not resolved sooner or later into a judicial question'. Today, his observation rings truer than ever. American social, economic and political life in the twenty-first century is dominated not just by the laws passed by Congress and the 50 states and implemented by the executive branch of government at federal, state and local levels, but also by a myriad of rulings by state and federal courts. In effect, these judicial decisions offer a rolling constitutional convention that constantly rewrites, amends and adds new text to that of the original document of 1787. Consequently, the law is as much a dominant feature of American politics as elections, coalitions, money and localism.

Contrary to formalistic legal models, however, courts are not composed of human computers that reconcile the facts of a case and existing law to give verdicts. Rather, they are made up of flesh-and-blood judges with their own particular backgrounds, beliefs and values. Can universities use racial preferences in admissions? Can states require parents to be notified before minors have abortions? Can children be allowed to recite prayers in state schools? Can states execute mentally retarded death row prisoners or 16-year-olds? Can grandparents exercise a constitutional right to visit their grandchildren? The answers to these and other questions that have a real-world impact on millions ultimately depend less on the express words of the Constitution than on the political and moral values of the judges appointed to the federal bench. Moreover, the answer to these questions increasingly depends on whether the president who picks those judges is a Democrat or a Republican.

The reasons for the crucial role of courts are clear. Built into the heart of American government is a profound and enduring tension between democratic and liberal values. On the one hand, America prides itself on its democratic form of government. The key foundation of this is the notion of making those who govern accountable to the governed through means of regular, fixed-term elections. On the other hand, Americans revere the rule of law, the federal constitution and the system of limited government that it established. How, then, can one reconcile the ability of majorities to see their will enacted with the requirement that the rights and liberties of minorities are guaranteed adequate protection? Democracy is not synonymous with majority rule and majorities can be as tyrannical as monarchs and dictators. Hence, government should be limited and no person should be above the law. Since those branches elected by the people cannot be trusted always to side with minorities, the most appropriate actors to safeguard the rights of the individual against the state and of minorities against majorities are the courts.

Much as some Americans may quibble with individual parts of the Constitution while accepting the whole, so the judicial system in general, and the Supreme Court in particular, wins widespread respect despite – and in an important sense, because of – handing down decisions that generate enormous political controversy. For example, in 1896, the Court ruled that racial segregation was constitutional (*Plessy v. Ferguson*) and then, in 1954, unconstitutional (*Brown v. Board of Education, Topeka*); that a woman's 'right to privacy' covered her decision to terminate a pregnancy in the first six months (*Roe v. Wade*, 1973), but not a gay person's right to engage in consensual adult sex in the home (*Hardwick v. Bowers*, 1986); that the president could be sued in office for an act of alleged sexual harassment that occurred before he entered the White House (*Jones v. United States*, 1998); and that the federal government could not ban the possession of guns within 1,000 feet of a school (*US v. Lopez*, 1995).

Although some of these decisions provoked nationwide outrage, the Supreme Court has managed to maintain the support and respect of the public. This tenacious ability to survive the political controversy that it generates is not so much despite, but more because of, its unelected character. A necessary myth surrounds the Court: that its justices merely seek to square the facts of cases that it considers with the Constitution to render a verdict; that it is a legal rather than a political body. But it is, intrinsically, both. Politics surrounds and pervades the court but so too does law, and the myth of judicial neutrality is a necessary one for its performing an effective role in America's democracy. In order to intervene in political matters, the Court needs to maintain an appearance of express distance from politics, even if the reality is more complex and ambiguous.

At times – not least since 1981 – that distance from conventional politics has appeared to be limited and fading fast. The decision in *Bush v. Gore* (2000), effectively handing the presidential election to Bush, was only the latest in a series of controversial rulings by the Supreme Court. The fear has hence arisen that, while the Founding Fathers intended American government to be limited, they did not envision an unlimited judicial role to secure this end. Concern exists that the courts have been transformed from what Alexander Hamilton termed 'the least dangerous branch' of government into an 'imperial judiciary'. Ironically, the contribution that these unelected figures make to a liberal democracy that prides itself on its representative character is enormous, enduring and invaluable. Without the judiciary, America would be a severely compromised and partial democratic regime.

THE ROLE OF THE COURTS

The key function of courts in liberal democracies is conflict resolution. Conflicts can take many forms, from the mundane and petty (a citizen's right to let his tree overhang a neighbour's garden) to the profound (divorce, child custody, violations of civil liberties and human rights, even genocide), but once the subject of litigation, it conventionally falls to courts to adjudicate on them. This adjudication can take several forms, but for our purposes, the key conflicts that American courts must resolve are those between:

- *The state and the individual citizen*. Individuals (and groups) often litigate in courts

Exhibit 8.1 Law versus politics?

The legal model

Is the Supreme Court merely a legal institution that seeks to find what the law says, apply this to a specific case, and thereby give a ruling? On this view (one that remains popular with many lawyers and judges), judges are no more than *la bouche de la loi* ('the mouth of the law'). With no significant discretion in rendering their decisions, they simply follow the standard formula:

R (rules or laws) + F (the facts of the case) = D (decisions or rulings).

Given the existing law and the relevant facts of the case, judges must simply square the two together in a statement of what the law says on this particular case.

The political model

Or is the Supreme Court a 'political' body? The leading British authority on the Court, Richard Hodder-Williams (1992), argues that we can identify six senses in which the court is political:

- *Definitional.* In reconciling competing claims, and as an appellate court of last resort, the Court necessarily allocates values (and sometimes powers) authoritatively.
- *Empirical.* Recognizing its potentially far-reaching power, other groups active in American political life – elected politicians, organized interest lobbies – seek to sway the Court in its decisions by litigation and by filing *amicus curiae* ('friends of the court') briefs with the court to try to sway Justices' opinions.
- *Influence-seeking.* The nine judges on the Court each want to prevail in arguments within the court and need to convince a majority to support their view of what the Constitution and the law requires. To do so often necessitates compromises, concessions and bargaining, a quintessentially political process. Justices are themselves strategic actors, tailoring their behaviour to seek to achieve their desired outcomes.
- *Prudential.* The Court does not operate in a social or political vacuum, but considers the likely consequences of its decisions before coming to a ruling. In the case of momentous decisions, such as *Brown* (1954), the justices strive to achieve a unanimous ruling to lend authority to the decision.
- *Policy-oriented.* The justices are said to use the law as a cover for advancing their preferred policy goals. Put simply, progressives vote the liberal lines, conservatives for conservative outcomes. Since the Constitution is so ambiguous, it is normally possible to find some type of constitutional support for almost any favoured policy position.
- *Systemic.* What the Court decides has consequences for the rest of the governmental and political system. In ruling on some issues, such as abortion or physician-assisted suicide, the Court introduces new questions to political life on which candidates, elected officials, bureaucrats and other figures must address. Conversely, by refusing to look at certain cases (such as segregation from 1896 to 1954 or direct challenges to the principle of capital punishment since 1976) the Court preserves the *status quo* against change.

because they are convinced that the state has intruded on their constitutional liberties or rights. For example, for the government to try to ban particular activities, such as flag-burning, is something that many citizens feel violates the right to free expression guaranteed by the First Amendment. Death row inmates may litigate against their sentence on the grounds that the Eighth Amendment prohibits 'cruel and unusual punishment'. Hence, courts are charged in such cases with deciding whether the state has infringed an individual's constitutional rights as a citizen of the United States.

- *Different branches of government at the same level.* Conflicts between the president and Congress are frequently referred to courts to adjudicate. Often, the courts refuse to do so on grounds that the conflict at hand is a 'political question' beyond the competence of the judiciary to resolve (such as the constitutionality of the 1973 War Powers Resolution).
- *Different tiers of government.* In a federal system, conflicts invariably arise between the state and the federal governments over which branch has the authority to legislate in particular areas. Again, it falls to the courts to resolve these disputes. When the Supreme Court ruled in *Printz v. US* (1997) that states could not implement the Brady Bill – requiring background checks on gun buyers – it was because the federal government did not have the authority to compel local officials to carry out its mandate.

Although these types of conflict are not unfamiliar in Europe, the American context remains unusual. The distinctive power of American courts is especially pronounced for three reasons:

- *Common law.* Unlike the tradition of civil law that holds sway in continental Europe, America's colonies inherited, and the republic subsequently built on, the English tradition of common law. In this respect, two bodies of law have significance: (i) the statutory laws passed by Congress and state legislatures; and (ii) 'judge-made' common law, in which precedent is built upon precedent as judges interpret what laws mean.
- *Judicial review.* The crucial power that federal courts exercise is that of constitutional judicial review. This is the power to hold unconstitutional, and hence unenforceable, any law, any official action based on a law, or any other action by a public official that a court deems to be in conflict with the basic or supreme law, that is, the US Constitution.
- *Constitutional amendment.* The third reason for the extraordinary influence of the courts is the difficulty of reversing a court ruling on constitutionality. This can only be achieved by formal amendment of the US Constitution, which, as we saw in Chapter 2, is extremely difficult to achieve and requires very broad public support. In the event that even 60 per cent of Americans disapprove of a court ruling, they are unable to overturn it by constitutional amendment (which needs two-thirds of both houses of Congress and three-quarters of the states). When courts decide cases, their rulings can have far-reaching political implications.

Two dilemmas arise immediately in regard to the judicial role. First, how much freedom do judges possess to create new laws? In theory, the legal duty is to find out what the law states, relate this to the facts of a given case, and provide a ruling. But as Exhibit 8.2 illustrates, the process of interpretation is open to different approaches, which can result in courts effectively initiating new policies in the manner traditionally performed by elected legislatures. In general, the less deference that judges show legislatures, and the more expansively and creatively they read the Constitution, the more likely it is that courts will engage in making new policies under the guise of judicial interpretation – not merely interpreting laws but initiating new public policies.

The second dilemma is closely related to the first and concerns the possibility that citizens could be subject to a 'government of

Exhibit 8.2 The problems of judging

Lack of clarity. Many provisions in the Constitution are unclear or ambiguous in meaning. Phrases such as 'commerce', 'equal protection' and 'due process of law' were penned in the eighteenth century and demand interpretation. But what interpretation to adopt is far less straightforward.

Conflicting provisions. Many constitutional provisions, when applied to 'real-world' cases, yield conflicting conclusions. For example, does the First Amendment's guarantee of free speech outweigh the provisions of the Constitution allowing states to make their own laws, including on matters of the press?

Relativity. Even constitutional guarantees are relative, not absolute. A decision has to be made as to what weight is accorded particular protections. The rights to freedom of speech, religion and to own firearms are not absolute ones that 'trump' any other consideration. Under certain conditions, laws that might seem to some to infringe those rights – outlawing the dissemination of literature about bomb-making or banning the sale of bazookas – may nevertheless be held to be constitutional.

Ambiguous intent. The intent of the Framers of the Constitution's provisions and of those who craft laws enacted today is often unclear. In many cases, the authors of such laws were, and are, themselves divided. Moreover, looking to the intent of the writers of particular laws is also problematic. Sometimes the supposed authors of legislation, for example, elected members of a particular congressional committee, did not know the full contents of legislation since the laws were penned instead by expert unelected professional staff and full-time bureaucrats.

judges'. Democracy depends on those in authority being accountable to the citizens they govern, typically by means of regular elections. Yet most (though not all) American judges are unelected and can exercise tremendous influence in ruling laws and actions by public officials constitutional or unconstitutional. In theory, then, courts can exercise awesome power. Most significantly, they can deny elected officials the fruits of their hard-won victories by striking down the laws that they pass as violating the Constitution. Reflecting such fears of a 'judicial dictatorship', conservative campaigner Pat Buchanan attacked the Supreme Court for protecting 'criminals, atheists, homosexuals, flag burners, illegal aliens – including terrorists – convicts, and pornographers' (O'Brien, 2000: 108). Others, however, contend that protecting minorities is exactly what the Court should be doing.

THE STRUCTURE OF THE COURT SYSTEM

The best way to envisage America's court system is as a pyramid with the Supreme Court at the top. It receives cases from the 13 United States Courts of Appeals, the Court of Military Appeals, and state courts. The Supreme Court receives and disposes of about 5,000 cases each year (or 'term'), most by a brief decision that the subject matter is either not appropriate or sufficiently important to warrant review by the full Court. Each year the Court decides about 150 cases (some but by no means all of great national importance) and about three-quarters of such decisions are announced in full published opinions.

Thousands of litigants try to get their cases before the Court each year, but only a handful end up being decided by the justices. These are the cases that were granted

Exhibit 8.3   The American court system

FEDERAL COURTS		STATE COURTS
US Supreme Court	Highest appellate courts	State Supreme Court
US Court of Appeals for The Federal Circuit Temporary Emergency Court of Appeals	Intermediate appellate courts	Courts of Appeals (exist in about two-thirds of all states; sometimes called Superior or District Courts)
US District Courts	Trial courts of general jurisdiction	District Courts
Examples include Rail Reorganization Court, Court of Federal Claims, Court of International Trade, Court of Veterans' Appeals and Tax Court	Trial courts of limited jurisdiction	Examples include Juvenile Court, Small Claims Court, Justice of the Peace, Magistrate Court and Family Court

certiorari (commonly called 'cert'). There are a few ways that a case may make it to a federal appeals court. Often it comes from a US district court, other times from a state or specialized court or a federal agency.

For example, consider a case heard and decided by a district court. If a party is dissatisfied with the decision rendered, it can have it reviewed in a court of appeals. If dissatisfied with the decision of the court of appeals, the party may seek additional review in the Supreme Court. But the Supreme Court only reviews cases that involve matters of national importance and accepts only a small number of cases each term.

When a case is taken to the Supreme Court, the nine justices must first decide whether they have jurisdiction – meaning that they are the correct court to decide the case. If the Supreme Court – or any other court – does not have jurisdiction, then it does not matter what the justices think about the plaintiffs, defendants or the merits of a case – what they decide will not be binding. If the Supreme

Court decides to hear a case, it will grant a writ of *certiorari* commanding the lower courts to convey records of the case up to the justices.

Two kinds of jurisdiction exist: original (meaning that the court can act like a trial court) and appellate (meaning that the court can review the decision-making of a lower court, on appeal). The Supreme Court has original jurisdiction in only a very small proportion of cases – ones that affect ambassadors and other public ministries and consuls and cases in which an individual American state is a party (typically involving disputes between two states).

In most cases, however, the Supreme Court acts as an appeals court. It may consider cases from most lower federal courts as well as appeals from the highest court of a state in which a judgment can be had, but only if the case involves an important question of federal law. Ultimately, the Court will only consider cases where it has to mitigate a dispute that cannot be brought in any other court or when the question being litigated rests on the interpretation of the Constitution or a federal law. The Supreme Court rarely engages in fact-finding (except when the lower court misapplied the law).

However, establishing jurisdiction does not automatically result in a case reaching the Supreme Court's docket. The Court rejects cases for various reasons. For example, it will not consider a hypothetical question – a case must be grounded in an actual dispute. Also, a Supreme Court decision is definitive. No further appeal is possible, although the Court may take the same issue up at a later time (and decisions can be overturned by constitutional amendment).

Exhibit 8.4   How the process works: hearing and writing the opinion

The term (or annual calendar)
The Court opens a new term on the first Monday in October. Justices hear oral arguments Monday through Wednesday for two straight weeks. Then, the Court recesses for two weeks to write opinions and take care of other business. The pattern of 'sitting' to hear arguments and 'recessing' to take care of opinions continues through the following April. After that point, the Court sits only to announce opinions and release orders. The term ends when the final opinion is released, usually at the end of June.

Oral argument before the Court
When a case goes to the Supreme Court, each side has just 30 minutes to speak to the Court and answer questions. The basic format is: the attorney states the nature and facts of the case, followed by an argument on the law. Often, justices will interrupt the attorney to ask a factual question or pose a hypothetical situation. The most difficult part of oral argument is for the attorneys to remain focused on the points that they want to get across to the Court. The Court may grant additional time for oral argument (as it did in November 2000 when it gave an additional 30 minutes to hear the case brought by George W. Bush about the contested Florida ballots in that year's presidential election), but generally cases are heard in one hour. The extensive process of reading written briefs outlining each side's arguments, and then circulating opinions on these, then takes place in earnest.

The Court debates a case
Conferences are held in the Chief Justice's chambers and are confidential. Only the justices attend. The Chief Justice begins the discussion, followed by the associate justices in order of seniority. A majority is required to decide a case, but the conference votes are not binding. Votes are final only when the final opinion is issued.

Writing opinions
The opinion-writing process is the most time-consuming and complicated process of the Court. The majority opinion is written either by the Chief Justice (if they have voted with the majority) or the most senior associate justice. A justice who writes an opinion must convince four other justices to join the opinion. So begins a long process of negotiation and compromise. Each draft is circulated among the other justices, who will edit and make suggestions. Law clerks do a great deal of work during this process, researching past cases and writing draft opinions.

If no majority exists, a plurality opinion may result. For example, if five justices agree on the result but only two or three agree on the reasoning, the opinion of those two or three is a plurality opinion. Justices who do not agree with the vote on a case typically write a dissenting opinion.

DENYING DEMOCRACY? THE CASE OF FLAG-BURNING

A paradigmatic example of how the Court works is the issue of flag-burning. The Stars and Stripes is a revered symbol, so much so that it is common to find the flag flown outside ordinary American homes. But citizens who are seeking to protest against some controversial action or policy sometimes express their views by burning the flag. Whoever commits such desecration, not surprisingly, deeply offends millions of Americans. As Robert Bork argues:

> The national flag is different from other symbols. Nobody pledges allegiance to the presidential seal or salutes when it goes by. Marines did not fight their way up Mount Suribachi on Iwo Jima to raise a copy of the Constitution on a length of pipe. Nor did forty-eight states and the United States enact laws to protect these symbols from desecration. (Bork, 1990: 128)

In 1989, a case reached the Court where a group of anti-Reagan protestors at the Republican national convention of 1984, in Houston, had burned the flag in contravention of a Texas law that prohibited flag desecration. The Supreme Court, however, ruled in *Texas v. Johnson* (1989) that the Texas law was unconstitutional because it violated the guarantee of freedom of expression that is offered by the First Amendment to the Constitution. As Justice Brennan wrote: 'If there is a bedrock principle underlying the First Amendment, it is that the Government may not prohibit the expression of an idea simply because society finds the idea offensive or disagreeable.'

In response, Congress overwhelmingly passed a new law – the Flag Protection Act of 1989 – that made flag desecration a federal (rather than a state) offence. The following year, in *United States v. Eichman* (1990) the Court once again struck down this new federal law, again for the same reasons about free expression. In a 5–4 decision, the majority once more objected to the suppression of free speech based on the content of the message being advanced.

Here is a prime example of what many Americans fear about the power accorded the courts. A measure supported by the overwhelming majority of Americans – 48 states and the federal government had enacted such anti-desecration laws – is frustrated by the votes of nine individuals (in this case, just five) who are unelected, unaccountable and in place until they either retire or die. Moreover, the justices are, by definition, an elite group. Conventionally, they have attended Ivy League universities such as Harvard and Yale and enjoyed a relatively privileged and affluent existence. They are, in this basic descriptive sense, hardly representative of Americans at large, yet the Constitution accords them the power to strike down the acts of the people's freely chosen elected officials. What type of democracy, then, is this?

Ironically, as Exhibit 8.5 shows, the fact that the Court can exercise such power has not meant that its members are well-known figures. Unlike the trial of O.J. Simpson, the Court's proceedings occur away from the glare of television cameras (the audio feed of oral argument about the 2000 presidential election case was the first time the Court was heard 'live' as its proceedings happened). This largely explains why the justices remain relatively invisible to many Americans, as well as helping to guarantee the institution a measure of dignity often denied members of Congress and the executive branch.

APPOINTING THE JUSTICES

Congress – not the Constitution – sets the number of justices that serve on the Court. The Court has had as few as five members and as many as ten. But since the Judiciary Act of 1889, the Court has consisted of nine members – eight associate justices and one Chief Justice. Justices have precedence according to the seniority of their commissions and each is assigned to one of the courts

Exhibit 8.5   Courting the public: name that judge

Should television cameras be allowed to cover court proceedings? Some argue that this is a necessary part of making a democracy transparent and even educating the public about the Constitution and the rule of law. Others contend that it erodes the dignity of the Court. Certainly, the absence of television seems to reinforce the public's limited awareness of the individuals who actually govern their lives.

Respondents able to name 1989 Supreme Court Justices:

O'Connor	23%
Rehnquist	9%
Kennedy	7%
Scalia	6%
Marshall	5%
Blackmun	4%
Brennan	3%
White	3%
Stevens	1%

(71 per cent of respondents to the survey could not name any justice; only two of 1,005 respondents correctly named all nine.)

Respondents able to name the judge of the TV show The People's Court:

Wapner	54%
Other	1%
Don't know	42%

Source: *Washington Post National Weekly Edition*, June 26–July 2, 1989, p. 37.

of appeals for emergency purposes (such as last-minute death row appeals). The Constitution specifies only one function of the Chief Justice: to preside over the impeachment trial of a president before the Senate (which has happened just twice, with Salmon P. Chase presiding over Andrew Johnson's trial in 1868 and William Rehnquist over Bill Clinton's in 1998–99).

The appointment of Supreme Court justices is one of the most important responsibilities that a president holds, for three reasons. First, typically, the judges will remain on the Court long after the president has departed Washington (federal judges are appointed for life and can be removed from office against their will only through 'impeachment for, and conviction for, treason, bribery or other

high crimes and misdemeanors'). Earl Warren, for example, was Chief Justice for 16 years (1953–69). His successor, Warren Burger, was Chief Justice for 17 years (1969–86) before William Rehnquist became Chief Justice. Burger and Rehnquist both faced four presidents during their tenure (Nixon, Ford, Carter and Reagan, and Reagan, Bush, Clinton and Bush, respectively). Burger's Court was also crucial in prompting Nixon (ironically, the man who had originally appointed Burger) to resign from the office of the presidency over the Watergate scandal.

Secondly, a Supreme Court justice is one of only nine members of the Court, meaning that, compared to the 435 members of the House and the 100 members of the Senate, the proportionate influence of one individual is much greater. This is especially so given that a bare majority of five judges can determine whether or not a law is constitutional.

Thirdly, since the Court can strike down laws and actions as unconstitutional, the power that a justice can wield is potentially very far-reaching. In areas as diverse as abortion and trade policy, the Court – in theory, at least – can exert a more lasting political influence than even a two-term president.

But, as Table 8.1 illustrates, not all presidents get to make nominations to the Supreme Court. Some fortunate ones may have several (Nixon had four, Reagan four, Bush two, and Clinton two), less fortunate others have none (Jimmy Carter became the first president in 80 years not to appoint a single Supreme Court justice and the only president serving a full term not to make a nomination).

The reason for this is not mere luck or happenstance. Justices are acutely aware of the influence they possess, and so often time their resignation with a view to shaping the type of successor likely to replace them on the bench. For example, Thurgood Marshall, the first black justice appointed by Lyndon Johnson in 1967, suffered a heart attack in 1976. Subsequently plagued by acute ill health, he refused to resign during the 1980s, since Republican presidents occupied the White House. Only in 1991, when he could tolerate the situation no longer, did he retire. As he had long feared would occur, President Bush nominated a strongly conservative

judge (and the second black justice on the Court), Clarence Thomas, to fill the vacancy.

Those presidents who do get the opportunity to make a nomination have no guarantee of success, however. The Constitution grants the president the power (in Article II, section 2, clause 2) to nominate justices with the 'advice and consent' of the Senate. Like many constitutional provisions, this has been the subject of intense disagreement over time, and has not been resolved. Defenders of presidential power argue that the appointment power is the president's prerogative alone. They stress the advice portion of the clause, but de-emphasize the consent provision: the Senate is entitled to offer its views but should be circumspect about asserting its power. The implication is that, in all but the most extraordinary circumstances, the Senate should defer to the president's wishes. Conversely, proponents of a meaningful congressional role argue that the constitutional clause amounts to a veto power that the Senate can wield against presidential nominees it dislikes, in much the same way that the Senate can reject treaties that the president has negotiated.

The historical record shows that it is the second interpretation that has held sway in practical politics. But the process by which the Senate exercises its power has changed significantly over time. What many Americans regard as normal practice is a relatively recent innovation. That is, once nominated, prospective justices are required to attend

TABLE 8.1   Presidential judicial appointments compared

	Nixon	Ford	Carter	Reagan	Bush	Clinton
Supreme Court	4	1	0	4	2	2
Circuit Court	45	12	56	78	37	49
District Court	182	52	202	290	148	246
Special Courts	7	1	3	10	0	4
Total	**238**	**66**	**261**	**382**	**187**	**301**

Source: O'Brien (2000: 116).

hearings before the Senate Judiciary Committee, which, in the modern era, are conventionally televised. The Committee then makes a recommendation to the Senate and the full Senate then votes to confirm or reject the nominee.

The importance of the Senate role is especially significant when one considers two factors: (i) the kinds of nominee that presidents select; and (ii) which party controls the Senate. In the first regard, the criteria for selection are many and varied, and the candidates often equally numerous and heterogeneous. There are no set requirements (constitutional or otherwise) to be a justice, although in practice it is overwhelmingly lawyers who have been nominated to the bench. Usually, the president takes into account the candidate's legal and judicial experience, educational background and professional reputation, but political considerations also play a very influential part.

In regard to the second factor, getting a nominee past the Senate can also be a tricky enterprise, especially when the chamber is in the hands of the party that does not control the White House. In these circumstances, the nomination of a justice can assume a symbolic status as a political virility test between the White House and Capitol Hill, a challenge of how powerful the president may be in regard to Congress. Sometimes, presidents are tempted to regard the nomination as a prerogative that they dare the Senate to refuse.

Senate rejections remain unusual events. From 1789 to 1997, only 29 of 147 nominations failed. But when they occur, they typically arouse marked political controversy. In some cases, presidents react extremely badly to a rejected nominee and petulantly propose an even less palatable successor to the Senate. Both Nixon and Reagan, for example, followed this course. In Nixon's case, such was the disastrous character of the Carswell nomination in 1970 that his principal sponsor in

the Senate, Roman Hruska (Republican, Nebraska) resorted to the ingenious argument that since there were a lot of mediocre Americans, they were entitled to representation on the Court in the form of a judicial mediocrity: 'Even if he is mediocre there are a lot of mediocre judges and people and lawyers. They are all entitled to a little representation, aren't they, and a little chance? We can't have all Brandeises, Cardozos, and Frankfurters and stuff like that there.'

Although exceptions to the rule, the most controversial nominations in recent years nevertheless provide a telling commentary on the politicization of the modern process. Robert Bork and Clarence Thomas differed somewhat in their approaches to constitutional interpretation, but both were ardently conservative in their political values and believed in 'originalism' – a search for what the Framers of the Constitution meant when they made their provisions. Nominated by Reagan in 1987, Bork became the subject of intense national controversy and a focus for strong tensions between the White House and Capitol Hill. Over 300 anti-Bork interest groups, and over 100 pro-Bork groups, sought to influence the views of the senators who held his fate in their hands. Over $15 million was spent over the summer of 1987 to try to sway their views. In the end, Bork was rejected by the largest margin of any nominee in history: 58–42. All but two votes supporting him were Republican; all but six opposing him were Democratic. The crucial swing group, the Southern Democrats, voted heavily against Bork. In their polling, they noted how vehemently African Americans – a crucial bloc of their biracial electoral coalitions – opposed Bork's nomination. They voted accordingly. Such was the level of antagonism over the nomination that a new verb entered the American vocabulary: 'to bork', meaning to derail a nomination through foul as well as fair means.

Four years later, the nomination of another

Exhibit 8.6   The strange story of Judge Robert Bork

When Reagan nominated Bork, Senator Edward Kennedy appeared on the Senate floor to denounce the judge. He claimed that Bork's America would be one of backstreet abortions and segregation. The effort was extraordinarily effective in mobilizing a broad coalition of liberals against the nomination. A television advertisement saw a family gazing in awe at the Supreme Court building in Washington while narrator Gregory Peck warned that Bork 'defended poll taxes and literacy tests, which kept many Americans from voting. He opposed the civil rights law that ended "Whites Only" signs at lunch counters. He doesn't believe the Constitution protects your right to privacy. And he thinks freedom of speech does not apply to literature and art and music.' Peck went on: 'Robert Bork could have the last word on your rights as citizens, but the Senate has the last word on him. Please urge your senators to vote against the Bork nomination, because if Robert Bork wins a seat on the Supreme Court, it will be for life – his life and yours.'

But the facts of the case were less clear-cut. Bork had opposed the Civil Rights Act of 1964, though he later changed his mind. As Solicitor General in 1974, he willingly carried out the orders of President Nixon (which his two predecessors had refused) to fire the Special Prosecutor into Watergate, Archibald Cox. But traditionally, only two criteria governed whether the Senate would confirm: legal expertise and ethical good standing. On both grounds, Bork was an impeccable nominee. His scholarship was well respected, if controversial, while his character was unimpeachable. During the hearings, Bork was suspected of having undergone a 'confirmation transformation', moderating his previously hard-line views to suit the more political preferences of the committee majority. Ultimately, Bork was left as something of a martyr to the American conservative movement, and went on to pen scathing critiques of modern judges and jurisprudence (*The Tempting of America: The Political Seduction of the Law*, 1990) and American culture and politics more broadly (the soberly entitled *Slouching Towards Gomorrah: Modern Liberalism and American Decline*, 1996). Richard Posner, one of the most respected and influential of current federal judges, noted that despite his differences on matters of constitutional interpretation with Bork, the judge should have been confirmed in 1987 and 'would have been an outstanding Justice' (Posner, 1998: 230 n2).

conservative judge proved equally controversial. Bush nominated Clarence Thomas, a judge whose record was not prestigious but who promised to divide the Democratic majority in the Senate, for while conservative, Thomas was also black. The nomination proved even more divisive when a scandal erupted concerning charges that Thomas had sexually harassed another African American, Anita Hill, a former employee who subsequently became a law professor. The subsequent nationally televised hearings presented another example of the combination of prurience and Puritanism so beloved of Americans. Witnesses gave testimony about whether Thomas had rented a porno movie featuring 'Long Dong Silver' and had 'jokingly' enquired about whether an employee had left pubic hair on a can of coke. During the confirmation battle Thomas was reportedly 'reduced to uncontrollable fits of weeping, vomiting, hyperventilating, and writhing on the floor' and suffered visions of people trying to kill him (Lazarus, 1999: 458). Ultimately, Thomas was narrowly confirmed (52–48) with the Southern Democrats again proving crucial. This time, they found that a majority of southern whites approved of Thomas's nomination (despite his race); and so too did a majority of blacks (despite his conservatism). It was not the Senate's finest hour, and Thomas subsequently proved a much more partisan than disinterested judicial figure on the bench.

AFTER THE APPOINTMENT: LIFE TENURE AND JUDICIAL INDEPENDENCE

Presidents not only face political hurdles before successful nominations win approval by the Senate. Frequently, they also encounter disappointment with justices who successfully win confirmation and make it to the Court. In many cases, the justices fulfil their role in a fashion that deeply irritates their presidential nominators: by exercising independent judgement. This is all the more galling for presidents since, unless Congress impeaches a justice, the judge is there for life. In an age when even many university professors no longer possess life tenure, Supreme Court justices do. Again, this reinforces the importance of careful selection for both the president and Senate.

THREE COURTS, THREE TYPES OF 'ACTIVISM'

Given its unelected composition and clearly defined adjudicative role, the judiciary is far more insulated from the pervasive societal influence that characterizes the rest of American government. But the Court is not hermetically sealed-off from the rest of the political system or society. Both specific decisions and the broader approach that the justices adopt to the law are profoundly affected by wider developments in American society. It has often been claimed that the

Exhibit 8.7   Judicial independence: the ones that got away

When they nominate justices to the Court, presidents want to achieve different goals: reward supporters; pay back political debts; achieve a more representative court; and place someone on the Court who reflects the president's own preferences. Unfortunately for them, this often does not prove to be the case:

Tom Clark. Truman appointed Clark and later reflected with typical Midwestern candour that 'it isn't so much that he's a bad man. It's just that he's such a dumb son-of-a-bitch. He's about the dumbest man I think I've ever run across. . . . I never will know what got into me when I made that appointment, and I'm as sorry as I can be for doing it.'

Earl Warren. The prime example of judicial independence: a former Republican Governor of California who had presided over the internment of Japanese Americans during the Second World War, Warren was a potential presidential candidate in 1952, but he supported Ike Eisenhower in return for a promise that he would receive the first vacancy on the Court that turned up. As it happened, that was Chief Justice. Warren then presided over some of the most innovative, controversial and liberal rulings in American history, inducing Ike to describe the nomination as the 'biggest damn fool mistake' he had made as president.

Warren Burger. Nixon appointed Burger Chief Justice in 1969, with the express intention to halt and then reverse the liberal rulings of the Warren Court, but Burger's court – sometimes against his objections, sometimes with his support – presided over several rulings that deeply antagonized Nixon: introducing busing for racial integration, establishing a woman's constitutional right to an abortion, and forcing Nixon – by a unanimous verdict in *United States v. Richard M. Nixon* (1974) – to give up the incriminating tapes of his involvement in the Watergate cover-up to the Special Prosecutor investigating the affair.

Court 'follows the election returns', meaning that the justices take notice of the dominant trends in public opinion expressed through federal and state elections and respond to them, albeit slowly, incrementally and sometimes reluctantly.

For many years, this approach seemed correct. For example, having struck down key parts of his New Deal, the Court in the mid-1930s faced a direct threat to its independence when President Franklin D. Roosevelt proposed adding a new justice for each one on the bench who reached 70 years of age – the so-called 'Court-packing plan'. Though defeated in Congress, the existing justices took note and the 'switch in time that saved nine' (a new majority supportive of the New Deal regulations) was a clear expression of the Court responding to public support for the New Deal's federal government intervention in tempering the unbridled free market.

However, this is less sure a guide to contemporary Court politics. Following the election returns assumes that those returns offer a clear guide and, in contemporary America, this is much less obviously the case in the era of divided party control of the federal government. Consequently, the Court too has been affected both by an apparent absence of public consensus on many key political questions and the sometimes bitter conflicts between Democrats and Republicans. This, in turn, has been manifest in the changing approaches of successive Courts (named after their Chief Justices).

The Warren Court (1953–69)

The Warren Court has been both celebrated and castigated as, respectively, the greatest advance for liberties and equality and the most heinous federal judicial intrusion on traditional rights and the autonomy of the individual states. Martin Shapiro (1990) argues that the Court initiated five controversial policies in much the way that elected legislatures conventionally make policy: desegregation, reapportionment, the rights of criminal defendants, birth control, and emasculating state obscenity laws. As he puts it:

Exhibit 8.8 Key cases under the Warren Court

Brown v. Board of Education (1954). A unanimous and momentous decision that struck down the state-sanctioned segregation of public schools in the South.

Roth v. United States (1957). Liberalized laws on obscenity such that only 'hard-core' pornography was unprotected speech under the First Amendment.

Baker v. Carr (1962). Mandated reapportioning of congressional districts on an equality principle despite the fact that some provisions of the Constitution (such as the composition of the US Senate and the Electoral College) contain expressly unequal modes of representation.

Griswold v. Connecticut (1965). Struck down a Connecticut state law that banned the use of contraceptives even by married couples. Although the law was no longer enforced, the elaboration in the decision of a 'right to privacy' would later be controversially extended to create a constitutional right to an abortion in 1973.

Miranda v. Arizona (1966). Expanded the rights of criminal defendants, mandating that police had to tell an arrested person of his or her rights (the famous list beginning, 'You have the right to remain silent . . .').

Loving v. Virginia (1967). Struck down state laws banning racial intermarriage on the basis of the 'equal protection' clause of the Fourteenth Amendment.

'Few American politicians would care to run on a platform of desegregation, pornography, abortion, and the "coddling" of criminals' (Shapiro, 1990: 48). Although Warren had previously been a Republican governor of California, his record as a Chief Justice was anything but conservative – much to Eisenhower's annoyance.

The Burger Court (1969–86)

While Warren boldly went where no Supreme Court had gone before, Burger ventured less confidently in his aftermath. In a sense, despite the landmark rulings and the controversies they generated, the political context for Warren had been less formidable than for Burger, for while the rulings that the Warren Court gave were often audacious and controversial, they tended to make declarations of fundamental principle. By contrast, Burger's court was left with the much more tricky and delicate task of implementing these rulings on the ground. Thus, for example, where Warren boldly declared segregated schools unconstitutional, Burger faced the (in some ways more challenging) task of ensuring how practically to achieve desegregated school systems in the face of white resistance and patterns of residential racial segregation that resulted not from *de jure* state law but from *de facto* historic housing patterns.

Such a problematic context largely explains what Victor Blasi (1983) characterizes as the 'rootless activism' of the Burger years. Rather than striking out in clear and bold directions, like Warren, Burger's rulings were a mixture

Exhibit 8.9   Key cases under the Burger Court

Swann v. Charlotte Mecklenberg Board of Education (1971). Allowed the busing of black and white students beyond their neighbourhood school in order to achieve racially balanced school systems.

Furman v. Georgia (1972). By a 5–4 majority the Court struck down the death penalty as violating the Eighth Amendment's prohibition on 'cruel and unusual' punishments.

Roe v. Wade (1973). Stated that the Constitution's 'right to privacy' protected a woman's right to terminate her pregnancy in the first six months of pregnancy.

Miller v. California (1973). An attempt to tighten obscenity law by stipulating that a work had to possess 'serious literary, artistic, political or scientific value' in order to be protected as speech by the First Amendment.

US v. Nixon (1974). Denied the applicability of 'executive privilege' and thereby forced President Nixon to surrender White House tapes revealing his involvement in the Watergate cover-up.

Gregg v. Georgia (1976). Approved new death penalty laws that provided for separate trials regarding guilt or innocence and then the sentence, stating that capital punishment was not always unconstitutional.

Bakke v. Regents of the University of California (1978). Ruled that formal racial quotas were impermissible but that race was an acceptable criterion to take into account in university admissions policies.

INS v. Chadha (1983). Struck down the 'legislative veto' that allowed executive agencies to act subject only to the House and Senate voting against them (but Congress and the executive essentially ignored the ruling).

of pragmatism, principle and precedent. For those conservatives hoping that the recent years of liberal advance by the judiciary would be reversed, Burger represented the disappointing 'counter-revolution that wasn't'. On some issues, such as capital punishment and abortion, Burger even extended the liberal assault on conservative state laws.

Partly as a result, the challenge of reshaping the federal judiciary became a prominent theme in the Reagan administration. Conservatives who railed against the Court's decisions on abortion, capital punishment, equal protection, church and state and obscenity, firmly believed that through making 'sound' appointments the policies that they disapproved of could be struck down through judicial intervention. This had the notable attraction that it could circumvent a Congress dominated by the Democrats.

The Rehnquist Court (1986–)

The Rehnquist Court was the focus for the hopes and fears of conservatives and liberals, respectively. Conservatives hoped that, with appointments made by successive Republican presidents, the Court would reverse many of the liberal decisions of prior years.

In particular, it was hoped that *Roe v. Wade*, affirmative action, prayer in school and pornography would all witness conservative responses. Liberals feared that this would indeed be the case. Both looked to Rehnquist as 'Warren in reverse' – an aggressively conservative Court.

However, the overall record was more mixed. The Rehnquist Court disappointed conservatives by failing to overturn *Roe* (although its critics contended that it had effectively gutted the meaning of the decision, leaving it as a largely symbolic ruling). It also upheld the right to burn the flag. Only by 1995 could the Court be said to have developed a clear and reasonably coherent conservative approach, particularly with regard to issues of states' rights (where it proved mostly deferential to state laws). Even then, as Exhibit 8.11 illustrates, some decisions suggested that a mostly conservative set of justices could still exercise independent judgment.

THE LIMITS TO COURT INFLUENCE

Much of the attention devoted to the Court naturally focuses on the many examples of

Exhibit 8.10   Key cases under the Rehnquist Court

Webster v. Reproductive Services (1989). A 5–4 majority upheld two of several restrictive provisions of a Missouri law regarding the use of public employees and facilities for non-therapeutic abortions and tests of foetus viability.

US v. Eichman (1990). Ruled that the Flag Protection Act of 1989 violated the right to free speech of the First Amendment.

Planned Parenthood v. Casey (1992). Although this did not overturn *Roe v. Wade*, the Court allowed more autonomy for states to regulate the conditions under which abortions could occur.

US v. Lopez (1995). Struck down the Gun Free School Zones Act of 1990 that had made possession of a firearm within 1,000 feet of a school a federal criminal offence.

Reno v. US (1997). A unanimous Court struck down the Communications Decency Act of 1996 (that sought to prevent the transmission of 'indecent' materials by e-mail and Internet) as an unconstitutional violation of the First Amendment.

Exhibit 8.11   Close calls: some key split decisions from the 1999–2000 term

Of 74 decisions issued by the Court in the 1999–2000 session, 21 were decided completely or in part in rulings of 5–4, including:

United States v. Morrison. The majority found that Congress exceeded its authority when it allowed women who were victims of violence to sue their attackers in federal court.

Stenberg v. Carhart. A narrow majority said a Nebraska law banning what abortion opponents call 'partial-birth' abortions was too broadly drawn and presented an undue burden on a woman seeking an abortion. The court also said it was unconstitutional because it did not contain an exception to protect the health of the woman.

Boy Scouts of America v. Dale. The majority found that requiring the Boy Scouts to admit homosexuals as scout leaders violated the group's free association rights.

United States v. Playboy Entertainment Group, Inc. The majority said that restrictions on the broadcasting of adult material, enacted by Congress in the 1996 telecommunications law, placed an undue burden on free speech.

FDA v. Brown and Williamson Tobacco Corp. The Court ruled that the Food and Drug Administration does not have the authority to regulate tobacco without a more specific authorization from Congress.

Apprendi v. New Jersey. On hate crimes, the court ruled that the Constitution requires that juries – not judges – determine whether a crime was motivated by bias. A jury must determine that a crime was motivated by bias beyond a reasonable doubt in order for a more severe sentence to be imposed.

the justices using their power to strike down the laws and actions of elected officials as unconstitutional. Although most of the Court's work is mundane and the major decisions it gives are a decided minority of the total, it is rare for a term to pass that does not feature at least a few politically controversial rulings. Lawyers and political scientists examine these in detail and increasingly attempt to examine how far judges' votes are merely covers for their personal policy goals.

However, some academics take a different approach and question whether the extent of the Court's political influence is very great, even on landmark rulings about abortion, civil rights and the death penalty. They argue that when one examines the real effect of Court decisions, the extent to which the justices actually affect practical policy outcomes is far more modest than is often assumed. Some even go so far as to argue that, as far as the Court being an engine of social change is

concerned, it represents merely a 'hollow hope' (Rosenberg, 1991). On this view, its actions are mostly symbolic rather than substantive. Why?

One fundamental reason is that the Court cannot enforce its own rulings. The Court lacks both the 'power of the purse' and the kinds of instrument of coercion – an army, police force or bureaucracy – that can implement its rulings, that can put those decisions into effect on the ground. As such, the Court can make pronouncements of constitutionality on particular laws, but whether these have any effect in the real world depends on two further, contingent factors: the response of other branches of government and the attitudes of the public at large. On this view, the Court can sometimes resemble a petulant child declaring what it wants but being dependent on its parents to deliver.

Other powerful constraints on the Court's influence also exist. As a legal body, the Court

Exhibit 8.12   Symbolism or substance? Abortion and desegregation

Abortion

The Court's decisions in 1973 established the constitutional right of a woman to terminate her pregnancy in the first trimester. This overturned 46 state laws that made abortion a criminal offence. But it did not mean that women across America who desired to obtain an abortion could do so. The Hyde Amendment of 1976 prohibited the federal government from using public funds to establish or support abortion clinics. In 1989 and 1992, two Court decisions permitted states to regulate the conditions surrounding abortion providing that they did not impose an 'undue burden' on the women concerned. In practice, the lack of federal and state funding has meant that many states lack abortion service providers, leaving the 'right' to an abortion as a very uncertain and location-dependent one.

Desegregation

When the Court declared southern school segregation to be unconstitutional in the *Brown* decisions of 1954 and 1955, it effectively struck down the way of life of an entire region of the United States that had existed since the latter part of the nineteenth century (which, of course, had followed the pre-Civil War era of slavery). But declaring segregated schooling unconstitutional was one thing, achieving the practical integration of the races in schools was immensely more difficult. Ten years after *Brown*, only 1 per cent of southern schools had mixed races together. Only when Congress passed the Civil Rights Act of 1964, and with the executive branch implementing its provisions, did a change begin to occur in the South. In a series of controversial rulings during the early 1970s, the Court allowed states to order schoolchildren to be bused beyond their local neighbourhood schools to more distant schools to achieve integration across America. However, many white parents simply took their children out of public schools and sent them to private and religious schools. By the beginning of the twenty-first century, black and white children were again being educated in mostly separate schools – a 'voluntary' return to the racial separatism of the first half of the previous century.

is obliged to follow the doctrine of *stare decisis* or precedent – it cannot simply make a new law that contradicts prior rulings. Similarly, the Court follows legal procedures and the justices can make a distinction between their personal preferences ('what would I like to happen?') and the demands of law ('what is required by law?'). Ultimately, democratic methods exist in which the Court can be curbed, either through a formal constitutional amendment to overturn a specific decision or through Congress removing its appellate jurisdiction over an entire area (dozens of bills have been introduced since 1973 to remove the appellate role of the Court on abortion, for example, but none successfully).

Having emphasized the difficulties that the Court faces, the controversies it is forced to

address, and the problems that it confronts in alienating sections of American society who do not approve of particular decisions, it is perhaps worth noting a simple but remarkable fact: most of the time, the Court manages to reach a settlement that reflects the views of most Americans. Admittedly, it does so slowly and circuitously quite often, but that it gets there in the end is a crucial mainstay of its public support.

Partly, this is a function of the generally acute political sensitivity of the justices. More important, though, is the centrality of the Constitution to American life. The Court is the most appropriate institution to adjudicate on what the document says. Imagine President Nixon being charged with deciding whether his actions in Watergate were unconstitutional, or 535 members of Congress deciding whether the president's waging war in Vietnam, Cambodia, Panama or Kuwait were constitutional. The proximity of lawmakers to electoral politics makes them unreliable guardians of constitutional rectitude. As such, whatever the Court decides in a case has an authoritative character absent from the views of even presidents, much less members of Congress.

This has helped to ensure a continuing role and respect for the Court in an otherwise election-heavy democracy. Such a contribution is vitally important. The American system was not designed as a purely majoritarian democracy. Nor was the Constitution intended to be unchangeable short of formal amendment. Protections against majority rule and guarantees of individual rights and liberties were entrenched in the Constitution. In rejecting the laws and actions of elected officials, the Court necessarily acts in a counter-majoritarian fashion – that makes its legitimacy precarious and shrewd judgement a necessity. But liberal democracy is not synonymous with majority rule, and the US Constitution established a democratic form of government that contained expressly anti-majoritarian features.

Moreover, it is not inappropriate that those individuals least pressured by the demands of electioneering should be entrusted with policing the boundaries between the different branches of the federal government, between the federal government and the 50 state governments, and between the citizen and the state. The record of the Supreme Court is far from unimpeachable and is deeply stained by its decisions about slavery, racial segregation and Japanese wartime internment in, respectively, *Dred Scott*, *Plessy* and *Korematsu*. That, however, is not an argument for abandoning the Court or curbing its power of constitutional judicial review, but rather for persevering with its role and preserving the principle that only the most accomplished justices should be privileged to sit on its bench.

A JURIDICIZED POLITICS AND A POLITICIZED JUDICIARY?

Whatever the political aspects to the judicial role, the myth of judicial neutrality has conventionally been seen as crucial to the effective functioning of the federal courts. The fear of many commentators – not least judges themselves – is that recent political controversies have eroded this myth. For judges to be 'political' to students of political science is one thing; for them to be seen by the public to be political is another. What is dangerous here is that if judges are regarded as essentially being just another type of politician, then they will be evaluated on the same basis, that is, instead of enquiring as to the experience and prestige of a judge, a potential appointee will be asked about his substantive political views. In place of broad themes of integrity and constitutional interpretation, the judge is asked about whether he supports a pro-choice position on abortion or an anti-quotas position on affirmative action.

Some critics argue that this is precisely what has occurred since 1981. With divided party control of the federal government, the institutional rivalries over the judiciary that were established by the Constitution became overlaid by partisan antagonisms. Initially, under Reagan and, to a lesser extent, Bush, this took the form of a Republican White House screening its prospective nominees to ensure that genuine conservatives were appointed, while from 1986 to 1992, a Democratic Senate challenged many of those nominations. One of Reagan's Attorney Generals, Edwin Meese, observed that the rigorous judicial selection process was designed 'to institutionalize the Reagan revolution so it can't be set aside no matter what happens in future presidential elections' (O'Brien, 2000: 96).

From 1994 to 2000, the roles were reversed, with President Clinton eager to encourage diversity on the bench challenged by a Republican Senate at least as keen to stop liberal appointees. According to a bipartisan group called Citizens for Independent Courts, the average time for Senate action on judicial nominations rose from 38 days in 1977–78 (when both the presidency and the Senate majority were Democratic) to 144 days in 1987–88 (when a Republican president faced a Democratic Senate) to 201 days in 1997–98 (when a Democratic President faced a Republican Senate). The judicial appointment process has become subject to increasing partisan and institutional conflict. Twenty-four of Bill Clinton's nominees to federal appeals courts from 1995 to 2001 were blocked by Republicans without even formal hearings being convened.

Clinton, both by design and unintentionally, accelerated this politicization further. As David O'Brien observes:

> Ironically, this constitutional law scholar turned politician who never was able to escape his past in office failed to give federal judgeships high priority or to view them as instruments of presidential power. Constantly moving from one crisis to another, he failed to achieve an overarching political vision. His administration's goals in judicial recruitment were limited from the outset, and they became increasingly constrained ... Clinton appointed two Supreme Court justices and a large number of lower court judges who were highly qualified and who increased the representation of women and minorities on the federal bench. Still, he abandoned a large number of judicial nominees, avoided confirmation battles, and, particularly in his second term, was forced to compromise presidential prerogatives in judicial selection by trading judgeships with Republican senators and appointing judges opposed to his political positions. In these and other ways, Clinton weakened the presidency. (O'Brien, 2000: 116)

Senators not of the president's political party know that it is a good bet that his nominees will rule in ways that they disapprove or even deplore, in a wide range of politically charged cases. Divisions in courts often, though not always, follow the party lines of those who appointed the judges.

Such judicial divisions reflect the increasing politicization of the law itself. As judges have extended their powers ever deeper into the realm of politics, any semblance of consensus on what were once called 'neutral principles of law' has disintegrated. For example, some liberal judges who stress the need to protect freedom of speech when the issue is government subsidies for sexually explicit art, embrace the use of 'harassment' laws to punish speech offensive to racial minorities or women and champion government discrimination against religious speech. Yet equally, some conservative judges who have emphasized 'judicial restraint' and fidelity to the plain text and original meaning of the Constitution, increasingly compromise their principles in an absolutist zeal to strike down racial preferences in education and employment or to expand states' rights on matters of gender or homosexual equality. At the same time, increasing numbers of law professors in America argue that every judicial decision is an essentially political projection of the judge's racial, sexual and economic perspective and, to this extent, is illegitimate.

Others, however, wholeheartedly reject these views. Criticism of 'political judging', while accurate as a description of what has happened, is misplaced in terms of its assessment of the merits and flaws of this phenomenon. On this view, there is nothing wrong with asking judges about their views on the issues that are salient to the public. After all, since we know as a matter of brute fact that courts now will often rule on abortion, civil rights and the death penalty, why not find out what a prospective judge, who will be charged with deciding such cases, actually thinks?

An alternative criticism is that, whatever the descriptive and normative validity of the 'politicized judiciary' case, it is simply ahistorical. The nineteenth century was full of examples of overtly partisan warfare over the courts, as was the critical period during the 1930s when the Court struck down key pieces of New Deal legislation (until, threatened by Roosevelt's notorious, though unsuccessful, court-packing plan, the justices reversed their opposition in 1937). On this line, then, a politicized judiciary is nothing new in America, however unwelcome its recent return and – arguably – increased scope may be.

In some senses, as in much of political life, where one stands on these issues depends largely on where one sits. That is, if the result of a ruling is favourable, the method by which that outcome is attained is unlikely to cause much concern. Liberals were alternately unhappy about the New Deal era Court (until 1937), pleased by the Warren Court, and increasingly dismayed by the Rehnquist Court's steady retreat from liberal judicial activism. Conservatives, mostly, felt the exact opposite. On specific issues, consistency is elusive. Liberals who oppose anti-desecration laws about the Stars and Stripes are considerably keener on laws that prohibit public display of the Confederate flag; conservatives who loathe protections for burning the national flag tend to look more generously on protections for the symbol of Dixie. Both camps resort to accusations of activism against decisions they dislike, while defending those they approve of in terms of appropriately modest judicial restraint.

Moreover, while the response of politicians may be to find nominees without strong political or ideological views, thereby keeping some of the best legal minds off the bench, this may not be all bad. Given that a lack of consensus exists on where law finishes and politics begins, it may be preferable to have judges who are reluctant to impose their own political and moral values on the body politic, deferential to the primacy of elected officials in making broad legislative choices, sensitive to competing arguments, and suspicious of absolutes and extremes.

But although this response is superficially compelling, it neglects an important point about the rule of law and the role of judges. Law is fundamentally about process. The results are, in this sense, secondary considerations. What is crucial is that the decisions have been arrived at in the appropriate manner. Judging in a 'creative' manner may

well yield results that please many in terms of the outcomes. The notion of the 'living Constitution' seems to sanction such practices. But such creativity also poses two types of problems.

One problem is that of stability. The merit of the law is its predictability. In principle, once the possibility of creative judging is opened, it is difficult to see where and what limits exist to its scope. A second difficulty then arises, in providing limits. For if proponents of the 'living Constitution' are correct, the Court should attend to what majority or 'civilized' preferences are on questions such as abortion. Yet the Bill of Rights was expressly designed to be independent of majority preferences. A court that bases its interpretation of the Bill of Rights on what majorities prefer abandons its role of protecting minorities.

The second problem is one of legitimacy. Political victories won through conventional democratic channels are likely to be more legitimate and enduring than ones secured through judicial routes. Yet there now exists scarcely any policy or issue – from gun control and tobacco regulation to the issue of 'grandparents' rights' – that Americans do not think appropriate subjects for resolution through litigation.

Neither liberals nor conservatives should welcome such a situation. Bork may be wrong to suggest that the law has been 'seduced' by politics, but it has certainly been more open to its advances than previously and has sometimes succumbed. A period of abstinence may now be in order but, in practice, the close embrace of law and politics remains a stark fact of American public life.

CONCLUSION

Criticism of the Court as the most, not the least, dangerous branch of American government is not new. In 1819 it was said that 'the Constitution . . . is a mere thing of wax in the hands of the judiciary, which they may twist and shape into any form they please'. In 1861, another complained that 'if . . . the policy of the Government upon vital questions affecting the whole people is to be irrevocably fixed by decisions of the Supreme Court . . . the people will have ceased to be their own rulers'. And in 1937, it was protested that 'the Court . . . has improperly set itself up as . . . a super-legislature . . . reading into the Constitution words and implications which are not there'. Thomas Jefferson, Abraham Lincoln and Franklin D. Roosevelt, respectively, were no strangers to an 'imperial judiciary'.

The broad and deep reverence in which the Court is popularly held is a by-product of the universal esteem Americans profess for the Constitution and the rule of law. But the justices are constantly aware of their own role and the formidable dangers that the Court confronts in handing down divisive and controversial decisions. The legitimacy of the Court depends on its remaining pragmatic, yet simultaneously adhering to proper modes of constitutional interpretation. That tension has become increasingly fraught over time as, to paraphrase de Tocqueville, scarcely any judicial question now arises which is not, sooner or later, turned into an explicitly political question.

To many critics, the Court remains the only appropriate institution of the federal government to interpret the Constitution. It is precisely through its distance from electoral politics that the Court can resist majoritarian pressures, adapt the Constitution to a changing society, and contribute to the political stability of America. When the election returns are themselves unclear, the Court's task becomes more difficult but no less central. The exercise of judicial review is anti-majoritarian and undemocratic, but democracy in general is not synonymous with majority rule and the Constitution established a system that was neither straightforwardly majoritarian nor wholly democratic. What is more, it remains open to other branches of government to challenge judicial interpretations since both the president and members of Congress take oaths to uphold the Constitution.

Ultimately, the Court's role is crucial to the apparent changelessness of the Constitution. In effect, the institution is a continuing constitutional convention, debating and redefining what the document means to a changing America. To charge that the Court is acting politically is therefore not so much inaccurate as irrelevant. Politics is inherent to judicial action and inextricable from a democracy that protects minorities as well as indulging majorities. It is ironic that it is only through the interventions of a body of unelected judges denying elected officials the fruits of their victories that America can claim to be a functioning constitutional democracy. The danger of straying too far from the Constitution, however, is the gradual erosion of the very authority that courts need to command in order to intervene to resolve disputes.

FURTHER READING

Kermit Hall (ed.), *The Oxford Companion to the United States Supreme Court* (1992) is a superb compendium of entries on all aspects of the top court, including cases, justices, and topics ranging from capital punishment to executive–legislative relations.

Richard Hodder-Williams, 'Six Definitions of Political and the US Supreme Court', *British Journal of Political Science*, 22 (1) (1992), in framing the discussion on abortion, is an excellent analysis of how the Court is a political institution.

Edward Lazarus, *Closed Chambers: The Rise, Fall, and Future of the Modern Supreme Court* (1999) is an excellent inside account of the Court's personalities and procedures, showing in detail how the legal body operates in a thoroughly political fashion.

Robert McKeever, *Raw Judicial Power? The Supreme Court and American Society* (2nd edition) (1995) is a balanced and readable discussion of some important controversies that the Court has tackled, including abortion, capital punishment and affirmative action.

John Maltese, *The Selling of Supreme Court Justices* (1998) is a well-written account of how presidents go about persuading the Senate to confirm their nominees.

David O'Brien, 'Judicial Legacies: the Clinton Presidency and the Courts', in Colin Campbell and Bert Rockman (eds), *The Clinton Legacy* (2000) is a detailed and clear assessment of Clinton's approach to the judiciary.

Terri Jennings Peretti, *In Defense of a Political Court* (1999) is an excellent book reviewing the different approaches to the Court's interpreting role and defending its political credentials.

Tinsley Yarbrough, *The Rehnquist Court and the Constitution* (2000) is an excellent scholarly analysis of the Court's mixed approach to constitutional interpretation.

WEB LINKS

US Supreme Court
http://www.supremecourtus.gov

Supreme Court information and rulings
http://www.law.cornell.edu/supct

US legal code
http://www.law.cornell.edu/uscode

Comprehensive guide to all aspects of the US Constitution, key cases and the American legal system
http://www.findlaw.com

American Bar Association
http://www.abanet.org

Hieros Gamos, guides to law organizations and governments
http://www.hg.org

Justice Department site about federal bench vacancies and nominees
http://www.usdoj.gov/olp

Official site of the federal court system
http://www.uscourts.gov

Brennan Center for Justice, New York University School of Law
http://www.brennancenter.org

A politically liberal site
http://www.independentjudiciary.com

A politically conservative site
http://www.judicialselection.org

A site about the lobbying of sitting judges
http://www.tripsforjudges.org

American Judicature Society
http://www.ajs.org

National Center for State Courts
http://www.ncsconline.org

QUESTIONS

- How far can the role of an unelected judiciary in America's democracy be defended?

- 'Since judges in America exercise such marked political influence, they should be elected by the people.' Discuss.

- What principles should guide judges in interpreting the Constitution?

- What limits, if any, exist to the power of federal courts?

- Is the Supreme Court too powerful an institution or is its influence overestimated by its critics?

9 Interest Groups

Americans of all ages, all stations of life, and all types of disposition are forever forming associations. There are not only commercial and industrial associations . . . but others of a thousand different types – religious, moral, serious, futile, very general and very limited, immensely large and very minute.

Alexis de Tocqueville, 1835

By a faction I understand a number of citizens, whether amounting to a majority or minority of the whole, who are united and actuated by some common impulse of passion, or of interest, adverse to the rights of other citizens, or to the permanent and aggregate interests of the community.

James Madison, *Federalist Papers*, No. 10

- Interest Group Activism
- A Typology of Interest Groups
- Interest Group Functions, Strategies and Tactics
- Approaches to Interest Group Influence
- The Best Democracy Money Can Buy?
- Conclusion

Chapter Summary

Interest groups are prominent and important participants in the American political system. The First Amendment guarantees the right of each citizen to petition the government. Today, thousands of interest lobbies of varying sizes do precisely that on every conceivable issue, from gun control to health care to US policy towards China. Most Americans belong to at least one interest group and many belong to several simultaneously. Such participation occurs for a variety of reasons and interest groups target the multiple access points that exist in the governmental system. But political scientists disagree about both the extent of interest group influence on American government and the merits of the influence that such groups exert. Pluralists tend to see the sheer number of interest groups as effectively cancelling each other out and allowing governments to play them off against each other. As such, the influence of interest groups and lobbies on policy is essentially benign and does not subvert what policymakers seek to achieve in the national interest. But elite theorists tend to argue that some groups are far more influential than others (particularly economic groups) and that, in particular, corporate interests invariably succeed in the American system at the expense of the public interest. Still other writers – such as Theodore Lowi – argue that the problem about interest group influence in America is that all groups (economic, non-economic, ideological, single-issue and more) are, to a greater or lesser extent, successful in influencing decision-making. On balance, competition within and between interest groups provides an important contribution to the quality of American democracy, ensuring that government is responsive to public concerns not just at election time but also between elections. Nevertheless, while clear evidence of politicians being 'bought' by vested interests is very difficult to muster, the influence of interest groups is highly uneven. In particular, a strong bias exists in the system towards the wealthy and affluent that is only partially compensated by other forms of mass political participation such as voting.

No matter how important elections may be to American democracy (and, as we saw in Chapter 4, this is a much contested issue), they are not the only method by which the citizenry can influence government in the United States. Political participation in America takes many important forms beyond voting: signing petitions, writing letters, joining demonstrations, sending e-mails and donating campaign contributions to candidates and parties. Among all of these activities, one of the most important is participating in interest groups – an activity that Americans partake of in very large numbers.

An interest (or pressure) group is an association of individuals or organizations that join together to advance or defend the particular interests they share. Unlike political parties, interest groups do not seek to occupy government, but many frequently seek to influence it. In this sense, for example, environmental pressure groups lobby the federal government (the executive, Congress and the Supreme Court) as well as state and local governments but, unlike the Green Party, do not offer candidates in elections (though they may endorse them, as well as sponsoring ref-erendums or citizen initiatives on environmental issues).

The importance of interest groups to American politics is immense, not least since politics in the United States is fundamentally coalitional in nature. The Constitution guarantees the right of American citizens both to assemble and to petition the government in its First Amendment, that is, the entitlement of groups to lobby government on behalf of particular interests is a constitutional right. Such rights were seen as important in assuring citizens of their ability to voice their views to government between, as well as in, elections. And as American government has grown substantially in its responsibilities since 1933, interest groups and pressure group activism have correspondingly expanded and diversified, driven in part by the fact that the separated and fragmented system of government offers numerous access points to the policymaking process from city councils and school boards to state and federal courts.

But in today's America the role and influence of interest groups are not generally seen by political scientists as benign, however important the constitutional guarantees remain to American citizens. Rather, interest groups have become highly controversial players in politics, being strongly criticized for compromising and even corrupting the democratic process. Rather than preserving the voice of the citizenry, pressure groups and lobbies have been viewed by some analysts as allowing minority opinions and interests to triumph over the majority will on issues as diverse as firearms regulation, defence policy and health care. In particular, through providing federal candidates, both presidential and congressional, with a large percentage of their campaign funding, the belief has developed among many Americans that American government in general (and Congress, especially) is in the grip of wealthy 'special interests'.

Among the most important and widely held aspects of this view of interest groups is that, either selectively or as a whole, they effectively 'buy' politicians. On this approach, American government is in thrall to influential lobbies that fund America's political class and place the needs and desires of special interests ahead of those of the nation. What is especially troubling about this notion is that many successful interest lobbies (such as the National Rifle Association and the American Association of Retired Persons) do not discriminate between the two major parties. As Chapters 3 and 4 noted, members of both the Republican and Democratic parties receive funds, advice and suggestions from such interest groups, many of which are markedly less interested in ideology than incumbency when it comes to influencing lawmakers. Consequently, when the energy corporation Enron collapsed in 2001, for example, it was not only the Bush administration and congressional Republicans who were tainted, but also the Clinton administration and congressional Democrats (many of whom had received campaign contributions from Enron).

Such popular notions raise two key problems for students of American politics. First, there exists a basic empirical problem – how much influence do American interest groups (generally and in terms of particular groups) possess, and why? Secondly, there exists a corresponding normative problem, that is, what are the implications of that influence for democratic governance in the United States? In particular, does the liberty to petition government now confer such a disproportionate influence on certain lobbies that political equality in America is undermined? Although it would be naive in the extreme to discount the influence of interest groups – especially powerful economic ones – this chapter will contest the accuracy of some of the conventional criticisms levelled at American pressure groups. Interest groups occupy an important position in American politics and the access that some have to leading decision-makers undoubtedly influences, but is not alone in determining, public policy in America.

INTEREST GROUP ACTIVISM

Several reasons exist why interest groups should be so numerous and active in America. Although James Madison warned against the dangers of 'faction' in *Federalist Papers* No. 10, the Founding Fathers established the basis for the legitimacy of interest lobbies in the Constitution itself. As Exhibit 9.1 notes, the First Amendment guarantees to each American citizen the freedom of assembly, association and petitioning the government – something that the federal government cannot infringe. Beyond this, the marked fragmentation of the American state that prior chapters have emphasized has ensured that multiple access points exist for interest groups to target – not simply federal, state and local governments, but also, within each tier, executive departments and agencies, legislative assemblies and courts. The fragmentation of government has an additional effect here in as much as, unlike many European states, American governing institutions have been chronically unable to impose

Exhibit 9.1 The legitimacy of interest group influence in America

The First Amendment to the US Constitution states: 'Congress shall make no law respecting an establishment of religion, or prohibiting the free exercise thereof; or abridging the freedom of speech, or of the press; or the right of the people peaceably to assemble, and to petition the Government for a redress of grievances.'

coherence or order on the interest group universe.

Societal developments have also played a major role in sustaining the plethora of American interest groups that exist. The historic weakness of class consciousness in America and the presence of cross-cutting cleavages such as race, religion, ethnicity and region have helped to ensure the proliferation of 'non-economic' groups, in particular. Since political parties have also been comparatively weak institutions (unable to devise and implement collective programmes of government) and the government fragmented, substantial incentives and opportunities exist for ethnic, social, economic and issue groups to influence the policymaking process.

More recently, with the growth of extensive government responsibilities (especially those of the federal government), a range of organized groups have arisen whose interests are affected by, or connected to, the government's operations, from farm workers affected by agricultural subsidies to abortion rights campaigners concerned by new government regulations on abortion services. Finally, since the later 1960s, think tanks, universities and even foreign governments have mushroomed in the extent to which they either lobby or hire other consultants to lobby the federal government on behalf of particular interests. The number of registered lobbyists in Washington more than doubled from 1975 to 1985 (Salisbury, 1990: 204) and doubled again by the later 1990s. By 2000, in excess of 20,000 lobbyists – more than 38 for each member of Congress – existed.

A TYPOLOGY OF INTEREST GROUPS

The American interest group universe is remarkably fragmented and competitive. Although political scientists' typologies of interest groups differ significantly in terms of their number and detail, in essence it is possible to identify five broad types of interest group that are active in America today.

- *Economic*. Economic interest groups encompass a variety of categories such as chambers of commerce, corporations (such as General Motors, Microsoft or Boeing), labour unions (such as the AFL-CIO), agricultural groups (such as the American Farm Bureau Federation and the National Farmers' Union) and professional bodies (such as the American Medical Association and National Education Association).
- *Public interest groups*. These groups tend to be associated with the promotion of particular causes. Common Cause, for example, has been a major advocate on behalf of American consumers' rights, especially in relation to car safety. Friends of the Earth has been highly active on ecological issues. The Children's Defense Fund has sought to advance protections for children.
- *Sectional groups*. These interest groups tend to represent the concerns of particular segments of the population. For example, the National Association for the Advancement of Colored People is the longest-established civil rights organization for African Americans. The National Organization for Women was established

in 1966 to represent issues of particular concern to American women (from abortion rights to sexual harassment). The American Association of Retired Persons (AARP) has been highly influential on behalf of the substantial number of Americans over 55 years of age (not least in discouraging politicians from reforming the social security system).

- *Attitude groups*. These groups advocate particular political positions, sometimes associated with a particular cause or more broadly with an ideological orientation. The Christian Coalition, for example, advances a broad agenda (from opposing same-sex unions to supporting tax incentives to encourage Americans to marry) based on the protection and promotion of traditionalist values. The American Civil Liberties Union takes a libertarian stance on issues concerned with free speech and individual liberties, opposing measures such as censorship. The National Rifle Association strongly opposes gun control measures, while Americans for Gun Safety supports selective tougher firearms laws.
- *Intergovernmental*. These groups combine public officials occupying particular positions so that they can pool ideas and exert pressure on other government institutions. One of the most important here is the National Governors' Conference, the association of the 50 state governors. Another is the US Conference of Mayors.

One important aspect of the American interest group universe, however, is the extent to which its internal fragmentation mirrors that of American government more broadly. Not only are the above groups distinguishable from each other, but they are also each internally fragmented. Unlike many traditional European interest group systems, where a single 'peak' organization (such as the Confederation of British Industry or the National Farmers' Union) dominates its particular sector, American interest groups have always been fragmented and competitive. Hence, within a given sector, such as

agriculture, there exist many competing pressure groups rather than a single, dominant organization.

INTEREST GROUP FUNCTIONS, STRATEGIES AND TACTICS

Interest groups can generally be seen to perform five broad functions in democratic political systems:

- *Representation*. Organized groups offer an important alternative to political parties by which Americans can articulate their views to government and seek redress of their grievances.
- *Citizen participation*. Pressure groups offer an opportunity, beyond voting in elections, for ordinary Americans to become active in the political life of the nation.
- *Public education*. Through their various efforts to influence government, organized interest groups can contribute to educating Americans about what the government is doing, what effects policies are having on the ground, and what can be done to alter existing problems.
- *Agenda-building*. Pressure groups can place previously neglected or ignored issues on the agenda of both the mass American public and local, state and federal government, forcing decision-makers to address important issues.
- *Programme monitoring*. By monitoring the programmes, laws and regulations that government operates, interest groups provide an additional check (beyond political parties, the media and the bureaucracy) to ensure that the government is conducting itself responsibly.

Not all organized interest groups perform all five of these functions simultaneously, but as a whole the contributions that pressure groups make on these criteria provides an important mechanism for enhancing the quality of American democracy.

As noted earlier, American interest groups

vary substantially, but most face a set of common strategies or tactics to employ in order to influence government. Unlike parliamentary systems such as the UK, where influencing the national government is essentially a matter of trying to persuade the executive to support a particular initiative (and within this, often trying to convince a particular minister to support it), the American system of fragmented and decentralized government offers many more opportunities for exerting influence. In essence, though, it may be said that there are three general ways in which interest groups try to bring pressure to bear on the government: through the vote at election time; by campaign finance contributions; and by an organizational entity that formulates the strategy for getting precise pieces of legislation passed, provides a focus of unity for like-minded individuals, forges alliances with other social forces towards shared political goals, monitors decisions to ensure that friends are rewarded and opponents punished, and offers feedback (information) to members so that the organization becomes more active and effective.

In relation to the federal government, three main avenues exist by which interest groups try to influence the policy process:

- *Congress*. Interest groups frequently attend and testify at congressional hearings on policy and even encourage lawmakers to commission such hearings or investigations if they believe it is advantageous to their concerns. They also develop regularized contacts with key members and their staffs. Some groups forge links with congressional caucuses (such as the Black Caucus) in order to coordinate strategies and tactics. Lastly, but by no means of least importance, pressure groups make extensive use of the relatively permissive campaign finance regime to donate funds to individual lawmakers' campaigns. There is no guarantee, of course, that such donations will influence a legislator's behaviour, either in terms of pursuing a particular priority or voting in a particular way on pending bills, but in many cases, such donations are, at a minimum, a rational device to ensure that the interest group at least remains as a 'player' in the decision-making process.

- *The executive branch*. As in all democracies, an important mechanism by which influence can be exerted is to target the executive bureaucracy – what is conventionally regarded as the government itself. Since bureaucrats (both political appointees and permanent public or civil servants) are responsible for implementing laws, regulations and executive orders, the federal bureaucracy has a crucial role in determining policy outcomes (the next chapter describes this in more detail). Interest groups therefore try to influence appointments to the bureaucracy to ensure that nominees who share their concerns and preferences are appointed to key Departments and agencies responsible for policy implementation in their area. Many interest groups are also keen to provide information to bureaucrats about the effects, merits and demerits of particular policies. This is a particularly valuable source of influence for some interest groups since, in many cases, the information and expertise that an interest group possesses may exceed that of the bureaucracy itself. In this way, federal bureaucrats – and their political masters – can gain valuable information that informs subsequent policy decisions.

- *Judiciary*. As Chapter 8 noted in detail, the role of state and federal courts in America is extensive and influential. As part of the tripartite arrangement of America's separated system of government, courts can and do exert a substantial say over policy. It therefore makes sense for many interest groups to target the judiciary as a means of shaping outcomes in a favourable direction. One mechanism to do this is, like the bureaucracy, to try to influence who actually sits on the judicial bench. By providing advice to lawmakers on appointments (and, as we saw in the Bork example, expending money on TV advertisements and campaign contributions), federal lawmakers can be swayed to vote for or against particular nominees. Beyond this, interest groups can themselves take out law suits and litigate cases through the courts. Finally, pressure groups frequently provide advice (such as 'friends of the court' briefs to the Supreme Court) to judges in an effort to convince them of the persuasiveness of their case.

But beyond this, American interest groups operate in many other ways. In some cases, groups seek to exert an indirect influence on decision-makers by seeking to sway American public opinion more broadly. Demonstrations (such as those of the civil rights movement during the 1950s and 1960s) and public marches (such as the Million Mom March in Washington, DC of May 16, 2000, which saw the largest-ever mass demonstration to protest against America's weak gun laws) often have a view to gaining television coverage for their cause. The civil rights movement's sit-ins, boycotts and peaceful rallies were all-important in gaining televised coverage of the brutality of southern segregation, and thereby persuading other Americans to support the cause of civil and political rights for black southerners. As a result, federal legislators came under substantial pressure to pass landmark legislation (in particular, the Civil Rights Act of 1964 and Voting Rights Act of 1965).

Abortion is another issue where both sides in the heated controversy have resorted to public marches and other measures to reach a wider American public and heighten

Exhibit 9.2   America's most powerful lobby? The National Rifle Association

America possesses the world's most heavily and legally armed civilian population. Estimates place the number of privately owned firearms at approximately 250 million in a total US population of about 270 million. Although most Americans do not own guns, one in six Americans owns a handgun. America's firearm regulation is extensive (over 20,000 laws and regulations exist at federal, state and local level) but it is also comparatively weak in content. For example, most states do not require a citizen to have a permit to purchase a gun, nor do they place limits on the total number of firearms an individual may purchase. Most Americans have consistently supported demands for stronger gun controls for decades, but the federal government has only rarely tightened up firearms laws. One of the main reasons for this is the activism of the National Rifle Association (NRA). With over three million members dispersed across America, the NRA is a formidable mass membership organization. Its Institute for Legislative Action constantly monitors federal and state governments for any attempts to introduce stronger controls regulating the ownership, sale and production of firearms (almost all of which the NRA can be relied on to oppose). Its membership is then issued an 'alert' to protest the measure by a telephone call, e-mail or visit to state and federal elected officials. Such activism ensured that by the summer of 2001 26 states had passed laws protecting gun manufacturers from lawsuits for the criminal and public health consequences of gun violence. By 2002, driven in large part by NRA campaigns, 42 of the 50 states had introduced laws allowing their citizens to carry guns concealed on their person or in their car. A survey of Washington political operatives for *Fortune* magazine in May 2001 saw the NRA displace the American Association of Retired Persons as the most influential lobbying force on Capitol Hill. The NRA is probably the clearest example of an instance where an influential non-economic interest group with a large and active mass membership base has managed to ensure that majority public preferences on a particular issue are not realized in public policy outcomes.

awareness of their particular cause. For example, 'pro-life' groups from 1974 onwards organized an annual protest outside the Supreme Court to commemorate (or rather castigate) the day that *Roe v. Wade* (1973) was decided. 'Pro-choice' groups in turn began convening counter-demonstrations to demand the retention and strengthening of abortion rights during the 1980s. During the 1990s some groups strongly opposed to abortion rights, such as Operation Rescue, even resorted to direct action (blocking access to clinics where abortions were performed) to gain media attention and – in their hopes – a sympathetic hearing from elected officials, judges and the broader American public.

Many interest groups also resort to mass mailings of their members, taking out press and television advertisements, and (increasingly) using the Internet. Some of these activities are designed merely to inform members of current developments, but often the activities have the purpose of stimulating political responses: writing letters, making telephone calls, attending public meetings, sending e-mails. As Exhibit 9.2 notes, the National Rifle Association (NRA) is one of America's most adept and influential interest groups in this regard, with a supremely informative and sophisticated Internet site and a highly active mass membership base that most elected politicians (especially at the federal level) rarely wish to offend.

APPROACHES TO INTEREST GROUP INFLUENCE

Political analysts have differed strongly on how to characterize the American interest group universe since the 1950s. While most agree on the types of role that interest lobbies perform, and the methods by which they seek to influence government, their actual success is hotly disputed.

The pluralist approach

The pluralist approach to interest groups is associated with the influential American political scientist, Robert Dahl. Dahl (1961) argued that the American political system was pluralistic. Although Dahl conceded the inequality between different types of organized interest groups, with business interests typically possessing greater financial resources than most non-economic groups, such resources were not cumulative. That is, no one type of organized group possessed an advantage in all available resources (for example, businesses were advantaged by money but labour and civil rights groups were advantaged in terms of sheer numbers). Implicit within this account is the notion that, overall, interest groups provide valuable contributions to the development of American public policies and the health of America's democracy. Since all interests in society could be organized into such groups, which would subsequently compete with each other but, of necessity, have to make concessions and compromise in order to secure a result, the ultimate product of such activity would be functional for America as a whole. In essence, policy outcomes would mirror the nation's collective priorities and preferences. As important representative forces, interest group activities assist in keeping elected politicians in touch with the needs and demands of distinct American social groups from farmers to auto workers. To the extent that one measure of good public policy is its responsiveness to the public at large, on this approach, interest groups assist in ensuring that responsiveness.

The elitism/unequal results approach

The most consistent and dismissive critique of pluralism has been offered by analysts (both liberal and conservative in their leanings) who identify America as a profoundly unequal society, not only in economic terms, but also in terms of the influence that particular interests wield in the American system.

One of the most influential versions of this argument was advanced by C. Wright Mills in a book entitled *The Power Elite* (1956). Mills emphasized the extent to which privileged interest groups – from weapons manufacturers to agricultural lobbies – cooperated with elites in government to advance their parochial concerns. Far from there being no barriers to entry to the interest group universe, as pluralists suggested, those many interests lacking sufficient financial resources were excluded from the nexus of decision-making. Not least, in many cases, policy was decided less by an open, transparent and democratic process – as American civics books typically teach young Americans – than by a closed decision-making environment. As Exhibit 9.3 notes, the classic example of this was the notion of the 'iron triangle'.

The end-of-liberalism approach

An alternative approach to the above two – associated with the American political scientist Theodore Lowi (1979) – turns the

Exhibit 9.3   The 'iron triangle'

Far from being benign and beneficial contributors to public policy, critics of the pluralist account have held that interest groups in fact distort the policy process, causing rather than resolving many public policy problems. One important notion here is that of the 'iron triangle', whereby interest groups form a mutually beneficial relationship with key congressional committees (and subcommittees) and bureaucratic agencies. The three points of the triangle are locked in a mutually rewarding relationship where the incentives that each face work to insulate policymaking from broader, more democratic forces. The classic examples of iron triangles were the defence and agricultural sectors. In his farewell address of 1961, for example, President Eisenhower (no radical) warned of the dangers posed in America by what he termed the 'military–industrial complex'. The defence iron triangle comprises the arms industry, the Pentagon and members of Congress representing constituencies whose economies are defence-oriented. Each party has a vested interest in ever larger defence expenditures. Arms manufacturers profit from federal purchases of weapons and technology. The Pentagon acquires increased resources and power. Lawmakers win votes from constituents working in defence-related industries or the armed forces. Eisenhower's case was that the national interest of America might well be poorly served by such an arrangement, with defence expenditures greater than was either necessary or affordable and weapon systems that are expensive and even ineffective. But the extent to which iron triangles continue to exist and determine policy, whether on defence or other areas, is contestable. For example, defence expenditures went down as well as up from 1947 to 2002, suggesting that factors other than the three points of the triangle (not least international threats to American national security, from the USSR to terrorists) intruded on policymaking. Moreover, in most policy sectors, an increasing range and diversity of participants has gained footholds in the policymaking process over the past two decades. In the agriculture sector, for example, environmental and ecological groups have expressed concerns over land usage and pesticides while consumer rights groups have raised issues of excessive subsidies to farmers, resulting in costs being passed on to the buyers of foodstuffs. While there is little doubt that the interests of pressure groups, bureaucrats and federal lawmakers in a given sector are frequently more complementary than competitive, this does not mean that policy is decided with no broader considerations or additional participants. That is, the broader features of American democratic structures do intrude and constrain what otherwise closed groups of decision-makers can achieve.

traditional criticisms of interest groups on their head. Lowi's case does not deny that substantial inequalities exist between affluent Americans and groups such as the unemployed, poor or homeless, but the main problem about interest group influence is that most organized interests succeed (to a greater or lesser degree) rather than fail in influencing public policy. What this means, then, is that because so many groups have stakes in existing policy, it becomes extremely difficult for government to alter policies in ways that may be beneficial to the nation as a whole. In essence, policies from welfare to health care are 'stuck' because of the inability of decision-makers to challenge vested interests.

THE BEST DEMOCRACY MONEY CAN BUY?

Perhaps the most important concern about interest groups is the extent to which their influence on government is connected to their ability to donate funds to elected politicians. While tourists in Washington frequently visit the White House, Capitol Hill, the FBI Building and the Supreme Court, official tours tend not to take them to K Street (just a few blocks from the White House), the location of hundreds of firms and offices whose business is to lobby the government. To many Americans, it is this process of lobbying that distorts and discredits the notion that government is 'of, by and for' all of the people.

Exhibit 9.4 The inequality of interest group influence

In 1960, the political scientist E.E. Schattschneider observed of the pluralist approach to interest groups, that 'the flaw in the pluralist heaven is that the heavenly chorus sings with a strong upper-class accent'. Although the interest group universe since the 1960s has witnessed a substantial influx of previously unrepresented groups (from women and gay and lesbian Americans to consumer rights groups, ethnic organizations and environmental lobbies), that assessment has received substantial support since then. The interest group system in America is without doubt open – in the sense that few formal barriers to associations exist – and it rarely impedes new or unconventional interests from organizing. But the interest group system is also biased in terms of class since employers and wealthier Americans are typically far more able to exploit opportunities to form and join such organized groups. Ironically, as the system became more diverse, so business increased its disproportionate overrepresentation within it. Approximately 70 per cent of interest groups with a presence in Washington, DC currently, for example, are corporate and business interests. Moreover, as Senator Bob Dole (Republican, Kansas) once noted, there are no PACs of the unemployed or the poor (though groups do exist that campaign for them). That class bias is compounded further by two factors. First, the costs of joining – much less organizing – interest lobbies can more easily be met by more affluent Americans. Secondly, a free-rider problem affects groups that seek to organize to pursue public goods that non-members cannot be excluded from enjoying. That is, if an individual can receive the benefit without expending efforts to achieve it, it is irrational to join the organization. The prospects of mass membership organizations developing to advance the interests of the unemployed, homeless, drug addicts, the poor, and welfare recipients are therefore much slimmer than those for organizations advancing the interests of Microsoft or Boeing. This need not mean that such a bias is automatically reflected in public policy, since competing factors – from votes to courts to other organized interests – exist, but it does mean that the American interest group universe is a highly imperfect reflection of the myriad 'interests' that actually exist in contemporary America.

Moreover, good reasons exist to be suspicious of the power and influence that organized interests can 'purchase' in government:

- *The testimony of lobbyists and former lawmakers*. Both lobbyists and members of Congress who have retired from politics have conceded that money plays a key role in the decision-making process for many lawmakers. Although most lobbyists deny that their activities amount to vote-buying, they generally concede that an organization with significant financial resources that makes contributions is actively seeking a 'return' on the investment. Federal lawmakers are busy individuals with multiple demands on their time. A financial contribution is one way (not sufficient but necessary in many lobbyists' eyes) to ensure that lawmakers will respond when contacted. As is often said on Capitol Hill, 'my vote is not for sale but it is available for rent'.

- *The unequal pattern of campaign contributions*. A large proportion of the money that is contributed to individual candidates for federal office, political parties and ballot committees (that sponsor referendums and citizen initiatives) comes from a relatively narrow range of interests: business corporations, professional Americans and wealthy individuals (Ross Perot, Steve Forbes, Bill Gates, John Paul Getty). Since these donors are sufficiently affluent to be able to make contributions, it is unlikely that the interests they pursue will be ones that challenge, rather than confirm, the existing social and economic order (with its profoundly unequal distribution of income and wealth).

- *The 'best Congress money can buy'*. The case that American politicians – especially (but not only) in Congress – are more or less bought by interest lobbies is one that many critics have made. As Exhibit 9.5 reveals, when the combination of donations from particular groups is compared to the votes by legislators on relevant issues of concern to those groups, a strong

case can be advanced that the two are related – even intertwined. As Chapters 3 and 4 noted, we also know that virtually all federal lawmakers now require substantial campaign budgets to run competitive races. Indeed, many try to scare off potential challengers through amassing such budgets well in advance of the next election. In order to do so, obtaining donations from interest groups eager to gain a hearing on Capitol Hill is a rational strategic activity for cash-strapped politicians.

But this apparently indisputable connection needs to be heavily qualified. Most obviously, while there exists a clear correlation between donations and votes, this by no means establishes the proof of a clear, causal relationship – that the donation caused the lawmaker to vote the way he or she did. Even in the cases that Stern (1988) cites, it may well be the case that the money donated is a reward for prior behaviour rather than an inducement for future votes, or that the legislator would have voted the same way even without a donation – whether for constituency reasons, from partisan considerations or because of presidential persuasion. For example, a lawmaker representing one of the districts in Detroit, Michigan, where General Motors had a sizeable plant in the 1970s and 1980s, would have had to have voted for the domestic content automobile legislation – for reasons of re-election, even if he or she received no interest lobby donations at all.

Moreover, it is very difficult to find clear evidence that a specific interest group (as opposed to 'interests' such as business in general) possesses anything approaching monopolistic power in the American system. What does appear to be reasonably certain is that, when decisions are reviewed, a strong bias towards business interests exists. For example, during the 1990s, two broad coalitions of interest groups sought to influence the Clinton administration's policy on granting 'Most Favoured Nation' (MFN) status to China (this normalized trade relations

Exhibit 9.5   The best Congress money can buy?

Of those receiving this amount from the sugar lobby in 1983–86	This percentage voted for sugar subsidies in 1985
More than $5,000	100
$2,500–$5,000	97
$1,000–$2,500	68
$1–$1,000	45
0	20

Of those receiving this amount from the American Medical Association in 1977–80	This percentage voted against containing hospital costs in 1979
More than $15,000	100
$10,000–$15,000	95
$5,000–$10,000	82
$2,500–$5,000	80
$1–$2,500	38
0	37

Of those receiving this amount from the Auto-workers' PAC in 1979–82	This percentage voted for the domestic content auto bill in 1982 (requiring all cars sold in the USA to contain a certain percentage of US-made parts)
More than $20,000	100
$10,000–$20,000	91
$2,500–$10,000	82
$1–$2,500	62
0	17

Estimated annual total costs to consumers and taxpayers

Sugar subsidy	$3 billion
Hospital costs	$10 billion
Domestic contents on autos	$4 billion
Total	$17 billion (per annum)

Source: Adapted from Stern (1988: 140–3).

between the two nations despite China's leadership being communist). The measure had to be authorized by Congress on an annual basis and became a focus for intense lobbying efforts. On one side, a broad coalition of business interests who sought access to China's growing market favoured the MFN measure. Against it was a coalition of human rights groups, religious organizations, labour unions and environmental pressure groups who, concerned at China's repression of religious freedom, poor labour laws and environmental record, opposed the measure. Every year that it received a vote, MFN gained a solid congressional majority, and in 2000 normal trade relations were voted as permanent. This strongly suggested that powerful corporate interests can shape not only domestic but also foreign policy.

But while the influence of economic interests in general cannot be denied, this is hardly unusual in a comparative perspective.

Moreover, the broader picture of interest group influence is less clear. Writers such as Robert Salisbury (1990) argue that the very proliferation of interest groups of every description since the 1960s has strongly diminished the chance that any one organized group can exert decisive influence on public policy. Still less is it the case that such a group can exercise such influence on a consistent basis. In essence, the argument from this perspective is 'more groups, less clout'. There are several reasons why this argument has substantial merit:

- *Empirical evidence about campaign finance contributions.* Political scientists have sought for several decades now to examine whether evidence exists that demonstrates the influence of campaign contributions. But the evidence is at best mixed. Frequently, what it demonstrates is a correlation between the interests of a donor and the vote on a relevant issue, but it does not prove causation – that the reason why the legislator voted that way was because of the donation.
- *Proportionality.* An individual PAC donation is typically less than 1 per cent of the overall campaign receipts of any member of Congress. In the context of elections where successful House candidates expend at least $1 million and Senate candidates at least $10 million (and in many cases much more), the notion that a donation of even $5,000 can decisively influence a lawmaker's vote is implausible.
- *The multiplicity of PACs and interest groups.* Approximately 10,000 Political Action Committees (PACs) currently exist in America. As Salisbury argues, the pronounced diversity of interest groups ensures that, on any particular issue, many competing groups are likely to be active. This allows substantial flexibility on the part of a federal lawmaker. For example, a vote on whether or not to tighten regulations on petrol emissions from vehicles will typically pit the automobile industry against environmental

groups. Legislators who received funds from the former and voted to tighten the regulations (against their preference) may well forfeit campaign funds from the auto industry in the future, but such a vote would simultaneously make the lawmakers the more likely recipient of funds from green groups. While neither the size of opposing coalitions nor the precise composition is likely to be perfectly matched on many issues (notoriously, the gun rights lobby has been far better funded than the gun control lobby), the existence of competing groups assures most lawmakers of some autonomy.

- *The obligation to donate.* Far from the lawmakers being bought, in many cases it is interest groups that face a political 'obligation' to donate to elected officials. That is, legislators' staffs will frequently note at receptions attended by lobbyists who does not contribute to the lawmakers' campaign funds. Indeed, when the Republican Party won control of Congress in 1994, Majority Leader Dick Armey (Republican, Texas) expressly informed a series of interest lobbies that had previously donated to the Democratic Party that access to the new congressional leadership would not be granted unless a change in the partisan pattern of donations was rapidly seen to occur.
- *Inertia.* As Chapter 7 noted, Congress is a highly decentralized institution within a highly fragmented system of government. The corollary of the existence of so many access points to government in America is that so many veto points to policy change also exist. In general, it is more difficult to initiate policies in the American system than to veto them, so the likelihood that a given interest group can achieve policy changes through funding activities is not great.
- *Access.* The most convincing research suggests powerfully that what interest groups achieve through donations is 'access' to decision-makers, not influence. By comparing lawmakers' votes on bills with the

campaign funding they received, money buys a hearing (a telephone call or a visit to the lawmaker's office to make a 10- or 15-minute presentation) and may even lead to a lawmaker devoting extra time to the particular issue, but at best influences voting only at the margins. That is, when lawmakers have no clear or strong preferences on an issue or when no competing pressures exist, a donation may exert an influence, but the probability of these conditions existing is minimal. Not only do lawmakers tend to have strong biases on most issues in terms of their partisan and ideological leanings, but competing influences frequently impinge on their calculations (not least the voters back home but also party leaders, committee colleagues, the president's position, staff views and the pressures of other interest groups).

In short, the notion that interest groups can 'buy' politicians is too simplistic and deterministic to be convincing. To take the most obvious examples, there is simply no way that a legislator representing Harlem would have voted against imposing sanctions on apartheid South Africa in the 1980s, no matter how much funding may be given his or her campaign war chest by American corporations with business interests in the republic (indeed, the imposition of sanctions against South Africa, Cuba, Iran, Libya and other nations during the 1980s and 1990s illustrated precisely how business interests that would profit from more open markets were 'trumped' by non-economic pressures – from fighting the Cold War to punishing the apartheid regime). To return to the gun control issue, many lawmakers vote against gun control not because of the NRA donations, but rather because many of their constituents own – and care about – firearms.

However, it is not necessary to resort to such extreme cases to disprove the buying hypothesis. As Chapter 7 noted, studies of congressional behaviour have demonstrated that American lawmakers must consider a variety of pressures in selecting which

committees to sit on, which bills to sponsor and what votes to cast: party, ideology, committee colleagues, party leaders, White House position, and so on. Some of these considerations may reinforce a vote in a particular group's favour, but others may well work against this, outweighing whatever donations and representations a particular group has made. In sum, the plurality of influences and considerations that pressure federal lawmakers limit, even if they do not eliminate, the extent to which a particular organized interest can induce support. As Exhibit 9.6 notes, even a supposedly influential lobby such as the Christian Right confronts powerful obstacles to influence in the fragmented American political system.

CONCLUSION

Interest groups are an essential part of the democratic process in America. Constitutional guarantees that protect an individual citizen's right to join with others in common endeavours and to voice views to government are crucial elements of a liberal democratic regime. Such activism ensures that political participation is something that does not simply occur at election time. More so than in most democracies, the extent to which such guarantees are protected in the United States – and the extent to which ordinary Americans take advantage of them by joining interest groups to protect or advance particular causes – is remarkable. Moreover, interest groups provide key vehicles for placing new issues on the public agenda, encouraging and facilitating all Americans to participate in their own government. Indeed, much as Americans decry Congress but approve of their particular lawmakers, so most Americans criticize special interests while valuing the role and influence of groups that represent their particular concerns.

Exhibit 9.6   Religion and politics: the Christian Right

The Christian Right had its origins in the mid-1970s. Opposed to what evangelical and fundamentalist Christians perceived as the declining place of religion in American public and private life, the Christian Right sought to reverse an alleged public philosophy of 'secular humanism' on issues such as abortion rights, marriage, pornography, gay rights, and the prohibition of prayer in public schools. The Christian Right was extremely active in raising funds, voter registration efforts, the distribution of guides for voting, mobilizing voters and party activism. In particular, Christian groups played a major role in selecting Republican Party candidates in primary elections in dozens of American states. The presidential candidacies of Ronald Reagan in 1980 and George W. Bush in 2000 were substantially assisted by such groups. But despite such activism, the policy influence of the Christian Right has been relatively limited. For example, in 1995–96 the Republican 104th Congress rejected seven of ten agenda items of the leading organization, the Christian Coalition's 'Contract with the American Family'. Although the organization's director, Ralph Reed, claimed to have achieved four major successes on retiring in 1996, this was rather unconvincing. Of the four that he cited: the welfare reform law of 1996 was not a specifically Christian Right issue; the Communications Decency Act 1996 (a blanket Internet anti-pornography measure) was partially voided by federal courts over subsequent years; the Defense of Marriage Act 1996 (that allowed but did not require states to refuse to recognize the legality of same-sex unions) proved unable to prevent some states, such as Vermont, recognizing same-sex unions in law; and the Partial Birth Abortion Act 1996 (that sought to make illegal a particular late-term abortion procedure) was vetoed by President Clinton. As these examples suggest, even a powerful and active interest group such as the Christian Coalition faces major hurdles to influencing policy consistently or decisively in America. Not only does it need to forge coalitions and alliances with other groups (which, given its relatively immoderate positions on many issues is not straightforward), but it also confronts active and influential opponents – some of these are liberal groups such as People for the American Way and the American Civil Liberties Union, others are religious organizations with more moderate views. With the existence of multiple veto points in a federal and separated system of government and weak political parties unable to implement (or even devise) clear programmes of government, even well-organized and mass membership non-economic groups face powerful obstacles. Some of these are strategic and tactical. In the 1988 Republican Party primaries, for example, southern fundamentalists and evangelicals were divided among themselves over which candidate to support (despite having one of their own preachers, Pat Robertson, running for the presidency), while in 1992 and 1996 the Christian Coalition did not support Pat Buchanan, the candidate closest to its own positions. On policy, some in the Coalition favour the Supreme Court overturning *Roe v. Wade* (which would return abortion policy to the individual states to decide), while others seek a constitutional amendment to prohibit it in all American states. But most obviously, as Steve Bruce argues, the barriers to the Coalition are as much about the nature of modern American society as the institutions of American government: 'About 70% of American women work. The chances of a first marriage ending in divorce are 50:50. Almost a quarter of American families are headed by a single parent. Most middle-aged Americans have experimented with soft drugs and many middle-class Americans still smoke dope. Extra-martial and pre-martial sexual intercourse are commonplace' (Bruce, 2000: 279).

While the essence of the pluralist case is, on balance, more or less valid, the central difficulty that accompanies high rates of participation in pressure groups is that political freedom effectively 'trumps' political equality in substance if not in form in contemporary America. The real inequality that exists between interest groups is undeniable and, moreover, many are not themselves models of inclusive or democratic decision-making (many well-organized groups are conventionally run by a few full-time leaders who only rarely consult rank-and-file members on policy issues). Certain groups, such as the poor and homeless, are accorded unequal political representation and, consequently, the American political system underrepresents the great diversity of interests that exist in the American polity. The result is that the system is rendered somewhat less democratic and the legitimacy of government is, at least partly, weakened. To paraphrase George Orwell's famous indictment of communism, although all Americans are formally equal before the law, in practice some are more equal than others thanks to the activism of organized interest groups.

FURTHER READING

Allan Cigler and Burdett Loomis (eds), *Interest Group Politics* (1995) is an excellent collection of essays on all aspects of interest groups in American politics today.

Robert Salisbury, 'The Paradox of Interest Groups in Washington – More Groups, Less Clout', Chapter 7 in Anthony King (ed.), *The New American Political System* (2nd edition) (1990) is a clear and simple case about the limits to interest lobbies' influence.

Graham Wilson, 'American Interest Groups', Chapter 9 in Jeremy Richardson (ed.), *Pressure Groups* (1993) is a comprehensive introduction to the US interest group universe.

Steve Bruce, 'Zealot Politics and Democracy: the Case of the New Christian Right', *Political Studies*, 48 (2) (2000), pp. 263–82 is an excellent, concise analysis of the limits to the influence of the Christian Right.

Larry Sabato, *PAC Power: Inside the World of Political Action Committees* (1985) is an old but excellent analysis of the use interest groups make of PACs.

Jeffrey Berry, *The Interest Group Society* (2nd edition) (1989) is a balanced and dispassionate assessment of the role and influence of interest groups in America.

Philip Stern, *The Best Congress Money Can Buy* (1988) is a strong argument that claims American politicians are indeed essentially 'bought' by interest groups.

WEB LINKS

American Civil Liberties Union
http://www.aclu.org

Christian Coalition
http://www.cc.org

National Association for the Advancement of Colored People
http://www.naacp.org

Nation of Islam
http://www.noi.org

Common Cause
http://www.commoncause.org

American Medical Association
http://www.ama-assn.org

US Conference of Mayors
http://www.usmayors.org

AFL-CIO
http://www.afl.cio.org

The Business Round Table
http://www.business-roundtable.com

National Association of Manufacturers
http://www.nam.org

QUESTIONS

- 'The existence of so many competing interest groups in America precludes the possibility of any one interest dominating the policy process.' Discuss.

- Under what conditions is interest group influence on government substantial?

- Was Madison right in *Federalist Paper*, No. 10 to be so wary of the influence of 'faction' in American politics?

- Do interest groups enhance or undermine the quality of American democracy?

- Are American elected officials 'bought' by influential 'special interests'?

10 The Federal Bureaucracy

Robert Singh and Mark Carl Rom

Government isn't the solution; government is the problem.

> Ronald Reagan, 1980

It is good for democracy but bad for an effective presidency – though by no means always for either – that the chief executive possesses a highly imperfect capacity to induce the vast officialdom of the executive branch to abide by his purposes and follow his directives.

> Louis Koenig, *The Chief Executive* (1996: 181)

- The Growth of the Federal Bureaucracy
- The US Constitution
- Bureaucratic and Democratic Values
- The Functions of the Federal Bureaucracy
- Structure and Composition
- Evaluating the Federal Bureaucracy
- Conclusion

Chapter Summary

The federal bureaucracy is an integral but problematic part of America's democracy. The bureaucracy has evolved in ways that the Founding Fathers could not have anticipated. In particular, although most Americans typically oppose 'big government', the United States has nevertheless developed a vast federal bureaucracy. The federal bureaucracy is far larger, more wide-ranging in scope and more complex than at the nation's founding – to the extent that the federal government is now the largest single employer in America, with a civilian workforce of almost two million individuals. To meet citizen demands for government to regulate the market to ensure the delivery of 'public goods' such as clean air and safe highways, the bureaucracy has three main functions: implementing laws, writing detailed rules that make those laws enforceable, and adjudicating disagreements over competing interpretations of such rules and regulations. Federal departments, independent regulatory commissions, independent executive agencies and government-sponsored corporations perform these functions with the powers and procedures given to them by statutes passed by Congress, through career civil servants directed by a small number of temporary political appointees. For better and worse, the federal bureaucracy has sufficient authority and influence to constitute a fourth branch of government. On the one hand, the bureaucracy provides American government with experienced and expert professionals who offer continuity and political neutrality to its operations: they literally make government work. On the other, the large size, extensive authority and substantial autonomy of the bureaucracy poses major problems in terms of its political control by both its titular head, the president, and Congress. Unlike civil servants in unitary and parliamentary regimes, American bureaucrats confront more than one political master and frequently forge alliances with other political actors (especially Congress) against the president to protect their personnel, programmes and budgets or to impede policy change.

As prior chapters have noted, Americans typically exhibit an ambivalent attitude towards government in general and the federal/national government in particular, being eager for its protection, services and benefits but wary of its reach. Even after the terrorist attacks of September 11, 2001 and the Bush administration's responses to them (entailing among other things an expansion of government budgets such as Defense and Homeland Security and a reorganization of federal government agencies), most Americans did not fully trust the federal government. But they nevertheless expect it to achieve important public goals.

An important part of this ambivalence encompasses the federal bureaucracy that is tasked with implementing national public policies. Like Congress, the bureaucracy provides a reliable focus for popular discontent (and even scorn). Americans typically expect and demand that the federal government guarantees a strong national defence, efficient and safe highways and airways, clean air and water, a stable currency and a growing economy (among many other public goods). But many Americans typically look poorly on the federal departments and agencies that work

on a daily basis to achieve these goals. In particular, popular discontents centre on the notions that the national bureaucracy is unduly powerful, inefficient, remote, politicized, self-serving and, as a 'captive' of those organized interests and clients with which it deals, beyond the control of elected officials in both the executive branch and Congress.

Contemporary public concerns about the quality of the federal bureaucracy are inextricably linked to its vast reach. Today the bureaucracy touches almost every aspect of life from birth to death through its involvement in education, the environment, national defence and the economy. In effect, while the Constitution established three branches of the federal government, the federal bureaucracy has developed as a necessary but problematic fourth branch: necessary because the federal bureaucracy clearly enhances the quality of American life by protecting Americans from poor air, poisonous foods, substandard highways and many other threats to health, safety, and well-being; but problematic because agencies from the Federal Bureau of Investigation to the Environmental Protection Agency have often resisted democratic control and acted in breach of their authority, sometimes infringing individual rights and often limiting the extent of individual liberties from government interference. Consequently, the bureaucracy occupies a position as an essential but poorly regarded part of the American system of government.

THE GROWTH OF THE FEDERAL BUREAUCRACY

The massive growth in the size and scope of the federal bureaucracy is one of the most important developments in American politics. When the first government was established under the new Constitution in 1789, President George Washington's Cabinet comprised just three departments (State, Treasury and War) and an attorney general. With the post office, these made up the entire federal executive branch. But with the establishment of a wide range of federal welfare, social security, urban and education policies, a massive growth in the federal government's regulatory role, and the growth of America's global power, the federal bureaucracy was transformed in size and scope. By 2002, although the number of federal government departments had increased to 14, dozens of independent agencies, commissions and government-sponsored corporations co-existed with them, responsible for the implementation of more than 1,400 federal government programmes. Ironically, when Bill Clinton declared in his 1996 State of the Union address that the 'era of big government is over', the 14 government departments alone employed almost 1.8 million staff (see Table 10.1).

As Exhibit 10.1 notes, however, the 'real' size of the federal bureaucracy is even larger than this when indirect as well as direct sources are taken into account. Political pressures and the populist appeal of anti-government messages since the mid-1960s have encouraged American politicians to claim that they have curbed the increase in government. (Some Republicans even suggest

that the phrase 'I'm from the government and I'm here to help' is a contradiction.) But while some activities formerly in the public sector have been delegated to private contractors, in many instances the ultimate source of payment or employment is the federal government in Washington, DC (but with offices, such as the one in Oklahoma City bombed by Timothy McVeigh in 1995, throughout the states). From research institutes receiving federal grants to conduct research on science or health matters to janitors who clean federal buildings, the federal government pays or contracts out numerous activities to a myriad of institutions and individuals. More people work for the federal government in today's America than for any other single organization and the bureaucracy affects literally all aspects of American life.

That this should be the case is not surprising. All industrialized democracies employ

TABLE 10.1   The 14 federal government departments

Department	Number of civilian employees
Agriculture	113,321
Commerce	36,803
Defense	830,738
Education	4,988
Energy	19,589
Health and Human Services	59,788
Housing and Urban Development	11,822
Interior	76,439
Justice	103,262
Labor	16,204
State	24,869
Transportation	63,552
Treasury	155,951
Veterans' Affairs	263,904
Total	1,781,230

Source: US Bureau of the Census (1996).

Exhibit 10.1 The federal government: how large?

The relative size of the federal bureaucracy (federal bureaucrats as a proportion of the total American workforce) has steadily declined since 1953. So too did the absolute number of permanent civilian federal bureaucrats from the 1970s on. In 2001, the federal bureaucracy comprised fewer employees at the end than at the start of President Clinton's two terms in office – approximately 1.8 million, compared to 3 million in the 1970s. (The trend was partially challenged by the nationalization of airport security in 2002 in response to the attacks of September 11, 2001, which gave the federal government the responsibility of hiring 40,000 new airport baggage screeners.) But the number of federal bureaucrats does not accurately reflect the total size of American government, which includes employees paid by federal tax dollars (who perform contracted services for the government or receive grants to do federal work) or those who perform functions for the federal government (those who fulfil federal requirements). For example, the rockets and space shuttles of the National Aeronautics and Space Administration (NASA) are designed, built and maintained by private corporations, not the federal government. A large amount of scientific research is funded by the National Science Foundation (NSF), while much health research is financed by federal grants from the National Institutes of Health (NIH). Although the recipients of such grants are not formally federal employees, it is nevertheless the federal government that ultimately pays their salaries. Beyond this, when state and local bureaucrats or private employees perform tasks required or mandated by the federal government – collecting data on compliance with federal laws such as environmental protection, for example – they are effectively working for the federal government. The actual size of the federal government therefore comprises some 15 million persons who can legitimately be counted as governmental workers, a far larger figure than the formal 1.8 million federal bureaucrats.

bureaucracies to perform government's key functions: implementing laws, collecting taxes and providing for public safety and national security. As the responsibilities of governments in industrialized nations have increased, more and more programmes have developed that require administration and implementation. For all the populist anti-government rhetoric that exists, America has not been immune from this common phenomenon. For political reasons (not least to exploit traditional anti-government sentiment among voters, sentiment that increased sharply from the late 1960s through to the 1990s), federal lawmakers and the president typically claim that they are restraining the growth of government or even reducing it, but Congress and the president simultaneously require the government to accomplish many important and diverse tasks. Ironically, then, the federal bureaucracy has been simultaneously shrinking in size but expanding in scope.

THE US CONSTITUTION

Like the term 'democracy', the US Constitution does not explicitly mention the bureaucracy, but the Constitution exerts a profound influence on the structure and performance of the federal bureaucracy. Indeed, to speak of 'the' bureaucracy is a little misleading. Fears of a potentially tyrannical government motivated the Framers of the Constitution to divide powers between federal, state and local governments as well as within the federal government. The result is that there exists not so much a single bureaucracy as multiple bureaucracies. Three influences are especially important in shaping these:

Exhibit 10.2   The growth of the federal bureaucracy: a brief history

The federal bureaucracy has developed incrementally (that is, without a grand design) since 1789 as American society's needs and priorities continually evolved and the global role and responsibilities of the United States increased. In broad terms, however, four important stages of expansion can be identified.

Phase One (1787–1863). Following the ratification of the US Constitution, Congress created the first federal government departments: the Department of War, the State Department (to deal with diplomacy and foreign policy), and the Treasury (to regulate the nation's finances). The first Congress also acknowledged that for an effective presidency to occur, the officials appointed to government departments should be appointed by the president, not Congress. Up to the time of the Civil War, virtually all federal government workers were located in the Post Office, delivering mail.

Phase Two (1863–1932). The size, scope and responsibilities of the federal government were transformed by the Civil War. A substantial growth in the federal bureaucracy occurred simply with the increase in soldiers that took place to fight the war. To ensure a reliable supply of food (and to assuage disgruntled farmers), Congress created the Department of Agriculture in 1862. In 1863 the National Currency Act and in 1864 the National Bank Act were passed, establishing a Comptroller of the Currency with the power to charter and supervise banks In 1866, the Pension Office was set up to pay benefits to Americans who had served in the northern armies. In 1870, the Department of Justice was established. In the later nineteenth century, the combination of a rapidly growing national economy, the development of large business corporations, and the pressure from populist and progressive reformers encouraged Congress to establish several new departments. In 1887, the Interstate Commerce Commission (ICC) was established to regulate disorderly competition between railroad companies. In 1903 the Department of Labor and Commerce were founded (split into separate departments in 1913). In 1913 Congress established the Federal Trade Commission to insulate small businesses from unfair competition and the Federal Reserve System to regulate banks, set interest rates and control the money supply.

Phase Three (1932–52). The Depression of the 1930s and the heavy demands of the Second World War (1939–45) caused the federal government to expand substantially in size, scope and complexity. As Chapter 1 noted, FDR's 'New Deal' set up a large number of agencies to provide jobs and economic support (such as the Tennessee Valley Authority), many of which remain in existence today (such as the Securities and Exchange Commission that regulates the stock market). Most of the vast increase in federal employment took place during this stage. Bowles (1998: 258) notes that whereas in 1933 there was one civil servant for every 280 Americans by 1953 there was one for every 80.

Phase Four (1952–2003). As postwar America evolved, a far-reaching set of bureaucratic reforms were ushered in because of growing public pressures on federal lawmakers to deal with problems ranging from city decay to industrial pollution. In 1953, the Department of Health, Education and Welfare was created, taking on board policy areas that had previously been left to state and local governments. This was later split into the Department of Health and Human Services and Department of Education in 1979. As part of Lyndon Johnson's 'Great Society' programme, the Department of Housing and Urban Development (1965) and Department of Transportation (1966) were created. The expansion continued under President Nixon with the Occupational Safety and Health Administration (1970), the Environmental Protection Agency (1970), the Consumer Product Safety Commission (1972), and the Nuclear Regulatory Commission (1974). The Department of Energy was created in 1977, as was the Federal Energy Regulatory Commission.

American political culture

As Chapter 1 noted, the basic values of most Americans, reflected in and reinforced by the Constitution, are anti-government. A corollary of this is that a strong anti-bureaucratic bias exists in the broader American political culture. Americans are suspicious of (and occasionally resentful towards) government departments and agencies instructing them what to do or how to do it. In some cases, such as the attitudes of National Rifle Association (NRA) members towards the Bureau of Alcohol, Tobacco and Firearms or of citizen militias towards the Federal Bureau of Investigation (FBI), this animus towards the bureaucracy can even assume violent forms. More generally, a combination of the cultural emphasis on individual freedom and belief in democratic control over government typically animates Americans against bureaucratic authority or expertise. Support for free market capitalism leads most Americans to assume that private businesses are preferable to public bureaucracies, and markets to governmental regulations. But while Americans invariably believe that bureaucracies should be more efficient ('business-like'), they nevertheless expect bureaucracies to make decisions through democratic processes involving public participation and consultation.

Checks and balances

The Constitution divides power between the three branches of the federal government. The bureaucracy therefore differs from those administrations in states with parliamentary governments. Both the president and Congress assert control whereas in parliamentary systems, executive and legislative functions are concentrated in the executive branch alone, the bureaucracy therefore having a single head. In America, this means that bureaucrats, in effect, have two political masters: the president who heads the executive branch to which they belong and the congressional lawmakers who exercise authority over the existence of, and funding for, particular agencies and programmes. As Exhibit 10.3 notes, each branch of the federal government therefore influences the shape, activities and role of federal bureaucrats.

First, Congress has the authority to establish (or abolish) agencies, give them legislative instructions, appropriate funds for their operations and conduct oversight of them. The Senate also confirms (or rejects) presidential appointments of senior executive posts. For example, the Senate rejected President Bush's nominee of former Republican Senator John Tower to be his Secretary of Defense in 1989 (on the grounds of Tower's alleged womanizing and boozing tendencies).

Secondly, the President is the chief executive officer in the executive branch of the federal government, appointing department and agencies' heads and directing them to achieve particular goals. Typically, presidents reward appointees who have strong ties to their party (in 2000, George W. Bush appointed Donald Rumsfeld as his Defense Secretary, a long-standing figure in the Republican Party establishment), who will appeal to the main groups that deal with a particular department (Clinton appointed the economically conservative Lloyd Bentsen as his first Treasury Secretary in 1993), or to consolidate a Cabinet that 'looks like America' in terms of racial, ethnic and gender criteria (Clinton appointed four women to his second administration, for example).

Thirdly, federal courts have the authority to rule on the legality and constitutionality of department and agency actions and to adjudicate disputes that are litigated against them.

Federalism

The Constitution divides power between different tiers or levels of government (federal, state, local) as well as between the branches at the federal level. Whereas in unitary systems such as the UK, local bureaucracies typically receive instructions and budgets from the national headquarters, in America,

Exhibit 10.3 The constitutional basis of bureaucratic authority

Congress has the constitutional authority to create agencies, fund them, and charge them with administrative responsibilities.

Article I, Section 8: 'The Congress shall have the Power To . . . provide for the common Defense and general Welfare of the United States. . . . To make all Laws which shall be necessary and proper for carrying into Execution the foregoing powers, and all other Powers vested by this Constitution in the Government of the United States, or in any Department or Officer thereof.'

The President has the authority to direct agencies and select their leaders (although Congress can impeach and convict these leaders in cases of maladministration).

Article II, Section 1: 'The executive Power shall be vested in a President of the United States of America.'

Article II, Section 2: 'The President . . . shall nominate, and by and with the Advice and Consent of the Senate, shall appoint . . . other public Ministers and Consuls . . . and all other Officers of the United States, whose Appointments are not herein otherwise provided for, and which shall be established by Law: but the Congress may by Law vest the Appointment of such inferior Officers, as they think proper, in the President alone . . . or in the Heads of Departments.'

Article II, Section 4: '[A]ll civil Officers of the United States, shall be removed from Office on Impeachment for, and Conviction of, Treason, Bribery, or other high Crimes and Misdemeanors.'

The judiciary has the authority to adjudicate claims against agencies.

Article III, Section 2: 'The judicial Power shall extent to all Cases, in Law and Equity, arising under this Constitution, the Laws of the United States . . . or which shall be made, under their Authority; – to all Cases affecting . . . other public Ministers; – to Controversies to which the United States shall be a Party. . . . In all Cases affecting . . . other public Ministers . . . the Supreme Court shall have original Jurisdiction.'

national, state and local governments may each have bureaucracies that are active on specific issues, such as education, transportation or health. The federal government relies on lower-level governments (and third parties such as private organizations receiving federal grants or working under contract to federal agencies) to deliver its programmes (almost nine out of every ten federal bureaucrats work outside, not in, Washington, DC). State and local bureaucracies possess their own budgets and do not merely take instructions from their federal/national counterparts (instead having their own masters in turn – state governors and state legislatures). Federal, state and local bureaucracies therefore engage in various patterns of conflictual, competitive and, sometimes, cooperative relations.

The cumulative result is that the Constitution has established a federal system with the fragmented national government having authority over some issues, the state governments over others, and power over still other issues shared between them. To take one important example, the president cannot fully control the content of his own administration's economic policy. This is not only a matter of Congress writing the annual budget for the federal government, but also, as Exhibit 10.4 notes, that control of interest rates and the money supply is in the hands of 'the Fed'.

Exhibit 10.4   The Federal Reserve Board and monetary policy

The Federal Reserve Board (or 'Fed') was established by Congress in 1913 and vested with the authority over US monetary policy. It is governed by a seven-member board whose members are appointed for staggered 14-year terms, nominated by the president subject to Senate confirmation. The presidents of 12 Federal Reserve banks supplement the Board. Both presidents and Congresses over the past two decades have deferred to the Fed for national economic management, with monetary policy accordingly emerging as the federal government's most important macro-economic instrument. At no time was this more clear than in President Clinton's first term. Clinton inherited a chairman of the Fed, Alan Greenspan, who had been appointed by President Bush to a second term of four years in March, 1992. Clinton favoured a reduction in long-term interest rates to stimulate the economy and increase employment, but was advised that Greenspan, whom he could not sack, would only lower interest rates on condition that the president made cuts in the federal budget. Greenspan's view was that the stock exchangers in government bonds would only feel confident in lowering their rates if the federal government's budget deficit was lowered. Clinton reportedly exploded with rage at the advice, astounded that 'the success of my program and my re-election hinges on the Federal Reserve' (Woodward, 1994: 84). Ironically, however, it was in large part through heeding the views of the independent Federal Reserve that a remarkable 103 successive months of economic growth was sustained over Clinton's two terms in office.

As was noted in Chapter 2, the Constitution is 'silent' about many important issues that the Framers did not anticipate arising which American government must now address: education, transportation and the environment, for example. National, state and local (including city) bureaucracies are all involved in addressing these issues. The federal government has a Department of Education (since 1979), for example, as do all of the 50 state governments. National and state governments all have departments of transportation, environmental protection agencies, and agencies that provide health care facilities. Federal and state governments commonly have similar priorities and work cooperatively but often state and national bureaucracies disagree with each other and must work to resolve conflicts of interest and opinion.

Since political control over the federal bureaucracy is so fragmented, however, America's bureaucracy is more independent of both the legislature and executive than is common in comparable democracies. The bureaucracy has no single nor undisputed

master and therefore it can, and does, frequently play legislative, executive and judicial branches against each other, as well as competing against other agencies within the same executive branch (indeed, frequently competing against agencies even within the same department). The making of public policy is therefore highly complex, lengthy and contested. Although Chapter 7 detailed a bill's movement through Congress, in many instances a bill's journey through the various subcommittees, committees and the full House and Senate are only part of the full 'legislative history'. Once a bill becomes law, another journey commences: the rules and regulations that turn policies into programmes must be written, debated and promulgated by the federal departments and agencies that must then enforce them.

The role of the bureaucracy here is therefore crucial. Almost all bills that make it through Congress and get signed by the president are vague, ambiguous and open to competing interpretations. This is partly a necessary function of winning a majority of the House, Senate and the president to compromise and agree a final, acceptable law. Overcoming controversy and finding common ground requires, more often than not, a mutual agreement to leave the details alone; but it is also a functional issue. Federal lawmakers cannot anticipate and provide for every contingency in statute law. Bureaucrats who must implement laws must therefore be allowed some discretion and are hence delegated powers to make rules that are published in the *Federal Register* (see Exhibit 10.5), that is, in implementing policy, bureaucrats necessarily make policy.

These political footballs do not vanish but instead land in another part of the playing field. The regulatory agency must then flesh out the details of laws passed by Congress by drawing up rules and regulations to clarify how laws are implemented (the Environmental Protection Agency (EPA), say, in drawing up a clean air regulation). Frequently, those who would be most affected by a new law, or a change in existing law, get a chance to 'comment' on how it should be put into effect (in the EPA case, this might involve representatives of industry, ecological interest groups and local citizens). In other words, they can lobby the agency, the Office of Management and Budget within the White House, and even the president as the rules are being drafted.

The congressional authors of the original legislation typically also contribute. If an agency's director is careful in safeguarding its future appropriations, he or she will typically pay careful attention to the author's (that is, the key members of Congress) interpretation of any vaguely written provision. In instances where the law and the regulation conflict – if the agency goes further than Congress intended, for example, in its mandate to regulate clean air standards or worker safety – the case typically falls to the third branch of government, the federal courts. Judges then examine the legislative history of the measure (hearing testimony, committee reports, speeches and floor debates) for clues to the original congressional intent, bringing the process full circle. Frequently the judges add their own political sensibilities to the equation, in effect making judgements as to the merits of the policy. But if the courts rule against a given department or agency, the agency can nevertheless seek additional authority from the Congress to restore the prior provision.

Exhibit 10.5 Making rules

Congress frequently delegates powers to federal agencies to draw up rules, regulations and judgments that are binding. Together with executive orders issued by the president, these are required by law to be published in a daily federal government publication, the *Federal Register*. For example, the Federal Aviation Administration (FAA) issues extensive regulations about airline safety (from the use of emergency exits and prohibitions on smoking to the detail of aircraft design). Notices of rules that an agency is intending to issue must be published in the *Federal Register*. Interest groups scrutinize these for regulations affecting them or their clients. In some cases, corporations take legal action to appeal against agency actions, some of which are resolved by the agencies themselves but others fall to courts to decide whether the rule was lawful and within the delegation of authority granted to the agency by Congress. Just as courts build case law and precedent, so bureaucracies build an impressive legacy of administrative law. In 1936, the *Federal Register* had a total of 2,400 pages. By 1976 it contained 60,000 pages and was increasing by over 5,000 pages per year. Although the Reagan administration (1981–89) was praised by conservatives for its 'deregulation', this came less from the abolition of regulating agencies than a slowdown in the growth of the rules and regulations they issued.

To take one notable example that illustrates the lengthy process of implementation, Congress passed the landmark Civil Rights Act in 1964, but it left undefined what constituted racial or sexual 'discrimination'. This task – defining not only what counts as discrimination but also what counts as evidence that this has occurred – was left for federal bureaucrats to identify. Initially, the Department of Labor's Office of Federal Contract Compliance – the primary regulator of employment conditions – adopted a policy of 'affirmative action' to meet the non-discrimination goals of the 1964 law. The OFCC issued guidelines in 1968 and 1971 establishing numerical goals and timetables by which members of particular minority groups were to be represented within certain occupations, before going on to rule that the existence of disproportionately low employment rates of these minorities would count as sufficient evidence of discrimination (that is, mere statistical disparities rather than proof of an intent to discriminate would suffice). Such bureaucratic autonomy and discretion can powerfully alter the practical consequences of laws whose authors may well not have favoured the intended result, but such is the price of ambiguity in statute law (which is, in turn, typically the price of gaining a congressional majority and presidential assent to passing a bill into law).

BUREAUCRATIC AND DEMOCRATIC VALUES

As the prior section implicitly suggested, a basic tension exists between bureaucratic and democratic values (in general, not simply in America). In terms of the former, bureaucrats tend to emphasize specialist knowledge, expertise, professionalism and rationality as essential attributes in making good public policy. Bureaucrats possess the information and knowledge as to how to devise rules and regulations that implement vaguely phrased or ambiguous laws. But in terms of democratic values, elected politicians frequently seek to impose policy changes to satisfy their particular electoral constituencies, that is, politicians frequently want to alter existing policies. It is therefore often the case that the bureaucrat's judgement of what constitutes 'good public policy' collides with the politicians' assessment of what policy should be.

More broadly, three aspects of the basic democratic character of American government condition and complicate how the federal bureaucracy functions:

- *Democratic control.* A central feature of American politics is that government – and hence the bureaucracy – must be subject to popular control. Bureaucratic decisions are legitimate only in as much as they result from democratic processes. The federal bureaucracy is charged with implementing the president's orders but has authority only when duly granted it by laws enacted by Congress. If a bureaucratic agency acts in breach of its legitimate authority, it will typically face a hostile public and disgruntled organized interests. It may also be subject to judicial intervention to reverse its actions.
- *Participation and transparency.* The American public expects to participate directly in bureaucratic decision-making, by contributing to the decision-making process (attending public hearings, for example) and gaining access to bureaucratic records about how decisions were made and implemented. Laws such as the Administrative Procedures Act (APA) and the Freedom of Information Act (FOIA) provide legal expressions and guarantees of the public role and access.
- *The right of redress.* Individual citizens believe that they should not be subject to arbitrary bureaucratic rulings, and should have the ability to litigate against federal agencies in court if their rights are infringed.

But the extent to which the federal bureaucracy is truly subject to full and effective democratic controls is notably unclear. First, popular control over the federal bureaucracy is neither straightforward nor total. As we saw above, elected politicians in both Congress and the presidency are typically neither willing nor able to specify exactly what federal bureaucrats should do in particular real-world cases. Instead, they invariably provide them with substantial administrative autonomy and discretion, delegating the authority to devise rules of implementation. Secondly, despite the above guarantees of access and information, the American public in general is mostly inattentive to the process of decision-making and public involvement in the process is usually minimal (although organized interest groups do scrutinize decisions carefully and are often heavily involved in rule-making and implementation, not least given their expert knowledge). Thirdly, many Americans view bureaucrats as antagonistic to the exercise of their individual freedoms. Even when the bureaucracy acts lawfully, it may face substantial public protests and ultimately be required by its political masters to change its regulations. As Exhibit 10.6 notes, federal bureaucrats have clearly acted illegally at different points in recent American history, such as when the Internal Revenue Service (IRS) harassed individual citizens for political purposes (an activity particularly

prevalent under the presidency of Richard Nixon from 1969 to 1974).

THE FUNCTIONS OF THE FEDERAL BUREAUCRACY

The federal bureaucracy as a whole serves three functions for the national government that essentially correspond to those that the Constitution conferred on the executive (implementation), legislature (rule-making) and judiciary (adjudication).

Executing laws

The Constitution requires in Article II, Section 2 that the executive branch must 'take care that the laws be faithfully executed'. The federal bureaucracy implements laws passed by Congress and signed by the president: the Post Office delivers the mail, the Internal Revenue Service (IRS) collects taxes, the Transportation Safety Administration (created in the aftermath of September 11) inspects baggage at the airports.

Creating rules

Because laws are normally vague (by accident or design), the bureaucracy is required

Exhibit 10.6   The Federal Bureau of Investigation (FBI)

One of the clearest examples of the autonomous power of a federal bureaucratic agency is that of the Federal Bureau of Investigation (FBI). A law enforcement agency within the Department of Justice, many Americans nevertheless believe it to be an independent and separate organization. The FBI, under its director J. Edgar Hoover, acted in effect as an autonomous arm of American government. Hoover was notoriously resistant to the preferences of his immediate boss, the Attorney General, as well as the president. Since he possessed compromising material on many politicians (including the Kennedys) and established a public reputation as a zealous pursuer of criminals and communists alike, few presidents dared politically to sack him. As an unelected bureaucrat Hoover was effectively an independent operator, able ruthlessly to pursue suspected communists and to order the illegal surveillance of many Americans (including Martin Luther King and Frank Sinatra). The 'war against terrorism' after September 11 re-ignited fears among some Americans that federal bureaucrats might conduct illegal surveillance of Americans to identify potential terrorists within the United States.

also to write specific rules that guide how the laws will be executed. But since America's economy and society have become more complex and the problems addressed by the federal government more complicated (from environmental protection to the regulation of the Internet), Congress has confronted substantial problems in specifying exactly what the federal bureaucracy should do. Beyond the problems plaguing innovative congressional action that were noted in Chapter 7, Congress is often reluctant to be exact in its legal provisions because it lacks either the information or expertise to be precise (despite the existence of substantial supporting institutions such as the General Accounting Office, Congressional Budget Office, and Congressional Research Service).

Adjudication

The federal bureaucracy is occupied in addressing many complex and controversial issues. Inevitably, disputes arise between parties subject to bureaucratic regulations. When settling these, agencies are required by law to act as if they were judicial bodies. Adjudication typically takes the form of a civil trial, with a judicial officer who is structurally and functionally separated from the other activities of the agency making the decisions. For example, the National Labor Relations Board (NRLB) attempts to resolve disputes concerning federal labour laws when management and labour present differing interpretations of what the laws require.

STRUCTURE AND COMPOSITION

The structure and composition of the federal government is determined by expressly political factors (in particular the goals and needs of the president and the Congress). As Exhibits 10.7 and 10.8 note, the federal bureaucracy is a massive and complex set of distinct agencies – in excess of 1,000 civilian agencies exist from the Federal Trade Commission to the Consumer Product Safety Commission.

Immense in size and extremely diverse in terms of its roles and operations, the hundreds of specialized departments, agencies, bureaux, offices and corporations that make up the federal bureaucracy directly employ nearly two million people and work with as many as 15 million more who act as recipients of grants and contracts or who fulfil mandates. Competition between agencies within departments – for control of programmes, personnel and funds – is intense and endemic.

Given the size, role and importance of the federal bureaucracy, the recruitment process is crucial to its effective operation. Until 1893, most federal employees were hired under a 'spoils system' – the party controlling the White House recruited workers as it chose, usually employing its particular supporters. If the other party won the presidency, it could replace these patronage appointees with its own supporters. The spoils system began to be eroded in 1883 with the enactment of the Civil Service Reform Act, to be replaced by a 'merit system' of appointment on the basis of success in competitive examinations. With successive laws and executive orders, the merit system expanded steadily to over 90 per cent of federal employees. The overwhelming proportion of federal bureaucrats are today career civil servants selected on the basis of competitive examinations or particular skills. Approximately 15,000 job skills (from nuclear physicists to typists) are represented within the federal workforce.

It is political appointees, however, who occupy the most senior positions in the vast majority of federal agencies (of the 3,000 or so that exist, approximately 1,200 require Senate confirmation for appointment; around 2,000 do not). The rationale for political appointments to top positions is that the federal bureaucracy should be directed by those with connections to the democratically elected president. However, this raises a key problem. Since few presidents (even particularly intellectual ones such as Clinton) have clear goals on all issues and the president typically

Exhibit 10.7   Components of the federal bureaucracy

Departments. In 2002, there existed 14 Cabinet Departments, employing about 60 per cent of the federal workforce and accounting for most federal spending. Each Department is headed by a Secretary, appointed by the president and confirmed by the Senate (except the Department of Justice, which is directed by the Attorney General.) The Secretary is tasked with establishing the Department's policies and administering its operation, consistent with congressional directives and presidential goals. Departments vary substantially in size and funding. The largest in terms of staff is the Department of Defense, which employs approximately 800,000 civilian Americans (about one-half of the entire federal civilian workforce) as well as approximately 1.4 million uniformed military personnel. The Department of Health and Human Services is the largest in terms of funding, accounting for approximately 40 per cent of all federal spending (mainly through the Social Security and Medicare programmes, which respectively provide pensions and medical services to the elderly). At the other end of the spectrum, the Department of Education employs about 5,000 civil servants and has a budget of about $42 billion.

Independent regulatory commissions. Although only 14 Departments exist, dozens of independent agencies and commissions operate within the bureaucracy, created by Congress. Each has responsibility for regulating particular sectors of the economy (the Securities and Exchange Commission and securities markets or the Food and Drug Administration and pharmaceuticals) or certain policy arenas (for example, the Federal Reserve Board and monetary policy). The commissions are granted authority by Congress to make, enforce and adjudicate rules. They are usually headed by a board of directors (or 'commission') rather than a single director, although the commission's chairman generally is the pre-eminent member. The Federal Reserve Board has extensive influence on economic policy through its power to set interest rates. The Equal Employment Opportunities Commission (EEOC) has developed extensive guidelines to combat sexual and racial discrimination in employment. The Federal Communications Commission (FCC) regulates broadcasting policy and determines national standards, while the Federal Election Commission (FEC) monitors and regulates the conduct of American federal elections.

Independent executive agencies. Resembling Cabinet Departments, independent executive agencies conventionally have narrower responsibilities. Like Departments, these agencies are led by a single director, appointed by the president and confirmed by the Senate, who serves at the pleasure of the president. The heads of these agencies report directly to the president, rather than to a Departmental Secretary.

Government-sponsored corporations. Beginning in the 1930s, Congress has established corporations to perform functions that might otherwise have been done by private firms (but, in the eyes of Congress, were not being done appropriately or at all). Examples include the Federal Deposit Insurance Corporation (which insures savings deposits in commercial banks) and Amtrak (which operates most of America's passenger trains). The largest is the US Postal Service.

knows relatively few of the appointees directly or closely, scope exists for autonomous action by appointees. Moreover, political appointees frequently have their own goals and preferences. The appointees mainly work in the agencies with career civil servants, not in the White House with the president and his immediate staff. Although political appointees generally act in ways that they believe are consistent with presidential wishes, they sometimes pursue their own policy goals or become sympathetic with the

Exhibit 10.8 Independent regulatory commissions, independent executive agencies and government-sponsored corporations, 1998

African Development Foundation	National Credit Union Administration
Central Intelligence Agency	National Foundation of the Arts and
Commodity Futures Trading Commission	Humanities
Consumer Product Safety Commission	National Labor Relations Board
Corporation for National and Community	National Mediation Board
Service	National Railroad Passenger Corporation
Defense Nuclear Facilities Safety Board	(Amtrak)
Environmental Protection Agency	National Science Foundation
Equal Employment Opportunity	National Transportation Safety Board
Commission	Nuclear Regulatory Commission
Export–Import Bank of the US	Occupational Safety and Health Review
Farm Credit Administration	Commission
Federal Communication Commission	Office of Government Ethics
Federal Deposit Insurance Corporation	Office of Personnel Management
Federal Election Commission	Office of Special Counsel
Federal Emergency Management Agency	Panama Canal Commission
Federal Housing Finance Board	Peace Corps
Federal Labor Relations Authority	Pension Benefit Guaranty Corporation
Federal Maritime Commission	Postal Rate Commission
Federal Mediation and Conciliation	Railroad Retirement Board
Service	Securities and Exchange Commission
Federal Mine Safety and Health Review	Selective Service System
Commission	Small Business Administration
Federal Reserve System	Social Security Administration
Federal Retirement Thrift Investment Board	Tennessee Valley Authority
Federal Trade Commission	Trade and Development Agency
General Services Administration	US Arms Control and Disarmament
Inter-American Foundation	Agency
Merit Systems Protection Board	US Commission on Civil Rights
National Aeronautics and Space	US Information Agency
Administration	US International Development Corporation
National Archives and Records	Agency
Administration	US International Trade Commission
National Capital Planning Commission	US Postal Service

Source: *United States Government Manual 1998–99* (1998: 22).

goals of the agency that they preside over – a phenomenon known as 'going native'.

EVALUATING THE FEDERAL BUREAUCRACY

The federal bureaucracy is typically criticized not only by the American public but also by political analysts. Six main charges are commonly levelled at federal bureaucrats:

- *Clientelism.* Agencies tend to serve the interests of those whom they are supposed to oversee, protecting them at the expense of the broader public interest.
- *Imperialism.* Agencies invariably seek to expand their powers and responsibilities at the expense of other agencies and

programmes, notwithstanding the issue of how public needs are best met.

- *Parochialism.* Bureaucracies tend to focus narrowly on their own goals rather than the 'big picture' of government or the national interest as a whole.
- *Incrementalism.* Most bureaucratic agencies are not renowned for creative or imaginative operations, instead acting slowly and cautiously and generally resisting major changes.
- *Arbitrariness.* In applying abstract rules to concrete cases, agencies often ignore the particular concerns or specific merits of those affected by the rules.
- *Waste.* Given their size and routinized procedures, bureaucracies tend to use resources less efficiently than private sector organizations.

Beyond these, American politicians from across the spectrum often charge the bureaucracy not simply with inefficiency or subversion of policy, but also with explicit political bias. But whether the federal bureaucracy has a clear partisan bias is highly contentious. There exist at least three reasons to doubt whether bureaucratic obstructionism, when it occurs, derives from overt partisan or ideological motivations:

- *Representativeness.* Most political scientists concur that bureaucrats' political views tend, on the whole, to mirror those of the American public more broadly. As noted in Chapters 3 and 4, Americans currently are fairly evenly divided in their partisan loyalties and views between Republicans and Democrats.
- *Respect for democratic values.* Beyond this, federal bureaucrats tend to vest both their own neutrality and democratic values more broadly with great significance. If their elected leaders are Republicans, they will pursue the goals that the Republicans establish; if their elected superiors are Democrats, they act accordingly. (This is complicated, of course, in conditions of divided party control of the federal government, when one party controls the

White House and the other party maintains a majority in one or both houses of Congress.)

- *Professionalism.* Many (if not most) federal bureaucrats are well-educated specialists in technical and managerial positions, 'white collar' professionals who take their responsibilities seriously, as engineers, lawyers, economists, technicians or analysts, rather than as partisans. Whether the incumbent in the White House is Democratic or Republican, most bureaucrats receive – readily – advice and guidance from elected officials and act in ways consistent with their professional training. If their political superiors seek conservative ends, the bureaucracy generally complies; if their elected leaders have a progressive bent, bureaucrats tend also to promote these objectives. Since elections are constant – and hence the possibility of new political masters in the White House and Congress is also a constant – it makes little sense for permanent bureaucrats to do otherwise than assist in the implementation of policy as elected officials demand.

Effective government and democratic accountability together require that presidents should be able to secure the implementation of their legitimate policy goals by the bureaucracy. But as we noted in Chapter 6, powerful obstacles exist to effective presidential leadership. Ironically, the federal bureaucracy that the president heads provides one of the most significant, a rival as potentially substantial as Congress.

But federal bureaucrats possess their own measure of legitimacy, despite their unelected role. The modern administrative state, comprising a myriad different agencies, places great emphasis on the values of professionalism, expertise, continuity and rationality. When political leaders seek to satisfy their particular electoral constituencies by making policy changes, bureaucrats may nevertheless raise legitimate concerns about the rationality of those reforms or their own ability to achieve an effective policy outcome. The trade-off between the democratic imperative and the need for rationality and effectiveness in policy, with the latter at least in part the province of expert professionals well versed in the field, is inescapably part and parcel of modern political life (not only in America).

What complicates and politicizes this general phenomenon in the US is the separated system. From the viewpoint of federal bureaucrats, loyalty is owed to the president as their day-to-day manager, but their very existence ultimately rests more with Congress, as the institution of government that structures and funds the bureaucracy. First, it is Congress that uses its legislative power to establish, merge or abolish departments, set up new programmes and agencies, and fix terms of appointment. Secondly, it is Congress that uses its appropriations power (the 'power of the purse') to finance departments, agencies and civil servants. Thirdly, Congress uses its power of oversight to investigate agencies within the executive branch, and then to reward or penalize these. Fourthly, given incumbency rates, lawmakers may be in place long after a president has departed the White House. Taken together, federal bureaucrats have every reason to fear members of key congressional committees and subcommittees at least as much as (and often more than) the president.

The operations of the federal bureaucracy therefore powerfully compound the extensive fragmentation of the American political system, reinforcing its decentralizing pulls. The costs of this in terms of democratic responsiveness and accountability are frequently substantial. But the lens through which the bureaucracy is viewed sharply alters the picture. In particular, American democracy provides for two co-equal elected partners, the presidency and Congress. The Framers deliberately sought to avoid a dictatorial or dominant presidency. Presidents during the twentieth century (not least, but not only, Richard Nixon) sought to use agencies such as the FBI and IRS to target political opponents. An influential and independent civil service, able to resist such abuses, can

therefore be regarded less as an impediment to democratic values than a necessary part of them. The inherent problem, however, is that the very size, scope and fragmentation of American government provides ample opportunities for bureaucrats to reinforce parochial and sectional policymaking at the expense of the broader national interest.

CONCLUSION

The federal bureaucracy is an active and independent participant in the American policy process, continually negotiating and bargaining with the presidency, Congress, courts and organized interest groups. Each bureaucratic agency possesses its own clientele, power base and authority, little of which derives directly from the president. Congress creates agencies, defines their powers and appropriates their funds. But once created, agencies take on a life of their own, defending themselves against those who threaten their powers or seek their abolition by bargaining with competing institutions of government and enlisting the support of their clientele to defend their existing role, budget and programmes.

Public demands for 'less bureaucracy' are as much a constant in American politics as the demands for solutions to pressing social and economic problems. But the irony here is that it is frequently bureaucrats who are charged with making and implementing those solutions. Moreover, for practical as well as political reasons, the 'parent' congressional committees that delegate powers to executive agencies consciously increase the autonomous power of those bureaucracies to form policy by implementing policy. While this is a common phenomenon across industrialized democracies, its impact is especially significant in the United States. Not only does bureaucratic fragmentation and competition often impede the chances of policy change, but the ability of agencies to resist democratic control compounds the parochialism that inheres in American government and politics.

FURTHER READING

Aberbach, J., *Keeping a Watchful Eye* (1990) is a clear analysis of the role of Congress in overseeing the bureaucracy.

Goodsell, C., *The Case for Bureaucracy: A Public Administration Polemic* (1994) is a robust defence of the role and effectiveness of federal bureaucrats.

Gormley, W., *Taming the Bureaucracy: Muscles, Prayers and Other Strategies* (1989) is an examination of how to enhance the performance of bureaucratic agencies.

Rourke, F., *Bureaucracy, Politics and Public Policy* (1984) is an excellent introduction.

Wilson, J.Q., *Bureaucracy: What Government Agencies Do and Why They Do It* (1989) is a comprehensive analysis that examines bureaucracies' internal characteristics and their external environment.

Woll, P., *American Bureaucracy* (1977) is a classic overview of the functions and effectiveness of bureaucratic agencies in America.

WEB LINKS

Bureau of the Census
http://www.census.gov

Department of Defense
http://www.dtic.dia.mi/defenselink

Department of Education
http://www.ed.gov

Department of Health and Human Services
http://www.os.dhhs.gov

Center for Disease Control
http://www.cdc.gov

National Institutes of Health
http://www.nih.gov

Department of Justice
http://www.usdoj.gov

Department of State
http://www.state.gov

Department of the Treasury
http://www.ustreas.gov

Central Intelligence Agency
http://www.is.gov

Environmental Protection Agency
http://www.epa.gov

FirstGov: provides information about federal agencies, programmes and
benefits and links to state government sites
http://www.firstgov.gov

Fedworld: connects to most federal departments, bureaux, commissions and
to governmental statistics and reports
http://www.fedworld.gov

Jefferson Project: includes academic analyses of the federal government.
http://www.voxpop.org

QUESTIONS

- Why is the federal bureaucracy so difficult for presidents to control?

- Are bureaucracies threats to freedom or guarantors of liberty?

- To what extent is the federal bureaucracy insufficiently powerful?

- Is bureaucratic fragmentation rational?

- 'The fact that federal bureaucrats are unelected officials suggests that their autonomy of action should be modest.' Discuss.

11 Domestic Policy

If one accepts the premise that tribalism is a human universal, then the incarceration of Japanese-Americans in World War II, the exclusion of Jews from universities and the professions in the 1920s and 1930s, the ruthless persecution of Mormons, the removal of Indian tribes, and the maintenance of a brutal, racial caste system in the pre-1960s South seem less remarkable than the eventual alleviation, reversal, or abandonment of all these social policies by the American political system. Looking, moreover, at the overall record of Western Europe during a comparable time period, it is not at all clear that despite its organizational singularities the American approach to democratic self-government suffers greatly by comparison.

Nelson Polsby (1997: 179)

American democracy ensures the public get their way, even if the result is not always pleasant.

Jonathan Freedland (1998: 31–2)

- Federalism
- Public Policy
- Economic Policy
- Social Policy
- Criminal Justice Policy
- Conclusion

Chapter Summary

Domestic policymaking in America is distinguished by three main characteristics. First, federalism makes America a 'compound republic', part national, part state and part local. Policymaking is therefore a complex and multi-level affair in which not only the federal/national government influences policy outcomes, but so too do a myriad (no less than 85,000) other state, local and city governments. Secondly, most domestic policies feature intense competition within and between several branches of government (executives, legislatures, judiciaries) as well as tiers to achieve distinct policy goals. Thirdly, the 'law of unintended consequences' frequently conditions policy outcomes. Although policies may originate with a clear design, the ambiguities of laws and the vagaries of their implementation often produces anomalies, surprises and unanticipated side-effects. The effect of the vertical division between the federal, state and local governments and the horizontal separation between different branches of government at the same level is to ensure that the central features of the policy process in America are fragmentation, competition and adversarialism. No single authority controls or determines policy outcomes. Not only does this ensure that the experience of individual Americans varies markedly according to where they happen to live and work, but it also means that there exists a constant political struggle to (re)shape existing public policies in different directions. Whether the subject is economic, social or criminal justice policy, the lack of a single source of national policy makes for a complex and diverse set of outcomes in which 'strong' or 'decisive' government on the Westminster model is precluded, but where the competing preferences of American citizens receive regular and substantial expression.

A good contemporary example of both the benefits and the problems posed by the fragmentation of American government that prior chapters outlined is the issue of human cloning. Cloned human embryos are made by combining a cell from a person with a human egg whose genetic material has been removed. The resulting embryo would be identical genetically to the person who donated the cell. Federal funds cannot currently be used for experiments involving cloned human embryos, but no federal law currently precludes such work being undertaken in America with private funds.

On April 10, 2002, President George W. Bush called on Congress to prohibit all types of human cloning. Declaring that 'life is a creation, not a commodity', Bush requested that the Democratic Senate pass legislation to outlaw the cloning of microscopic human embryos for research into new medical therapies, in addition to outlawing the creation of cloned babies. Although the federal government supported a broad range of research involving stem cells derived from animal embryos and adults, Bush declared that

human cloning was contrary to medical ethics, its purported benefits were highly speculative and any law allowing human cloning would be virtually impossible to enforce adequately.

But in response, a bipartisan group of senators on Capitol Hill led by Dianne Feinstein (Democrat, California) announced that they intended to pass a bill that would permit cloning for research purposes. Although most agreed that it should be illegal to create cloned human beings, they strongly defended the right of medical researchers to use cloned human embryos that showed potential for developing treatments for debilitating illnesses and conditions such as Parkinson's disease, spinal cord injuries, and diabetes. Forty Nobel laureates from the US scientific community also issued a joint statement that the ban Bush sought would exert a 'chilling effect' on all scientific research in America. At the same time, Senators Sam Brownback (Republican, Kansas) and Mary Landrieu (Democrat, Louisiana) announced that another bill that they were sponsoring – to prohibit both 'reproductive' and 'therapeutic' cloning – had the support of around 40 senators.

Although the issue is a particularly complex and emotive one, the differences expressed on cloning are merely one instance of the complexity of passing and implementing laws and public policies to address pressing social and economic problems in America. Most Americans endorse the general goals set forth in the preamble of the US Constitution (national unity, justice, law and order, national security, welfare and liberty), which, as Chapter 1 noted, are rooted in their Creedal values – liberty, equality before the law, equality of opportunity – but the prospects of assuring that those goals are realized are arguably weakened by the combination of a markedly diverse social base, a supremely fragmented system of government, weak political parties, an active interest group universe, and powerful courts and bureaucracies. President Bush could request, but not compel, Congress to act on human cloning. Congress itself was internally divided, as were the main parties. And even if a bill was eventually agreed, its details would be delegated to federal bureaucrats to refine and its constitutionality would almost certainly be tested in the federal courts.

Yet despite the extensive fragmentation of government, the United States has recorded an impressive history of economic growth, prosperity, educational distinction and (as the next chapter details) international influence. If America's governmental system is plagued by localism, division and competition, it may nevertheless seem that other less successful nations may well usefully imitate these. Whether American economic and international successes have occurred more despite than because of the fragmentary system of government is questionable, but what is certain is that domestic policymaking in America is complex, competitive and adversarial. In particular, domestic policymaking is distinguished by three main characteristics.

First, the federal nature of the American system of government makes the policy process a complex and multi-level affair. The vertical divisions between the federal, state and local governments preclude there being either one particular policy applicable nationwide or the control of the policy process by a single tier of government. The process is instead blurred and ambiguous, with constant pressures between a range of actors with very different interests and constituencies. The conflicts built into the architecture of government demand cooperation between different tiers of government in order to facilitate effective policymaking on matters as varied as social insurance, law enforcement and health and safety at work.

Secondly, most American public policies feature intense competition between several branches of government (as well as tiers) at federal, state and local levels. No single institution (executive, legislature or judiciary) determines policy alone. Congress and the White House are frequently in conflict at the federal level, especially in conditions of divided party control, but so too are the House and Senate and the parties (and factions) within each. Bureaucratic agencies, organized interest lobbies and courts also play an active and influential role within the process, competing and forging coalitions with other actors with similar interests or goals as they see fit. And these divisions are, moreover, replicated at state and local levels.

Thirdly, the 'law of unintended consequences' frequently conditions policy outcomes. Precisely because so many institutional influences exist on the policy process and the opportunities for participation are so extensive, clear, lasting and unambiguous, policy results are infrequent but unanticipated results, surprises and side-effects can frequently occur. For example, it was a national security shock – the launch by the Soviet Union of the first space satellite, Sputnik, in 1957 – that led Congress to pass the National Defense Education Act (NDEA) of 1958. That measure provided federal aid for science teaching in the public schools and NDEA scholarships for advanced students in science, mathematics and engineering. In short, a policy designed to assist with America's defence policy (so that the US would not be left behind in the 'space race') ended up having substantial beneficial effects on expanding America's higher education system and increasing its cohort of college graduates.

In an important respect, as the NDEA example suggests, it no longer makes sense (indeed, even during the Cold War it was somewhat misleading) to speak of 'domestic' policy as something separate from foreign policy. Few policy areas exist in America (or other industrialized market democracies) that are unaffected by international factors, from foreign direct investment in America to environmental regulations. Nonetheless, to the extent that the dominant elements remain internal to America, we can assess the key domestic features of policies in particular, and the policy process more broadly. In this chapter, we concentrate on three very different areas to illustrate the many pressures on policymakers and the diversity of policy results: economic policy, social policy and criminal justice policy. Before we move on to these, though, some initial remarks should be made about America's federal system, which exerts a pervasive influence on all domestic policy questions.

FEDERALISM

At the heart of the domestic policy process is the federal nature of the union. Federalism refers to a political arrangement in which, as well as the national/federal government, local units of government (territorial, regional, provincial, state, municipal, and more) exist that can exercise final decisions on certain government activities and whose existence is specially protected (both in formal constitutional terms and by the established habits and preferences of citizens). In unitary systems such as the UK, even devolved powers (such as those to the Scottish Parliament and Welsh Assembly) can be altered or abolished by the national government, but in America, as Justice Anthony

Kennedy put it, the US Constitution 'split the atom of sovereignty' into two. As neither a centralized nation-state like France nor a loose confederation of independent sovereign states like the European Union, sovereignty in America is shared between both specially protected state and local governments and the federal authority. As Table 11.1 notes, over 85,000 distinct government units co-exist in the American system, staffed by some 500,000 elected officials (537 federal, approximately 8,000 state and 494,000 local officials).

In comparative terms, what this means is that American policymaking invariably involves the operation of a 'compound republic', one that is partly national and partly state and local in character. Although, as the previous chapter noted, the federal government has accumulated vast powers and a large bureaucratic apparatus, it spends most of its money and enforces its rules not directly on individual citizens but on other units of government. Whether the matter is the welfare system, programmes to assist central cities, the interstate highway system or clean water programmes, the federal government seeks less to govern directly as to persuade or coerce the states and localities – through regulations, grants and incentives – to govern according to national standards or goals.

Federalism therefore pits national policy and national citizenship rights against state and local policies and sub-national community preferences. States do not have 'rights' in the same sense that individual citizens do, but the central question informing debates on federal–state relations is a practical one: which allocation of power between states and the federal government best meets desired public policy goals?

For the Founding Fathers, federalism secured both liberty and public goods. Dividing power allowed state and federal governments to check each other to preserve individual freedoms through a double security, while at the same time ensuring that some goals are secured at federal, others at state, level. In particular, certain public goods are

TABLE 11.1 The administrative structure of American government

Type of government unit	Number
Federal/national government	1
State government	50
Local government:	
County	3,043
Municipal (city)	19,279
Township/town	16,656
School district	14,422
Other special district (e.g. airport authority, sewage treatment)	31,555
Total local government	84,955
Total	85,006

Source: US Bureau of the Census (1996: 295).

best provided by the federal government, since individual states are unlikely to pay for them when others can 'free ride' on their benefits. For example, missiles located in North Dakota also protect citizens in Texas and Virginia, but North Dakota would be unlikely to pay for their cost alone. Beyond national defence, the federal government provides, through federal taxes and borrowing, for interstate highways, space exploration, the Post Office, the Coast Guard, air traffic control, national parks, and most medical research. As the previous chapter noted, federal agencies also ensure the policing of goods, persons and businesses across state lines. National programmes and minimum federal standards – from child labour laws to social security and unemployment insurance – also mitigate against the existence of the most egregious differences in social provision between the individual states.

Beyond these important broad federal government functions, the individual states remain essentially autonomous. From the regulation of firearms and free speech to the imposition of taxes and delivery of welfare services, federalism ensures that the quality of life and extent of personal freedoms for American citizens differs significantly according to which state and locality they reside in.

If states wish to enact more protection for individual liberties or clean air than the federal government provides, they can do so. Similarly, in what Justice Louis Brandeis termed 'laboratories for experiment', states can innovate public policies without requiring a national policy. For example, Wisconsin has pioneered innovations in industrial compensation, unemployment insurance and welfare reform, California in higher education, New York in community policing and Hawaii in universal health care that other states then imitated. As Exhibit 11.1 suggests, compared to policymaking in a unitary state or one with devolved powers, federal systems therefore feature much more multi-layered policy processes. More opportunities exist to influence policy and to innovate, and a wider range of participants is typically active in seeking to exert influence.

As was emphasized in Chapter 1, the chief characteristic of America's social base in general – both between and within the 50 states – is difference. Depending on whether a citizen lives in Alabama or Illinois, the types of public services, levels of taxes, and even regulations on the most private of matters (sex, for example, as Exhibit 11.2 notes) differ substantially. These differences reflect, in large measure, the social composition of the particular

Exhibit 11.1   Varieties of federalism

Confederation. An arrangement in which ultimate government authority is vested in the states that make up the nation. Whatever power the national government has is derived from the states being willing to give up some of their authority to a central government.

Co-operative federalism. A period of cooperation between state and national government that began during the Great Depression. The national government assumed new responsibilities, and state and local officials accepted it as an ally, not an enemy.

Dual federalism. The perspective on federalism that emerged after the Civil War. It saw the national and state governments as equal but independent partners, with each responsible for distinct policy functions and each barred from interfering with the other's work.

Federation (federal system). A mixture of confederation and unitary systems in which the authority of government is shared by both the national and state governments. In its ideal form, a federal constitution gives some exclusive authority over some governmental tasks to the national government, while giving the states exclusive authority over other governmental matters. There would also be some areas where the two levels of government would share authority.

New Federalism. (Partially successful) attempts by Presidents Nixon and Reagan to return power to the states through block grants.

Unitary system. A form of government in which ultimate authority rests with the national government (such as the UK). Whatever powers state or local governments have under this type of government are derived from the central government.

states. In states where religious fundamentalism and 'traditional values' are important influences, such as Alabama, restrictive laws on abortion rights co-exist with permissive regulations on gun ownership. If citizens of one state feel oppressed by its policies, migration offers a potential escape (hence the concentration of libertarians in New Hampshire, Mormons in Utah and environmentalists in Oregon). But what is crucial here is that the experiences that condition the lives of most Americans are primarily related to local and state circumstances, not Washington, DC.

For example, take the issue of same-sex unions. Some states during the 1990s moved to legalize same-sex relationships, to allow gay and lesbian couples the same legal status, rights and government benefits as married ones. But many American traditionalists – or 'social conservatives' – objected strongly to such moves. This was not only because of their moral beliefs about gay and lesbian

relationships, but also because such actions had the potential to nationalize the policy by default. States have been obliged to recognize the legality of, for example, marriages, divorces, birth certificates and driving licences legally obtained in other states, but in the case of same-sex unions (which some states such as Vermont have now legalized), Congress intervened in 1996 by passing the Defense of Marriage Act – signed into law by President Clinton – which 'inoculated' states against mutual recognition of such unions. A gay couple from Mississippi who marry in Vermont will not be recognized as married if they return to reside in the Deep South state.

The federal government therefore has a substantial and important, but still limited, role in shaping policy in the 50 states. The broad framework of criminal and civil law remains a state and local matter. It is the individual states that determine the age at which a resident may leave school, drive a car, drink

Exhibit 11.2 The state in American bedrooms

Although often considered the quintessential private activity, sex in America is 'blanketed by laws' to the extent that crossing a state boundary can involve 'stepping into a different moral universe' (Posner and Silbaugh, 1998: 1–2). Oral sex, for example, was illegal in 15 of the 50 states as late as 1999. Adultery remained a crime in 24 of them. Eight states had prohibited the sale, though not the use, of 'marital aids'. Thirty-three states had no statutes relating to fornication but in 17 it was considered a misdemeanour or felony. Incest was a felony in 48 states but only a misdemeanour in Virginia and did not even merit a statute in Rhode Island. Prostitution was only a misdemeanour in most states, but the strongest condemnatory language in American sex law ('unnatural', 'lascivious' and 'a crime against nature') was reserved for 'sodomy', although 23 states had no statutes at all pertaining to the practice. Theoretically, the state of Alabama allows sex with donkeys and corpses (no state law exists against either bestiality or necrophilia), but punishes oral sex between husbands and wives (there exists a law against oral sex that does not discriminate between married and unmarried persons or heterosexuals and homosexuals). Most of these laws are of course unenforced and – absent of a totalitarian state – unenforceable. Nevertheless, the differences illustrate how domestic regulations can differ sharply even on the most intimate and private of matters according to the particular state's moral traditions and political culture.

alcohol or marry. Everyday matters, from the provision of street lights to the disposal of sewage, remain mostly dependent on state and local provision. And although all Americans are subject to federal taxes on incomes, their liability to other tax burdens varies according to where they live. Sales and property taxes are common though their rates vary, and most states now operate a state income tax. New York City also imposes a city income and a city sales tax. In some states, elected officials decide tax policy, while in others state constitutions require tax increases to be approved by the people in a referendum. In 1978, Proposition 13 in California was approved by voters, amending the state constitution by cutting property taxes, limiting the authority of local government to raise taxes, and requiring a two-thirds vote in the California legislature before state taxes could be increased.

Since the states therefore remain central to most Americans' daily lives and the political system as a whole (for instance, citizens vote in federal elections as their states determine, and no national referendum exists), much of the federal government's interventions consist not in directly imposing policy solutions on the states but rather devising incentives and penalties to induce individual states to adopt particular standards or policies, such as speed limits. But the remarkable growth of federal government responsibilities since the New Deal (noted in Chapter 10) has offered three opportunities for an extensive assertion of the federal government role:

- *Funding transfers.* First, the federal government transfers substantial amounts of national funds to the states. As Exhibit 11.3 notes, how it does this can vary greatly. Funds can be granted for specific policy goals, apportioned on the basis of certain eligibility criteria, or given as a block for the states to decide how best to use the funds.
- *Mandates.* The federal government can require that states undertake a specific activity (such as reducing lead levels in drinking water or providing job training for recipients of welfare benefits). Most mandates concern civil rights and environmental protection. For example, various pollution-control laws require states to

Exhibit 11.3 Federal government transfers to state governments

Block grants. Money given to the states by Congress that can be used in broad areas and is not limited to specific purposes like categorical grants. A means introduced in the mid-1960s to give states greater latitude in how the funds are to be spent.

Categorical, or conditional, grants. Money given to the states and localities by Congress that can be used for limited purposes under specific rules detailing how funds are to be spent.

Formula grants. Grants given to states and localities on the basis of a specific funding formula (such as population density, number of eligible persons, per capita income or other factors).

Grants-in-aid. A general term for transfers given by Congress to state and local governments for a specific spending purpose.

comply with federal standards for clean air, pure drinking water and sewage treatment. But two general problems exist with mandates. First, many mandates are written in vague terms, effectively leaving federal administrative agencies the power to determine what state and local governments must do. For example, the Americans with Disabilities Act was one of 20 mandates signed into law by President Bush in 1990, and required businesses and state and local governments to provide the disabled with equal access to services, employment, buildings and transportation systems. However, the law provided no clear definition of 'equal access', no clear instruction as to how this was to be administered and no reliable estimate of its cost. Secondly, by the early 1990s, Congress had mandated over 150 such actions on the states without providing additional funds for them. Under the 1995 Unfunded Mandates Relief Act, when Congress requires states to implement new legislation that entails substantial expenditures without transfers of federal funds to assist, a separate vote must occur to determine if Congress wishes to impose the unfunded mandate on the states.

- *Prohibitions.* The federal government can restrain or prohibit states from pursuing certain courses. For example, the federal Clean Water Act allows federal authorities to prohibit states from highway construction that endangers certain wetland conservation areas.

From the New Deal era, even when federal intervention in a new area was seen as needed or desirable, it was generally viewed as, at best, a necessary evil. But with the activism and 'creative federalism' of LBJ's 'Great Society' programmes of 1964–68, some Americans saw federal participation in new areas as a positive way to mobilize and employ resources. Previously, federal initiatives had typically had to be justified (frequently on national defence grounds) to legitimize intervention in areas traditionally left to state and local governments (education, land-use controls and law enforcement, for example), but the 1960s saw many Americans endorse a federal role as legitimate provided simply that Congress held it to be so. The past three decades have witnessed profound changes in the federal system. Partly, these reflect changes in the relative financial and political status of the various governments in the federal system, but they also stem from changes in the economic geography of America, in demographics and in expectations of government. In regard to the latter, in particular, two important breaks can be identified.

Whereas prior to 1964 federal grant pro-grammes were intended to implement state and local goals, the Great Society programmes spelt out national goals in areas ranging from racial equality to health care. These national goals were to be implemented not directly by the federal government but through a variety of federal aid recipients, including local governments and non-governmental organizations. Moreover, as we saw in the previous chapter, regulatory activities became increasingly important and extensive as the federal government moved into areas such as consumer, worker and environmental protection, which brought the federal government into areas previously regulated – if regulated at all – by state governments. Between 1960 and 1966 federal grants to the states doubled, did so again between 1966 and 1970, and doubled yet again from 1970 to 1975. By 1985, in excess of $100 billion annually was spent through federal grants, administered through over 400 distinct programmes (with the five largest – housing assistance for low-income families, Medicaid, highway construction, services to the unemployed, and welfare programmes for mothers with dependent children and the disabled – accounting for over half of the total sums).

But a steady reaction against the growth of the federal government's interventions then ensued from the later 1970s to today. The major changes occurred with Reagan's election in 1980 and the Republican Congress of 1995–96. Reagan sought a fundamental change in the role of the central government which would shrink in size, function, tax revenues and influence on domestic matters. A greater reliance on state governments and fewer and weaker federal–state relationships was to be matched by reduced federal regulation of state and local government. The Omnibus Budget Reconciliation Act of 1981 consolidated 57 categorical grants into nine block grants, reducing funding for many grant programmes and abolishing a number of programmes such as intergovernmental

personnel grants. But there was ultimately no reduction in total outlays under Reagan's presidency: federal spending – domestic and military – increased during the Reagan years, and the initial cut in personal income tax rates of 1981 was partially offset by increases in social security and business taxes in subsequent years.

Reagan's unsuccessful assault nevertheless emboldened Republicans to attempt subsequently to limit the federal government's reach. The Republican 104th Congress made some important changes, not least in reforming the unfunded mandates system (above) and welfare assistance to the states (see below). However, American politics and public policy remains markedly more nationalized than it was in the 1930s, with the federal government – and especially, as we saw in Chapter 8, the federal courts – imposing increasingly uniform standards on the states in the forms of mandates and conditions of federal aid. Federalism means that citizens living in different parts of America will be treated differently, not merely in spending programmes such as welfare, but also in legal systems that assign different penalties to similar offences or that enforce civil rights laws differently (see below). But federalism also ensures that more opportunities exist to participate in decision-making, from influencing school curricula to deciding where highways are to be constructed.

Even here, however, the competitive pressures that are an inevitable by-product of a complex and fragmented government structure ensure that policy can rarely be decided in a clear and consistent fashion. If one examines the federal government alone, an array of departments and agencies compete to determine policy on the economy, social welfare, criminal justice (and, as Exhibit 11.4 notes, the environment). As such, the relative coherence and simplicity of government in unitary states such as France and the UK is decidedly absent from America.

Exhibit 11.4 American environmental policy

The refusal of the administration of George W. Bush to abide by the Kyoto Protocol on global warming prompted stinging international criticism of America. However, environmental policy is not determined by a presidential mandate. Instead, the responsibility for environmental protection is scattered across the executive branch, Congress, the courts and an array of independent and quasi-independent bureaucratic agencies. Some states, such as California and Oregon, have enacted tougher environmental protection laws than others and have even gone beyond federal requirements. But within the federal government, competition is itself endemic. Environmental protection is a matter that encompasses the Departments of Energy, Transport, Interior and, indirectly, Commerce, Agriculture and Health. No Department for the Environment exists but the Environmental Protection Agency (EPA) is charged with the regulatory task of enforcing legislation such as the National Environmental Protection Act, 1970 and the Clean Air Acts of 1970 and 1990, respectively, as well as implementing policies on toxic waste and dangerous chemicals. But the EPA is only one of several agencies involved in environmental protection. The main laws setting out US environmental policy are each enforced by separate agencies with distinct priorities, preferences and operating procedures. For example, the Clean Air Act is administered by the Department of Transport, the Endangered Species Act by the US Fish and Wildlife Agency and the NEPA by the Environmental Protection Agency. Environmental rules and policies are therefore frequently not the result of clear and consensual decision-making but of bureaucratic turf wars between environmental agencies over which agency 'owns' a particular issue and how it should best be implemented. Moreover, as noted in the last chapter, agencies do not simply follow the instructions of their nominal congressional or presidential masters. Many environmental laws are drafted in general terms, leaving agencies substantial autonomy and discretion to draft the implementing rules and regulations. The result is one in which the traditional picture of intense competition is vividly apparent. Had Al Gore become president in 2001 rather than Bush, the US response to Kyoto would likely have been more positive, but the ability of the president to determine policy on the environment more broadly would have been similarly subject to powerful limits.

PUBLIC POLICY

Public policy is 'the sum of government activities, whether acting directly or through agents, as it has an influence on the lives of citizens' (Peters, 1993: 4). As the previous section noted, although the federal government has grown vastly in size and responsibilities, the federal nature of American government provides substantial influence for the states and local governments on policy outcomes. But even within the federal government alone, competition, fragmentation and overlapping authority is endemic. The next sections deal with three of the most significant examples of such complexity: economic, social and criminal justice policy.

ECONOMIC POLICY

The American market economy is the largest and most productive in the world. For several decades after the end of the Second World War, the United States dominated the world economy. Its dynamic and diverse economy, high standard of living and impressive productivity were much envied abroad. New products – from televisions to computers – were frequently produced first in America before being introduced elsewhere.

The US dollar was the international currency, displacing gold and other currencies. US foreign aid and private investment were important to the economic development of the rest of the world. American economic growth was also determined almost entirely by domestic developments – foreign trade and investment had a marginal impact.

During the 1970s and 1980s, however, some analysts described America as being in 'decline'. Japan's economy had exploded from virtually zero at the end of 1945 to being the second most productive in the world. Economic growth in western Europe exceeded that of America in the late 1970s. For most of the 1980s America ran a huge trade and budget deficit and relied considerably on foreign investors to maintain its living standards. Moreover, international actors increasingly influenced domestic economic developments.

From the vantage point of the twenty-first century, however, predictions of American decline were – to paraphrase Mark Twain – greatly exaggerated. The American economy grew in an unprecedented fashion in the 1990s, experiencing 107 consecutive months of growth. Output and productivity exceeded all its international competitors and – although America depends more on the cooperation of other nations and international organizations to achieve its economic, military and political goals – the United States continues to possess more freedom of action than any state primarily because of its size, productivity and dynamism.

But if America's market economy is remarkably successful, it is also complex and certainly not 'free'. Federal, state and local governments continually condition its operation through bureaucratic regulations, laws, court decisions and arbitration (see Exhibit 11.5). The federal government in particular regulates the national currency – the dollar –

Exhibit 11.5 Economic policy: taxing, spending and regulating

Economic policy is the collection of principles and programmes adopted by government to influence economic activity. Although, as noted below, the compilation of the annual federal budget is the most important aspect of this, it is not the only one. When the federal government decides federal tax rates, how much money should be in circulation in America, and what federal regulations should govern where and how corporations, individuals and non-government organizations operate, it is continually making economic policy.

- *Fiscal policy.* This comprises tax policy (raising government funds) as expressed in laws and regulations as well as spending policy as contained in the federal budget.
- *Monetary policy.* This consists of government activities that influence the overall amount of economic activity by increasing or decreasing the supply of money (the amount of money circulating and available to consumers, producers and government for buying and selling goods and services). When more money is in circulation, interest rates tend to decline and demand for goods and services tends to increase. Rising demands often lead to increasing prices of limited goods and services, fuelling inflation. Reducing the money supply has the reverse effect, slowing the economy and reducing inflation, but often increasing unemployment.
- *Regulatory policy.* This consists of the laws, rules and regulations that govern the conduct of producers, traders and consumers. For example, anti-monopoly laws seek to prevent one corporation from exercising disproportionate influence in a particular sector of the economy, while consumer protection laws seek to guarantee standards for goods and services purchased by the public.

and procures (or purchases) goods and services from the private sector. It also raises public monies from private citizens and American corporations through taxation. Government (or public) expenditure, however, accounts for a smaller proportion of total national economic output than in most industrialized market democracies.

The decisions of federal, state and local governments about fiscal and labour market policies condition the character of national, regional and local economies. In particular, the federal government – as the government with the largest budget – powerfully influences America's output, employment and investment policies and outcomes. Federal government activities currently account for in excess of 20 per cent of Gross National Product (GDP). The federal budget is also important because the US Constitution does not require the budget to be balanced or in surplus, whereas the constitutions of several states prohibit a fiscal deficit.

As with other domestic policies, the structural features of federalism and the separation of powers provides for a highly fragmented process of economic decision-making. The authority to formulate economic policy is scattered between separate branches and tiers of government. For example, no single authority exists to set taxation rates (as noted above, state and local governments frequently administer income, property and sales taxes, on goods such as books, for example). This exacerbates the general pattern of competitive politics in America because the importance of economic policy is so great. The decisions that public officials make about taxation and spending are invariably surrounded by intense public interest. Moreover, elected officials are frequently judged by voters primarily on the state of the economy.

America has also been affected by the

Exhibit 11.6 Key participants in economic policymaking

At the federal level, three players are especially influential in determining economic policy:

The executive branch. The president and his key economic advisers, in particular, the Secretary of the Treasury and the Director of the Office of Management and Budget (OMB), play a crucial role in developing policy options, forecasts of their likely effects, and in persuading other branches of government to change programmes, funding levels and taxation rates.

Congress. With the constitutional 'power of the purse', Congress oversees and evaluates the federal government's budget. The Congressional Budget Office (CBO), established in 1974, forecasts the development of the economy and provides Congress with its own estimates of the cost of proposed programmes. Congress can therefore rely on its independent source of information and advice, separate from the OMB. Such independence is politically important. For example, when the Clinton administration proposed major health care reform after the 1992 elections, the CBO analysed prospective costs and the feasibility of reforms offered by the White House (and groups in Congress). It advised that the White House's comprehensive plan would be too complex and costly while less ambitious congressional proposals would make little difference to how many Americans possessed health insurance and how affordable such coverage would be. The advice, combined with the massive lobbying effort of organized groups such as the American Medical Association and insurance companies, helped to doom comprehensive reform in 1994.

The Federal Reserve. As we noted in the last chapter, the Fed sets monetary policy by controlling the money supply and setting interest rates.

transformative trends that are loosely termed 'globalization'. The US government depends on foreign governments and investors to buy the US Treasury bonds that finance most of the annual US budget deficit and the accumulated national debt (the annual deficits combined since 1789). America also depends on foreigners to hold the dollars Americans pay them for the foreign-made goods that they purchase since America has a large and persistent trade deficit (the foreign-produced goods imported into America typically exceed the US-made goods that are sold abroad). Moreover, American exports depend on the competitiveness of US industry. Taxes on corporations can be passed on to consumers in the form of higher prices, but can also raise the production costs of industry, making goods less competitive in foreign markets and worsening the trade deficit.

The annual federal budget details how the nation's income, raised from taxes on individuals and corporations and government bonds, will be spent. The budget is the supreme political document, determining national priorities, shaping congressional and election debates, and allocating benefits to national, state and local interests. As Exhibit 11.7 explains, the budget process is not only highly politicized (several of the Reagan administration's annual budgets were deemed 'dead on arrival' by Democrats in Congress during 1981–89), but is also complex and lengthy.

Rather than there being 'the' budget process, there exist several processes that produce two or more budgets (and rarely on schedule). About 20 months prior to the beginning of the target fiscal year, administration officials send spending guidelines to the array of executive agencies that make up the federal bureaucracy. Thousands of federal bureaucrats then prepare policy options and cost estimates for every agency and each federal programme administered. Officials in the Office of Management and Budget (OMB) then integrate these estimates into the budget proposal the president submits to Congress in the February before the October in which the budget is expected to take effect. The executive branch budget is typically thousands of pages in length and weighs several pounds.

Congressional committees that deal with each federal programme and agency then have approximately one month to submit their responses to the executive budget and to suggest changes to the House and Senate Budget Committees. Each of the budget committees must prepare a 'budget resolution' that sets target spending levels for the fiscal year, to be agreed to by each chamber by April. House appropriations committees then develop and try to persuade the chamber to pass 13 appropriations bills that make up the actual budget (these craft whatever changes in tax laws and spending programmes are required by the budget resolution). The Senate in turn examines these from July to September. By October both chambers are expected to have agreed – through conference committees that reconcile any differences between the House and Senate bills – the final contents of the 13 bills, which are then sent to the president for signature (or veto).

Clearly, this is a convoluted and lengthy process. Moreover, it is complicated by partisan and institutional politics. In particular, with the presidency occupied by one party and Congress held by another, reaching an agreement in full and on time is extremely difficult. Compromise and concessions are requisite amid a constant bargaining process that occurs within as well as between the two branches. If the president vetoes one or more of the appropriations bills, Congress must revise them to make acceptable changes or a partial shutdown of government will occur until an agreed version is reached. This occurred in November 1995 when President Clinton and the Republican 104th Congress were deadlocked on the budget. Although essential services such as national defence and tax collection continued, government employees were unable to work and many federal services were temporarily halted.

Until the late 1960s most Americans believed that the federal budget should be

Exhibit 11.7 The federal budget process(es), 1995–97

Phase One: The President's Budget

March–June 1995	Office of Management and Budget (OMB) develops budget guidelines and calls for estimates of needs from each executive agency.
July–September 1995	Agencies formulate requests and submit them to OMB.
October–December 1995	OMB reviews requests and negotiates changes with agencies.
December 1995–January 1996	The president approves the final totals.
January 1996	The final budget for the executive branch is compiled and printed.
February 1996	The president presents/sends his budget to Congress.

Phase Two: The Congressional Budget

March 1996	Congressional committees submit their responses and proposed changes to the budget committees of the House and Senate.
April 1996	The formal deadline for both houses to agree a budget resolution for FY1997.
May–July 1996	The House draws up its appropriations bills.
July–September 1996	The Senate draws up its appropriations bills.
September 1996	Conference committees between the House and Senate produce a reconciled/compromise budget consisting of 13 large bills.

Phase Three: The Final Agreement

October 1996	The fiscal year (a 12-month accounting period) begins under a new budget or under a 'continuing resolution' if work has not been completed on all 13 appropriation bills.
October 1996–September 1997	Executive agencies spend the appropriated funds.
January 1997–September 1997	The president can propose changes in appropriations, subject to approval by Congress, and Congress may make additional appropriations at the request of the president throughout the fiscal year.

balanced except in times of crisis (such as war or recession), but since then the primary goal of American policymakers has shifted towards encouraging economic growth, even at the cost of budget deficits. Although Ronald Reagan publicly supported balanced budgets, his administrations' taxing and spending policies – aimed at economic growth – produced the largest budget deficits in American history, turning the world's largest creditor into its largest debtor nation by 1986. The deficit began to decline only when President Clinton and congressional Republicans, buoyed by favourable economic conditions, pursued an agenda of serious deficit reduction, ultimately concluding a balanced budget agreement in 1997.

Approximately 70 per cent of federal revenue comes from individual Americans' incomes in the forms of individual income

TABLE 11.2 The federal tax burden

Annual family income (in $)	Tax rate (percentage)
0–10,000	8.0
10,000–20,000	8.8
20,000–30,000	13.3
30,000–50,000	17.5
50,000–75,000	19.9
75,000–100,000	21.1
100,000–200,000	22.0
200,000 and over	23.7
Average	20.1

Source: *Economic Report of the President, 1996* (Washington, DC: US Government Printing Office), p. 83.

taxes and Social Security and Medicare 'contributions'. Reflecting a marked bias against progressive taxation policies, only about 12 per cent stems from taxes on corporations. Moreover, as Table 11.2 illustrates, although the tax burden appears to be fairly equitable in percentage terms, the result is one of profound inequality. A millionaire pays 23.7 per cent while someone making $30,000 pays 17.5 per cent. In terms of outlays, approximately 60 per cent of federal spending goes in direct payments for individual Americans' health, education and veterans' benefits. Approximately 16 per cent goes on military spending, and 4 per cent each on physical resources (transportation, environment and energy) and other federal government operations. Around 11 per cent services the interest on the accumulated national debt.

What this means is that almost two-thirds of the annual federal budget consists of 'uncontrollables' – spending commitments that neither the president nor Congress can avoid honouring without making politically problematic changes in the law. For example, 'entitlement' programmes provide benefits to individuals who have an established legal right to them (such as social security, pensions for retired government workers and military personnel, Medicare, Medicaid and veterans' benefits). As the ranks of the eligible increase, as they have done with the ageing of the 1960s 'baby boom' generation, the outlays necessarily grow accordingly. To alter such programmes is politically extremely difficult, given the large number of recipients.

Another important and persistent 'uncontrollable' is interest payments on the national

TABLE 11.3 Breakdown of federal expenditures (FY2001)

Federal outlays	Percentage of total federal budget
Social Security	23
Non-defense discretionary	19
Defense discretionary	16
Medicare	12
Net interest on national debt	11
Medicaid	7
Means tested entitlements	6
Other mandatory	6

Source: *A Citizen's Guide to the Federal Budget of the US Government, Fiscal Year 2001* (Washington, DC: US Government Printing Office).

debt (the cumulative total of all annual budget deficits since America's founding, less any annual surpluses). When the federal government enjoyed a brief annual budget surplus at the end of Clinton's period in office, politicians therefore differed on what to do with it. Many Democrats favoured using it to pay off some of the $5 trillion of national debt. Many Republicans, by contrast, favoured using it to provide tax cuts to Americans to stimulate greater economic activity.

In sum, only about one-third of the annual federal budget is 'discretionary', that is, sums that Congress and the president can alter without major changes in existing programmes. Even here, this is more or less evenly divided between defence expenditure and non-defence commitments. Partly as a result, although the budget process consistently occupies a central place in economic policy and drives partisan divisions over the (re)distribution of American resources, it is only one part. The role of the Fed in controlling interest rates and setting monetary policy and of state and local governments in their taxing and spending policies also exert a crucial influence beyond what the federal government decides are its budgetary priorities and preferences on American economic prosperity, inequalities and growth.

SOCIAL POLICY

Social policy encompasses areas such as health, social insurance, welfare and education. The federal role in the regulation of these areas has grown enormously since the 1930s, and especially since the Democratic administrations of the 1960s, but it remains relatively limited in comparative terms. The traditional self-reliance and individualism that make up 'the American way' have caused most Americans to view government 'handouts' with suspicion – especially welfare benefits – even as millions have come to view certain sources of government benefit provision (particularly cash payments to, and

medical assistance for, the elderly) as tantamount to a 'right'.

It was during the New Deal of the 1930s that the federal government first established a framework for providing national welfare and social security benefits for the poor and old in America. Although the scope and amount of welfare coverage has remained comparatively modest, it has grown substantially. Welfare was initially limited to aid to families with dependent children (AFDC) and distributed to the states on a matching federal–state formula that saw, and continues to see, vast disparities in the amounts received. Not until the 1960s did health care provision and housing assistance become elements of federal social policy. Since then 'welfare' has become a politicized issue, often employed by Republicans to attack Democrats as favouring government 'handouts' over individual responsibility. In 2000, the major welfare programmes constituted only 6 per cent of total federal government spending.

As Exhibit 11.8 notes, from the New Deal to the 'Great Society' of Lyndon Johnson's 1965–69 administration, a series of landmark social policies were enacted. Public support for these has been varied between programmes and over time but in some cases – most notably social security benefits (especially for widows, widowers, the disabled and the old) and Medicare (a programme offering medical aid to the old) – elected politicians would be politically unwise to risk suggesting changes, much less abolition. Other programmes, however, such as Medicare (providing medical care for the poor), food stamps and AFDC, have been the subject of intense political pressure for many years. There now exists an essentially bifurcated or two-tier welfare system, in which public support for social insurance is extensive and robust while popular support for welfare is much more limited and politically contentious.

The main element of the American welfare system, Social Security (involving direct cash payments to the poor), came into existence on

Exhibit 11.8 Main federal social policy landmarks

1935 – The Social Security Act introduced the programme of assistance to the old, unemployment insurance and assistance to 'widows and orphans' (that later became AFDC).

1937 – The Public Housing Act provided federal grants for the construction of municipal housing.

1964 – The food stamps programme allowed the poor to exchange certified stamps for food.

1965 – Medicare (care for the old) and Medicaid (for the poor) were set up as part of LBJ's Great Society programme, while the Elementary and Secondary Education Act provided federal aid to local school authorities in poorer areas.

1968 – The Housing Act provided housing subsidies to renters and owners of low-income housing.

1971 – The Supplementary Security Income (SSI) provided welfare benefits for older citizens.

August 14, 1935 when FDR signed the Social Security Act. A response to the mass economic and social deprivation of the Great Depression, Social Security guaranteed old people a basic income against all eventualities and provided federal cash payment for 'widows and orphans'. That entitlement evolved into the Aid to Families with Dependent Children (AFDC) programme, which paid benefits to over 14 million Americans annually by the early 1990s (10 million of whom were children).

But federalism profoundly informs American social policy as much as it does any other. In particular, AFDC was originally designed on a matching formula so that the federal benefits matched those of the individual states. The result was that benefits varied substantially, depending on the relative affluence and generosity of the individual states. For example, by the mid-1990s, the maximum monthly benefit for a one-parent family of three in Alaska was $923, compared to $120 in Mississippi. The combined federal and state programmes provided family incomes ranging from 46 per cent of the poverty line in impoverished Mississippi to 95 per cent in relatively affluent Connecticut and Vermont.

Recent studies of welfare provision also reveal its complex dynamics. Some American families go on and off welfare rolls several times during a few years, entries and exits being determined by the availability of employment, costs of day care assistance and access to health insurance, the addition of a child to the family, and the collapse or repair of marriage. About 30 per cent of Americans spend less than three years on AFDC after first enrolling; but another 30 per cent end up on the programme for eight years or more (approximately 65 per cent of total recipients). Beyond AFDC, non-cash payments such as food stamps were also available to some 27 million Americans, as were school lunch programmes for poor children and forms of housing assistance (Golay and Rollyson, 1996: 75).

The central policy problem in social policy, however, is less that of welfare reform than the danger of insolvency in the Social Security system as a result of an increasing mismatch between the retiring 'baby-boom' generation and the comparatively fewer workers left in the labour market who replace them; that is, the number of net contributors to programmes such as Social Security and Medicare is due to decline in the early twenty-first century as the number of beneficiaries increases. As more payroll taxes are paid into the programmes, a surplus initially emerges but when the outlays for the retirees are then factored in, the programme becomes insolvent around 2025.

The federal government's response to this dilemma has encompassed two main reactions. First, Republicans and, latterly, 'New Democrats' such as Clinton have successfully sought to reform welfare policy to reduce the number of claimants. In 1988 Congress passed the Family Support Act, which required the states to provide work or training programmes for all welfare recipients (so-called 'workfare'). In 1996, Clinton, having pledged in 1992 to 'end welfare as we know it', signed the Personal Responsibility and Work Opportunity Reconciliation Act (see Exhibit 11.9) which prohibited welfare recipients from receiving benefits after five years on the rolls and narrowed the eligibility criteria for receipt of food stamps, Supplementary Security Income and other welfare benefits.

Secondly, Democrats and Republicans have fought to a stand-off on issues of social insurance reform. Despite recognizing the looming insolvency crisis, attempts by Reagan in 1982 to cut social security benefits and by the Republican 104th Congress in 1995–96 to limit the increasing costs of Medicare were rapidly abandoned in the face of intense political opposition from Democrats and powerful interest lobbies such as the American Association for Retired Persons (AARP). Most Americans expect to receive these benefits at some stage, whatever their economic position, and hence few politicians can afford electorally to be seen as threatening the programmes. With elderly voters distributed throughout the nation, represented by powerful lobby groups such as the AARP, and influential in key Electoral College states such as Florida, reform of the programmes is extremely difficult to contemplate – however necessary in financial terms.

Exhibit 11.9   'To end welfare as we know it'?

A popular belief outside the United States sees America as a nation that is essentially heartless in terms of its social policy, refusing to provide assistance to the needy. But although state assistance is not generous, it does exist. For example, Aid to Families with Dependent Children was a measure that was financed by open-ended federal matching payments that went to the states. The more welfare recipients added to a state's roll, the greater the federal matching funds. Such funding was often criticized for providing incentives to states to add clients to their welfare rolls, since the states' share of the costs was often less than half for each client added. In 1996, Congress passed, and President Clinton reluctantly signed into law, the Personal Responsibility and Work Act, which substantially altered the purpose and funding of the federal welfare programme. The measure replaced AFDC with Temporary Assistance for Needy Families (TANF). Under the latter, the federal block grant for each state is fixed. States cannot use federal funds for clients who have been on welfare benefits for more than five years. States that assist clients to leave the welfare rolls by job training or other methods may retain the federal funds that would otherwise have been spent on welfare benefits. If the rolls are not reduced, states risk the federal government reducing the size of their block grants. Although the unprecedented economic boom of 1993–2001 played a large role in reducing the welfare numbers, the change of incentives – capping federal funds so that states would not gain funds by expanding welfare rolls – also assisted. But critics feared two flaws existed in the measure. First, with only very modest provisions to assist with funding childcare facilities, 'workfare' remained an unrealistic option for many American families. Secondly, the prospect of a tighter labour market or economic downturn after 2001 would likely return many millions of Americans to relying heavily on welfare assistance.

Exhibit 11.10 Health care in America

America's health care provision is offered by a three-tiered system. First, approximately 95 million Americans take out private health insurance schemes. Secondly, some 140 million Americans belong to Health Maintenance Organizations (HMOs) that employ market criteria to cost health care provision by doctors and hospitals. Thirdly, about 35 million Americans (about 15 per cent of the total US population) possess no coverage at all. Bill Clinton made the extension of health care provision a priority of his first two years in office, delegating the design of the administration's plan to his wife Hillary. The Health Care Security Act extended coverage to the entire US population, required employers to provide health care coverage and placed price controls on insurance policies. But support for the measure stalled and then died in Congress over 1994. Criticized as too bureaucratic, as imposing excessive costs on business (especially small business) and as ineffective in limiting the spiralling costs of medical coverage, alternative plans developed by Republicans and Democrats in Congress themselves proved unacceptable to the White House. Here, then, was a prime example of a fragmented political system unable to reach a consensus on an issue of supreme importance to millions of Americans: not only those paying too much for medical cover, but also, more importantly, to those entirely lacking medical insurance.

The result is that American social policy remains a national patchwork of limited and varied provision. Since reform of existing programmes entails either increases in taxation (opposed by most Republicans) or reductions in social spending and insurance/welfare benefits (opposed by most Democrats), neither the dismantling of Social Security and Medicare nor the extension of government provision of welfare assistance to universal health care provision are likely in the immediate future (see Exhibit 11.10).

CRIMINAL JUSTICE POLICY

The issues of crime and punishment in America are at least as politically controversial in America as those of economic and social policy. From 1968, when Richard Nixon popularized the demand for 'law and order' amidst sharp increases in the crime rates, political assassinations, city riots and political violence, crime emerged as an important national issue. In particular, appeals to 'law and order' became a signal to millions of white voters about broader issues of criminal and social disorder, declining morality, irresponsibility and race.

But issues of criminal justice and public order pit core features of the American value system against each other. Public concern about the consequences of unrestrained individualism has accorded government an important, though not exclusive, role in the preservation of life, liberty and public order. Public policies on crime are dominated at federal and state levels by a 'punitive paradigm' that heavily favours retribution, penal institutions and lengthy prison sentences over prevention and treatment. The land of the free has especially embraced mass incarceration. Although it possesses only 5 per cent of the global population, for example, America possesses 25 per cent of the world's total prison population. Approximately one in 142 Americans is in prison, and America's rate of 690 prisoners per 100,000 people is over five times that of the UK. Official statistics noted a marked decrease in crime rates by 2001 but the violent crime rate remains more than three times the level during the 1950s. America appears to many to be subject to an excess of law and an absence of order.

Against these concerns for being 'tough' on crime has been pitted a pronounced respect for individual civil rights and liberties against government intrusion. Over half of the rights guaranteed in the Bill of Rights concern crime and punishment. The Fourth, Fifth, Sixth, Seventh and Eighth Amendments contain protections that specify how the federal government must act in criminal proceedings. Federal court interpretations of these constitutional guarantees since the 1950s have also expanded the rights of criminal defendants and required major reforms in the ways that local and state police forces conduct themselves.

But, as one would expect of a federal and separated system of government, criminal justice policy has been affected by the more general federalizing tendencies of the post-New Deal years and it also differs greatly between (and within) the 50 states. In regard to the former, for example, over 3,000 federal – that is, national – crimes now exist (compared to fewer than 12 in 1787), more than 40 per cent of which were enacted after 1970. These range from the serious (terrorism) to the absurd (disrupting rodeos). In regard to the latter, the qualities of justice and mercy differ between and within states. For example, jury sizes vary from state to state, while federal cases require a jury of 12 persons. The federal government requires a unanimous verdict for conviction in many criminal justice proceedings whereas this is not required in many state trials. In three areas of criminal justice policy, especially, the complexity and diversity of practice in America's federal system are apparent.

First, the criminal justice system differs between the states in terms of what counts as criminal behaviour and the punishments for convictions. For example, 25 states adopted habitual offender statutes by the 1990s, such as 'three strikes and you're out' laws that sentenced repeat offenders to life imprisonment after their third felony conviction (the constitutionality of which was finally challenged in the Supreme Court in 2002–03). Federal and state governments passed 'mandatory minimums' statutes that limited judges' discretion on sentencing by requiring minimum prison terms for certain offences. 'Truth in sentencing' laws in several states, requiring that prisoners serve their full sentence, in effect abolished prison parole. Gang membership and recruitment became criminalized. 'Megan's Law' statutes also required communities to be notified of convicted sex offenders and 'sexual predator' laws provided for the civil detention of those offenders who remained dangerous at the end of their criminal term.

Secondly, America is now the only democratic nation (other than Japan) to allow and implement capital punishment. The death penalty is a legal punishment in 38 states and also for the federal government, although 12 states and the District of Columbia prohibit capital punishment. Although it is only a marginal element of the criminal justice system as a whole, the political symbolism of capital punishment is powerful – as a proxy for being 'tough' on crime and punishment in general. Although ruled unconstitutional by the Supreme Court by a 5–4 vote in *Furman v. Georgia* (1972), the Court changed its view just four years later in *Gregg v. Georgia* (1976). Most states restored their death penalty laws.

In 2000, 85 death row prisoners were executed. Almost 90 per cent of these took place in the South. Of the 38 death penalty states, 24 carried out no executions and only three non-southern states (Arizona, California and Missouri) conducted any. Texas, headed by the then Governor George W. Bush, executed 40 prisoners, almost as many as the rest of the states combined (in his six years as governor from 1995 to 2001 Bush saw 152 convicted murderers executed). Four defendants who were under the age of 18 at the time they committed their crimes were executed in 2000, while 25 of the 38 death penalty states allowed the execution of mentally retarded prisoners (the Supreme Court ruled the practice unconstitutional in 2002). Concern for the rights of victims of crimes – rather than those of criminal defendants – intensified so that 34 of Texas's 40 executions had the victims' families in attendance.

The US Constitution allows but does not require capital punishment. The Fifth and Fourteenth Amendments allow 'deprivation of life' providing that this occurs according to 'due process' of law (essentially a fair trial). Although the Eighth Amendment prohibits 'cruel and unusual punishments', this has been interpreted by federal courts to apply only to the methods, not the principle, by which the death penalty is administered. While the United Nations, the European Union, Amnesty International and the Pope have also raised concerns about executions (both generally and in particular cases), domestic public opinion remains broadly supportive. Indeed, even in the 12 states that abolished the death penalty, federal prosecutors can now seek capital sentences for certain crimes involving drug trafficking and murder as a result of laws passed in 1994 and 1996 (even if the states have not passed laws against these crimes).

Thirdly, support for self-defence has translated into the most heavily and legally armed civilian population in the world. Private access to guns is a distinctive and fundamental feature of American political culture. Fear not only of criminals, but also of government, informs a widespread enthusiasm for firearms, while belief in the Second Amendment remains strong among many, if not most, Americans. To many Americans, the widespread legal access to guns represents 'freedom's insurance policy'. Not only do millions of Americans see no conflict between the private legal ownership of guns and social order, but many view the former as the method by which the latter is achieved. Proposals to regulate gun ownership, sales and use therefore invariably excite intense political opposition.

To many millions within and outside America, however, the fact that gun controls remained so weak as gun massacres became increasingly routine over the later 1990s bemuses and infuriates. Deaths from gun violence – murders, suicides and accidents – exceeded 30,000 every year during the 1990s (although over 98 per cent of gun owners clearly do not murder, perpetrate crimes, commit suicide or have accidents with their guns).

The regulation of firearms, however, remains primarily a state and local, rather than a federal, matter. Over 20,000 laws and regulations governing the manufacture, distribution and sale of firearms exist but mostly at state and local level. More importantly, most of these tend to be very weak and permissive in terms of their substantive content. Over the 1980s and 1990s, for example, 42 American states introduced laws allowing the carrying of concealed guns, effectively privatizing American security to the level of the individual citizen. The logic of such laws was 'more guns, less crime'. Similarly, while 16 states required prospective gun buyers to wait several days before completing their purchase (while checks for possible criminal records were made), 14 states had an instant check system and 20 states ran no checks at all.

Although the majority of Americans tend consistently and by decisive margins to want stronger gun controls, this rarely occurs. The diversity in regulation is mirrored by two constants in gun politics since 1968: crises, when demands are made for stronger controls (most typically after assassinations or mass killings such as that at Columbine High School in Littleton, Colorado, on April 20, 1999); and the dominance of organized gun rights lobbies such as the National Rifle Association (NRA). For example, in 1999–2000, the Republican 106th Congress refused to pass bills that would have imposed a three-day waiting period on would-be gun buyers at otherwise unregulated travelling gun shows.

Measures to require child-proof trigger locks on handguns and to ban the import of large-capacity ammunition clips were also rejected.

As these three examples illustrate, national action by the federal government not only requires concerted public support, but also runs against localized opposition, constitutional tests of legitimacy, and countervailing pressures from lobbies, lawmakers, judges and bureaucrats. Even on matters of life and death, domestic policy is driven by state and local preferences at least as much as by national imperatives.

CONCLUSION

Domestic policies in America consistently reflect a compromise between the broad collective goals of the nation (national unity, justice, law and order, national security, welfare and freedom) and the competing and divergent interests of American individuals and organized interests on specific public policy questions. But the defining characteristics of policymaking are fragmentation and competition. Power and responsibility for policymaking is scattered among and within different tiers and branches of government, each facing distinct constituencies, operating procedures and goals. Fragmentation is assured in a federal system and is the inevitable result of a system in which the responsibility for formulating and implementing policy is shared between several layers and branches of government. Federal laws are often vague and subject to competing interpretations, not only because of the compromises struck in Congress, but also because when laws are initially passed the knowledge needed to allow more precise rules is not always available.

The politics of domestic policymaking has nevertheless altered in one vitally important regard since the 1970s. A combination of an expanded domestic policy agenda, in which the federal government has a policy on almost every conceivable subject, an active interest group universe, a semi-autonomous federal bureaucracy and a powerful Congress has meant that policy discussion in Washington now is less about radical innovation than managing and tinkering in incremental ways with existing policies. For example, in the 1960s debate was centred on whether the federal government should pass civil rights and Medicare laws. Today, the issue is the content of the former (non-discrimination or 'positive' discrimination for minorities?) and restraining the growing costs of the latter. Even on as vexed an issue as capital punishment, where debate in the later 1960s and early 1970s focused on its constitutionality, discussion is now centred more on shoring up its administration (to allow DNA evidence at trial) than on its abolition.

The costs of this 'compound republic' approach are two-fold. First, the relative coherence that a unitary state can bring to the provision of health care or environmental protection is typically absent in America's patchwork of laws and regulations. Secondly, the quality of national citizenship – from levels of welfare benefits to legal entitlements to civil rights – varies according to state and local residence. But the benefits that federalism offers are at least as important. A diverse population is admitted not only freedom from commonly imposed national constraints, but can also participate in decision-making to ensure that localized opinions receive expression in law and public policy. The integrity of the states – reflected in their equal representation in the Senate and the indirect method of presidential election through the Electoral College – remains central to American politics. Moreover, for those analysts who are critical of American policy processes, the comparative question must be whether alternative systems have performed better in terms of achieving public goods and collective goals from clean air and economic security to medical care. On that issue, at least, the comparative jury remains out.

FURTHER READING

Daniel Elazar, *American Federalism: A View from the States* (1984) is an excellent analysis of the relationship between the federal government and the individual states.

James Gosling, *Politics and the American Economy* (2000) is a detailed but readable introduction to the politics of economic policymaking.

B. Guy Peters, *American Public Policy: Promise and Performance* (1993) is a detailed and thorough analysis of public policies from economic policy to the environment.

Jonathan Freedland, *Bring Home the Revolution: The Case for a British Republic* (1998) is an excellent, highly readable overview of the differences between America and the UK on a range of policies.

Hugo Adam Bedau (ed.) *The Death Penalty in America* (1997) is an excellent collection of essays on all aspects of the capital punishment regime.

Robert Spitzer, *The Politics of Gun Control* (1995) is a very readable and clear overview of firearms policy and politics.

Alan Brinkley, Nelson Polsby and Kathleen Sullivan, *New Federalist Papers: Essays in Defense of the Constitution* (1997) comprises 19 short and provocative essays on American democracy, most providing a robust defence of the federal and separated system and its public policy results.

WEB LINKS

The Office of Management and Budget
http://www.whitehouse.gov/WH/EOP/omb

Congressional Budget Office
http://www.cbo.gov

House Budget Committee
http://www.house.gov/budget

House Appropriations Committee
http://www.house.gov/appropriations

The Federal Reserve
http://www.federalreserve.gov

National Institutes of Health
http://www.nih.gov

Environmental Protection Agency
http://www.epa.gov

Department of the Interior
http://www.doi.gov

Food and Drug Administration
http://www.fda.gov

Coalition opposing human cloning
http://www.stemcellresearch.org

Social Security Administration
http://www.ssa.gov

Official government site for data on Medicare and Medicaid
http://www.cms.gov

The Federal Reserve's 'Beige Book' on the state of the economy
http://www.bog.frb.fed.us/

National Rifle Association
http://www.nra.org

Coalition to Stop Gun Violence
http://www.csgv.org

National Committee to Prevent Wrongful Execution
http://www.constitutionproject.org

Citizens for a Moratorium of Federal Executions
http://www.federalmoratorium.org

Site supportive of capital punishment
http://www.prodeathpenalty.com

QUESTIONS

- Is the system of government too fragmented to produce coherent or rational public policies?

- To what extent do policy outcomes mirror the preferences of the general public in America?

- What are the main features of domestic policymaking in America?

- Has American economic, social and military success come about more despite than because of its fragmented system of government?

- Is federalism an asset or a hindrance to effective policymaking in America?

12 Foreign Policy

A multicultural America is impossible because a non-Western America is not American. A multicultural world is unavoidable because global empire is impossible. The preservation of the United States and the West requires the renewal of Western identity. The security of the world requires acceptance of global multiculturality.

Samuel Huntington, *The Clash of Civilizations* (1996: 318)

The war against terror will not end in a treaty. There will be no summit meeting, no negotiations with terrorists. This conflict can only end in their complete and utter destruction.

Vice President Dick Cheney, February 15, 2002

- The Historical Context
- Making Foreign Policy
- The US Constitution
- The Executive Branch
- Congress
- The Military–Industrial Complex
- Intermediary Organizations
- Conclusion

Chapter Summary

America today is the world's most powerful nation-state and sole 'mega-power'. Having expended enormous resources to defeat the Soviet Union during the Cold War, the end of the Cold War promised Americans a new era of peace and prosperity. But the terrorist attacks of September 11 shattered such notions and ushered in a new lodestar for American foreign policy: the 'war against terrorism'. Even prior to the attacks, however, American hegemony in the international system was clear, despite the content of American foreign policy and the processes by which it is made having changed significantly in the post-Cold War era. A broader set of issues from trade to the environment and an expanded set of players emerged to ensure that although the president remains the central and dominant figure in foreign policymaking, he cannot be said fully to 'control' American foreign policy. Congress, state governments, interest groups, the mass media and public opinion all play important roles in shaping America's international policies from trade policy to foreign aid. Whether the post-September 11 era will re-establish an enduring presidential dominance – not simply primacy – in foreign policy remains to be seen, but the institutional and political pressures on presidential foreign policy are many and impressive. Nevertheless, the image of a fragmented and competitive policymaking process is less applicable to foreign than domestic policy.

Because the United States is currently the world's leading global power, its internal politics matters not only to Americans but also to the rest of the world. The old aphorism that 'when America sneezes, the rest of the world catches a cold' remains more valid than ever. Few policy areas now exist where the priorities and preferences of the United States do not matter significantly to other nations and the international system as a whole. From international trade to immigration, environmental policy to exchange rates and, most significantly, in cases of war and peace from Colombia through Afghanistan to Iraq, America remains the premier military, economic and diplomatic force in the world. Such is America's current technical and logistical superiority that 'superpower' no longer adequately captures the extent to which American military, economic and cultural influence exceeds all its allies and rivals. America is now the world's first 'megapower', comparable in its dominance to the Roman and British empires at their respective heights.

As September 11 made crystal clear, the protection of national security is the imperative of American foreign policy and the defence of US national interests is at the heart of the foreign policymaking process. From 1947 to 1991, American foreign policy had been defined by the Cold War with the Soviet Union and its communist allies. Not just America's relations with the rest of the world, but also its domestic political and social life were shaped by the overriding national imperative of containing the expansion of

communism. But the end of the Cold War made it more difficult to articulate what exactly constituted the American national interest. With the terrorist attacks of September 11, some observers argued that a new era was ushered into being, although most of the contours of US policy were in fact unchanged by the tragedy. Not least, the fundamental predicament for America since 1945 – whether to accept a role as global policeman while being castigated abroad as a global bully – remained inescapable.

But if the international system is rarely stable, the mechanisms by which US foreign policy is formulated exhibit significant continuity. The Constitution left the control of foreign policy as 'an invitation to struggle' between the president and Congress. During the 1990s, that struggle reached an intensity and bitterness rarely seen in the post-Second World War era. With post-Cold War foreign policy increasingly encompassing issues that broadened the definition of 'national security' – trade, drugs, environment, the proliferation of weapons of mass destruction – many more lawmakers felt compelled by domestic pressures and partisan imperatives to take an active interest in international matters. American foreign policy is therefore a product of the competition and compromises between the White House and Capitol Hill that have always been the hallmark of domestic policy. Even in the aftermath of 9/11 and a resurgent foreign policy presidency under George W. Bush, competition and coalition-building remained prominent and integral features of the foreign policy process.

THE HISTORICAL CONTEXT

In his farewell address as America's first president, George Washington famously warned his compatriots against 'foreign entanglements', but those warnings subsequently went unheeded by his successors. In a fashion that the Founding Fathers could not have anticipated, America had, by the second half of the twentieth century, established a 'national security state': a polity with a permanent and massive military establishment, a powerful Central Intelligence Agency authorized not only to collect intelligence information but to engage in covert action, and a set of interested actors – weapons manufacturers, lawmakers with military bases or ports in their districts and states, international allies and organizations such as NATO – for whom the maintenance and expansion of America's military might made extremely good financial, political and even moral sense.

Contrary to popular notions of American isolationism, and despite the influence of a traditional notion that political differences between Democrats and Republicans should 'end at the water's edge', America's world role has been the subject of intense domestic disagreements since the republic's founding. In part, this was related to the nature of American identity that was discussed in Chapter 1. Many immigrant Americans escaped oppression and looked to America to build a new future. For some, the 'exceptional' nature of the United States made concern for other parts of the world undesirable. With only about one-sixth of Americans owning passports, the people of America have acquired an international reputation for being inward-looking and insular, unconcerned by the rest of the world except in times of war. For many, as Exhibit 12.1 suggests, the Middle East is Kansas and the Far East is Maine.

Against this, however, needs to be set the values that underpin American national identity, not least ideals of human rights and democracy that Americans cherish at home and take as an example for other nations to follow. The flip side of being an immigrant nation is that particular ethnic Americans have often looked to their homelands or that of their ancestors and sought to pressure decision-makers to act according to their interests. From German Americans and Italian Americans pressuring decision-makers to avoid involvement in Europe during the 1930s, to African Americans pushing for sanctions against South Africa in the 1980s and Irish Americans encouraging active US involvement in the peace process in Northern Ireland during the 1990s, ethnic and racial lobbies have complemented business, labour, religious and ideological

Exhibit 12.1 The Middle East: Kansas?

- 1964: 58% of Americans knew that the USA was a member of NATO; 40% believed the USSR was also.
- 1983: 45% believed the US government supported the Sandinistas in Nicaragua.
- 1985: 28% believed the US and USSR fought each other in the Second World War.
- 1985: 37% did not know the US had supported South Vietnam.
- 1993: only 25% could identify the Serbs as having conquered much of Bosnia.
- 1994: 46% believed foreign aid was one of two biggest items in the federal budget (at 1%).
- 2000: Only 33% of Americans could identify their Secretary of State, Madeleine Albright, but 76% could identify Cuban leader Fidel Castro.

Source: Kegley and Wittkopf (1996: 265–6); *National Journal*, June 3, 2000, p. 1775.

advocacy groups in seeking to shape foreign policy.

An additional factor that encouraged America's engagement with the world was brute self-interest: national security and economic prosperity. As Exhibit 12.2 notes, four traditions have existed in American foreign policy, offering contrasting prescriptions for America's role in the world. As such, and although the term has often been used to characterize US foreign policy, Americans have never been entirely 'isolationist'. Rather, for most of American history, the nation's foreign policy was unilateralist – whether or not America decided to intervene in the wider world was a matter that Americans would decide alone, free from the 'entangling alliances' of which Washington had warned, and interventions would rely on American forces rather than multilateral ones. On occasion, presidents would even announce a national 'doctrine' on foreign policy – not so much a sophisticated, strategic blueprint as a warning to other nations of what US national interests were and when the United States would act to defend them by force. The earliest, the Monroe Doctrine of 1823, announced America's intentions of safeguarding her own hemisphere in North and South America from European influence.

In reality, however, international conflicts were relatively rare intrusions on a comparatively insular nation that was mostly preoccupied by domestic concerns. Not until the Second World War, with the Japanese attack on Pearl Harbor on December 7, 1941, did America, under FDR, assume the international responsibilities that it would not subsequently relinquish after 1945. Left at the end of that war as the world's only economic and military superpower, but confronted by an adversary in the Soviet Union that was intent – to many influential Americans – on global domination, the years since 1941 have seen the United States embrace internationalism. But it is important to note that even at the conclusion of the Second World War, the Truman administration moved to demobilize America's armed forces. The notion that Americans, a people instinctively suspicious of concentrated power, eagerly embraced a national security state and global role does not stand up to close scrutiny.

The onset of the Cold War (deliberately hastened by Truman in and after 1947 as US disillusion with the USSR intensified) ultimately led to a broad agreement between the main two political parties on the content of foreign policy and the key institutional

Exhibit 12.2   The four traditions of American foreign policy

Walter Russell Mead (2001) argues that there exist four distinct traditions in US foreign policy:

- *Hamiltonians* advocate a strong alliance between the federal government and big business as crucial to domestic prosperity and success abroad, focusing on the need to integrate America into the global economy.
- *Wilsonians* argue that the US should focus on spreading American democratic and social values internationally, to create a peaceful and democratic international community that respects the rule of law.
- *Jeffersonians* argue that US foreign policy should be concerned more about safeguarding domestic democracy than promoting it abroad, disliking anything that increases the risk of war.
- *Jacksonians* hold that the US should prioritize the physical security and domestic well-being of Americans and act exclusively to achieve those ends.

actor to achieve policy goals. Broad bipartisan support for the containment of communism as the guiding principle of foreign policy was accompanied by bipartisan acceptance of the presidency's pre-eminent role in prosecuting that policy – through economic, military, diplomatic and covert means – from 1947 to 1966. While Congress continued to influence foreign policy (controlling funds, ratifying appointments, etc.), it mostly actively supported or reluctantly acquiesced in presidential leadership from Truman to Johnson.

However, partisan differences did not disappear entirely. Republicans made important political gains at the Democrats' expense during the McCarthy era of the late 1940s and early 1950s – none more so than Congressman and then Senator Richard Nixon. Having been charged by Republicans as responsible for the 'loss of China' in 1949, the Korean War (1950–53), and allowing communist subversion to spread at home, Democratic officials – especially presidential candidates – felt obliged to adopt strongly anti-communist principles in election campaigns and in office. From 1948 to 1968, Democrats such as John F. Kennedy and Lyndon Johnson actively feared being tarred by their opponents as 'soft on communism'. While, ironically, that fear ultimately led to the disastrous war in Vietnam (see Exhibit 12.3), the corresponding confidence of Republican presidents facilitated unusually positive steps towards erstwhile foreign enemies. As Nicol Rae argued:

> The presidential majority assembled by Eisenhower and the Republicans, largely on the basis of national security issues, would give the GOP a lock on the White House for much of the next quarter-century. As long as the Cold War persisted and the profile of the presidency in foreign and security policy remained high, the Republicans held a crucial advantage in presidential politics over a Democratic Party that was never quite able to overcome the suspicion of naivete in foreign affairs. Ironically, the perception of the Republicans as hardliners on foreign policy

allowed Republican presidents to be far more flexible and innovative in international affairs than their Democratic counterparts during the Cold War. By contrast, fears of a resurgence of Republican McCarthyism contributed to the decisions of the Democratic Kennedy and Johnson administrations to escalate American involvement in Vietnam. (Rae, 1998: 54)

As the popular saying had it, 'only Nixon can go to China'.

Much as the Cold War affected both parties, so its end dramatically affected domestic politics. Although conflicts over foreign policy had increased substantially from 1968 to 1992, the collapse of the Soviet Union in 1991 left America as a superpower without a clear world role. Moreover, the post-Cold War world added divisions over foreign policy to existing differences on domestic issues among the two parties. But perhaps the most important consequence was to reduce the salience of foreign policy to the American public in federal elections. Thereby, the end of the Cold War helped to neutralize a problematic issue for Democratic presidential candidates. Despite the victory of US forces in the Gulf War of 1991, President George Bush's foreign policy record could not prevent his electoral defeat in 1992. Indeed, the perception that Bush was overly interested in international issues rather than domestic American problems contributed substantially to his defeat. As we will see later, President George W. Bush's response to 9/11 was shaped not only by America's international needs, but also by partisan politics at home.

MAKING FOREIGN POLICY

The making of foreign policy differs from that of domestic policy in several key respects. Presidential authority is greater, congressional influence more limited, judicial interventions are unusual, and non-economic interest group input is rarely decisive in determining outcomes. But, as with all

Exhibit 12.3 America and Vietnam

The impact of defeat in Vietnam can be gauged from the many novels and movies that continue to deal with America's growing and ultimately failed involvement in Southeast Asia from 1954 to 1975 (from *Apocalypse Now* to *Born on the Fourth of July*). The conflict was a national trauma that persisted until US forces were withdrawn from South Vietnam in 1975 by President Ford.

- It was the first war that America unequivocally lost. Over 58,000 Americans died during the war, the largest loss of American military life in history.
- The war was the first televised US conflict. Although its effects are strongly disputed, there is little doubt that the television coverage of a losing war powerfully concentrated American politicians' minds. Not least, political and military leaders subsequently devoted careful attention to both the 'CNN effect' (the ability of television to place issues on the public agenda) and the 'Body Bag effect' (the aversion to loss of military lives). Both are less significant than popularly imagined, but elite perceptions of their existence have shaped policy from 1975 to 2001.
- The war was deeply polarizing and divisive in America, pitting 'doves' and 'hawks' against each other, making foreign policy a salient issue in elections, and contributing to the erosion of the Democrats' New Deal coalition.
- The war ended the Cold War norm of bipartisanship in foreign policy. Although the extent to which the two main political parties from 1945 to 1966 agreed on foreign policy has often been exaggerated, their differences prior to Vietnam were relatively modest. After Vietnam, Republicans and Democrats came increasingly to disagree over the content of foreign policy (on matters such as détente, human rights, and containment), the regional priorities for US strategic interests (Central America, Europe, the Middle East, Africa and China) and the instruments by which foreign policy should be carried out (direct military engagement, covert activity, or foreign aid).

Despite this, 'revisionist' writers such as Michael Lind (1999) now see Vietnam as a 'necessary' conflict that, like the crises over Berlin from 1958 to 1963 and the Cuban Missile Crisis of October 1962, managed to avoid a direct confrontation between American and Soviet forces that could have turned 'hot'.

aspects of American politics, the US Constitution exerts a profound influence on the process by which foreign policy is made.

THE US CONSTITUTION

As early as the 1830s, de Tocqueville argued that democracies are much less effective than despotic regimes in regard to foreign affairs. Following his lead, contemporary critics frequently point to the constitutional division of powers between the executive and legislature as inhibiting an effective foreign policy. Just as with his powers in domestic policy, the president's constitutional authority in foreign affairs is limited and checked. Whether America is at peace or war, the assertion by Congress of its formal powers is a constant. But, as is often the case in politics, which viewpoint is embraced depends heavily on whose ox is being gored. Arguably, by encouraging competition between and within the executive and legislative branches, the prospects for effective policies to emerge are actually greater in democratic than in non-democratic systems (where countervailing options to those in power are fewer).

THE EXECUTIVE BRANCH

Along with the growth in the federal government's role and responsibilities, foreign policy has been the crucial bulwark in the development of the executive branch in general and the modern presidency in particular. Had the extension of the federal government's responsibilities not occurred during the New Deal, the international context would nevertheless have compelled a substantial increase in presidential power. The embrace of an ongoing global role during and after the Second World War was the main reason for the vast increase in the importance of the presidency in the constitutional order that has continued to the present day.

In constitutional terms, the presidency retains important formal and informal powers that render the occupant of the White House especially influential on the world stage:

- *Constitutional powers*. The president's formal powers as Commander-in-Chief, chief diplomat, and Head of State and Head of Government make him the key figure in foreign policy. Only the president negotiates treaties with foreign states and it is for the president to nominate and receive ambassadors and nominate the key personnel to conduct foreign policy (the Secretary of State, Secretary of Defense, National Security Adviser, and head of the CIA).
- *Nuclear weapons*. The development of the world's most extensive and sophisticated nuclear arsenal powerfully elevated the president's authority within and outside the United States. When commentators speak of the presidency as the most powerful political office in the world, this is a large part of the explanation. A single individual holds the capacity to destroy the world several times over.
- *Media attention*. Television and newspaper journalists often focus on the president as the sole shaper of foreign policy. This is inaccurate, since a vast bureaucratic network exists that collates information, makes recommendations, and is charged with implementing foreign policy decisions. However, what America stands for is typically associated with the president's priorities and preferences, as the only nationally elected figure and the only official with a national constituency.
- *Information*. Thanks to the array of executive branch departments and agencies with a foreign focus, the president possesses easily the most comprehensive and sensitive collection of information and intelligence on the international system. Combined with the need for secrecy, efficiency and clarity in decision-making, this informational advantage confers on the president a uniquely influential role. Not only does the president possess exceptional political legitimacy, but his authority is augmented by the possession of information that his competitors in Congress and elsewhere lack.
- *Legal authority*. As Exhibit 12.4 documents, rather than constraining the president, many laws passed by Congress have – either intentionally or inadvertently – given the president additional authority to prosecute foreign policy by conferring powers with respect to specific nations, issues or institutions. That is, the powers that successive presidents have claimed have been granted (or at least, not withheld) rather than seized.

Taken together, the combination of formal constitutional powers, legal authority and the growth of America's international role make the president a formidable player on the world stage. But of course, the powers by themselves imply nothing about the wisdom with which they are used. Few presidents leave office without some failures in international affairs. In some cases, these can be relatively modest, but in others they can be of an immense magnitude (JFK and LBJ and Vietnam, for example). This is especially important since, even when initiatives fail,

Exhibit 12.4   Select laws on foreign sanctions

The following laws passed by Congress gave the president the authority to impose a wide range of sanctions (from total economic embargoes to bans on sales of specific weapons) against other nations.

- *Trading with the Enemy Act (1917)*. The First World War law allowed the president to impose economic restrictions during war or national emergency. Provisions include authority to control foreign exchange, gold and foreign property.
- *Export–Import Bank Act (1945)*. Prohibited the bank from supporting countries involved in terrorism, nuclear proliferation or human rights abuses.
- *Foreign Assistance Act (1961)*. Allowed the restriction of foreign aid in cases of illegal activities such as human rights violations, press censorship or limits on religious freedom.
- *Arms Export Control Act (1968)*. Permitted sanctions against countries that spread nuclear arms or when the president deemed sanctions were necessary for world and US security.
- *International Emergency Economic Powers Act (1977)*. Amended the Trading with the Enemy Act to remove wartime as a necessary condition for the president to restrict overseas financial transactions or freeze foreign assets; allows export embargoes during national emergency and economic embargoes.
- *International Security and Development Cooperation Act (1985)*. Authorized the president to ban imports from countries involved in terrorism.
- *Iran–Iraq Arms Non-Proliferation Act (1992)*. Imposed sanctions on governments and companies that transferred technology to Iran or Iraq that could be used to develop advanced weaponry.
- *Cuba Sanctions (Helms–Burton) Act (1996)*. Codified the long-standing US economic embargo on Cuba, effectively prohibiting normal trade while Fidel Castro remained in power.
- *Iran–Libya Sanctions Act (1996)*. Imposed sanctions against foreign companies that invest in the oil industries of Iran or Libya or that sell weapons or other goods to Libya.

presidents can be tempted to take action in international affairs to boost their standing at home. Even genuine foreign policy disasters, such as the Bay of Pigs in 1961 and the seizure of American hostages in Iran in 1979, can result in an increase in presidential popularity at home.

But, as Table 12.1 notes, presidential foreign policy powers are checked and balanced under the Constitution. Only Congress has

TABLE 12.1   The separation of powers in foreign policy

Formal powers of the president	Formal powers of Congress
• Commander-in-Chief of armed forces	• Power to declare war
• To negotiate treaties	• To ratify/reject treaties (Senate only)
• To nominate ambassadors and key foreign policymakers (e.g. Secretary of State, Defense, CIA Director)	• To confirm or reject presidential nominees (Senate only)
• To 'receive' representatives of foreign governments	• To 'raise and support' armies

the power to declare war (although most US military engagements have not been accompanied by declarations of war, including Korea, Vietnam, Afghanistan and the 'war on terrorism'). The president can negotiate treaties but the Senate must ratify these for them to become law (notoriously, the Senate rejected the Treaty of Versailles in 1919 that President Wilson had negotiated, while more recently a Republican Senate in 1999 rejected the Comprehensive Nuclear Test Ban Treaty negotiated by the Clinton administration). The president can make nominations but the Senate must confirm these (in 1996 the nomination of former Massachusetts Governor William Weld to be Ambassador to Mexico was held up by Senator Jesse Helms (Republican, North Carolina) because Weld was too 'soft' on drugs and sympathetic to gay rights). Finally, whatever a president seeks to do, the power of the purse – the authority to pay for actions in international affairs – is vested with Congress.

One of the distinguishing features of foreign policy is also the marked judicial reluctance to enter the 'political thicket' on foreign policy. In contrast to domestic affairs, where (as Chapter 8 noted) federal courts have been an important influence, only rarely has the federal judiciary intervened on matters of foreign policy. One of the most famous was when the Supreme Court, in *US v. Curtiss-Wright Export Corporation* (1936), stated that the president 'acts as the Sole organ of the federal government in the field of international relations'. More recently, the Court has regularly refused to adjudicate conflicts between Congress and the president over the exercise of war powers.

In some respects, this latter refusal is especially problematic. The issue of whether, when and how to send military forces to war is surrounded by controversy. The intentions of the Founding Fathers were reasonably clear in this regard. For example, in *Federalist Papers*, No. 69, Alexander Hamilton wrote that:

The president is to be commander in chief of the army and navy of the United States. In this respect his authority would be nominally the same with that of the king of Great Britain, but in substance much inferior to it. It would amount to nothing more than the supreme command and direction of the military and naval forces, as the first general and admiral of the confederacy; while that of the British king extends to the declaring of war and to the raising and regulating of fleets and armies; all which, by the Constitution under consideration, would appertain to the legislature.

Similarly, Thomas Jefferson wrote to James Madison in 1789 that: 'We have already given in example one effectual check to the dog of war by transferring the power of letting him loose from the executive to the legislative body, from those who are to spend to those who are to pay.' Madison in turn wrote to Jefferson in 1793 that: 'the Constitution supposes what the history of all governments demonstrates, that the executive is the branch of power most interested in war, and most prone to it. It has accordingly, with studied care, vested the question of war in the legislature.'

Contemporary practice has therefore tilted far away from what was intended by the Constitution's authors. Michael Glennon even argued that the Gulf War of 1991 (when the US and 27 other nations acted to expel Iraqi forces from Kuwait) 'represented a textbook example of how an audacious executive, acquiescent legislature and deferential judiciary have pushed the Constitution's system of separation of powers steadily backwards toward the monopolistic system of King George III' (Glennon, 1991: 84). Although, as Exhibit 12.5 notes, Congress after Vietnam attempted to impose constraints on the president's ability to wage war without consultation, these have been mostly ineffective.

The Constitution ensures that presidential authority is in theory checked and balanced by Congress in many ways, but on the issue of implementing foreign policies, Congress is hampered by possessing only some fairly

Exhibit 12.5 Curbing presidential wars? The War Powers Resolution

In 1973, Congress passed the War Powers Resolution (WPR), overriding President Nixon's veto. A direct response to the conduct of the Vietnam War by Presidents Johnson and Nixon, the WPR was a deliberate attempt to restrain the authority of the president, as Commander-in-Chief, to wage what were, in effect, undeclared wars. The WPR required that the president report to Congress within 48 hours if hostilities – either actual or imminent – involving US military personnel broke out. Once the report was issued, the president was required to win congressional approval for the authorization of force within 60 days. If this did not occur, the president then had a further 30 days in which to end the military action (a total 90-day cut-off).

However, the WPR has proven singularly ineffective in achieving its goals. Successive presidents have ignored its provisions and cast doubt on its constitutionality. The reasons for the lack of teeth of the WPR include:

- Ironically, the WPR gave the president the legal authority to wage war without a congressional declaration for the first time in American history, albeit only for 90 days.
- No president of either political party has fully recognized the constitutionality of the WPR.
- The federal courts have refused to pass a clear ruling on the WPR's constitutionality, sometimes describing the issue as a 'political question' beyond judicial competence, at other times stating that Congress could make the WPR effective if it wished simply to act to that end.
- Presidents since Vietnam have been shrewd in their use of military personnel. Most conflicts involving American forces have generally been short and avoided large-scale deployment of ground forces (such as the invasions of Grenada in 1983 and Panama in 1989–90).
- The political will has not existed in Congress to enforce the WPR or to strengthen its provisions. Most legislators are reluctant to vote against the president at times of war, especially once the military are already deployed. To do so would be likely to court electoral damage or even defeat.

blunt weapons. In particular, neither writing new laws nor withholding funds from the executive are politically easy to achieve. Not only is it difficult to muster majority support in the two chambers, but also, since the president can veto ordinary legislation, Congress must obtain 'super-majorities' to overcome presidential resistance. This is difficult on domestic issues but when questions of foreign policy are at stake it becomes particularly problematic to achieve.

As in domestic politics, the existence of an array of Departments and agencies within the executive branch also serves as both a resource and a constraint on presidential power in foreign affairs. As Chapter 10 noted, the federal bureaucracy is a vast and complex entity whose agencies frequently find themselves in conflict and competition with each other, and who serve two political masters: president and Congress. On foreign affairs, too, Congress possesses the ability to determine the budgets of key Departments such as Defense as well as the power to investigate agencies' activities. As such, the bureaucrats who staff the foreign policy establishment must attend not only to presidential directives but also congressional pressures.

In diplomacy, it is formally the Department of State that is charged with formulating and implementing American policy. In practice, however, presidents since Truman have tended to rely more on the National Security Council and its head, the National Security

Exhibit 12.6 The Clinton foreign policy

As the governor of a small, rural southern state, President Clinton had minimal experience of foreign policy on entering office in 1993. He had also run an election campaign focused on domestic policy concerns. Clinton's defenders point to some important accomplishments during his two terms: the passage of the North American Free Trade Agreement (NAFTA), the successful bail-out of Mexico in 1995, more or less cordial relations with Russia and China, continued containment of Iraq, successful intervention in Kosovo in 1999, and important achievements in the peace processes in Northern Ireland and the Middle East. But critics argue that Clinton squandered opportunities to assert a more effective American role in the world after the collapse of communism. As Emily Goldman and Larry Berman observed:

Absent a strategic guidepost, Clinton's foreign policy has been broad but shallow; many international initiatives underway but few resources and little time devoted to any one because of a lack of priorities. Absent enlargement, all we are left with is engagement, with no sense of why we should engage or how we should engage. The tendency of the administration to juxtapose engagement with isolation is a false one that only succeeds in polarizing the foreign policy debate further. (2000: 252)

Clinton's failure to prioritize counter-terrorism, along with U-turns on the defence budget and national missile defence, added strongly to the picture of a president only intermittently interested in – and relatively poorly equipped to manage – foreign policy at a point of transition in the international system.

Adviser, than on the State Department. Competition between the Department and the Agency can be intense, to the extent that Nixon deliberately chose William Rogers as his Secretary of State because he would be outwitted by his NSA, Henry Kissinger. Equally, the Department of Defense, or 'Pentagon', is a frequent antagonist of the State Department, while other executive players, such as the Commerce Department, may also pursue separate political goals. For example, while the Pentagon lobbied against the sale of 'dual use' technology to Iraq before and after 1991 on grounds of national and regional security, the State and Commerce Departments both supported bids by US companies to be allowed licences to export goods.

The result is that competition within the executive branch, while not as severe as on domestic policy, is still endemic. In the aftermath of September 11, for example, 'hawks' such as Donald Rumsfeld and his deputy Paul Wolfowitz were strongly in favour of an aggressive military response to terrorism, encompassing not only Al Qaeda terrorists in Afghanistan but also so-called 'rogue states' such as Iraq. By contrast, Secretary of State Colin Powell was far more wedded to the construction of an international coalition, multilateral action with allies, and non-military mechanisms of exerting influence in the international arena. Such competition can be functional for US policy – the administration's response to the terrorist attacks saw one of the most impressively coordinated and coherent approaches in postwar foreign policy – but, as Exhibit 12.6 notes, without a clear presidential lead, such competition can also be ill-suited to coherent and consistent policymaking.

CONGRESS

The role of Congress in international affairs is altogether more complex and contested than in domestic politics. Traditionally, Congress has had little influence over crisis-level policies, more over strategic policy and the greatest on structural policies (see Exhibit 12.7). With the Vietnam War and then the end of the Cold War, the role of Congress became stronger than at any time since the 1930s.

Increasing congressional activism on international matters since the late 1960s has been driven by:

- *Constituency pressures.* As the foreign policy agenda has broadened to encompass issues with a direct effect on local districts and states, such as trade, drugs and immigration, the incentives for lawmakers to take up an active international role have grown. With substantial inward financial investment into America, this is especially the case. For example, a representative from Alabama with a major source of employment in Mercedes Benz cannot afford to ignore issues affecting the auto trade – from gas emissions to sanctions on foreign nations trading with Cuba to laws on labour union recognition and plant closures.
- *Partisanship.* Some groups are particularly strong supporters of particular parties. For example, the consistent support offered to the Democrats by African Americans and Jews has encouraged Democratic lawmakers to take up active positions on matters such as sanctions against apartheid South Africa and support for Israel (although, ironically, the most vociferous American supporters of Israel – Christian evangelicals – are also among the most loyal supporters of Republican presidents and Congresses).
- *Complexity of legislation.* By the 1990s, much legislation that appears ostensibly 'domestic' in focus in fact contains an international dimension. For example, federal government subsidies to farmers also raises issues of fair trade and tariffs, while reform of the CIA has knock-on effects for the intelligence community as a whole.

Exhibit 12.7   Three levels of foreign policy

- *Structural policies* – deployment of resources or personnel. Congress has conventionally played an especially powerful role here, largely due to the re-election benefits that can accrue from winning the allocation of new military bases, the building of new ports for the Navy, and the expansion of weapons-manufacturing plants and research and development contracts.
- *Strategic policies* – to advance the nation's interests militarily or diplomatically. Although most lawmakers have tended not to take an active interest in diplomacy, some legislators have always been interested in foreign affairs. For example, black members of Congress lobbied over many years to impose sanctions against apartheid-era South Africa, while Latino lawmakers have lobbied over immigration reform (though not in the same direction). Increasingly, lawmakers take up foreign policy issues to appeal to particular active lobbies within their constituencies or particularly generous campaign donors, such as the Christian Coalition.
- *Crisis policies* – to protect America's vital interests against specific threats. Congress is least well equipped to intervene on crisis matters such as wars, terrorist attacks and hostage-taking. In part, this is a function of its size – reaching a quick and decisive agreement for action among 535 members is impossible. Partly, Congress lacks the extensive and often sensitive information that the executive possesses, and partly, Congress is notoriously 'leaky' – sensitive information can reach the press and even opponents of the vital interests of the US.

- *Organized interest activity.* Congress is a fragmented and open legislature and, as Chapter 9 noted, this means there exist many points of contact for organized groups to make their case. Some of these are economic interests (from Microsoft to mushroom growers). Some are religious and advocacy groups (Christian groups and human rights groups seeking to pressure the government on China). Others are ethnic or racial groups; for example, Frank Pallone (Democrat, New Jersey) represents a district that includes a large Indian American population and he joined other New Jersey lawmakers in establishing the House India Caucus in 1993.
- *Media.* Given the global reach of news organizations today, concerns that might have been ignored in the 1930s can now become visible overnight in the living-rooms of ordinary Americans. The 'CNN effect' means that television coverage can provide instant and graphic attention to famines, civil wars and environmental catastrophes. By placing such events before the American public, the media can advance (or retard) international matters on the agenda of Congress, although the extent to which mere coverage of an issue determines the response of governing institutions has been contested.

Because so many competing pressures are brought to bear on Congress, the national legislature can rarely speak with one voice on foreign policy – another reason why many foreign policy observers prefer to see a strong presidency making the running on international matters. But advocates of presidential power need to remember that Congress is a co-equal branch of government under the Constitution. The fact that the source of political legitimacy and authority for Congress is different from that of the president does not, and should not, marginalize the congressional role in international matters. On foreign as well as domestic affairs, the Framers opted for certainty of action over speed. As Exhibit 12.8 notes, matters such as whether the president can negotiate free trade agreements are ones that Congress has a legitimate role in influencing (such 'fast track' authority allows presidents to make an agreement that must then be voted up or down – without allowing any amendments – by the two houses of Congress).

THE MILITARY–INDUSTRIAL COMPLEX

As we noted in Chapters 9 and 10, the reality of who makes policy can often be different from the formal democratic theory. In particular, 'iron triangles' or 'sub-governments' can exert a parochial force on policymaking. President Eisenhower in particular warned about the danger of the 'military–industrial complex' on leaving office in 1961. Fearing that the development of a 'garrison state' could destroy the small-town America that he cherished and even undermine democracy, he cautioned that the

> conjunction of an immense military establishment and a large arms industry . . . new in American experience, exercised a total influence . . . felt in every city, every state house, every office of the federal government . . . In the councils of government, we must guard against the acquisition of unwarranted influence, whether sought or unsought, by the military–industrial complex.

Ike's theme has been regularly repeated since 1961, but mostly by individuals far to the left of the conservative general. In its milder versions, critics have questioned whether particular defence expenditures were warranted by the international context (see Exhibit 12.9). In its more extreme and lurid versions, writers from Noam Chomsky to Gore Vidal have popularized the claim that American foreign policy is determined not by the nation's actual national security needs but more by the combined – and mutually beneficial – interests of weapons producers and their bureaucratic allies in the Pentagon.

Exhibit 12.8 The history of 'fast track'

1974. The 1974 Trade Act created expedited procedures for congressional approval of non-tariff trade agreements. The president was required to give 90-day notices before entering into a trade pact and had to consult with appropriate congressional committees. Congress had a maximum of 90 days to vote up or down on the implementing legislation (without amendments).

1979. A law implementing the Tokyo Round of multilateral trade negotiations extended fast-track procedures until January 3, 1988.

1988. The omnibus trade bill re-authorized fast-track procedures until May 31, 1991, with a two-year extension possible, barring disapproval by either chamber. The extension was contingent on the president submitting reports to Congress about the negotiations.

1991. In response to intense White House lobbying, Congress rejected an attempt to disapprove of the two-year extension. President Bush wanted the extension to continue talks on the General Agreement on Tariffs and Trade (GATT) and to commence talks on a US–Mexico free trade pact.

1993. Congress extended fast-track authority to April 15, 1994, for the sole purpose of completing the GATT agreement. President Clinton wanted the bill enacted before he attended a summit of industrial nations in Tokyo in July. The focus on GATT allowed him to avoid a fight with Congress over broader fast-track authority.

1994. Clinton tried but failed to get a long-term extension of fast-track authority as part of legislation implementing the GATT agreement. Republicans objected to Clinton's attempts to include labour and environmental requirements for trade talks.

1995. The House Ways and Means Committee approved a fast-track renewal bill that was good until December 31, 1999 with a possible two-year extension. Clinton wanted the renewal to facilitate talks with Chile, but objected to provisions that would have barred trade negotiations from dealing with labour and environmental issues.

1997. The Senate easily passed a fast-track bill acceptable to Clinton but the House version was shelved after Clinton was unable to rally support from Democrats, who were under strong pressure from organized labour to defeat the measure.

1998. The House defeated an attempt by Clinton to renew fast-track procedures. Opponents had turned the debate into a referendum on NAFTA, dooming the bill. The Senate Finance Committee approved a trade bill that included fast-track authority but the full Senate never considered the issue.

2001. In December the House of Representatives voted by a one-vote margin to approve 'trade promotion authority' for President George W. Bush.

But how far the thesis is valid is questionable. It would certainly be naive in the extreme to ignore the mutual interests shared by members of the 'iron triangle': the Department of Defense requires the best military hardware for its formidable fighting forces, Pentagon bureaucrats wish to maintain and expand their own programmes, while weapons manufacturers naturally have a self-interest in an expansive military establishment employing (and increasing) the range of its products. The location of military, scientific and space bases is also strongly connected to the home districts and states of the lawmakers sitting on the relevant congressional committees (in particular the armed services committees). As Exhibit 12.10 notes, instances abound of legislators supporting a particular weapons system whose manufacturer just happened to be based in their state or district. Nothing new or novel here – simply Congress as usual at work.

Having conceded that much, though, the extent to which policy is determined, rather

Exhibit 12.9 A military–industrial complex?

- Employment in America is significantly linked to military expenditure: one in ten jobs is – directly or indirectly – linked to such expenditures by the Pentagon, arms manufacturers and related sources of employment.
- Congress has sometimes gone beyond presidential requests in voting defence appropriations. Congress was responsible for increasing expenditures on the MX missile from $150 million to $600 million per missile in the 1980s.
- Defence industry profits are higher than those in most other manufacturing sectors. This is in large part due to the generous manner in which the Pentagon treats defence contractors, handing out millions of dollars in grants and interest-free loans, repaying the costs of even unsuccessful bids, and allowing tax deferments on profits.
- Sheer extravagance, waste and fraud has been identified, most notoriously the Lockheed corporation being paid $640 by the federal government for an aeroplane toilet seat.
- Universities, which should keep a critical oversight of the military–industrial complex, are seduced by it, accepting millions of dollars' worth of research and development contracts connected to defence expenditures.
- Defence industry consulting firms and think tanks have mushroomed – most employ former Pentagon and Armed Forces personnel, whose advice usually supports the military–industrial complex's priorities and preferences.
- Defence expenditures have remained a priority even in times of massive budget deficits.

Source: Kegley and Wittkopf (1996: 302–4).

than influenced, by the three-pronged complex outlined in Exhibit 12.11 is far less clear. A plausible case can be made to the contrary: that over the course of American history, the external environment casts the crucial influence on the size of the military budget. Perceptions of threats (real and imagined) play a powerful role in conditioning policy responses. Some international events came as genuine shocks to Americans: the launch of Sputnik in 1957, the Soviet invasion of Afghanistan of 1979, the Iranian revolution of 1979, the collapse of the Eastern European and Soviet communist bloc, German reunification, the Iraqi invasion of Kuwait, and most notably the terrorist attacks of September 11,

Exhibit 12.10 'Rivers Delivers'

Mendell Rivers (Democrat, South Carolina) represented Charleston, South Carolina from 1941 to 1970. During that time he used his position on the House Armed Services Committee to transform the city's naval yard into a major Atlantic Fleet base. The base acquired squadrons of destroyers and nuclear submarines, an Army depot, Air Force base, Marine air station and veterans' hospital. His campaign slogan was 'Rivers Delivers'. When he took over as chairman of the committee, Charleston's share of the annual Navy construction budget more than doubled. A congressional colleague once advised him, 'You put anything else down there in your district, Mendel, it's gonna sink' (Anton and Thomas, 1999: 65).

Exhibit 12.11 'The 'iron triangle' on defence policy

Congress

House National Security and Senate Foreign Relations Committees
Armed Services Committees; Defense Appropriations Committee
Subcommittees
Joint Committee on Defense Production
Joint Economic Committee
Government Operations Committee
House and Senate members from districts/states with interest in the defence industry

Executive Agencies
Department of Defense
NASA
Department of Energy

Defence Contractors
Boeing, Lockheed
Martin, Northrop
Grumman, McDonnell
Douglas, Hercules

2001 on New York City and the Pentagon itself in Virginia. Events can and do drive policy.

Take, for example, the issue of national ballistic missile defence (a system to intercept ballistic missiles launched against America). Although the notion of such a defence was proposed by President Reagan in 1983 (the Strategic Defense Initiative, rapidly dubbed 'star wars' by its critics), with the end of the Cold War, American planners faced an entirely new strategic context. States such as Iran, Iraq and North Korea attempted to develop the capacity for nuclear, chemical and biological weapons of mass destruction while states such as Russia and China assisted the spread of nuclear technology and ballistic hardware to other nations. For most of the 1990s, the Clinton administration did relatively little in terms of a military response to this new context, holding that diplomacy and increasing economic ties might ameliorate the situation. Yet in Clinton's final year in office, and especially when George W. Bush became president, the focus of attempting to deploy a defensive shield gained greater urgency. Under heavy congressional pressure from Republicans, Clinton signed the National Missile Defense Act into law in 1999. With the attacks of 9/11, the defence

budget in general gained a substantial boost that simply could not have been viable prior to the atrocities.

But perhaps the clearest rebuke to the military–industrial thesis is the simplest one. That is, were the thesis accurate, we would expect to see a linear upward increase in the defence budget. This is not the case. As Tables 12.2 and 12.3 indicate, the levels of military expenditure, commitments and types of force have ebbed and flowed sharply over time. This is not to deny or minimize the significance of the connections between lawmakers, bureaucrats and interest lobbies, but it is to suggest that the key to the making of policy lies less in an iron triangle and more in successive administrations and Congress's perceptions of the national interests of the United States at large in the world.

The end of the Cold War, in particular, ushered in substantial reductions in America's military personnel, bases and equipment. As Table 12.4 shows, the defences of the United States experienced a substantial 'downsizing' between 1989 and 1999. It is difficult, then, in the light of such data, to accept the claims that a sinister cabal of Pentagon bureaucrats, hawkish lawmakers and profiteering arms makers is behind a consistent

TABLE 12.2   Federal expenditures on national defence, 1960–96

Year	Total ($bn)	Percentage of federal outlays	Percentage of GDP
1960	53.5	52.2	9.5
1965	56.3	42.8	7.5
1970	90.4	41.8	8.3
1975	103.1	26.0	5.7
1980	155.2	22.7	5.1
1985	279.0	26.7	6.4
1990	328.4	23.9	5.5
1996	303.3	16.9	3.6

Source: US Bureau of the Census, 1996.

TABLE 12.3   US Navy active ship force levels, 1917–2000

Year	Number of ships
1933	311
1936	322
1939	394
1945	6,768
1950–53	1,122
1964	859
1973	641
1989	592
1990	529
2000	315

Source: *CQ Weekly*, April 15, 2000, pp. 876–7.

attempt to expand America's military re-sources and expenditures.

INTERMEDIARY ORGANIZATIONS

The end of the Cold War not only increased the conflicts between and within the executive branch and Congress but also ended the era of bipartisanship in foreign policy that had existed from 1941 to 1966. In some respects this had ceased as early as 1966, when Senator William Fulbright (Democrat, Arkansas) commissioned hearings on the Vietnam War and progressive elements within the party mobilized for a withdrawal. Subsequently, Presidents Nixon, Ford, Carter, Reagan, George H.W. Bush and Clinton faced an influential chorus of critics from both parties. Even with the war on terrorism and overwhelming public support, President George W. Bush had to cajole and persuade key actors within his administration and Congress to support his objectives during 2001–02.

Strong elements of bipartisanship persist on foreign policy. The Democratic and Republican parties as a whole have not polarized in the dramatic ways that have occurred on domestic policy issues such as gun control and abortion. For example, most of the members of the two parties are committed to internationalism – only a few seek an isolationist policy that sees a wholehearted American withdrawal from a global role. However, some important changes have occurred. In particular, as Exhibit 12.12 notes, two cross-cutting axes on international affairs – on traditional national security concerns and trade/economic policy – have yielded four broad positions on foreign policy within the two parties.

Broadly speaking, the Democratic Party is

TABLE 12.4   America's downsized defences: 1989 v. 1999

	1989	1999
Active-duty military personnel	2.2m	1.4m
Military bases	495	398
Strategic nuclear warheads	10,563	7,958
Army		
Main battle tanks	15,600	7,836
Armoured personnel carriers	27,400	17,800
Navy		
Strategic submarines	36	18
Tactical submarines	99	66
Air Force		
Tactical fighter squadrons*	41	52
Long-range combat aircraft	393	206

* Squadrons contain from 12–24 aircraft.

Source: Defense Department, Arms Control Association, International Institute for Strategic Studies (*The Military Balance 1988–89 and 1998–99*).

Exhibit 12.12   Contemporary positions on US foreign policy

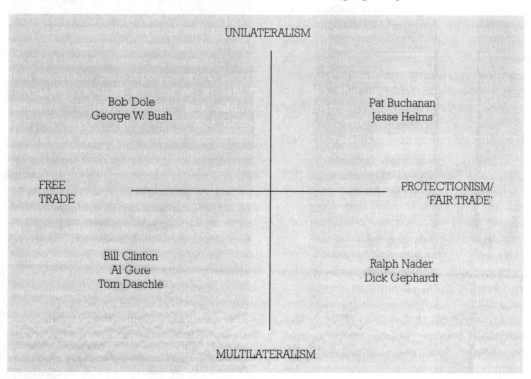

multilateralist and idealist on foreign policy. Democrats tend to favour humanitarian interventions, support strongly international organizations such as the United Nations, and want to act with allies in pursuit of international goals such as environmental protection. On trade, however, most congressional Democrats tend to support 'fair trade' rather than untrammelled free trade. Many favour attaching provisos to free trade treaties that mandate protections for workers and for the environment. As such, a majority of Democrats in Congress opposed President Clinton when he sought ratification of NAFTA, and the imposition of a 30 per cent steel tariff on European steel exporters in 2002 reflected George W. Bush's concern to win over the electoral support of traditionally Democratic-leaning states such as West Virginia, Pennsylvania and Ohio.

The Republican Party is, by contrast (and despite Bush's uncharacteristic stance on the steel tariffs), typically more unilateralist on security issues and more committed to free trade. Although most Republicans are strongly internationalist, many have grave reservations about multilateral action and supra-national institutions such as the United Nations, the World Trade Organization, and the International Monetary Fund. They tend to favour a strong military but are wary of expansive commitments to military intervention, particularly where the use of ground troops is employed. On trade, most in the GOP are keen for the expansion of free trade and new markets for American producers. Clinton owed ratification of NAFTA to the support of a majority of congressional Republicans, who joined with a minority of Democrats to support the treaty. Although a significant minority of Republicans opposed the permanent normalization of trade relations with China in 2000 – on both human rights and military grounds – the party is generally pro-free trade agreements, whether bilateral or regional.

The parties' positions have been powerfully influenced in turn by their particular electoral coalitions and allied organized interests. It was noted earlier that ethnic lobbies have traditionally sought to play a role in making foreign policy. Some popular perceptions even hold that American foreign policy is compartmentalized into ethnic enclaves: policy towards Israel being driven by the Jewish lobby, towards Ireland being driven by the Irish lobby, towards Cuba by Cuban Americans, and so on.

But, as with the military–industrial thesis, such claims need to be evaluated carefully. In particular, the outcomes of policy need to be analysed according to what policymakers determined to be America's national interests. Tony Smith (2000) argues persuasively that there have been three periods of ethnic influence on American foreign policy but that the zenith of such influence has occurred with the end of the Cold War (see Exhibit 12.13). As a result both of increased activism by ethnic lobbies and the apparent legitimacy that the influential public philosophy of multiculturalism accords such activism, US foreign policy is ripe for sectional influences to be felt.

Smith's argument is powerful and persuasive but, as with domestic politics, we should generally be cautious in equating activism with influence. There is often a tendency to infer back from foreign policy towards a given region or state to the activism of a particular domestic American lobby, and then to conclude that the policy was a response to that lobby's pressure. But the fact that a lobby has access to decision-makers within executive departments, agencies and Congress, and that policy is congenial to it, need not indicate proof of influence. As Exhibit 12.14 notes, there are often multiple factors at work in determining American foreign policy.

One particularly important consideration here concerns the existence of a countervailing lobby. Ethnic lobbies can influence policy much more easily if no opposing domestic

Exhibit 12.13   Three periods of ethnic group influence on US foreign policy

1910–41. Influential immigrant groups within America exerted a 'drag' on the nation's commitment to an internationalist role. In particular, German and Italian immigrants were hostile to US participation in the First World War and tempered American intervention in Europe during the 1930s.

The Cold War. From 1947 to 1991, many ethnic groups consolidated America's 'rise to globalism'. Polish, Italian and Cuban Americans were strongly opposed to communism and helped successive administrations to take a clear stand for containment.

The post-Cold War era. From 1992 to the present, the glue of anti-communism that had held ethnic lobbies together now broke apart. As a result, a range of ethnic lobbies competed to influence US policy: Armenian Americans, Jews, Cubans, Indian and Pakistani Americans.

lobby exists. For example, although many Anglophile Americans have expressed concern about groups such as NORAID, no organized anti-Irish republican lobby of consequence exists in America. Similarly, despite the increasing pressures brought by American farmers and other producers to relax relations with Cuba, no organized pro-Castro lobby exists in America, effectively ceding policy influence to the strongly anti-Castro Cuban American lobby with its stronghold in Miami, Florida.

Alternatively, one can refer back to the example of Israel. Traditionally, the powerful Israeli lobby has faced no counterpart on the side of Arab Americans. George W. Bush did

Exhibit 12.14   US policy towards Israel

Critics of American policy towards the Middle East frequently charge that the policy is driven, even determined, by the influence of American Jews. While there is no doubt that the political activism of Jewish Americans has helped to shore up US support for Israel since 1948, the key to American policy has been more strategic (American vital interests in the region) than domestic. It is highly likely that, even if no Jewish Americans existed in the United States, US policy towards Israel would have been broadly similar to the one that has in fact obtained. The reasons for this are several:

* A common biblical heritage (most Arabs are Muslim).
* A shared European value system (most Arabs take values from Islam).
* The democratic nature of Israel's political system (most Arab nations are monarchies or dictatorships).
* The Israeli role as a key regional ally of the US (Arab states have historically proven either unreliable allies for the US, such as Nasser's Egypt, or were clearly under the Soviet sphere of influence during the Cold War, such as Iraq).
* The sympathy extended Jews as victims of genocide in the Nazi Holocaust and the Russian pogroms (by contrast, and long before September 11, Arabs have sometimes been portrayed in America as terrorists, fanatics and ruthless exploiters of the US economy through their control of substantial oil resources).

TABLE 12.5   A typology of conditions for ethnic interest group influence on US foreign policy: the case of Israel

Conditions	Pro-Israel forces?	Pro-Arab Americans?
• Do group goals conform to US strategic interests?	Yes	No
• Is the group well assimilated into American society?	Yes	No
• Does the group display a high level of political activity?	Yes	No
• Is the group internally homogeneous?	Yes	No
• Does the group command the support of American public opinion?	Yes	No
• Is the group able to exert political clout?	Yes	No

make strong overtures to the Arab American population concentrated in Detroit, Michigan (a key swing state) in the 2000 election, but political support for Israel in Washington is bipartisan and strong. As Table 12.5 shows, on balance, and with America's strategic global and regional interests as the priority, the most important conditions that generally shape American policy strongly favour the pro-Israel forces rather than Arab Americans.

Overall, the picture of ethnic influence is highly complex and more subtle than popular coverage often admits. Ethnic lobbies are active and, in some case, influential. In the latter regard, some lobbies are strong forces, others weak, and many are episodic. But regardless of the group, it is very difficult to point to any lobby that can actually determine policy on a consistent basis. America's vital interests, and the plurality of competing pressures on policymakers, preclude such an outcome. Under some conditions – when decision-makers in government are divided, for example – ethnic lobbies can exert an influence at the margins. But the ultimate test of such influence is simply whether or not the group's goals are consistent with the national interests of the US.

CONCLUSION

Foreign policy remains subject to a constitutional 'invitation to struggle', but that invitation has rarely been refused in the post-Second World War era. Post-Vietnam, and especially with the Cold War's end, America has seen a steady expansion of the struggle over its role and purpose in international affairs that is at once institutional, partisan, ideological, and informed strongly by domestic as well as global political considerations. The breakdown of bipartisanship on both foreign policy goals and institutional means of securing those goals has not been wholesale, but it has been substantial.

At the same time, and well before September 11, 2001, presidential leadership in foreign policy remains largely intact – albeit still vulnerable to regular challenge on many fronts. The 'two presidencies' thesis has been undermined and the president must manage not only his relations with Congress, but also the many conflicts that regularly arise within his own administration. The president must also face a number of competing actors in foreign policy, not only from congressional allies and opponents but also interest lobbies of many types, national, sub-national and supranational economic actors, and international organizations of all descriptions. However, the president remains the key player in the policymaking process on international questions, largely because there is simply no other political force in the United States either able or willing to supplant him.

FURTHER READING

John Dumbrell, *The Making of US Foreign Policy* (1990) is a good introduction to the institutions that formulate and implement US policy.

John Lewis Gaddis, *We Now Know: Rethinking Cold War History* (1997) is an excellent and elegant survey of the theory and practice of US foreign policy in the Cold War.

Tony Smith, *Foreign Attachments: The Power of Ethnic Groups in the Making of American Foreign Policy* (2000) is an elegant and rich study of ethnic group influence on American policy during the twentieth century.

James Scott (ed.), *After the End: Making US Foreign Policy in the Post-Cold War World* (1998) is an excellent collection of essays addressing a range of questions about the effects of the end of the Cold War on the way in which US foreign policy is made.

Odd Arne Westad, *Reviewing the Cold War: Approaches, Interpretations, Theory* (2000) is an impressive collection of essays on most aspects of the Cold War conflict from its origins to arms control.

WEB LINKS

Department of State
http://www.state.gov

The Pentagon
http://www.defenselink.mil

Congressional Research Service reports on US foreign policies
http://www.fas.org/man/crs/

US Navy
http://www.navy.mil

US Air Force
http://www.af.mil

US Army
http://www.army.mil

US Marine Corps
http://www.usmc.mil

Center for Security Policy (pro-national missile defense)
http://www.security-policy.org

Federation of American Scientists
http://www.fas.org

NASA
http://www.nasa.gov

CIA
http://www.cia.gov

The CIA's 'World Factbook'
http://www.odci.gov/cia

US–China Business Council
http://www.uschina.org

Human Rights Watch
http://www.hrw.org/asia

QUESTIONS

- Who makes US foreign policy?

- Should the War Powers Resolution be repealed or reinforced?

- What effects did the end of the Cold War have on the content and construction of US foreign policy?

- 'American foreign policy is determined more by domestic politics than by the international interests of the United States.' Discuss.

- Compare and contrast the opportunities for, and limits on, the influence of TWO ethnic lobbies on American foreign policy in the post-Cold War era.

13 Conclusion

If one constant critical observation can be relied on in most assessments of government and politics in the United States, it is that the system is in flux. Pressures for political change, the complex constellation of personnel and groups within and outside American government institutions, and the activism of millions of citizens combine with a constant election cycle to produce a democratic regime that rarely seems settled for long. In the aftermath of September 11, 2001, in particular, the sense that a new era had been entered – not only in American foreign policy but also in domestic politics – was one that animated many observers of the United States.

But what is perhaps most striking is less the change that the tragedy ushered into being than the remarkable continuity in American government and politics. Domestic politics was placed on a strikingly brief hold before familiar features of the post-1968 era of divided government resurfaced vividly: the centrality of economic concerns to a post-industrial workforce in flux, the intensity of partisan conflict between two political parties whose electoral coalitions are more closely matched than at any time since at least 1945, and the seemingly intractable coordination problems confronting a supremely fragmented system of government still operating under the aegis of an eighteenth-century constitution.

That President George W. Bush and his administration benefited from the immediate public responses to September 11 cannot be doubted. The president's approval ratings rose rapidly and maintained their standing for several successive months into the summer of 2002, making the once-intense controversy over the 2000 presidential election a distant and fading memory. Bush's strategy of interweaving foreign policy with issues of economic security over 2002 cast his Democratic opponents in the unenviable position of fearing a return to the pattern of the Cold War years, in which Republican advantages on national security issues often trumped Democratic advantages on economic ones in presidential elections. Moreover, the nature of the terrorist threat against America – one in which the continental United States, with 8,633 miles of coastline, 300 ports of entry and more than 7,500 miles of border with Canada and Mexico, was now explicitly declared a target by Al Qaeda and its allies – ensured that homeland security was the first priority of the administration into the foreseeable future.

But at the same time as America under Bush declared war on terrorism and a desire to confront an 'axis of evil' in Iraq, Iran and North Korea, so American politics was strongly punctuated by 'business as usual'. In December 2001, the Republican House of Representatives passed the trade promotion authority for Bush ('fast track') by just one vote. In February 2002, the collapse of the corporate energy giant Enron prompted Congress's General Accounting Office to take the administration to court – for the first time in American history – and to demand that Vice President Cheney hand over details of his 2001 energy policy task force's closed hearings with oil executives. In March 2002, as

Chapter 11 noted, a bipartisan group of US senators rebuffed Bush's call for bans on human cloning only hours after he delivered it. So much, then, for new eras. The midterm elections of 2002 – if not the 2004 presidential contest – hinged fundamentally on domestic, not global, concerns.

A dispassionate and balanced analysis of American politics – one that neither focuses exclusively and emotively on the past and current ills of the United States nor praises America's achievements while neglecting the nation's darker dimensions – should not yield too many surprises at this state of affairs. The values instilled by a self-conscious revolution against arbitrary rule and despotic government continue to inform new generations of Americans to embrace individualism, private enterprise, and the defence of limited government and a republican democracy. The remarkable political stability and constitutional longevity that underpin the governmental system have helped to convince Americans that the United States stands apart in the world. The nation's success has only reinforced the sense that 'the American way' is indeed exceptional. As I have argued elsewhere (Singh, 2001), for all their joyously subversive and satirical swipes, even popular cartoons such as *The Simpsons* and *South Park* ultimately affirm core American values more than they reject them.

America has now achieved an unprecedented position of dominance in the current international system. However much non-Americans may fear and resent it, it remains a fact that no nation has been as dominant culturally, economically, technologically and militarily in the history of the world since the Roman Empire. For some American analysts, the lesson of September 11 was that American 'imperialism' is to be embraced – that the attack was a result of insufficient American involvement and ambition and the solution was to be more expansive in the US's global goals and more assertive in their implementation. Although America tends to operate not through brute force but through economic,

cultural and political means, the effect of the projection of American power is not unlike the effect of the projection of Victorian British power or Roman power. Future historians may well look back on the twenty-first-century United States as an empire as well as a republic, however different from that of Rome and every other empire throughout history.

But simultaneously, the fundamental contours of American government and politics that this book has traced remain intact: the ubiquity of constitutional influences that condition the architecture of government and the outcomes of the policy process; the vertical and horizontal divisions that render America a federal and a separated system, in which conflict is built into the heart of the democratic process; and the intense competition between and within government institutions and intermediary organizations from courts to bureaucracies that shape public policy outcomes. President Bush is unquestionably the most powerful government official in the world, but his ability to compel a vast and decentralized system to bend to his will is as nothing compared to Prime Minister Blair in the UK. An American empire – if it is that – is presided over by a figure who cannot remotely be described as imperial in his authority and power.

That, of course, is precisely as the Founding Fathers intended and as today's Americans desire. Even during wartime, the American system of government is a separated, not a presidential, one. Congress is a co-equal branch of government to the presidency, not an inferior one. Its composition is plural, rather than singular, and its modes of election, processes and procedures are dissimilar to those of the executive branch. But the Constitution did not establish a presidential system. Equally, the states have important grants of authority that the federal government as a whole cannot infringe. Policed by the federal and state courts, the American system of government is not reducible to the priorities and preferences of whoever occupies the White House – however much that occupant might wish this were the case and however much popular coverage of American politics frequently suggests that it is the case.

That such a complex system – checked and balanced, dividing rather than concentrating power, and demanding the forging of coalitions to reach consensus rather than empowering transient majorities to impose 'decisive' solutions – has left myriad social, economic and political problems unresolved cannot be denied. But which industrialized democracy today has fully resolved the problems of industrial decay, unemployment, poverty, homelessness, environmental degradation and more? On most comparative indices, America has achieved impressive results. Moreover, where many non-Americans view the United States as either irrational or callous – not least on matters such as health care provision, gun control and capital punishment – the policy outcomes typically reflect a divided sentiment within America. It is ultimately as inaccurate as it is patronizing to treat contemporary America as a homogeneous whole, any more so than any other nation.

Indeed, to the extent that this book has offered a qualified defence of America's system of government, diversity is its crux – not that the system 'works' rapidly in completely resolving pressing social and economic problems (though its achievements are impressive, if incomplete), but that the system has evolved steadily and surely to encompass and adapt to a transformed social base. It is probably doubtful, were the Framers of the Constitution to be magically transported back to the America of 2003–04, that they would approve of the top two foreign policy

positions in the Bush administration being held by black Americans (and one a woman at that!), of states legalizing same-sex unions, or of twenty-one-year-olds being able to carry handguns concealed in the streets of 42 states. At the same time, however, they would probably marvel that the nation has not only become the world's foremost power, but that it also continues to operate under the same constitutional design that they brought into being in 1787.

That a new global role, foreign policy objectives and heightened urgency on the part of the United States post-September 11 should co-exist with a familiar picture of domestic divisions, partisan squabbling and institutional rivalry within and between Congress, the executive and the courts therefore sits well with American history. America is a divided democracy and the American people are a diverse, heterogeneous and fractured citizenry. That Americans are united in opposing terrorism against the United States and its allies is a given, but how and what instruments to employ to that end – the size of the defence budget, the need for tax or spending cuts, the appropriate roles of the CIA and FBI, the correct balance between security and civil liberties – are all matters on which Americans disagree. The virtue of the American system is that such disagreements can find ample expression and that only consensus and compromise can yield clear and lasting policy results. However frustrating that is for the president, lawmakers and citizens, it is a powerful safety valve for marrying the protection of individual liberties and rights to the need for effective government in a liberal democratic regime.

Appendix I: Glossary

Adjudication. Court-like decision-making by the federal bureaucracy as to whether an individual or organization has complied with or breached federal regulations.

Administrative discretion. The ability of bureaucrats to make decisions that translate broad statute laws into specific rules.

Advice and consent. Provision of the Constitution conferring on the Senate the power to approve or reject presidential nominations to the executive and judicial branches of government.

Affirmative action. A set of procedures that attempts to correct the effects of past discrimination against minority groups and that can include specific goals and quotas for hiring minority applicants.

Agency. A term for any administrative unit of the federal government.

Aid to Families with Dependent Children (AFDC). Federal funds, administered by the states, for children living with parents or relatives who fall below state standards of need.

American exceptionalism. The notion that the United States is different from other nations. At its strongest, exceptionalism suggests that America is unique. In its weaker sense, exceptionalism points to certain features of American political development that distinguish it as different.

Amicus curiae. Written briefs submitted to the Supreme Court by third-party individuals or organizations – who are not party to a lawsuit – that want their opinions to be considered by the Court in reaching a decision. Latin for 'friend of the Court'. The number of such briefs increased steadily with the judicial activism of the Warren Court, and reached notable peaks in the *Bakke* and *Webster* cases.

Anti-Federalists. Those forces who favoured strong state governments and a weak national government and who were opponents of the constitution proposed at the Constitutional Convention of 1787.

Appellate courts. Courts that reconsider the decisions made by trial courts, at the request of the losing party seeking to appeal.

Articles of Confederation and Perpetual Union. Adopted by the Continental Congress in 1777 and ratified in 1781 as the United States' first constitution – established a loose union of states and a Congress with few powers, and provided the formal basis for America's national government until 1789, when they were supplanted by the US Constitution.

Bicameral. A legislature divided into two separate houses, such as Congress.

Bill of attainder. A legislative act declaring a person guilty of a crime and setting punishment without the benefit of a formal judicial hearing or trial; prohibited by Article I, Section 10 of the Constitution.

Bill of Rights. The first ten Amendments to the Constitution, which collectively guarantee the fundamental liberties and rights of citizens from abuse by the national government. Over time, American courts have 'incorporated' the Bill of Rights so that the first eight Amendments apply to the state, as well as the federal, governments.

Block grants. Money given to the states by Congress that can be used in broad areas and is not limited to specific purposes like categorical grants. A means introduced in the mid-1960s to give states greater freedom.

***Brown v. Board of Education of Topeka, Kansas* (1954)**. The Supreme Court unanimously struck down the 'separate but equal' doctrine as fundamentally unequal. It eliminated state power to use race as a criterion of discrimination in law and provided the national government with the power to intervene by exercising strict regulatory policies against discriminatory actions.

***Brown v. Board of Education of Topeka, Kansas (Brown II)* (1955)**. The Supreme Court issued a mandate for state and local school boards to proceed 'with all deliberate speed' to desegregate schools.

***Buckley v. Valeo* (1976)**. The Court limited congressional attempts to regulate campaign finance by declaring unconstitutional any absolute limits on the freedom of individuals to spend their own money on campaigns.

Budget deficit. The case when expenditures exceed revenues.

Budget surplus. The case when budget revenues exceed expenditures.

Bureaucracy. Any large, complex organization in which employees have specific job responsibilities and work within a hierarchy. Often used to refer to both government agencies and the people who work in them.

Cabinet. An official advisory board to the president, composed of the heads (secretaries) of the 14 major departments of the federal government. The secretaries, or chief administrators, are appointed by the president with the consent of the Senate. Approval is normally taken for granted, but recent years have seen rejections.

Candidate-centred campaign. A campaign in which paid consultants or volunteers co-ordinate campaign activities, develop strategies and raise funds. Political parties play a secondary role.

Capital punishment. The execution of convicted criminals by the state for certain types of crime. Currently legal in 38 states and for the federal government, the death penalty is constitutional. Although the courts have ruled certain types of execution to be a violation of the Eighth Amendment's prohibition on cruel and unusual punishments, the principle of capital punishment has not been so ruled since 1976.

Casework. Work done by members of Congress to provide constituents with personal services and help through the maze of federal programmes and benefits.

Categorical, or conditional, grants. Money given to the states and localities by Congress that was to be used for limited purposes under specific rules.

Caucus (congressional). An association of members of Congress based on party, ideology, interest or demographic characteristics such as gender, race and ethnicity. The most influential congressional caucuses include the Congressional Black Caucus and the Caucus on Women's Issues.

Caucus (political). A forum of a political or legislative group, normally closed to the public until the early 1900s, to select candidates, plan strategy or make decisions on legislative matters. Contemporary party caucuses are local party meetings which are open to all who live in the precinct and in which citizens discuss and then vote for delegates to district and party conventions. Party caucuses in Congress comprise the rank-and-file members, and party leadership posts and committee chairmanships are now subject to caucus ratification.

Central Intelligence Agency (CIA). The agency responsible for gathering and analysing information for policymakers.

Checks and balances. The principle that lets the executive, legislative and judicial branches share some responsibilities and that gives each branch some control over the others' activities. The major support for checks and balances comes from the Constitution's distribution of shared powers. Key examples are the presidential veto power over congressional legislation, the power of the Senate to approve presidential appointments, and judicial review of laws and executive orders.

Civil liberties. Areas of personal freedoms, most of which are spelled out in the Bill of Rights, that protect individuals from excessive or arbitrary government interference.

Civil rights. Rights that guarantee protection of individuals by the government against discrimination or unreasonable treatment by other individuals or groups.

Civil servant. A federal bureaucrat who is not politically appointed.

Class action suit. A lawsuit in which large numbers of persons with common interests join together under a representative party to bring or defend a lawsuit, such as hundreds of workers together suing a company.

Clear and present danger test. The proposition proclaimed by the Supreme Court in *Schenck v. United States* (1919) that the government had the right to punish speech if it could be shown to present a grave and immediate danger to the government's interests.

Closed primary. A primary election that allows voters to obtain only a ballot of the party for which they are registered.

Closed rule. A provision by the House Rules Committee limiting or prohibiting the introduction of amendments during floor debate on a bill. It emerged as an important tool by which party leaders controlled legislative outcomes and was used extensively after 1981.

Cloture. The rule for ending debate in the Senate that requires a vote of at least two-thirds or three-fifths of the members in a legislative body to set a time limit on debate over a given bill (currently, three-fifths are required – 60 senators – to cut off discussion in the 100-member Senate). Although cloture votes sometimes succeed, each senator has an individual incentive not to vote for cloture, as infringing a senatorial privilege that may be personally useful at some later date.

Coat-tail effect. Result of voters casting their ballots for president or governor and 'automatically' voting for the remainder of the party's ticket. With divided party control of the federal government the norm since 1968, the coat-tail effect has become an increasingly rare phenomenon in national American politics.

Cold War. The post-Second World War period characterized by ideological and policy confrontations between the American-led West and the Soviet-led East. Scholars differ over dating the Cold War: from 1917–91; 1947–91; and 1947–62. Although the Cold War achieved a 'long peace' in the sense that American and Soviet military forces did not engage in direct military conflict, a succession of 'hot' wars occurred as proxies for the main conflict.

Commerce power. The power of Congress to regulate trade among the states and with foreign nations.

Common law. Also called judge-made law, it refers to law based on the precedent of lower and prior court decisions.

Concurrent powers. Those powers the Constitution grants the national government but does not deny to the states, for example, to lay and collect taxes.

Concurring opinion. Opinion written by Supreme Court justices that agrees with the conclusion but not the reasoning of the majority opinion.

Confederation. An arrangement in which ultimate government authority is vested in the states that make up the nation. Whatever power the national government has is derived from the states being willing to give up some of their authority to a central government.

Conference committees. Temporary joint committees that are formed to reconcile differences between the House and Senate versions of a bill.

Confirmation. The power of the US Senate to approve or disapprove a presidential nominee for an executive or judicial post.

Congressional authorization. The power of Congress to provide the president with the right to carry out legislated policies.

Constituents. Members of the district from which an official is elected.

Constitutional government. A system of rule in which formal and effective limits are placed on the powers of the government.

Constitutionalism. An approach to legitimacy in which the rulers give up a certain amount of power in return for their right to utilize the remaining powers.

Containment. The foreign policy pursued during the Cold War by the US that called for preventing the Soviet Union from making expansionist moves.

Cooperative federalism. A period of cooperation between state and national government that began during the Great Depression. The national government assumed new responsibilities, and state and local officials accepted it as an ally, not an enemy.

Covert actions. Activities ranging from gathering intelligence to assassinating foreign leaders that are intentionally hidden from public view and may be of questionable legality.

Critical electoral realignment. The point in history when a new party supplants the ruling party, in turn becoming the dominant force. It tended to occur approximately every 32–36 years in America until 1968.

De facto segregation. Racial segregation that is not a direct result of law or government policy, but is instead a reflection of residential housing patterns, income distributions or other social factors.

De jure segregation. Racial segregation that is a direct result of law or government policy rather than residential housing patterns or other voluntary decisions by the races.

Declaration of Independence. The document declaring the colonies to be free and independent states that was adopted by the Second Continental Congress in July 1776. Written by Thomas Jefferson, the Declaration also articulated the fundamental principles under which the new nation would be governed, such as the consent of the governed and natural rights (among them life, liberty, and the pursuit of happiness). The document was both a catalyst for the revolutionary war and provided its intellectual rationale.

Deficit. An annual debt incurred when the government spends more than it collects. Each yearly deficit adds to the nation's total debt.

Deficit financing. Usually refers to deficits that are deliberately incurred as part of an effort to fight off a deflationary phase of the business cycle. Deficits are financed by borrowing. Despite his professed belief in a balanced budget, President Ronald Reagan took deficit spending to unprecedented heights and made America the world's largest debtor nation during 1981–89.

Delegated powers. Sometimes referred to as 'enumerated powers', these are the powers the Constitution gives the Congress that are specifically listed in the first 17 clauses in Section 8 of Article I. Assigned to one government agency but exercised by another agency with the express permission of the first.

Department. The major federal bureaucracies that are given this name by the Congress, are led by a Secretary, and serve as part of the president's Cabinet.

Department of Defense. Also know as 'The Pentagon', after the shape of the building in which it is located. The agency most closely linked with military policymaking. It includes the Departments of the Army, Navy, Air Force and Marines.

Department of State. The Cabinet department responsible for day-to-day operation of embassies, the protection of US interests abroad, formal negotiations between the US and other nations, and the provision of assistance and advice to the president.

Deregulation. A policy of reducing or eliminating regulatory restraints on the conduct of individuals or private institutions.

Détente. The relaxation of tensions between nations. The name for President Nixon's policy – formulated closely with his National Security Advisor, Henry Kissinger – of taking a more cooperative approach with the Soviets while enhancing American security arrangements with its allies.

Deterrence strategy. The build-up and maintenance of nuclear and conventional forces and large stockpiles of weapons to discourage any potential enemy from attacking the United States or its allies.

Dissenting opinion. A decision written by a justice in the minority in a particular case in which the justice wishes to express his or her reasoning in the case. Dissenting opinions are publicly available and can provide the rationale for political opposition and future judicial rulings that overturn majority holdings.

Divided government. The condition when the presidency is controlled by one party while the opposing party controls one or both houses of Congress. Political scientists disagree over both the causes and consequences of divided government. Some see the causes as purposeful, in that the American electorate is consciously voting to split control. Others contend that the result is an 'accident' of the electoral system. For some American critics, the division exacerbates existing problems of the separated system, making accountability impossible, leading to gridlock and encouraging political irresponsibility. However, scholars such as David Mayhew (1991) argue that divided government makes no difference in terms of the passage of major legislation.

Double jeopardy. Trial more than once for the same crime. The Constitution guarantees in the Sixth Amendment that no citizen shall be subjected to double jeopardy.

Dred Scott v. Sandford **(1857)**. The most infamous case in the history of the Supreme Court. Chief Justice Roger Taney wrote that black Americans were not citizens and that they 'were never thought of or spoken of except as property'. In a futile attempt to settle the slavery issue, which was threatening to tear the nation apart, the Court went further to rule that the Missouri Compromise was unconstitutional and Congress could not bar slavery from the territories. The ruling, in many critics' views, hastened the onset of the Civil War. It was overturned by the ratification of the Fourteenth and Fifteenth Amendments to the Constitution.

Dual federalism. The perspective on federalism that emerged after the Civil War. It saw the national and state governments as equal but independent partners, with each responsible for distinct policy functions and each barred from interfering with the other's work.

Due process. To proceed according to law and with adequate protection for individual rights. Guaranteed as a citizenship protection under the Fifth and Fourteenth Amendments. Due process has become the main vehicle by which the Bill of Rights is incorporated so that its protections apply to state governments as well as the federal authority.

Elastic clause. See 'necessary and proper clause'.

Electoral coalitions. Groups of loyal supporters who agree with the party's stand on most issues and vote for its candidates for office.

Electoral College. The system set up by the Constitution that provides for the people to elect a number of electors in each state equal to the number of US senators and representatives for that state. The electors from each state meet in their respective state capitals after the popular election to cast ballots for president and vice president. The presidential candidate winning the plurality vote in a state receives all its Electoral College votes.

Electorate. All of the eligible voters in a legally designated area.

Elite theory. The theory that public policies are made by a relatively small group of influential leaders who share common values, goals and beliefs.

Entitlement programmes. Government programmes that pay benefits to all eligible recipients. The amount of money spent depends on the number of those eligible rather than on some predetermined figure.

Entitlements. Automatic payments to any person or government meeting the requirements specified by law, such as social security benefits and military pensions.

Environmental impact statement. Since 1969, all federal agencies must file this statement demonstrating that a new programme or project will not have a net negative effect on the human or physical environment.

Equal employment opportunity. Federal programmes developed under civil rights legislation that prohibit workplace and other forms of discrimination on the basis of race, sex, religion, national origin or handicapped status.

Equal Protection Clause. A clause in the Fourteenth Amendment that requires that states provide citizens with the 'equal protection of the laws'.

Equal time rule. A Federal Communications Commission requirement that broadcasters provide candidates for the same political office an equal opportunity to communicate their messages to the public.

Equality of opportunity. A universally shared American ideal that all people should have the freedom to use whatever talents and wealth they have to reach their fullest potential. It embraces a conception of equality that is focused on process rather than results, but has been used by both liberals and conservatives, respectively, to support and attack policies such as affirmative action.

Exclusionary rule. The principle that evidence, no matter how incriminating, cannot be used to convict someone if it is gathered illegally in violation of the Fourth Amendment. The rule was established by the Supreme Court in *Mapp v. Ohio* (1961). Conservatives view the rule as an excessive protection for criminals and an unwarranted constraint on legitimate law enforcement activity.

Exclusive powers. All the powers that the states are in effect forbidden to exercise by the Constitution, that rest exclusively with the national government.

Executive agreements. Agreements with other nations made by the president without the Senate's consent. They have all the legal force of treaties but, unlike treaties, are not binding on succeeding presidents. Since they do not require Senate approval, executive agreements have come to exceed treaties by a ratio in excess of 40:1.

Executive order. A rule or regulation issued by the president that has the effect of law.

Executive privilege. The traditional right, claimed by presidents since George Washington, to withhold information from Congress and the courts.

Faction. A group of people with common interests, usually in opposition to the aims or principles of a larger group or the public. The Constitution was designed in part to minimize the influence of factions. The most influential party faction during the middle of the twentieth century was the cohort of Southern Democrats who opposed moves towards desegregation by the federal government.

Fairness doctrine. A Federal Communications Commission requirement for broadcasters who air programmes on controversial issues to provide time for opposing views.

Federal government. The national government of the United States. Although millions of Americans readily accept the distributive benefits offered by the federal government, most remain physically as well as psychologically distant from its principal seat in Washington, D.C..

Federal Register. The publication that contains all proposed and final federal regulations.

Federal Reserve Board. The governing board of the Federal Reserve System comprising a chair and six other members, appointed by the president with the consent of the Senate. The independent central bank that controls interest rates. Under its chairman, Alan Greenspan, the Fed was widely credited with maintaining the remarkable economic growth and stability of the 1990s.

Federal Reserve System (The Fed). Consisting of 12 Federal Reserve Banks, the Fed facilitates exchanges of cash, cheques and credit, regulates member banks and uses monetary policies to fight inflation and deflation. Alan Greenspan's successful chairing of the Fed made him a national (and international) figure of enormous repute and influence.

Federalist Papers. A series of editorials written by James Madison, Alexander Hamilton, and John Jay in 1788 to support the ratification of the Constitution in New York State. Now regarded as a major source of information on what the Framers were thinking when they wrote the Constitution and an important work in political philosophy.

Federalists. Those forces who supported a stronger national government and only reluctantly agreed to a Bill of Rights as the price of ratifying the new Constitution of 1787.

Federation (federal system). A mixture of confederation and unitary systems in which the authority of government is shared by both the national and state governments. In its ideal form, a federal constitution gives some exclusive authority over some governmental tasks to the national government, while giving the states exclusive authority over other governmental matters. There would also be some areas where the two levels of government would share authority.

Feudalism. A medieval political economic system in which landless families secured protection and the use of farmland in exchange for providing services and resources to the land's owner.

Filibuster. A prolonged debate in the Senate that is intended to kill a bill by preventing a vote. Once given the floor, senators have unlimited time to speak, and it requires a cloture vote of three-fifths of the chamber to end the filibuster.

Fiscal policy. The management of government expenditures and tax rates as a means of conducting national economic policy. Policymakers raise or lower government spending and taxes to execute fiscal policy.

Foreign aid. Assistance provided by the United States to another country. This usually takes the form of a grant of money or supplies, but it can also be a low-interest loan. By the later 1990s foreign aid assumed less than 1 per cent of the total US federal budget outlays, the major recipients remaining Israel, Egypt and Ireland.

Formula grants. Grants given to states and localities on the basis of population, number of eligible persons, per capita income or other factors.

Franking privilege. The power of members of Congress to send out mail free of charge, allowing incumbents to cultivate a favourable image among constituents.

Freedom of Information Act. A law enacted in 1996 that guarantees the public access to information about bureaucratic policies and activities.

Full faith and credit. Article IV of the Constitution requires that each state respect in all ways the acts, records and judicial proceedings of the other states. It has ensured that driving licences and divorces must be recognized as legal despite differences in individual state laws.

Gerrymandering. Apportionment of voters in districts in such a way as to give unfair advantage to one political party.

Going public. A strategy that attempts to mobilize the widest and most favourable climate of opinion within the United States.

Government. Institutions and procedures through which a territory and its people are ruled.

Grand Old Party (GOP). The Republican Party.

Grants-in-aid. A general term for funds given by Congress to state and local governments.

Gridlock. A term used to describe the state of affairs when the executive and legislative branches of government cannot agree on major legislation and neither side will compromise.

Gross Domestic Product (GDP). An index of the total output of goods and services. A very imperfect measure of prosperity, productivity, inflation or deflation, but its regular publication both reflects and influences business conditions.

Habeas corpus. A court order demanding that an individual in custody be brought into court and shown the cause for detention. Habeas corpus is guaranteed by the Constitution and can be suspended only in cases of rebellion or invasion.

Hatch Act. The federal law enacted in 1929 that makes it illegal for federal bureaucrats to take an active part in political campaigns or run for elective office. It was modified in 1993 to expand the political rights of federal workers.

Ideology. The combined doctrines, assertions and intentions of a social or political group that justify its behaviour. Americanism itself has been considered as an ideology.

Immigration and Naturalization Service (INS) v. Chadha **(1983)**. The first of two cases since 1937 in which the Supreme Court invalidated an act of Congress on constitutional grounds, declaring the legislative veto unconstitutional.

Impeachment. Formal charge of misconduct brought against a federal public official by the House of Representatives. If found guilty of those charges by the Senate, the official is removed from office.

Implied powers. Those powers given to Congress by Article I, Section 8, clause 18 of the Constitution that are not specifically named but are provided by the 'necessary and proper' clause.

Impoundment. Efforts by presidents to thwart congressional programmes that they cannot otherwise defeat by refusing to spend the funds that Congress has appropriated for them. Congress placed limits on impoundment in the Budget and Impoundment Control Act of 1974 after a series of controversial impoundments by President Nixon in 1973.

Independent agency. A federal bureaucracy that is not part of the president's Cabinet. They are considered 'independent' because, although the president appoints the agency head, the president may not remove him or her.

Independent counsel. A prosecutor appointed under the terms of the Ethics in Government Act of 1978 to investigate criminal misconduct by members of the executive branch. The legislation had been a response to the Watergate scandal and led, indirectly, to the (ultimately unsuccessful) impeachment of President Clinton in 1998–99.

Indirect election. Provision for election of an official where the voters first select the delegates or 'electors', who are in turn charged with making the final choice. The presidential election is an indirect election.

Inflation. A consistent increase in the general level of prices.

Injunction. A court order requiring an individual or organization either to cease or to undertake some form of action to prevent a future injury or to achieve some desirable state of affairs.

Interest group liberalism. A theory of governance that, in principle, all claims on government resources and action are equally valid, and that all interests are equally entitled to participation in and benefits from government. Associated especially with Theodore Lowi's 1979 book, *The End of Liberalism*.

Intergovernmental lobby. The many individuals and groups that have a special interest in the policies and programmes implemented through the growing intergovernmental relations system. These lobbyists represent private, consumer and business groups.

Interpretation. The process wherein bureaucrats implement ambiguous statutes, requiring agencies to make educated guesses as to what Congress or higher administrative authorities intended.

Interpretivism. An approach to constitutional interpretation that demands some search for what the Constitution actually says, either in its plain meaning, its original meaning or in terms of the intentions of the authors of particular provisions.

Iron triangle. The stable and cooperative relationships that often develop between a congressional committee or subcommittee, an administrative agency, and one or more supportive interest groups. Not all of these relationships are triangular, but the 'iron triangle' formulation is perhaps the most typical.

Judicial activism. The concept that the Supreme Court has a right and obligation to practise judicial review, especially in defence of political minorities.

Judicial restraint. Limited and infrequent use of judicial review – advocated on the grounds that unelected judges should not overrule the laws of the elected representatives.

Judicial review. The power of the courts to declare an act of a legislature constitutional or unconstitutional.

Judicial supremacy. The claim that the influence of courts in America is so great as to make the judiciary the supreme lawmaking, as well as law-interpreting, body.

Jurisdiction. The authority of a court initially to consider a case. It is distinguished from appellate jurisdiction, the authority to hear appeals from a lower court's decision.

Korematsu v. United States **(1944)**. The Supreme Court held that it was not unconstitutional to impose legal restrictions on a single racial group, in this case wartime measures prohibiting persons of Japanese ancestry from living in certain areas.

Legislative intent. The supposed real meaning of a statute as it can be interpreted from the legislative history of the bill.

Legislative supremacy. The pre-eminence of Congress among the three branches of the federal government, as established by the Constitution.

Legislative veto. A device in a bill that allows Congress or a congressional committee to veto the actions of an executive agency or the president in an area covered by the bill. It was declared unconstitutional by the Supreme Court in 1983 in *Immigration and Naturalization Service v. Chadha*. However, Congress continues to enact legislation incorporating such a veto.

Legitimacy. The belief of citizens in a government's right to pass and enforce laws.

Libel. The use of print or pictures to harm someone's reputation. An offence that is punishable by criminal law and subject to civil prosecution for damages.

Liberal. A liberal generally supports political and social reform, extensive governmental intervention in the economy, the expansion of federal social services, more vigorous efforts on behalf of the poor, minorities and women, and greater concern for consumers and the environment.

Line-item veto. The power of a president to veto portions of a bill but sign the rest of it. Without a line-item veto, a governor must accept or reject an entire bill.

Lobbying. Strategy by which organized interests seek to influence the passage of legislation by exerting direct pressure on members of the legislature.

Lochner v. New York **(1905)**. Seeking to protect businesses from government regulation, the Supreme Court invalidated a New York State law regulating the sanitary conditions and hours of labour of bakers on grounds that the law interfered with liberty of contract.

Logrolling. A legislative practice wherein reciprocal agreements are made between legislators, usually in voting for or against a bill. Unlike bargaining, logrolling unites parties that have nothing in common but their desire to exchange support.

Majoritarianism. The belief that public policies should be decided either primarily or exclusively by majority vote.

Majority Leader. The second-ranking party position in the House (the first in the Senate). The Majority Leader schedules floor action of bills and guides the party's legislative programme through the House.

Majority rule. Rule by at least one vote more than half of those voting.

Majority system. An electoral system in which, to win a seat in the parliament or other representative body, a candidate must receive a majority of all the votes cast in the relevant district.

Mandate. A claim made by a victorious candidate that the electorate has given him or her special authority to carry out campaign promises.

Marbury v. Madison **(1803)**. The landmark case in which Chief Justice Marshall established that the Supreme Court had the right to rule on the constitutionality of federal and state laws, despite the fact that judicial review was not explicitly granted by the Constitution.

Marshall Plan. A plan proposed in 1947 by Secretary of State George Marshall to provide financial aid and low-cost loans to help rebuild Europe after the Second World War. Over $34 billion was spent for relief, reconstruction and recovery.

Massive retaliation. The military strategy favoured by the Eisenhower administration during the 1950s, which warned the Soviet Union and its allies that any military confrontation could produce an annihilating nuclear attack on Moscow and other Soviet cities.

Matching grants. Programmes in which the national government requires recipient governments to provide a certain percentage of the funds needed to implement the programmes.

McCulloch v. Maryland **(1819)**. The first and most important case favouring national control of the economy over state control. In his ruling, John Marshall established the 'implied powers' doctrine enabling Congress to use the 'necessary and proper' clause of Article I, Section 8, to interpret its delegated powers. This case also concluded that when state law and federal law conflicted national law took precedence.

Means testing. Procedure by which potential beneficiaries of a public assistance programme establish their eligibility by demonstrating a genuine need for the assistance.

Medicaid. A federally funded, state-operated programme for medical services to low-income persons.

Medicare. National health insurance for the elderly and the disabled.

Merit system. The method for hiring federal workers based on their performance in open, competitive examinations. It replaced the spoils system.

Military–industrial complex. A concept coined by President Eisenhower in his farewell address of 1961, in which he referred to the threats to American democracy that may arise from too close a friendship between major corporations in the defence industry and the Pentagon.

Minority Leader. The head of the minority party in the Senate. Also the leader of the minority party in the House, who represents its interests by consulting with the Speaker and Majority Leader over the scheduling of bills and rules for floor actions.

Miranda v. Arizona **(1966)**. The Warren Court ruled that anyone placed under arrest must be informed of the right to remain silent and to have counsel present during interrogation.

Monroe Doctrine. An American policy established in 1823 that warned European nations not to interfere in Latin America while promising that the United States would not interfere in European affairs.

Multilateralism. A foreign policy that seeks to encourage the involvement of several nation-states in coordinated action, usually in relation to a common adversary, with terms and conditions usually specified in a multi-country treaty, such as NATO.

Multiple-member constituency. Electorate that selects all candidates at large from the whole district; each voter is given the number of votes equivalent to the number of seats to be filled.

Mutually Assured Destruction (MAD). The strategy that evolved during the 1960s whereby each of the nuclear powers would hold the other in check by maintaining the ability to annihilate the other in any major nuclear confrontation. Superbly satirized by the Stanley Kubrick movie starring Peter Sellers – *Dr Strangelove* (1964).

Nation-centred federalism. The view that the authority of the national government goes beyond the responsibilities listed in Article I, Section 8, of the Constitution. It is based on the necessary and proper clause and the principle of national supremacy.

National Economic Council (NEC). A council patterned after the National Security Council created by President Clinton to coordinate foreign and domestic economic policy matters. The NEC is headed by the national economic council advisor, who is expected to facilitate coordination of relevant policy concerns.

National Security Adviser. The head of the NSC staff, who may sometimes have a strong influence on foreign and defence policies.

National Security Agency (NSA). A highly secret intelligence-gathering agency operated by the Department of Defense.

National Security Council (NSC). Created by Congress in 1947 to advise the president on foreign policy and to coordinate its implementation.

National supremacy. The principle, stated in Article VI as the 'supremacy clause', that makes the Constitution and those laws and treaties passed under it the 'supreme law of the land'.

Nationalism. The widely held belief that the people who occupy the same territory have something in common, that the nation is a single community.

Nation-state. A political entity comprising a people with some common cultural experience (nation), who also share a common political authority (state), recognized by other sovereignties (nation-states).

Necessary and proper clause. Article I, Section 8 of the Constitution, which enumerates the powers of Congress and provides Congress with the authority to make all laws 'necessary and proper' to carry them out; also referred to as the 'elastic clause'.

New Federalism. Attempts by Presidents Nixon and Reagan to return power to the states through block grants.

New Jersey plan. A framework for the Constitution which called for equal representation in the national legislature regardless of a state's population.

Nomination. The process through which political parties select their candidates for election to public office.

North American Free Trade Agreement (NAFTA). An agreement among the nations of Canada, Mexico and the United States that promotes economic cooperation and abolishes many trade restrictions between the three nations.

North Atlantic Treaty Organization (NATO). A 1949 treaty tying US security interests to those of Western European and other member nations. It represented a major break in the US commitment to unilateralism.

Open primary. A primary election in which the voter can wait until the day of the primary to choose which party to enrol in to select candidates for the general election.

Opinion. The written explanation of the Supreme Court's decision in a particular case.

Original jurisdiction. The authority to hear a case before any other court does.

Originalism. An approach to constitutional interpretation.

Oversight. The effort by Congress, through hearings, investigations and other techniques, to exercise control over the activities of executive agencies.

Partisan primary. A primary election in which candidates run for their own party's nomination.

Partisanship. Loyalty to a particular political party.

Party identification. The tendency of people to think of themselves as Democrats, Republicans or independents.

Party machines. Local party organizations that control urban politics by mobilizing voters to elect the machines' candidates.

Party vote. A roll-call vote in the House or Senate in which at least 50 per cent of the members of one party take a particular position and are opposed by at least 50 per cent of the members of the other party. Party votes were fairly common in the nineteenth century, became increasingly rare over the twentieth, only to recover somewhat in the 1980s and 1990s.

Party whips. Members of Congress who support the party leaders in the House and Senate by communicating the party positions to the membership and keeping the leaders informed of members' views.

Party-as-organization. With few members, this primarily consists of state and county chairpersons and ward and precinct captains who work for the party throughout the year, recruiting candidates and participating in fundraising activities.

Party-centred campaigns. A campaign in which the party coordinates activities, raises money, and develops strategies.

Party-in-the-electorate. Includes anyone who identifies with a particular party, tends to vote for that party's candidates and may even contribute to its campaigns.

Party-in-government. The individuals who have been elected or appointed to a government office under a party label. They play a major role in organizing government and in setting policy.

Patronage. The resources available to higher officials, usually opportunities to make partisan appointments to offices and confer grants, licences, or special favours to supporters.

Pendleton Act. The federal law enacted in 1883 that replaced the patronage system with the merit system.

Plaintiff. The individual or organization who brings a complaint in court.

Platforms. Statements of party goals and specific policy agendas that are taken seriously by the party's candidates but are not binding.

Plessy v. Ferguson **(1896)**. In an infamous case, the Supreme Court held that the Fourteenth Amendment's 'equal protection of the law' clause was not violated by racial distinction as long as the 'separate' facilities were 'equal'.

Pluralism. The view that political power is and should be dispersed among many elites that share a common acceptance of the rules of the game.

Plurality system. An electoral system in which, to win a seat in parliament or other representative body, a candidate need only win the most votes in the election, not necessarily a majority of votes cast.

Pocket veto. An action whereby the president fails to sign a bill during the last ten days of a term and thereby effectively kills the bill.

Police powers. The powers of state governments over the regulation of behaviour within their borders. These police powers were used to justify state jurisdiction over economic matters.

Policy adoption. The stage of policymaking at which a struggle to gain government support occurs, typically demanding much bargaining and compromise.

Policy evaluation. The last stage in the policymaking process: looking at government actions and programmes to see whether goals have been achieved or to assess a policy's effectiveness and efficiency.

Policy formulation. Policymakers and their staffs deliberate the pros and cons of each issue in a process that may take years to complete.

Policy implementation. The carrying out of policy mandates through public programmes and actions.

Political Action Committee (PAC). An independent organization that interest groups, officeholders, and political candidates can establish for the sole purpose of contributing money to the campaigns of candidates who sympathize with its aims. PACs are the result of federal laws that prohibit most interest groups from donating money to political campaigns.

Political consultant. An individual, trained in public relations, media or polling techniques, who advises candidates on organizing their campaign.

Political culture. A set of values, beliefs and traditions about politics and government that are shared by most members of society. Political culture in the United States includes faith in democracy, representative government, freedom of speech and individual rights.

Political efficacy. The perception of one's ability to have an impact on the political system.

Political ideology. A pattern of complex political ideas presented in an understandable structure that inspires people to act to achieve certain goals.

Political participation. Encompasses a broad range of activities, from involvement in learning about politics to engagement in efforts that directly affect the structure of government, the selection of government authorities, or the policies of government.

Political parties. A coalition of people organized formally to recruit, nominate and elect individuals to office and to use elected office to achieve shared political goals.

Political socialization. The process by which individuals acquire political values and knowledge about politics. It is strongly influenced by people with whom the individual has contact from early childhood through adulthood.

Polity. A society with an organized government; the 'political system'.

Poll tax. A state-imposed tax upon the voters as a prerequisite to registration. It was rendered unconstitutional in national elections by the Twenty-fourth Amendment and in state elections by the Supreme Court in 1966.

Popular sovereignty. The concept that the best form of government is one that reflects the general will of the people, which is the sum total of those interests that all citizens have in common. First described by Jean-Jacques Rousseau at the time of the American Revolution.

Populism. A late 1870s political and social movement of western and southern farmers that challenged eastern business interests; a set of ideological beliefs that tends to favour government intervention in both economic and personal affairs.

Pork-barrel legislation. Legislation that appropriates funds for local projects in an area that a member of Congress represents.

Power. The capacity and ability to influence the behaviour and choices of others through the use of politically relevant resources.

Precedents. Prior cases whose principles are used by judges as the bases for their decisions in present cases.

Precinct. The bottom of the typical local party structure: a voting district that generally covers an area of several blocks.

Preferential primary. A primary election in which the elected delegates to a convention are instructed, but not bound, to vote specifically for the presidential candidate preferred by the voters on a separate part of the ballot.

Presidency. Although relegated to the second article of the federal Constitution, the presidency has emerged as the fulcrum of American government. The New Deal expanded the responsibilities of the federal government and the role of the executive branch in administrating federal programmes, while American participation in the Second World War – and the rapid transformation of that conflict into the Cold War – sustained the importance of foreign affairs to the United States. Although the presidential dominance of the era from 1941 to 1966 has been eroded since, the presidency remains the single most important office in American government.

Primary election. An election in which party members select candidates to run for office under the party banner.

Priming. The capacity of the mass media to isolate particular issues, events or themes in the news as the criteria for evaluating politicians.

Privileges and immunities clause. A provision in Article IV of the Constitution stating that the citizens of one state will not be treated unreasonably by officials of another state. That is, citizens of one state are guaranteed the 'privileges and immunities' of every other state, as though they were citizens of that state.

Progressive/regressive taxes. A judgement made by students of taxation about whether a particular tax hits the upper brackets more heavily (progressive) or the lower brackets more heavily (regressive).

Project grants. Grants awarded to states and localities for a specific programme or plan of action.

Proportional representation. The electoral system whereby legislative seats are assigned to party candidates in proportion to the percentage of the vote that the party receives in the election.

Public law. Cases in private law, civil law or criminal law in which one party to the dispute argues that a licence is unfair, a law in inequitable or unconstitutional, or an agency has acted unfairly, violated a procedure or gone beyond its jurisdiction.

Public policies. Actions taken by government officials in response to problems and issues raised through the political system.

Racial gerrymandering. Redrawing congressional boundary lines in such a way as to divide and disperse a minority population that otherwise would constitute a majority within the original district.

Realignment. A major shift by voters from one party to another that occurs when one party becomes dominant in the political system, controlling the presidency and Congress as well as many state legislatures.

Reapportionment. The redrawing of election districts and the redistribution of legislative representatives due to shifts in population after each ten-year census.

Red tape. The complex bureaucratic rules and procedures that make it difficult to get things done.

Referendum. The practice of referring a measure proposed or passed by a legislature to the vote of the electorate for approval or rejection.

Regulation. The rules that the federal bureaucracy develops to implement legislation.

Regulatory agencies. Departments, bureaux or independent agencies, whose primary mission is to eliminate or restrict certain behaviours defined as being undesirable in themselves or undesirable in their consequences.

Regulatory commissions. Federal agencies led by presidentially appointed boards that make and enforce policies affecting various sectors of the US economy. Formally independent of the White House to avoid presidential interference, these agencies employ large professional staffs to help them carry out their many functions.

Regulatory techniques. Techniques that government uses to influence the conduct of people.

Reinventing government. An approach to bureaucratic reform adopted by the Clinton administration that emphasized empowerment and decentralization in order to enhance the performance of government agencies and programmes.

Religiosity. The scope and intensity of religious beliefs among Americans. The United States remains distinguished by resistance to the secularizing trends that have affected European nations in the modern era. One important consequence has been to sustain issues such as abortion, school prayer, pornography and gay rights as salient issues in American politics.

Representative democracy. A system of government that provides the populace with the opportunity to make the government responsive to its views through the selection of representatives who, in turn, play a significant role in government decision-making.

Republic. A form of government in which decisions are made democratically by elected or appointed officials.

Republicanism. A doctrine of government in which decisions are made by elected or appointed officials who are answerable to the people; decisions are not made directly by the people themselves.

Reserved powers. Sometimes called 'residual powers', these are the powers that the Constitution provides for the states, although it does not list them specifically. As stated in the Tenth Amendment, these include all powers not expressly given to the national government or denied to the states.

Retrospective voting. The process by which individuals base their voting decisions on the candidates' or parties' past record of performance, not its promises for the future.

Revenue acts. Acts of Congress providing the means of raising the revenues needed by the government. The Constitution requires that all such bills originate in the House of Representatives.

Revenue sharing. A scheme to allocate national resources to the states according to a population and income formula.

Riders. Provisions that Congress knows the president opposes but that Congress attaches to bills the president otherwise desires.

Roe v. Wade **(1973)**. One of the most famous cases, in which the Court held unconstitutional all state laws making abortion a crime. The Court ruled that states could not interfere in a woman's 'right to privacy' and her right to choose to terminate a pregnancy.

Roll-call vote. A vote in which each legislator's yes or no vote is recorded as the clerk calls the names of the members alphabetically.

Rule of law. The principle that there is a standard of impartiality, fairness and equality against which all government actions can be evaluated. More narrowly, the concept that no individual stands above the law and that rulers, like those they rule, are answerable to the law. It was one of the most important legacies of the Framers of the Constitution.

Run-off primary. An election between the two top primary vote getters that determines the party's candidate in a general election. It is held in the southern states, where a majority of the vote is needed to win the primary. It is criticized as a device for excluding black candidates from winning nominations.

Select, or special, committees. Temporary committees established by the House of Representatives or the Senate to study particular problems.

Seniority system. A tradition through which the member of the majority party with the longest continuous service on a committee automatically becomes its chair. A neutral method of selection which privileges those members of Congress most successful at re-election (or those with the least competitive contests). For much of the twentieth century, this accorded white southern segregationists disproportionate influence in Congress. Although the power of committee chairs was undermined by the reforms of the 1970s, seniority remains the principle which – with few, but significant, exceptions – still determines who occupies the leadership of committees.

Separation of powers. The division of the powers to make, execute and judge the law among the three branches of American government: the Congress, the presidency and the courts. This principle was adopted by the Framers to prevent the tyranny and factionalism in the government. However, no actual separation exists, since this was deliberately compromised by the establishment of checks and balances. What does exist is a separation of personnel, such that no member of one branch of government can simultaneously hold office in another branch – another means by which the independence of the three branches is buttressed.

Simple majority. Fifty per cent plus one of those actually voting.

Single-issue group. An activist group that seeks to lobby Congress on a single or narrow range of issues.

Single-member district electoral system. The system of election used in America in all national and state elections and most local elections. Officials are elected from districts that are served by only one legislator, and a candidate must win a plurality – more votes than any other candidate, but not necessarily a majority – to win election.

Slander. Injury by spoken word which, like libel, is outside First Amendment protection and punishable by criminal law and civil prosecution.

Social Security. A contributory welfare programme into which working Americans contribute a percentage of their wages, and from which they receive cash benefits after retirement.

Soft money. Money contributed directly to political parties for voter registration and organization.

Solicitor General. The top government lawyer in all cases before the appellate courts where the government is a party.

Sound bite. A word or phrase that is meant to convey a larger meaning or image; used by political candidates to describe briefly their stand on issues.

Speaker of the House. The only House position created by the Constitution. The Speaker is chosen by a vote of the majority party and is the presiding officer of the House, the leader of its majority party, and second in line to succeed the president. Some Speakers have acted as effective prime ministers during periods of divided government. Most notably, Jim Wright and Newt Gingrich assumed aggressive, pro-active policy roles.

Split-ticket voting. The practice of casting ballots for the candidates of at least two different political parties in the same election. Voters who support only one party's candidates are said to vote a straight party ticket.

Spoils system. The system by which the party controlling the White House is able to hire its supporters as federal employees.

Standing. The right of an individual or organization to initiate a case.

Standing committees. Permanently established committees that consider proposed legislation in specified policy areas and decide whether to recommend passage by the larger body.

Stare decisis. Latin for 'let the decision stand'. A previous decision by a court applies as a precedent in similar cases until that decision is overruled.

State. A community that claims the monopoly of legitimate use of physical force within a given territory; the ultimate political authority or sovereign.

Statute. A law enacted by a state legislature or by Congress.

Straight party vote. The practice of casting ballots for candidates of only one party.

Sub-governments. Alliances among specific agencies, interest groups and relevant members of Congress. In their most extreme forms, called 'iron triangles', these alliances may effectively exercise authority in a narrow policy area, such as tobacco price supports. Other forms of sub-governments, called issue networks, involve a large number of participants with different degrees of interest.

Subsidies. Governmental grants of cash or other valuable commodities, such as land, to individuals or organizations. Subsidies can be used to promote activities desired by the government, to reward political support or to buy off political opposition.

Substantive due process. A judicial doctrine used by the appellate courts, primarily before 1937, to strike down economic legislation the courts felt was arbitrary or unreasonable.

Suffrage. The right to vote.

Supremacy clause. A provision in Article IV declaring the Constitution the supreme law of the land, taking precedence over state laws.

Supreme Court. The highest court in a particular state or in the United States. It serves primarily an appellate function.

Tariffs. Taxes on goods brought into the country from abroad that are often intended to protect growing domestic industries from foreign competition.

Three-fifths Compromise. Agreement reached at the Constitutional Convention of 1787 that stipulated that for purposes of the apportionment of congressional seats, every slave would be counted as three-fifths of a person.

Ticket-balancing. Strategy of party leaders to nominate candidates from each of the major ethnic, racial and religious affiliations.

Ticket-splitting. The practice of voting for candidates of different parties on the same ballot.

Treaties. Legally binding pacts by which two or more nations formalize an agreement reached through negotiation.

Trial court. The first court to hear a criminal or civil case.

Turnout. The percentage of eligible individuals who actually vote.

Unfunded mandates. Required actions imposed on lower-level governments by federal and state governments that are not accompanied by money to pay for the activities being mandated.

Unicameral. A legislature composed of only one house.

Unilateralism. The policy of taking action independently in foreign affairs, avoiding political or military alliances.

Unitary system. A form of government in which ultimate authority rests with the national government. Whatever powers state or local governments have under this type of government are derived from the central government.

United States v. Nixon **(1974)**. The Supreme Court declared unconstitutional President Nixon's refusal to surrender subpoenaed tapes as evidence in a criminal prosecution. It held that executive privilege did not extend to data in presidential files or tapes bearing on a criminal prosecution.

Veto. An important presidential check on the power of Congress. It is the president's power to reject legislation passed by Congress. The veto can be overruled, however, by a two-thirds vote of both chambers of Congress. In 1995, Congress passed a limited line-item veto that gave the president power to strike specific provisions of appropriation and tax bills but this was subsequently ruled unconstitutional by the Supreme Court.

Virginia Plan. A framework for the Constitution, introduced by Edmund Randolph, which called for representation in the national legislature based upon the population of each state.

Voting Rights Act (1965). The Voting Rights Act was passed in 1965 and represents one of the landmark legislative measures in civil rights history. By allowing black Americans in the South to register to vote with federal registrars rather than their local courthouses, the measure contributed to a steep increase in the black electorate and, largely as a consequence, a steady increase in the number of black elected officials at local, state and federal level. Amended by Congress in 1975 and 1982, judicial interpretations of its provisions against minority vote 'dilution' yielded several congressional districts whose boundaries were drawn in order to elect a minority representative to the House of Representatives.

Wall of separation. An interpretation of the establishment clause that requires a complete separation of government and religion.

War Powers Resolution (WPR) (1973). Passed by Congress over the veto of President Nixon, the WPR was a response to the conduct of the Vietnam War under Johnson and Nixon and the development of the 'imperial presidency'. Successive presidents ignored or contested the constitutionality of the WPR, and the Supreme Court has consistently refused to offer a clear ruling on the question. More important in limiting American military interventionism has been the legacy of Vietnam – the 'Vietnam syndrome' – that cautioned presidents against using ground troops in large numbers against a powerful or tenacious opponent.

Wards. City council districts that are, in the party organization, a level below that of the citywide level.

Whip system. Primarily a communications network in each house of Congress. Whips poll the rank-and-file membership to learn their voting intentions on specific legislative issues and to assist the majority and minority leaderships in various tasks.

White House Office. An agency within the Executive Office of the President that comprises the president's key advisors and assistants who help him with the daily requirements of the presidency.

Appendix II: The Constitution of the United States Of America

Preamble

We the People of the United States, in Order to form a more perfect Union, establish Justice, insure domestic Tranquillity, provide for the common defense, promote the general Welfare, and secure the Blessings of Liberty to ourselves and our Posterity, do ordain and establish this Constitution for the United States of America.

Article I

Section 1.

All legislative Powers herein granted shall be vested in a Congress of the United States, which shall consist of a Senate and House of Representatives.

Section 2.

The House of Representatives shall be composed of Members chosen every second Year by the People of the several States, and the Electors in each State shall have the Qualifications requisite for Electors of the most numerous Branch of the State Legislature.

No Person shall be a Representative who shall not have attained to the age of twenty five Years, and been seven Years a Citizen of the United States, and who shall not, when elected, be an Inhabitant of that State in which he shall be chosen.

Representatives and direct Taxes shall be apportioned among the several States which may be included within this Union, according to their respective Numbers, which shall be determined by adding to the whole Number of free Persons, including those bound to Service for a Term of Years, and excluding Indians not taxed, three fifths of all other

Persons. The actual Enumeration shall be made within three Years after the first Meeting of the Congress of the United States, and within every subsequent Term of ten Years, in such Manner as they shall by Law direct. The Number of Representatives shall not exceed one for every thirty Thousand, but each State shall have at Least one Representative; and until such enumeration shall be made, the State of New Hampshire shall be entitled to chuse three, Massachusetts eight, Rhode-Island and Providence Plantations one, Connecticut five, New-York six, New Jersey four, Pennsylvania eight, Delaware one, Maryland six, Virginia ten, North Carolina five, South Carolina five, and Georgia three.

When vacancies happen in the Representation from any State, the Executive Authority thereof shall issue Writs of Election to fill such Vacancies.

The House of Representatives shall chuse their Speaker and other Officers; and shall have the sole Power of Impeachment.

Section 3.
The Senate of the United States shall be composed of two Senators from each State, chosen by the Legislature thereof, for six Years; and each Senator shall have one Vote.

Immediately after they shall be assembled in Consequence of the first Election, they shall be divided as equally as may be into three Classes. The Seats of the Senators of the first Class shall be vacated at the Expiration of the second Year, of the second Class at the Expiration of the fourth Year, and of the third Class at the Expiration of the sixth Year, so that one third may be chosen every second Year; and if Vacancies happen by Resignation, or otherwise, during the Recess of the Legislature of any State, the Executive thereof may make temporary Appointments until the next Meeting of the Legislature, which shall then fill such Vacancies.

No Person shall be a Senator who shall not have attained to the Age of thirty Years, and been nine Years a Citizen of the United States, and who shall not, when elected, be an Inhabitant of that State for which he shall be chosen.

The Vice President of the United States shall be President of the Senate but shall have no Vote, unless they be equally divided.

The Senate shall chuse their other Officers, and also a President pro tempore, in the Absence of the Vice President, or when he shall exercise the Office of President of the United States.

The Senate shall have the sole Power to try all Impeachments. When sitting for that Purpose, they shall be on Oath or Affirmation. When the President of the United States is tried the Chief Justice shall preside: And no Person shall be convicted without the Concurrence of two thirds of the Members present.

Judgment in Cases of Impeachment shall not extend further than to removal from Office, and disqualification to hold and enjoy any Office of honor, Trust or Profit under the United States: but the Party convicted shall nevertheless be liable and subject to Indictment, Trial, Judgment and Punishment, according to Law.

Section 4.

The Times, Places and Manner of holding Elections for Senators and Representatives, shall be prescribed in each State by the Legislature thereof; but the Congress may at any time by Law make or alter such Regulations, except as to the Places of chusing Senators.

The Congress shall assemble at least once in every Year, and such Meeting shall be on the first Monday in December, unless they shall by Law appoint a different Day.

Section 5.

Each House shall be the Judge of the Elections, Returns and Qualifications of its own Members, and a Majority of each shall constitute a Quorum to do Business; but a smaller Number may adjourn from day to day, and may be authorized to compel the Attendance of absent Members, in such Manner, and under such Penalties as each House may provide.

Each House may determine the Rules of its Proceedings, punish its Members for disorderly Behavior, and, with the Concurrence of two thirds, expel a Member.

Each House shall keep a Journal of its Proceedings, and from time to time publish the same, excepting such Parts as may in their Judgment require Secrecy; and the Yeas and Nays of the Members of either House on any question shall, at the Desire of one fifth of those Present, be entered on the Journal.

Neither House, during the Session of Congress, shall, without the Consent of the other, adjourn for more than three days, nor to any other Place than that in which the two Houses shall be sitting.

Section 6.

The Senators and Representatives shall receive a Compensation for their Services, to be ascertained by Law, and paid out of the Treasury of the United States. They shall in all Cases, except Treason, Felony and Breach of the Peace, be privileged from Arrest during their Attendance at the Session of their respective Houses, and in going to and returning from the same; and for any Speech or Debate in either House, they shall not be questioned in any other Place.

No Senator or Representative shall, during the Time for which he was elected, be appointed to any civil Office under the Authority of the United States, which shall have been created, or the Emoluments whereof shall have been encreased during such time; and no Person holding any Office under the United States, shall be a Member of either House during his Continuance in Office.

Section 7.

All Bills for raising Revenue shall originate in the House of Representatives; but the Senate may propose or concur with amendments as on other Bills.

Every Bill which shall have passed the House of Representatives and the Senate, shall, before it become a law, be presented to the President of the United States: If he approve he shall sign it, but if not he shall return it, with his Objections to that House in which it shall have originated, who shall enter the Objections at large on their Journal, and proceed to reconsider it. If after such Reconsideration two thirds of that House shall agree to pass the Bill, it shall be sent, together with the Objections, to the other House, by which it shall likewise be reconsidered, and if approved by two thirds of that House, it shall become a Law. But in all such Cases the Votes of both Houses shall be determined by Yeas and Nays, and the Names of the Persons voting for and against the Bill shall be entered on the Journal of each House respectively. If any Bill shall not be returned by the President within ten Days (Sundays excepted) after it shall have been presented to him, the Same shall be a Law, in like Manner as if he had signed it, unless the Congress by their Adjournment prevent its Return, in which Case it shall not be a Law.

Every Order, Resolution, or Vote to which the Concurrence of the Senate and House of Representatives may be necessary (except on a question of Adjournment) shall be presented to the President of the United States; and before the Same shall take Effect, shall be approved by him, or being disapproved by him, shall be repassed by two thirds of the Senate and House of Representatives, according to the Rules and Limitations prescribed in the Case of a Bill.

Section 8.

The Congress shall have Power To lay and collect Taxes, Duties, Imposts and Excises, to pay the Debts and provide for the common Defense and general Welfare of the United States; but all Duties, Imposts and Excises shall be uniform throughout the United States;

To borrow Money on the credit of the United States;

To regulate Commerce with foreign Nations, and among the several States, and with the Indian Tribes;

To establish an uniform Rule of Naturalization, and uniform Laws on the subject of Bankruptcies throughout the United States;

To coin Money, regulate the Value thereof, and of foreign Coin, and fix the Standard of Weights and Measures;

To provide for the Punishment of counterfeiting the Securities and current Coin of the United States;

To establish Post Offices and post Roads;

To promote the Progress of Science and useful Arts, by securing for limited Times to Authors and Inventors the exclusive Right to their respective Writings and Discoveries;

To constitute Tribunals inferior to the Supreme Court;

To define and punish Piracies and Felonies committed on the high Seas, and Offences against the Law of Nations;

To declare War, grant Letters of Marque and Reprisal, and make Rules concerning Captures on Land and Water;

To raise and support Armies, but no Appropriation of Money to that Use shall be for a longer Term than two Years;

To provide and maintain a Navy;

To make Rules for the Government and Regulation of the land and naval Forces;

To provide for calling forth the Militia to execute the Laws of the Union, suppress Insurrections and repeal Invasions;

To provide for organizing, arming, and disciplining, the Militia, and for governing such Part of them as may be employed in the Service of the United States, reserving to the States respectively, the Appointment of the Officers, and the Authority of training the Militia according to the discipline prescribed by Congress;

To exercise exclusive Legislation in all Cases whatsoever, over such District (not exceeding ten Miles square) as may, by Cession of Particular States, and the Acceptance of Congress, become the Seat of the Government of the United States, and to exercise like Authority over all Places purchased by the Consent of the Legislature of the State in which the Same shall be, for the Erection of Forts, Magazines, Arsenals, dock-Yards and other needful Buildings; – And

To make all Laws which shall be necessary and proper for carrying into Execution the foregoing Powers and all other Powers vested by this Constitution in the Government of the United States, or in any Department or Officer thereof.

Section 9.
The Migration or Importation of such Persons as any of the States now existing shall think proper to admit, shall not be prohibited by the Congress prior to the Year one thousand eight hundred and eight, but a Tax or duty may be imposed on such Importation, not exceeding ten dollars for each Person.

The Privilege of the Writ of Habeas Corpus shall not be suspended, unless when in Cases of Rebellion or Invasion the public Safety may require it.

No Bill of Attainder or ex post facto Law shall be passed.

No Capitation, or other direct, Tax shall be laid, unless in Proportion to the Census of Enumeration herein before directed to be taken.

No Tax or Duty shall be laid on Articles exported from any State.

No Preference shall be given by any Regulation of Commerce or Revenue to the Ports of one State over those of another: nor shall Vessels bound to, or from, one State, be obliged to enter, clear or pay Duties in another.

No Money shall be drawn from the Treasury, but in Consequence of Appropriations made by Law; and a regular Statement and Account of the Receipts and Expenditures of all public Money shall be published from time to time.

No Title of Nobility shall be granted by the United States: And no Person holding any Office of Profit or Trust under them, shall, without the Consent of the Congress, accept of any present, Emolument, Office, or Title, of any kind whatever, from any King, Prince or foreign State.

Section 10.

No State shall enter into any Treaty, Alliance, or Confederation; grant Letters of Marque and Reprisal; coin Money; emit Bills of Credit; make any Thing but gold and silver Coin a Tender in Payment of Debts; pass any Bill of Attainder, ex post facto Law, or Law impairing the Obligation of Contracts, or grant any Title of Nobility.

No State shall, without the Consent of the Congress, lay any Imposts or Duties on Imports or Exports, except what may be absolutely necessary for executing its inspection Laws: and the net Produce of all Duties and Imposts, laid by any State on Imports or Exports, shall be for the Use of the Treasury of the United States; and all such Laws shall be subject to the Revision and Controul of the Congress.

No State shall, without the Consent of Congress, lay any Duty of Tonnage, keep Troops, or Ships of War in time of Peace, enter into any Agreement or Compact with another State, or with a foreign Power, or engage in War, unless actually invaded, or in such imminent Danger as will not admit of delay.

Article II

Section 1.

The executive Power shall be vested in a President of the United States of America. He shall hold his Office during the Term of four Years, and, together with the Vice President, chosen for the same Term, be elected, as follows:

Each State shall appoint, in such Manner as the Legislature thereof may direct, a Number of Electors, equal to the whole Number of Senators and Representatives to which the State may be entitled in the Congress: but no Senator or Representative, or Person holding an Office of Trust or Profit under the United States, shall be appointed an Elector.

The Electors shall meet in their respective States, and vote by Ballot for two Persons, of whom one at least shall not be an Inhabitant of the same State with themselves. And they shall make a List of all the Persons voted for, and of the Number of Votes for each; which List they shall sign and certify, and transmit sealed to the Seat of the Government of the United States, directed to the President of the Senate. The President of the Senate shall, in the Presence of the Senate and House of Representatives, open all the Certificates, and the Votes shall then be counted. The Person having the greatest Number of Votes shall be the President, if such Number be a Majority of the whole Number of Electors appointed; and if there be more than one who have such Majority, and have an equal Number of Votes, then the House of Representatives shall immediately chuse by Ballot one of them for President; and if no Person have a Majority, then from the five highest on the List the said House shall in like Manner chuse the President. But in chusing the President, the Votes shall be taken by States, the Representatives from each State having one Vote; a quorum for this Purpose shall consist of a Member or Members from two thirds of the States, and a Majority of all the States shall be necessary to a Choice. In every Case, after the Choice of the President, the Person having the greatest Number of Votes of the Electors shall be the Vice President. But if there should remain two or more who have equal Votes, the Senate shall chuse from them by Ballot the Vice President.

The Congress may determine the Time of chusing the Electors, and the Day on which they shall give their Votes; which Day shall be the same throughout the United States.

No Person except a natural born Citizen, or a Citizen of the United States, at the time of the Adoption of this Constitution, shall be eligible to the Office of President; neither shall any person be eligible to that Office who shall not have attained to the Age of thirty five Years, and been fourteen Years a Resident within the United States.

In Case of the Removal of the President from Office, or of his Death, Resignation, or Inability to discharge the Powers and Duties of the said Office, the Same shall devolve on the Vice President, and the Congress may by Law provide for the Case of Removal, Death, Resignation or Inability, both of the President and Vice President, declaring what Officer shall then act as President, and such Officer shall act accordingly, until the Disability be removed, or a President shall be elected.

The President shall, at stated Times, receive for his Services, a Compensation, which shall neither be increased nor diminished during the Period for which he shall have been elected, and he shall not receive within that Period any other Emolument from the United States, or any of them.

Before he enter on the Execution of his Office, he shall take the following Oath or Affirmation: – 'I do solemnly swear (or affirm) that I will faithfully execute the Office of President of the United States, and will to the best of my Ability, preserve, protect and defend the Constitution of the United States.'

Section 2.
The President shall be Commander in Chief of the Army and Navy of the United States, and of the Militia of the several States, when called into the actual Service of the United States; he may require the Opinion, in writing, of the principal Officer in each of the executive Departments, upon any Subject relating to the Duties of their respective Offices, and he shall have Power to Grant Reprieves and Pardons for Offences against the United States, except in Cases of Impeachment.

He shall have Power, by and with the Advice and Consent of the Senate, to make Treaties, provided two thirds of the Senators present concur; and he shall nominate, and by and with the Advice and Consent of the Senate, shall appoint Ambassadors, other public Ministers and Consuls, Judges of the supreme Court, and all other Officers of the United States, whose Appointments are not herein otherwise provided for, and which shall be established by Law: but the Congress may by Law vest the Appointment of such inferior Officers, as they think proper, in the President alone, in the Courts of Law, or in the Heads of Departments.

The President shall have Power to fill up all Vacancies that may happen during the Recess of the Senate, by granting Commissions which shall expire at the End of their next Session.

Section 3.

He shall from time to time give to the Congress Information on the State of the Union, and recommend to their Consideration such Measures as he shall judge necessary and expedient; he may, on extraordinary Occasions, convene both Houses, or either of them, and in Case of Disagreement between them, with Respect to the Time of Adjournment, he may adjourn them to such Time as he shall think proper; he shall receive Ambassadors and other public Ministers; he shall take Care that the Laws be faithfully executed, and shall Commission all the Officers of the United States.

Section 4.

The President, Vice President and all Civil Officers of the United States, shall be removed from Office on Impeachment for and Conviction of, Treason, Bribery, or other high Crimes and Misdemeanors.

Article III

Section 1.

The judicial Power of the United States, shall be vested in one supreme Court, and in such inferior Courts as the Congress may from time to time ordain and establish. The Judges, both of the supreme and inferior Courts, shall hold their Offices during good Behaviour, and shall, at stated Times, receive for their Services, a Compensation, which shall not be diminished during their Continuance in Office.

Section 2.

The judicial Power shall extend to all Cases, in Law and Equity, arising under this Constitution, the Laws of the United States, and Treaties made, or which shall be made, under their Authority; – to all Cases affecting Ambassadors, other public Ministers and Consuls; – to all Cases of admiralty and maritime Jurisdiction; – to Controversies to which the United States shall be a Party; – to Controversies between two or more States; – between a State and Citizens of another State; – between Citizens of different States; – between Citizens of the same State claiming Lands under Grants of different States, and between a State, or the Citizens thereof, and foreign States, Citizens or Subjects.

In all Cases affecting Ambassadors, other public Ministers and Consuls, and those in which a State shall be Party, the Supreme Court shall have original Jurisdiction. In all the other Cases before mentioned, the supreme Court shall have appellate Jurisdiction, both as to Law and Fact, with such Exceptions, and under such Regulations as the Congress shall make.

The Trial of all Crimes, except in Cases of Impeachment, shall be by Jury; and such Trial shall be held in the State where the said Crimes shall have been committed; but when not committed within any State, the Trial shall be at such Place or Places as the Congress may by Law have directed.

Section 3.

Treason against the United States, shall consist only in levying War against them, or in adhering to their Enemies, giving them Aid and Comfort. No Person shall be convicted of Treason unless on the Testimony of two Witnesses to the same overt Act, or on Confession in open Court.

The Congress shall have Power to declare the Punishment of Treason, but no Attainder of Treason shall work Corruption of Blood, or Forfeiture except during the Life of the Person attainted.

Article IV

Section 1.

Full Faith and Credit shall be given in each State to the public Acts, Records, and judicial Proceedings of every other State. And the Congress may by general Laws prescribe the Manner in which such Acts, Records and Proceedings shall be proved, and the Effect thereof.

Section 2.

The Citizens of each State shall be entitled to all Privileges and Immunities of Citizens in the several States.

A Person charged in any State with Treason, Felony, or other Crime, who shall flee from Justice, and be found in another State, shall on Demand of the executive Authority of the State from which he fled, be delivered up, to be removed to the State having Jurisdiction of the Crime.

No Person held to Service or Labor in one State, under the Laws thereof, escaping into another, shall, in Consequence of any Law or Regulation therein, be discharged from such Service or Labor, but shall be delivered up on Claim of the Party to whom such Service or Labor may be due.

Section 3.

New States may be admitted by the Congress into this Union; but no new State shall be formed or erected within the Jurisdiction of any other State; nor any State be formed by the Junction of two or more States, or Parts of States, without the Consent of the Legislatures of the States concerned as well as of the Congress.

The Congress shall have Power to dispose of and make all needful Rules and Regulations respecting the Territory or other Property belonging to the United States; and nothing in this Constitution shall be so construed as to Prejudice any Claims of the United States, or of any particular State.

Section 4.

The United States shall guarantee to every State in this Union a Republican Form of Government, and shall protect each of them against Invasion; and on Application of the Legislature, or of the Executive (when the Legislature cannot be convened) against domestic Violence.

Article V

The Congress, whenever two thirds of both Houses shall deem it necessary, shall propose Amendments to this Constitution, or, on the Application of the Legislatures of two thirds of the several States, shall call a Convention for proposing Amendments, which, in either Case, shall be valid to all Intents and Purposes, as Part of this Constitution, when ratified by the Legislatures of three fourths of the several States, or by Conventions in three fourths thereof, as the one or the other Mode of Ratification may be proposed by the Congress; Provided that no Amendment which may be made prior to the Year One thousand eight hundred and eight shall in any Manner affect the first and fourth Clauses in the Ninth Section of the first Article; and that no State, without its Consent, shall be deprived of its equal Suffrage in the Senate.

Article VI

All Debts contracted and Engagements entered into, before the Adoption of this Constitution, shall be as valid against the United States under this Constitution, as under the Confederation.

This Constitution, and the Laws of the United States which shall be made in Pursuance thereof; and all Treaties made, or which shall be made, under the Authority of the United States, shall be the supreme Law of the Land; and the Judges in every State shall be bound thereby, any Thing in the Constitution or Laws of any state to the Contrary notwithstanding.

The Senators and Representatives before mentioned, and the Members of the several State Legislatures, and all executive and judicial Officers, both of the United States and of the several States, shall be bound by Oath or Affirmation, to support this Constitution; but no religious Test shall ever be required as a Qualification to any Office or public Trust under the United States.

Article VII

The Ratification of the Conventions of nine States, shall be sufficient for the Establishment of this Constitution between the States so ratifying the same.

Amendments to the Constitution of the United States of America

Articles in addition to, and amendment of, the Constitution of the United States of America, proposed by Congress, and ratified by the several states, pursuant to the Fifth Article of the original Constitution.

Amendment I

Congress shall make no law respecting an establishment of religion, or prohibiting the free exercise thereof; or abridging the freedom of speech, or of the press; or the right of the people peaceably to assemble, and to petition the government for a redress of grievances.

Amendment II

A well regulated Militia, being necessary to the security of a free State, the right of the people to keep and bear Arms, shall not be infringed.

Amendment III

No Soldier shall, in time of peace be quartered in any house, without the consent of the Owner, nor in time of war, but in a manner to be prescribed by law.

Amendment IV

The right of the people to be secure in their persons, houses, papers, and effects, against unreasonable searches and seizures, shall not be violated, and no Warrants shall issue, but upon probable cause, supported by Oath or affirmation, and particularly describing the place to be searched, and the persons or things to be seized.

Amendment V

No person shall be held to answer for a capital, or otherwise infamous crime, unless on a presentment or indictment of a Grand Jury, except in cases arising in the land or naval forces, or in the Militia, when in actual service in time of War or public danger; nor shall any person be subject for the same offence to be twice put in jeopardy of life or limb; nor shall be compelled in any criminal case to be a witness against himself, nor be deprived of life, liberty, or property, without due process of law; nor shall private property be taken for public use, without just compensation.

Amendment VI

In all criminal prosecutions, the accused shall enjoy the right to a speedy and public trial, by an impartial jury of the State and district wherein the crime shall have been committed, which district shall have been previously ascertained by law, and to be informed of the nature and cause of the accusation; to be confronted with the witnesses against him; to have compulsory process for obtaining witnesses in his favor, and to have the Assistance of Counsel for his defense.

Amendment VII

In Suits at common law, where the value in controversy shall exceed twenty dollars, the right of trial by jury shall be preserved, and no fact tried by a jury, shall be otherwise re-examined in any Court of the United States, than according to the rules of the common law.

Amendment VIII

Excessive bail shall not be required, nor excessive fines imposed, nor cruel and unusual punishments inflicted.

Amendment IX

The enumeration in the Constitution, of certain rights, shall not be construed to deny or disparage others retained by the people.

Amendment X

The powers not delegated to the United States by the Constitution, nor prohibited by it to the States, are reserved to the States respectively, or to the people.

Amendment XI

The Judicial power of the United States shall not be construed to extend to any suit in law or equity, commenced or prosecuted against one of the United States by Citizens of another State, or by Citizens or Subjects of any Foreign State.

Amendment XII

The Electors shall meet in their respective states and vote by ballot for President and Vice-President, one of whom, at least, shall not be an inhabitant of the same state with themselves; they shall name in their ballots the person voted for as President, and in distinct ballots the person voted for as Vice-President, and they shall make distinct lists of all persons voted for as President, and of all persons voted for as Vice-President, and of the number of votes for each, which lists they shall sign and certify, and transmit sealed to the seat of the government of the United States, directed to the President of the Senate; – The President of the Senate shall, in the presence of the Senate and House of Representatives, open all the certificates and the votes shall then be counted; – The person having the greatest Number of votes for President, shall be the President, if such number be a majority of the whole number of Electors appointed; and if no person have such majority, then from the persons having the highest numbers not exceeding three on the list of those voted for as President, the House of Representatives shall choose immediately, by ballot, the President. But in choosing the President, the votes shall be taken by states, the representation from each state having one vote; a quorum for this purpose shall consist of a member or members from two-thirds of the states, and a majority of all the states shall be necessary to a choice. And if the House of Representatives shall not choose a President whenever the right of choice shall devolve upon them, before the fourth day of March next following, then the Vice-President shall act as President, as in the case of the death or other constitutional disability of the President – The person having the greatest number of votes as Vice-President, shall be the Vice-President, if such number be a majority of the whole number of Electors appointed, and if no person have a majority, then from the two highest numbers on the list, the Senate shall choose the Vice-President; a quorum for the purpose shall consist of two-thirds of the whole number of Senators, and a majority of the whole number shall be necessary to a choice. But no person constitutionally ineligible to the office of President shall be eligible to that of Vice-President of the United States.

Amendment XIII

Section 1. Neither slavery nor involuntary servitude, except as a punishment for crime whereof the party shall have been duly convicted, shall exist within the United States, or any place subject to their jurisdiction.

Section 2. Congress shall have power to enforce this article by appropriate legislation.

Amendment XIV

Section 1. All persons born or naturalized in the United States and subject to the jurisdiction thereof, are citizens of the United States and of the State wherein they reside. No State shall make or enforce any law which shall abridge the privileges or immunities of citizens of the United States; nor shall any State deprive any person of life, liberty, or property, without due process of law; nor deny to any person within its jurisdiction the equal protection of the laws.

Section 2. Representatives shall be apportioned among the several States according to their respective numbers, counting the whole number of persons in each State, excluding Indians not taxed. But when the right to vote at any election for the choice of electors for President and Vice President of the United States, Representatives in Congress, the Executive and Judicial officers of a State, or the members of the Legislature thereof, is denied to any of the male inhabitants of such State, being twenty-one years of age, and citizens of the United States, or in any way abridged, except for participation in rebellion, or other crime, the basis of representation therein shall be reduced in the proportion which the number of such male citizens shall bear to the whole number of male citizens twenty-one years of age in such State.

Section 3. No person shall be a Senator or Representative in Congress, or elector of President and Vice-President, or hold any office, civil or military, under the United States, or under any State, who, having previously taken an oath, as a member of Congress, or as an officer of the United States, or as a member of any State legislature, or as an executive or judicial officer of any State, to support the Constitution of the United States, shall have engaged in insurrection or rebellion against the same, or given aid or comfort to the enemies thereof. But Congress may by a vote of two-thirds of each House, remove such disability.

Section 4. The validity of the public debt of the United States, authorized by law, including debts incurred for payment of pensions and bounties for services in suppressing insurrection or rebellion, shall not be questioned. But neither the United States nor any State shall assume or pay any debt or obligation incurred in aid of insurrection or rebellion against the United States, or any claim for the loss or emancipation of any slave; but all such debts, obligations and claims shall be held illegal and void.

Section 5. The Congress shall have power to enforce, by appropriate legislation, the provisions of this article.

Amendment XV

Section 1. The right of citizens of the United States to vote shall not be denied or abridged by the United States or by any State on account of race, color, or previous condition of servitude.

Section 2. The Congress shall have power to enforce this article by appropriate legislation.

Amendment XVI

The Congress shall have power to lay and collect taxes on incomes, from whatever source derived, without apportionment among the several States, and without regard to any census or enumeration.

Amendment XVII

The Senate of the United States shall be composed of two Senators from each State, elected by the people thereof, for six years; and each Senator shall have one vote. The electors in each State shall have the qualifications requisite for electors of the most numerous branch of the State legislatures.

When vacancies happen in the representation of any State in the Senate, the executive authority of such State shall issue writs of election to fill such vacancies: Provided, That the legislature of any State may empower the executive thereof to make temporary appointments until the people fill the vacancies by election as the legislature may direct.

This amendment shall not be so construed as to affect the election or term of any Senator chosen before it becomes valid as part of the Constitution.

Amendment XVIII

Section 1. After one year from the ratification of this article the manufacture, sale, or transportation of intoxicating liquors within, the importation thereof into, or the exportation thereof from the United States and all territory subject to the jurisdiction thereof for beverage purposes is hereby prohibited.

Section 2. The Congress and the several States shall have concurrent power to enforce this article by appropriate legislation.

Section 3. This article shall be inoperative unless it shall have been ratified as an amendment to the Constitution by the legislatures of the several States, as provided in the Constitution, within seven years from the date of the submission hereof to the States by the Congress.

Amendment XIX

The right of citizens of the United States to vote shall not be denied or abridged by the United States or by any State on account of sex. Congress shall have power to enforce this article by appropriate legislation.

Amendment XX

Section 1. The terms of the President and Vice President shall end at noon on the 20th day of January, and the terms of Senators and Representatives at noon on the 3d day of January, of the years in which such terms would have ended if this article had not been ratified; and the terms of their successors shall then begin.

Section 2. The Congress shall assemble at least once in every year, and such meeting shall begin at noon on the 3d day of January, unless they shall by law appoint a different day.

Section 3. If, at the time fixed for the beginning of the term of the President, the President elect shall have died, the Vice President elect shall become President. If a President shall not have been chosen before the time fixed for the beginning of his term, or if the President elect shall have failed to qualify, then the Vice President elect shall act as President until a President shall have qualified; and the Congress may by law provide for the case wherein neither a President elect nor a Vice President elect shall have qualified, declaring who shall then act as President, or the manner in which one who is to act shall be selected, and such person shall act accordingly until a President or Vice President shall have qualified.

Section 4. The Congress may by law provide for the case of the death of any of the persons from whom the House of Representatives may choose a President whenever the right of choice shall have devolved upon them, and for the case of the death of any of the persons from whom the Senate may choose a Vice President whenever the right of choice shall have devolved upon them.

Section 5. Sections 1 and 2 shall take effect on the 15th day of October following the ratification of this article.

Section 6. This article shall be inoperative unless it shall have been ratified as an amendment to the Constitution by the legislatures of three-fourths of the several States within seven years from the date of its submission.

Amendment XXI

Section 1. The eighteenth article of amendment to the Constitution of the United States is hereby repealed.

Section 2. The transportation or importation into any State, Territory, or possession of the United States for delivery or use therein of intoxicating liquors, in violation of the laws thereof, is hereby prohibited.

Section 3. This article shall be inoperative unless it shall have been ratified as an amendment to the Constitution by conventions in the several States, as provided in the Constitution, within seven years from the date of the submission hereof to the States by the Congress.

Amendment XXII

Section 1. No person shall be elected to the office of the President more than twice, and no person who has held the office of President, or acted as President, for more than two years of a term to which some other person was elected President shall be elected to the office of the President more than once. But this Article shall not apply to any person holding the office of President, when this Article was proposed by the Congress, and shall not prevent any person who may be holding the office of President, or acting as President, during the term within which this Article becomes operative from holding the office of President or acting as President during the remainder of such term.

Section 2. This article shall be inoperative unless it shall have been ratified as an amendment to the Constitution by the legislatures of three-fourths of the several States within seven years from the date of its submission to the States by the Congress.

Amendment XXIII

Section 1. The District constituting the seat of Government of the United States shall appoint in such manner as the Congress may direct: A number of electors of President and Vice President equal to the whole number of Senators and Representatives in Congress to which the District would be entitled if it were a State, but in no event more than the least populous State; they shall be in addition to those appointed by the States, but they shall be considered, for the purposes of the election of President and Vice President, to be electors appointed by a State; and they shall meet in the District and perform such duties as provided by the twelfth article of amendment.

Section 2. The Congress shall have power to enforce this article by appropriate legislation.

Amendment XXIV

Section 1. The right of citizens of the United States to vote in any primary or other election for President or Vice President, for electors for President or Vice President, or for Senator or Representative in Congress, shall not be denied or abridged by the United States or any State by reason of failure to pay any poll tax or other tax.

Section 2. The Congress shall have power to enforce this article by appropriate legislation.

Amendment XXV

Section 1. In case of the removal of the President from office or of his death or resignation, the Vice President shall become President.

Section 2. Whenever there is a vacancy in the office of the Vice President, the President shall nominate a Vice President who shall take office upon confirmation by a majority vote of both Houses of Congress.

Section 3. Whenever the President transmits to the President pro tempore of the Senate and the Speaker of the House of Representatives his written declaration that he is unable to discharge the powers and duties of his office, and until he transmits to them a written declaration to the contrary, such powers and duties shall be discharged by the Vice President as Acting President.

Section 4. Whenever the Vice President and a majority of either the principal officers of the executive departments or of such other body as Congress may by law provide, transmit to the President pro tempore of the Senate and the Speaker of the House of Representatives their written declaration that the President is unable to discharge the powers and duties of his office, the Vice President shall immediately assume the powers and duties of the office as Acting President.

Thereafter, when the President transmits to the President pro tempore of the Senate and the Speaker of the House of Representatives his written declaration that no inability exists, he shall resume the powers and duties of his office unless the Vice President and a majority of either the principal officers of the executive department or of such other body as Congress may by law provide, transmit within four days to the President pro tempore of the Senate and the Speaker of the House of Representatives their written declaration that the President is unable to discharge the powers and duties of his office. Thereupon Congress shall decide the issue, assembling within forty-eight hours for that purpose if not in session. If the Congress, within twenty-one days after receipt of the latter written declaration, or, if Congress is not in session, within twenty-one days after Congress is required to assemble, determines by two-thirds vote of both Houses that the President is unable to discharge the powers and duties of his office, the Vice President shall continue to discharge the same as Acting President; otherwise, the President shall resume the powers and duties of his office.

Amendment XXVI

Section 1. The right of citizens of the United States, who are eighteen years of age or older, to vote shall not be denied or abridged by the United States or by any State on account of age.

Section 2. The Congress shall have power to enforce this article by appropriate legislation.

Amendment XXVII

No law varying the compensation for the services of the Senators and Representatives shall take effect, until an election of Representatives shall have intervened.

Bibliography

Aberbach, J. (1990) *Keeping a Watchful Eye*. Washington, DC: Brookings Institution.

Aldrich, J. (1995) *Why Parties? The Origin and Transformation of Party Politics in America*. Chicago, IL: The University of Chicago Press.

Anton, G. and J. Thomas (1999) 'The Politics of Military Base Closures', in E. Wittkopf and J. McCormick (eds), *The Domestic Sources of American Foreign Policy* (3rd edition). Lanham, MD: Rowman and Littlefield Publishers, pp. 61–70.

Bedau, H.A. (ed.) (1997) *The Death Penalty in America*. New York: Oxford University Press.

Berry, J. (1989) *The Interest Group Society* (2nd edition). Glenview, IL: Scott, Foresman/Little, Brown.

Blasi, V. (1983) 'The Rootless Activism of the Burger Court', in V. Blasi (ed.), *The Burger Court: The Counter-Revolution That Wasn't*. New Haven, CT: Yale University Press, pp. 198–217.

Bodenhamer, D. and J. Ely, Jr. (eds) (1993) *The Bill of Rights in Modern America after 200 Years*. Bloomington: Indiana University Press.

Bork, R. (1990) *The Tempting of America: The Political Seduction of the Law*. New York: The Free Press.

Bork, R. (1996) *Slouching Towards Gomorrah: Modern Liberalism and American Decline*. New York: Harper Collins.

Bowles, N. (1998) *Government and Politics of the United States* (2nd edition). Basingstoke: Macmillan.

Brennan, W. (1985) 'The Constitution of Un-United States: Contemporary Ratification', in *Davis Law Review, Volume 2*. University of California.

Brinkley, A., N.W. Polsby and K.M. Sullivan (1997) *New Federalist Papers: Essays in Defense of the Constitution*. New York: W.W. Norton and Company.

Bruce, S. (2000). 'Zealot Politics and Democracy: the Case of the Christian Right', *Political Studies*, 48 (2): 263–82.

Burnham, W.D. (1970) *Critical Elections and the Mainsprings of American Politics*. New York: W.W. Norton and Company.

Campbell, C. and B. Rockman (eds) (2000) *The Clinton Legacy*. New York: Seven Bridges Press.

Ceaser, J. and A. Busch (2001) *The Perfect Tie: The True Story of then 2000 Presidential Election*. Lanham, MD: Rowman and Littlefield Publishers.

Cigler, A. and B. Loomis (eds) (1995) *Interest Group Politics*. Washington, DC: CQ Press.

Cullen, J. (1997) *Born in the USA: Bruce Springsteen and the American Tradition*. New York: Harper Collins.

Dahl, R. (1961) *Who Governs?* New Haven, CT: Yale University Press.

Davidson, R. (ed.) (1992) *The Postreform Congress*. New York: St Martin's Press.

Dumbrell, J. (1990) *The Making of US Foreign Policy*. Manchester: Manchester University Press.

Elazar, D. (1984) *American Federalism: A View from the States*. New York: Harper and Row.

Esler, G. (1997) *The United States of Anger*. London: Michael Joseph.

Fenno, R. (1978) *Home Style: House Members in their Districts*. Boston: Little, Brown.

Fiorina, M. (1992) *Divided Government*. Boston, MA: Allyn and Bacon.

Foley, M. (1991). *American Political Ideas*. Manchester: Manchester University Press.

Foner, E. (1998) *The Story of American Freedom*. New York: W.W. Norton and Company.

Freedland, J. (1998) *Bring Home the Revolution: The Case for a British Republic*. London: Fourth Estate Limited.

Frymer, P. (1999) *Uneasy Alliances: Race and Party Competition in America*. Princeton, NJ: Princeton University Press.

Gaddis, J.L. (1997) *We Now Know: Rethinking Cold War History*. Oxford: Oxford University Press.

Glendon, M. (1991). *Rights Talk: The Impoverishment of Political Discourse*. New York: The Free Press.

Glennon, M. (1991) 'The Gulf War and the Constitution', *Foreign Affairs*, 70 (2): 84–101.

Golay, M. and C. Rollyson (1996) *Where America Stands 1996*. New York: John Wiley and Sons.

Goldman, E. and L. Berman (2000) 'Engaging the World: First Impressions of the Clinton Foreign Policy Legacy', in C. Campbell and B. Rockman (eds), *The Clinton Legacy*. New York: Seven Bridges Press, pp. 226–53.

Goodsell, C. (1994) *The Case for Bureaucracy: A Public Administration Polemic*. Chatham, NJ: Chatham House.

Gormley, W. (1989) *Taming the Bureaucracy: Muscles, Prayers and Other Strategies*. Princeton, NJ: Princeton University Press.

Gosling, J. (2000) *Politics and the American Economy*. New York: Longman.

Gould, L. (2000) 'Reconsidering LBJ', *The Wilson Quarterly*, 25 (2): 80–3.

Greenstein, F. (2000) *The Presidential Difference: Leadership Style from FDR to Clinton*. New York: Martin Kessler Books.

Hall, K. (ed.) (1992) *The Oxford Companion to the United States Supreme Court*. New York: Oxford University Press.

Harris, F. (1995) *In Defense of Congress*. New York: St Martin's Press.

Herrnson, P. (1995) *Congressional Elections: Campaigning at Home and in Washington*. Washington, DC: CQ Press.

Hodder-Williams, R. (1992) 'Six Definitions of Political and the US Supreme Court', *British Journal of Political Science*, 22 (1): 1–20.

Huntington, S. (1981) *American Politics: the Promise of Disharmony*. Cambridge, MA: Harvard University Press.

Huntington, S. (1996) *The Clash of Civilizations and the Remaking of World Order*. New York: Simon and Schuster.

International Institute for Strategic Studies (1988) *The Military Balance 1988–89*. New York: Oxford University Press.

International Institute for Strategic Studies (1998) *The Military Balance 1998–99*. New York: Oxford University Press.

Jacobson, G. (1983) *The Politics of Congressional Elections*. Boston, MA: Little, Brown.

Jones, C.O. (1994) *The Presidency in a Separated System*. Washington, DC: Brookings Institution.

Jones, C.O. (1995) *Separate but Equal Branches: Congress and the Presidency*. Chatham, NJ: Chatham House Publishers.

Kegley, C. and E. Wittkopf (1996) *American Foreign Policy: Pattern and Process* (5th edition). New York: St Martin's Press.

King, A. (1997) *Running Scared: Why America's Politicians Campaign Too Much and Govern Too Little*. New York: Martin Kessler Books.

King, A. (2000) 'Distrust of Government: Explaining American Exceptionalism', in S.J. Pharr and R.D. Putnam (eds), *Disaffected Democracies: What's Troubling the Trilateral Countries?* Princeton, NJ: Princeton University Press, pp. 74–98.

King, D. (2000) *Making Americans: Immigration, Race, and the Origins of the Diverse Democracy*. Cambridge, MA: Harvard University Press.

Koenig, L. (1996) *The Chief Executive*. Fort Worth, TX: Harcourt Brace.

Kramnick, I. (1987) 'Editor's Introduction', in J. Madison, A. Hamilton and J. Jay, *The Federalist Papers*. New York: Penguin Books.

Ladd, E.C. (1997) 'The 1996 Vote: The "No Majority" Realignment Continues', *Political Science Quarterly*, 112: 1–28.

Lamis, A. (1990) *The Two-Party South*. New York: Oxford University Press.

Lazare, D. (1996) *The Frozen Republic: How the Constitution is Paralyzing Democracy*. New York: Harcourt Brace.

Lazarus, E. (1999) *Closed Chambers: The Rise, Fall, and Future of the Modern Supreme Court*. New York: Penguin Books.

Lee, F. and B. Oppenheimer (1999) *Sizing Up the Senate: The Unequal Consequences of Equal Representation*. Chicago, IL: The University of Chicago Press.

Lind, M. (1999) *Vietnam, the Necessary War: A Reinterpretation of America's Most Disastrous Military Conflict*. New York: The Free Press.

Lipset, S.M. (1990) *Continental Divide: the Values and Institutions of the United States and Canada*. New York: Routledge.

Lipset, S.M. (1996) *American Exceptionalism: A Double-Edged Sword*. New York: W.W. Norton.

Lowi, T. (1979) *The End of Liberalism: The Second Republic of the United States* (2nd edition). New York: W.W. Norton.

Lowi, T. (1995) *The End of the Republican Era*. Norman, OK: University of Oklahoma Press.

Maltese, J. (1998) *The Selling of Supreme Court Justices*.

Baltimore, MD: The Johns Hopkins University Press.

May, E. and P. Zelikow (eds) (1997) *The Kennedy Tapes: Inside the White House during the Cuban Missile Crisis.* Cambridge, MA: Harvard University Press.

Mayer, W. (ed.) (1996) *In Pursuit of the White House: How We Choose Our Presidential Nominees.* Chatham, NJ: Chatham House Publishers.

Mayhew, D. (1974) *Congress: the Electoral Connection.* New Haven, CT: Yale University Press.

Mayhew, D. (1991) *Divided We Govern: Party Control, Lawmaking, and Investigations, 1946–1990.* New Haven, CT: Yale University Press.

McKeever, R. (1995). *Raw Judicial Power? The Supreme Court and American Society* (2nd edition). Manchester: Manchester University Press.

McSweeney, D. (1995). 'Parties and Presidential Nominations', in A. Grant (ed.), *Contemporary American Politics.* Aldershot: Dartmouth, pp. 193–213.

Mead, W.R. (2001) *Special Providence: American Foreign Policy and How It Changed the World.* New York: Alfred Knopf.

Mills, C. Wright (1956) *The Power Elite.* Oxford: Oxford University Press.

Neustadt, R. (1990) *Presidential Power and the Modern Presidents: The Politics of Leadership from Roosevelt to Reagan* (6th edition). New York: The Free Press.

O'Brien, D. (2000) 'Judicial Legacies: the Clinton Presidency and the Courts', in C. Campbell and B. Rockman (eds), *The Clinton Legacy.* New York: Seven Bridges Press, pp. 96–117

O'Neill, T. with W. Novak (1987) *Man of the House: The Life and Political Memoirs of Speaker Tip O'Neill.* New York: Random House.

Peretti, T.J. (1999). *In Defense of a Political Court.* Princeton, NJ: Princeton University Press.

Peters, B.G. (1993) *American Public Policy: Promise and Performance.* Chatham, NJ: Chatham House Publishers.

Polsby, N. (1977) 'Constitutional Angs: Does American Democracy Work?' in A. Brinkley, N. Polsby and K.M. Sullivan (eds), *New Federalist Papers: Essays in Defense of the Constitution.* New York: W.W. Norton and Company.

Polsby, N. and A. Wildavsky (1988) *Presidential Elections.* New York: The Free Press.

Posner, R. (1998) *Overcoming Law.* Cambridge, MA: Harvard University Press.

Posner, R. (2001a) *Breaking the Deadlock: The 2000 Election, the Constitution and the Courts.* Cambridge, MA: Harvard University Press.

Posner, R. (2001b) *Public Intellectuals: A Study of Decline.* Cambridge, MA: Harvard University Press.

Posner, R. and K. Silbaugh (1998) *A Guide to America's Sex Laws.* Chicago, IL: The University of Chicago Press.

Putley, J. (1997). 'The Moral Vacuum and the American Constitution', *The Political Quarterly,* January: 68–76.

Rae, N. (1994) *Southern Democrats.* New York: Oxford University Press.

Rae, N. (1998) 'Party Factionalism, 1946–1996', in B. Shafer (ed.), *Partisan Approaches to Postwar American Politics.* New York: Seven Bridges Press, pp. 41–74.

Rose, R. (1988) *The Postmodern President: The White House Meets the World.* Chatham, NJ: Chatham House Publishers.

Rosenberg, G. (1991) *The Hollow Hope: Can Courts Bring About Social Change?* Chicago: The University of Chicago Press.

Rourke, F. (1984) *Bureaucracy, Politics and Public Policy.* Boston, MA: Little, Brown.

Sabato, L. (1985) *PAC Power: Inside the World of Political Action Committees.* New York: W.W. Norton.

Salisbury, R. (1990) 'The Paradox of Interest Groups in Washington – More Groups, Less Clout', in A. King (ed.), *The New American Political System* (2nd edition). Washington, DC: American Enterprise Institute, pp. 203–29.

Scalia, A. (1997) *A Matter of Interpretation: Federal Courts and the Law.* Princeton, NJ: Princeton University Press.

Schattschneider, E.E. (1960) *The Semi-Sovereign People.* New York: Holt, Rinehart and Winston.

Schlesinger, A. (1974) *The Imperial Presidency.* London: André Deutsch.

Schlesinger, A. (1997) 'Rating the Presidents: Washington to Clinton', *Political Science Quarterly,* 112 (2): 179–90.

Schudson, M. (2000) 'America's Ignorant Voters', *The Wilson Quarterly,* 25 (2): 16–22.

Scott, J. (ed.) (1998) *After the End: Making US Foreign Policy in the Post-Cold War World.* Durham, NC: Duke University Press.

Shafer, B. (1983) *Quiet Revolution: The Struggle for the Democratic Party and the Shaping of Post-Reform Politics.* New York: Russell Sage Foundation.

Shafer, B. (ed.) (1991) *The End of Realignment? Interpreting American Electoral Eras.* Madison, WI: University of Wisconsin.

Shafer, B. (ed.) (1998) *Partisan Approaches to Postwar American Politics*. New York: Seven Bridges Press.

Shapiro, M. (1990) 'The Supreme Court from Early Burger to Early Rehnquist', in A. King (ed.), *The New American Political System* (2nd edition). Washington, DC: American Enterprise Institute Press, pp. 47–85.

Shogun, R. (2000) *The Double-Edged Sword: How Character Makes and Ruins Presidents, from Washington to Clinton*. Boulder, CO: Westview Press.

Singh, R. (1998) *The Congressional Black Caucus: Racial Politics in the United States Congress*. Thousand Oaks, CA: Sage.

Singh, R. (2001) 'Subverting American Values? *The Simpsons, South Park* and the Cartoon Culture War', in R. Singh (ed.), *American Politics and Society Today*. Cambridge: Polity Press, pp. 206–29.

Smith, T. (2000) *Foreign Attachments: The Power of Ethnic Groups in the Making of American Foreign Policy*. Cambridge, MA: Harvard University Press.

Spitzer, R. (1995) *The Politics of Gun Control*. Chatham, NJ: Chatham House Publishers.

Stanley, H. and R. Niemi (1990) *Vital Statistics on American Politics*. Washington, DC: CQ Press.

Stern, P. (1988) *The Best Congress Money Can Buy*. New York: Pantheon Books.

US Government (1996) US Bureau of the Census. Washington, DC: Government Printing Office.

US Government (1996) *Economic Report of the President*. Washington, DC: Government Printing Office.

US Government (2001) *A Citizen's Guide to the Federal Budget of the US Government, Fiscal Year 2001*. Washington, DC: Government Printing Office.

United States Government Manual (1998–99) Washington, DC: Government Printing Office.

Ware, A. (ed.) (1987) *Political Parties: Electoral Change and Structural Response*. Oxford: Basil Blackwell.

Ware, A. (1996) *Political Parties and Party Systems*. Oxford: Oxford University Press.

Wattenberg, M. (1996) *The Decline of American Political Parties, 1952–1994*. Cambridge, MA: Harvard University Press.

Wayne, S. (2000) *The Road to The White House 2000: The Politics of Presidential Elections*. Boston, MA: Bedford/St Martin's Press.

Westad, O.A. (2000) *Reviewing the Cold War: Approaches, Interpretations, Theory*. London: Frank Cass Publishers.

Wildavsky, A. (1996) 'The Two Presidencies Thesis', *Transaction*, 4: 7–14.

Wilson, G. (1993) 'American Interest Groups', in J. Richardson (ed.), *Pressure Groups*. Oxford: Oxford University Press, pp. 131–44.

Wilson, G. (1998) *Only in America? The Politics of the United States in Comparative Perspective*. Chatham, NJ: Chatham House Publishers.

Wilson, J.Q. (1989) *Bureaucracy: What Government Agencies Do and Why They Do It*. New York: Basic Books.

Woll, P. (1977) *American Bureaucracy*. New York: W.W. Norton and Company.

Woodward, B. (1994) *The Agenda: Inside the Clinton White House*. New York: Simon and Schuster.

Yarbrough, T.E. (2000) *The Rehnquist Court and the Constitution*. New York: Oxford University Press.

Index